VLSI Chip Design with the
Hardware Description Language VERILOG

Springer
Berlin
Heidelberg
New York
Barcelona
Budapest
Hong Kong
London
Milan
Paris
Santa Clara
Singapore
Tokyo

Ulrich Golze

VLSI Chip Design with the Hardware Description Language VERILOG

An Introduction Based on a Large RISC Processor Design

With Peter Blinzer, Elmar Cochlovius, Michael Schäfers, and Klaus-Peter Wachsmann

Prof. Dr. Ulrich Golze

Department of Integrated Circuit Design (E.I.S.)
Technical University of Braunschweig
P.O. Box 33 29
D-38023 Braunschweig, Germany
E-mail: golze@eis.cs.tu-bs.de

Ulrich Golze received a Diploma in Mathematics and a PhD in Computer Science at the University of Hannover, Germany, an M.A. of Computer and Communication Sciences at the University of Michigan, Ann Arbor, Michigan, USA, and an M.B.A. of Business Administration at the European Business School INSEAD in Fontainebleau, France.

With 176 Figures and 80 Tables
Includes Diskette

ISBN 3-540-60032-9 Springer-Verlag Berlin Heidelberg New York

Library of Congress Cataloging-in-Publication Data applied for

Die Deutsche Bibliothek - CIP-Einheitsaufnahme

VLSI chip design with the hardware description language VERILOG : an introduction based on a large RISC processor design / Ulrich Golze. - Berlin ; Heidelberg ; New York ; · Barcelona ; Budapest ; Hong Kong ; London ; Milan ; Paris ; Santa Clara ; Singapore ; Tokyo : Springer.
ISBN 3-540-60032-9
NE: Golze, Ulrich

Buch. - 1996

Cover Design: Meta Design, Berlin
Typesetting: Camera ready by author
SPIN 10502185 45/3142 – 5 4 3 2 1 0 – Printed on acid-free paper

Preface

The art of transforming a circuit idea into a chip has changed permanently. Formerly, the electrical, physical, and geometrical tasks were predominant. Later, mainly net lists of gates had to be constructed. Nowadays, designing with hardware description languages (HDL) similar to programming languages is at the center of digital circuit design. HDL based design is one of the centers of this book.

The successful design of small circuits is no problem today, but the demands on a design team are high when designing *large* real circuits. The second center is therefore a *complete* design of a real modern RISC processor with an efficiency in the range of a SPARC.

After an introduction also considering the economic importance of chip design as a key technology, Chapter 2 gives an overview of VLSI design (Very Large Scale Integration). The third chapter leads to modern RISC processors and prepares coarse design decisions. Due to the central role of hardware description languages, Chapter 4 contains a short and Chapter 11 an extensive introduction to the HDL VERILOG and to typical modeling techniques. Numerous examples as well as a VERILOG simulator are included on the disk.

The RISC processor TOOBSIE to be designed is specified externally in Chapter 5 by its behavior, its instructions, and an HDL interpreter as a reference. The internal specification in the next chapter determines a coarse architecture. The central HDL model is the Coarse Structure Model that is completely and executably included on the disk in 🖫3. The datapath pipeline of this model is explained in Chapter 7.

The Coarse Structure Model is suited for a semi-automatic translation into a Gate Model based on the component library of the silicon vendor. This Gate Model will be synthesized in Chapter 8 using selected examples. Finally, Chapter 9 treats the subjects testing, testability, tester, and testboard and discloses, whether the produced processor is actually functioning. A general outline concludes the volume.

This book is addressed to computer scientists and electrical engineers, but also managers, hence to practitioners designing chips or considering their application. It introduces

- modern VLSI design;
- semi-custom design of large chips;
- the hardware description language VERILOG HDL;
- the design of a modern real RISC processor;
- HDL modeling of large designs;
- specification, behavior, structure, HDL model, gate model, test, and testability.

As a textbook, this volume is self-contained and complete. Experts, however, may want to understand the RISC processor design at selected points or even completely, possibly as a base for the development of their own CAD tools and design methods. For this expert, there is an expert volume also containing all graphical "schematics" of the Gate Model (p. 359).

Figures and tables are numbered together per chapter. Chapter numbers beginning with an H such as H5.3 refer to the more *h*ardware-oriented expert volume.

The Team of a Large Project

A project of this size is developed in a team, even worse, in a changing team. The figure on the next page shows a hierarchy without "up" and "down", and every level without a first or last position. Without the assistants of the second ring, the project would not have been accomplished. The students of the third ring were particularly engaged. Peter Blinzer has moved by unusual commitment from the outer to the middle ring.

It all began with an idea of Michael Schäfers, which the author declared as impractical, not only for reasons of cost. He developed together with Klaus-Peter Wachsmann the training processor and predecessor TOOBSIE1. Later, the daily project management was done by Michael Schäfers and also by Klaus-Peter Wachsmann. Together with Elmar Cochlovius joining the team later, they have worked out the external and internal specification with all architectural details (Chapters 5 and 6).

The documentation of a large project is often unpopular, but often also decisive for the project. Elmar Cochlovius has managed (not only) this task; he was documenting by himself, and – more difficult – has motivated others to prepare documentation as a base for this book. In addition to the practical chip design, all three assistants have performed PhD research on design methodology (Chapter 10). As just one example, we mention the research of Elmar Cochlovius on high-level specification with statecharts.

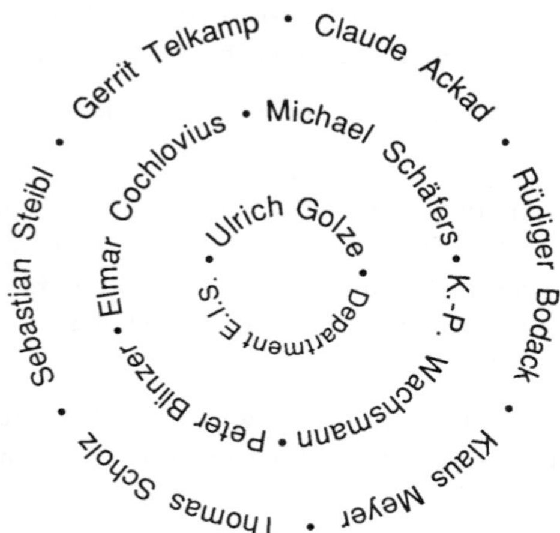

Peter Blinzer, Rüdiger Bodack, Klaus Meyer, and Sebastian Steibl have worked out the VERILOG models, in particular the Coarse Structure Model, and have commented on them (Chapters 7, H3, H4, 💾2, and 💾3). Peter Blinzer was also the major force for the Gate Model (Chapters 8 and H5).

Gerrit Telkamp has designed simple and complicated testboards and has tested the processor in the tester and on the board. Together with Peter Blinzer, he has prepared Chapter 9 on test. The latter has worked out the production test.

Claude Ackad has prepared as a book within the book the extensive VERILOG introduction (Chapters 4 and 11) and has become unpopular as a quality assurer of our documentation. Thomas Scholz designed operating systems for various testboards.

Matthias Bodenstein did not lose his joy in designing graphics until the last figure. Jürgen Hannken-Illjes transformed technical schematics into printable figures using methods of pattern recognition.

Karsten Dageförde, Matthias Mansfeld, Gerrit Mierse, Frank Prielipp, Jörg Reitner, Heiko Stuckenberg, Dirk Wodtke, and Florian Buchholz have delivered important contributions on the (invisible) fourth ring.

The project was performed at the Department of Integrated Circuit Design (E.I.S.) at the Technical University of Braunschweig. It was enabled by the support of LSI Logic Corp., the ESPRIT project EUROCHIP, the Lower Saxony Ministry of Science and Culture (MWK) and the Federal Ministry of Education and Science (BMBW), and a Volkswagen grant.

We are especially grateful to Wellspring Solutions Corp. for offering the simulator VeriWell to the readers of this book. It is included on the disk without any warranty; there are no restrictions on the use and application purpose.

Without encouragement and criticism of my publisher Springer, this work would not have been completed.

I started learning German at the age of 1 or so, English at 10, and began to prefer American at 24 when studying at the University of Michigan. Unfortunately, it will never be possible to make up for this delay of 9 years. I apologize for all those phrases that you as the reader would have expressed more smoothly.

Formerly, I doubted the value of dedications in books, until I myself started neglecting my family for my book: for Barbara, Christian, and Fabian.

Braunschweig, September 1995 Ulrich Golze

Contents

1 Introduction 1

2 Design of VLSI Circuits 9

2.1 Technological Foundations and Design Styles 9
2.2 The Design Process 14
2.3 The Design Phases 17

3 RISC Architectures 25

3.1 A Simple RISC Processor 27
3.2 Selection of a Processor Architecture 31
3.2.1 Proposals for Architectural Extensions 32
3.2.2 Evaluation of Proposals 34
3.2.3 Summary of Extensions Accepted 36

4 Short Introduction to VERILOG 39

5 External Specification of Behavior 47

5.1 The RISC Processor at Work 48
5.1.1 The Assembler 48
5.1.2 The Testboard 49
5.2 The Instruction Set 49
5.2.1 Class LD/ST of Load and Store Instructions 52
5.2.2 Class CTR of Branch Instructions 53
5.2.3 Class ALU of Arithmetic and Logic Instructions 55
5.2.4 Instructions of Class Special 56
5.2.5 Synthetic Instructions 57
5.2.6 External Specification of Interrupts 57
5.3 An Interpreter as a VERILOG HDL Model 59
5.3.1 Overview 61
5.3.2 Components 63
5.3.3 Application 66
5.4 Specification of Test Strategy 69
5.5 Quantitative Specifications 70

6 Internal Specification of Coarse Structure 73

6.1 Data Flow 74
6.1.1 Execution of Instructions in the Datapath 75
6.1.2 A Pipeline for the Datapath 75
6.1.3 Pipeline Features Visible in Applications 76

6.2 Timing 79
6.2.1 A Simple Clocking Scheme 79
6.2.2 The Bus Protocol 80

6.3 Pipeline Stages 84
6.3.1 Scheme and Naming of a General Pipeline Stage 84
6.3.2 Instruction Fetch Stage IF 87
6.3.3 Instruction Decode Stage ID 88
6.3.4 Execute Stage EX 92
6.3.5 Memory Access Stage MA 94
6.3.6 Write-Back Stage WB 95
6.3.7 Summary of Pipeline Actions 96

6.4 Caches and Register File 98
6.4.1 Multi-Purpose Cache MPC 99
6.4.2 Branch-Target Cache BTC 100
6.4.3 Cooperation of MPC and BTC with the Pipeline 107
6.4.4 The Register File 109

6.5 Internal Specification of Interrupts 110

7 Pipeline of the Coarse Structure Model 113

7.1 The Processor CHIP 118

7.2 The Instruction Fetch Unit IFU 123
7.2.1 I_BUS Multiplexer 126
7.2.2 IFU_ADDR_BUS Multiplexer 127
7.2.3 NPC_BUS Multiplexer 128
7.2.4 Branch-Target Cache BTC 128
7.2.5 Multi-Purpose Cache MPC 129
7.2.5.1 Instruction Write Logic IWL 130
7.2.5.2 Instruction Cache ICACHE 131
7.2.6 Branch Decision Logic BDL 132
7.2.7 Program Counter Calculator PCC 133
7.2.8 Pipeline Disable Logic PDL 134
7.2.9 Instruction Decode Logic IDL 135
7.2.10 Serial-Mode Controller SMC 137
7.2.11 External PC Logic EPL 138

7.3 The Instruction Decode Unit IDU 139
7.3.1 Decode Group DG1 141
7.3.2 Decode Group DG2 142
7.3.3 Decode Group DG3 143
7.3.4 Decode Group DG4 144
7.3.5 Decode Group DG5 145
7.3.6 Decode Group DG6 146

7.4 The Arithmetic Logic Unit ALU 147
7.4.1 Module ARITHMETIC 151
7.4.2 Module LOGIC 152
7.4.3 Module SHIFT 152

7.5 The Memory Access Unit MAU 152

7.6 The Forwarding and Register Unit FRU 154
7.6.1 Register Address Converter RAC 157
7.6.2 Forwarding Comparator CMP 157
7.6.3 Forwarding Selection Logic FSL 159
7.6.4 Register Access Logic RAL 160
7.6.5 Data and Address Pipeline 161
7.7 Building a Complete Processor 161

8 Synthesis of Gate Model 163

8.1 The Library of the Silicon Vendor 164
8.1.1 Gates 164
8.1.2 Internal Buffers 165
8.1.3 Flip-Flops 165
8.1.4 Latches 166
8.1.5 Input Clock Drivers 166
8.1.6 Input Buffers 166
8.1.7 Unidirectional Output Buffers 166
8.1.8 Bidirectional Tristate Output Buffers 166
8.1.9 Test Cell as a Megafunction 166
8.1.10 Adder as a Megafunction 167
8.1.11 Shifter as a Megafunction 167
8.1.12 Custom-Specific RAM Library as a Megafunction 167
8.1.13 Internal Buffers as Self-Developed Library Cells 167
8.1.14 Flip-Flops as Self-Developed Library Cells 167
8.1.15 Multiplexers as Self-Developed Library Cells 168
8.2 Manual Synthesis 169
8.2.1 Synchronous Data Transfer 169
8.2.2 Registers with Combinational Logic 171
8.2.3 Register Pipeline 171
8.2.4 Multiplexers for Data Selection 175
8.2.5 Constant Assignment 177
8.2.6 Variable Assignment 177
8.2.7 Indirect Synthesis of Behavioral Parts 179
8.3 Support by Logic Synthesis 181
8.3.1 Synthesis Tools 181
8.3.2 Example of a Logic Synthesis 181
8.4 A Larger Example 185
8.4.1 Synchronous Data Transfer 185
8.4.2 Combinational Logic 187
8.4.3 Multiplexers for Data Selection 189
8.4.4 Indirect Synthesis 191
8.4.5 Variable Assignment 194
8.5 The Asynchronous Bus Protocol as a Special Case 197
8.6 Statistics and Experiences 197
8.7 Simulation and Optimization of the Gate Model 199
8.7.1 Verification 200
8.7.2 Optimization 201
8.7.3 Timing Simulation 202

9 Testing, Testability, Tester, and Testboard 205

9.1 Fault Models and Fault Coverage 206

9.2 Automated Tester (ATE) 209
9.2.1 Set-up and Operation of Tester 210
9.2.2 Formats and Templates 212

9.3 Design for Testability 214
9.3.1 Multiplexers for Memory Test 215
9.3.2 Scanpath 216
9.3.3 Signature Analysis 216
9.3.4 Test Circuits of the Silicon Vendor 217

9.4 Functional Test 220

9.5 Extraction of Test Data 223
9.5.1 Requirements on Test Patterns and Test Blocks 223
9.5.2 Tristate, Quiescent Current, Process, and Memory Test 224
9.5.3 Functional Test 225
9.5.4 Evaluation of Test Patterns 226
9.5.5 Preparation of ATE Test Data 227

9.6 ATE Test 230
9.6.1 Set-up of DUT Card 230
9.6.2 Conducting the Tests 232
9.6.3 Test Results 233

9.7 Testboard 235
9.7.1 Backplane 237
9.7.2 PC-Interface Card and Bus-Interface Card 238
9.7.3 Memory Card 241
9.7.4 CPU Card 242
9.7.5 Evaluation 243

9.8 To Be Honest... 244

10 Summary and Prospect 247

10.1 Efficiency and Complexity 249

10.2 Specification, Analysis, and Simulation of Large VLSI Designs with Statecharts and Activitycharts 251

10.3 Fault Models and Test Patterns for HDL Models 254

HDL Models for Circuits and Architectures – A Supplementary Introduction Based on the Hardware Description Language VERILOG 259

11 HDL Modeling with VERILOG 261

11.1 Syntax Format EBNF 262
11.2 VERILOG Statements 263
11.2.1 Structural Statements 264
11.2.2 Variable Declaration 270
11.2.3 Operations 276
11.2.4 Program Control 284
11.2.5 Miscellaneous Statements 296
11.2.6 Verilog-XL Statements 297
11.3 Basic Modeling Concepts 302
11.3.1 Parallelism and Event Control of the Simulator 302
11.3.2 Time Control 305
11.3.3 Hierarchies of Modules and Instances 309
11.3.4 Behavior and Structure Models 310
11.3.5 Arrays of Variables 311
11.3.6 Modules and Groups 311
11.3.7 Bidirectional Communication 312
11.3.8 Some Practical Guidelines 315
11.4 Examples 315
11.4.1 A Simple Pipeline 315
11.4.2 A Complex Pipeline 318
11.4.2.1 Interfaces 319
11.4.2.2 FIFOs 319
11.4.2.3 ALU 320
11.4.2.4 Test Module 320
11.4.2.5 VERILOG Model 322
11.4.2.6 Simulation Output 327
11.4.3 Behavior Model of Processor ASIC 327
11.4.3.1 Instructions 327
11.4.3.2 VERILOG Model 328
11.4.3.3 Simulation Output 331
11.4.4 Structure Model of Processor ASIC 332
11.4.4.1 Module `memory` 332
11.4.4.2 Module `regcntr` 333
11.4.4.3 Module `alu` 333
11.4.4.4 Module `controller` 334
11.4.4.5 Module `system` 335
11.4.4.6 Module `application` 335
11.4.4.7 VERILOG Model 335
11.4.4.8 Simulation Output 343
11.5 EBNF Syntax of Statements 343

Bibliography 347

Index 353

Expert Volume 359

DISK

0 Read Me First

1 VERILOG Examples

2 VERILOG Source Code of the Interpreter Model

3 VERILOG Source Code of the Coarse Structure Model

3.1 Processor CHIP
3.2 Instruction Fetch Unit IFU
3.3 Instruction Decode Unit IDU
3.4 Arithmetic Logic Unit ALU
3.5 Memory Access Unit MAU
3.6 Forwarding and Register Unit FRU
3.7 Pipeline Control Unit PCU
3.8 Bus Control Unit BCU
3.9 System Environment SYSTEM
3.10 Service Modules
3.10.1 Control File TEST
3.10.2 Statistics TRACE
3.10.3 Memory and Register Output DUMP
3.10.4 Graphic Output GRAPHWAVES
3.10.5 Bus Monitor CHECKBUS
3.10.6 Control MCTRL

4 An Operating System and Larger Examples

4.1 Operating System VOS
4.2 Example Programs
4.2.1 Ackermann Function
4.2.2 Factorial
4.2.3 Quicksort
4.2.4 Dhrystone
4.3 Control File TEST

5 Simulator VeriWell for PC

6 Simulator VeriWell for SUN Sparc

1 Introduction

Nothing could be finer than to receive a large chip from the silicon vendor after many months of designing. Nothing could be sweeter than to have it functioning right away (and nothing could be more embarrassing...). The likelihood of this desired case of *first time right* is today quite large for experienced design teams in a known technology and in a proper CAD environment. Nevertheless, over the years there is a competition such that on the one hand, the largest possible chips and circuits become always more complex and hence more at risk of fault, and on the other hand, design methodology and design support tools become more and more powerful and elaborate. This competition is by no means decided, and for large circuits, the design methodology is clearly behind the technological opportunities.

Not only experts know about the importance of electronics today with chip design as a key technology. In figures, electronics have reached in 1992 with a market of $1,000 billion a share of 10% of the worldwide gross product. Of this, semiconductors participate with about $80 billion [Courtois 1993].

In the year 2000, electronics will be the leading industrial sector with predicted $3,000 billion. Of this, 43% will be in data processing, 22% in consumer electronics, 14% in telecommunications, 12% in industrial electronics, and 6% in automotive electronics, to mention only the most important applications [Courtois 1993]. For integrated circuits (ICs), not only the absolute turnover figures are important, but even more the size of the dependent electronic markets.

In the market of integrated circuits, custom or *application specific ICs* (*ASICs*) participate with roughly 18% with an increasing tendency [Eschermann 1993]. This book concentrates on the design of ASICs or chips developed for a particular application, as opposed to standard circuits as memories or microprocessors, which generally are sold in high volume. (From the design methodology, there is no principal difference between ASICs and standard circuits, but the latter ones justify a higher design and optimizing effort and are marketed differently.)

VLSI stands for *Very Large Scale Integration* or circuits with an *integration density* of up to one million transistors per chip. With historic predecessors of small, medium, and large scale integration (SSI, MSI, and LSI in Figure 1.1), the ULSI technology (U for Ultra) as the successor of VLSI has partially become reality with 10^8 transistors per chip. More than the state of a technology with a certain integration density, the *tendency* of microelectronics is typical for which we propose the name *ALSI*: Always Larger Scale Integration. Following a prediction of Moore in the 1960s, the integration density has doubled in less than two years for many decades.

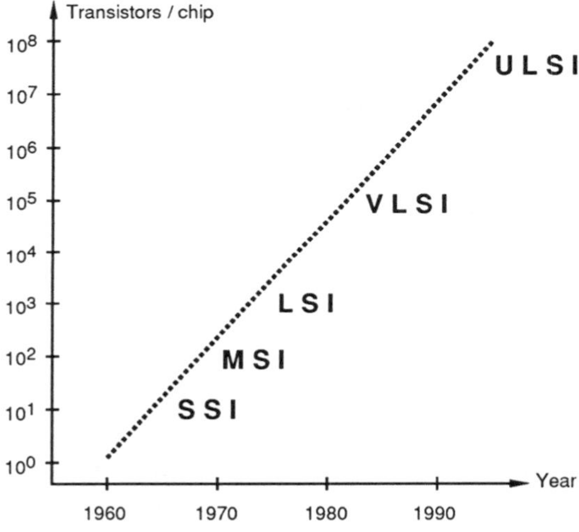

Figure 1.1 Integration density

The reason for the exponential increase of functions per chip lies primarily in the continuous decrease in size of the transistors integrated, from several micrometers in the early 1980s down to about 0.5 μm effective structure width, with a predicted technological limit of 0.3–0.2 μm. The increasing chip complexity was also supported by an increase of reliability of the circuit elements involved, allowing even an increase of the meaningful chip area.

Chip design as the art of transforming a circuit idea into a functioning piece of silicon has permanently changed during the last 30 years. From the first transistor integration around 1960 to the late 1970s, chip design was in the care of very experienced electrical engineers and semiconductor specialists who knew and applied quite a few rules. Also nowadays, these experts are required for the development of more and more powerful technologies or for the design of analog circuits.

In the digital domain, there was a major change around 1978, when Carver Mead and Lynn Conway [Mead, Conway 1980] enabled a decoupling of design and technical realization by defining, rather like a least common denominator, a simple interface applicable to most silicon vendors. This Mead-Conway movement led at American universities, with appropriate national support, to a fast popularization of chip design. ("Just" five years later, similiar movements started in Europe ...)

In the process, the interface between designer and silicon producer moved "upward" towards higher abstraction for the first time. In *full-custom* design, all details of a circuit had now to be designed, the transistors had to be dimensioned and composed to meaningful geometrical *layouts* which were afterwards verified by an *analog simulator*. A layout is a true-to-scale template for the structures to be produced, however strongly enlarged.

Even though this geometric design and the development of suitable geometric CAD tools gave an almost aesthetic satisfaction, the development of larger circuits remained an extremely time-consuming matter.

Around the middle of the 1980s, *semi-custom* design style became the workhorse of VLSI design. With the user interface again moving upward, the semi-custom design employs optimized library cells, typically logic gates, adders, etc., composes them to logic wiring diagrams (gate netlists, *schematics*) and *simulates* them *logically*. The transformation into a geometric layout is achieved by efficient *placement and routing* programs. The designer, in general, is not involved with single transistors, he does often not even know the internal structure of the library cells used. The dominant role of semi-custom design on the ASIC market is demonstrated by Figure 1.2 [Elektronik 1991], where the programmable circuits can almost be considered as semi-custom design with respect to design methodology.

Also at the gate level, however, large circuits finally became too impractical, so that in the following years, *hardware description languages* (*HDL*) have penetrated semi-custom design. HDLs are higher programming languages, extended by constructs of parallelism, time, and hardware-suited data structures. They support circuit descriptions on varying abstraction levels, starting with a first behavioral specification of the problem to be solved, introducing more and more hardware structure in a process of stepwise hierarchical refinement until the gate level is reached. On each level, an HDL description is not only a precise documentation, but it can also be executed or *simulated*. Once an HDL model is precise enough, it can be transformed into a placeable and routable gate model manually or by *logic synthesis*. The research on *high-level synthesis* tries to move the entry level for synthesis upward.

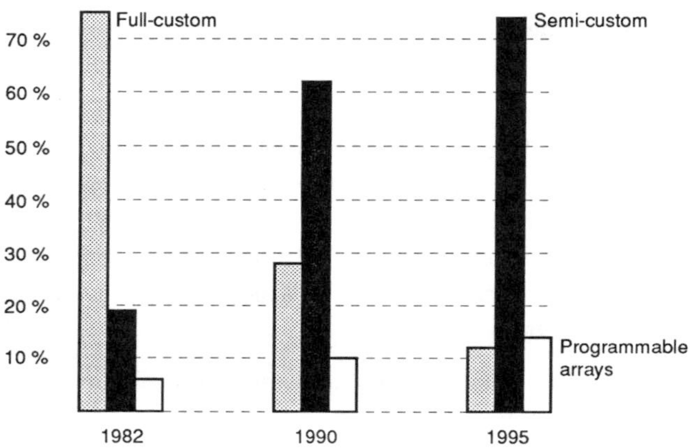

Figure 1.2 Fraction of semi-custom design of total ASIC turnover

Modern computer architecture is no longer engaged only with the components of a computer, but is much more strongly coupled "upward" with suitable instruction sets, compilers, and operating systems and "downward" with appropriate methods and structures of chip design. By VLSI design moving upward and computer design (also) moving downward, both areas have come very close, and even cover each other in many aspects.

The most radical change in the field of computer architecture in the last decade was the appearance of RISC processors. These are marked by relatively simple homogeneous instruction sets that are efficiently executable in parallel pipelines.

This book treats modern semi-custom VLSI design by developing a RISC processor as a large consistent example until production maturity. It is not a toy processor or a small class room example. The following short specification will later be explained for the less experienced reader.

It is a semi-custom design of a 32-bit RISC processor. The underlying technology is a 0.7μ-CMOS process for a gate-array with two metal layers (sea-of-gates). The array has 210 000 transistors. A RISC typical 3-operand load-store instruction set is realized. The targeted efficiency is 30 MIPS (million instructions per second) with less than one cycle per instruction on average (CPI). Employing a classical von-Neumann architecture enables a low pin-count for the processor chip, with the disadvantage, however, of a bottleneck caused by a single common data and instruction bus to the main memory. This disadvantage is compensated by a multi-purpose instruction cache on-chip. Further important architectural features are a five-stage pipeline, a branch-target cache, a flexible treatment of branch delays and a transparent forwarding mechanism. Finally, scanpath techniques with signature registers and various interrupt mechanisms are employed to support a good testability on the hardware and software side.

One may ask why it has to be such a large example and why it will be a RISC processor. The realization of a small circuit is easily possible today. Various textbooks treat the relevant questions individually, often in an academically interesting depth. We are aiming, however, at the design of *large* circuits. As in software design, designing in the large is hard to teach. This will be confirmed by anybody who has really participated in a large project. *Learning by doing* is the best experience, which in chip design, however, is often too expensive. As the second best method, we recommend *learning by watching doing*, i.e., the study of an actually and successfully performed larger project.

This distinguishes ours from other textbooks. Thereby, however, we choose the thorny way of treating many partially boring details and presenting something which will never be complete or perfect, never free of faults – a feature of *all* large designs, even when successful. On the other hand, the reader may and must choose for herself or himself whether she or he wishes

- to get just a first insight,
- to understand the project on a high functional level or the important architecture components,
- to study the HDL description or later even the gate-level netlist,
- to analyze the whole design "down to the last bit", or
- to use it as a starting point and raw data for her or his own research.

We proudly present our design of the processor TOOBSIE *completely*. Academic institutions have often neither funds nor time for a large design, whereas successful industrial design teams suppress the design details for obvious competitive reasons. For further development of CAD tools and of a general design methodology, however, large realistic examples are urgently required.

We have chosen a RISC processor as a large example in spite of the fact that RISC architectures have been researched to a large extent. Basic knowledge of classical computers is widespread, so not many prerequisites are required.

Although we have developed a processor with several architectural novelties that is as fast as a SPARC processor of today (which definitely will not be the case tomorrow), we do not intend to compete in the market. Rather we have developed a large example, whose pipeline data flow as well as the complex controller of the pipeline exceptions and the caches may be helpful for quite a few different designs. As opposed to a video chip, for instance, also involving many transistors but relatively simple algorithms for wide data streams, our example is inherently complex to an extent almost enforcing modeling and verification supported by a hardware description language.

This book is meant to give knowledge and experience of

- VLSI design of semi-custom ASICs;
- architectures of RISC processors and of caches (intelligent on-chip memories);
- CAD tools for chip design, particularly the hardware description language VERILOG XL;
- the design of *large* circuits.

This is neither a book on foundations of VLSI design nor a work on computer architecture nor a comparative study of various hardware description languages, as each subject requires (and has) its own textbooks. Our intent is to offer to the reader many aspects of a large project, not to put theory in the foreground but also not to remain at the level of small examples that are hard to apply in the large.

As the target group of this book, we think of computer scientists and electrical engineers, but also managers, in short practitioners interested in designing chips or applying them. We hope that both the beginner, with basic knowledge in computer systems and in programming, and the design specialist will find interesting parts.

The present volume contains foundations and an extensive course on the HDL VERILOG. First, the processor TOOBSIE is externally specified by its instruction set and defined by an executable HDL interpreter, so that it can be tested for the first time. Subsequently, an internal specification fixes the coarse processor architecture containing pipelines, caches, a register file, forwarding, etc., again first verbally and afterwards in a pretty large Coarse Structure Model on an HDL base. This model already permits a rather precise prediction of the future processor and constitutes the creative part of the design.

We explain the transformation of the internal specification into a Coarse Structure Model for some selected components, and likewise for the subsequent transformation into the Gate Model. Parallel to the chip design, the practical processor test after production is prepared, first by test patterns for a tester and then by a system environment with main memory and periphery for a real and long test.

The enclosed disk contains all examples of the VERILOG introduction in Chapter 11 (Chapter 🖫1), the Interpreter Model (🖫2), and the complete Coarse Structure Model (🖫3) in VERILOG. The reader may thus select interesting parts in the partially large models using a PC editor; he or she may try some of the many examples using the enclosed simulator VeriWell (without warranty).

An expert volume for design specialists contains not only the extensive documentation of the instructions (Chapter H2), but also the complete printed models with additional comments (H3 to H5); this includes the rather large Gate Model with about 150 graphical schematics based on the library of the silicon producer LSI Logic.

The disk includes also an operating system for the Coarse Structure Model and various simulation experiments, but as it is not in the actual scope of this book, we include it with only a few comments (Chapter 🖫4).

TOOBSIE, by the way, stands for Technical University of Braunschweig Integrated Engine and just incidentally recalls Dustin Hoffman's charming movie character TOOTSIE.

2 Design of VLSI Circuits

After a short introduction to technology and design styles, this chapter presents basic ideas on the design of VLSI circuits. This includes levels of design abstraction as well as model behavior and model structure by hierarchical decomposition. A large design requires a careful planning of project time and method, particularly the organization of phases and milestones with expected models and documents.

2.1 Technological Foundations and Design Styles

A digital chip may today be designed in a "semi-custom" style without deeper knowledge of semiconductor technology or electrical properties of transistors and basic circuits. For the technological and electrical foundations, we refer to appropriate textbooks [e.g., Fabricius 1990, Mukherjee 1986].

About 2 out of 3 application-specific circuits are based on the CMOS technology (complementary MOS), the name of the MOS transistor coming from the layers **M**etal, **O**xide, and **S**ilicon on the chip, the "C" indicating the use of two complementary transistor types, the p- and the n-transistor. Metal is today normally replaced by polysilicon. The CMOS technology will in the middle future remain the work horse of digital circuit design, followed by bipolar technology with about 20% of all designs, BiCMOS circuits where CMOS is augmented by bipolar drivers, and to a small extent by fast gallium arsenide circuits. CMOS chips are characterized by a high integration density, acceptable switching speed, and low power consumption.

An overview of various types of digital circuits and design styles is shown in Figure 2.1. Already in Chapter 1, we excluded *standard circuits* such as memory components from the target of this book, for which an intensive design effort is possible due to high volume.

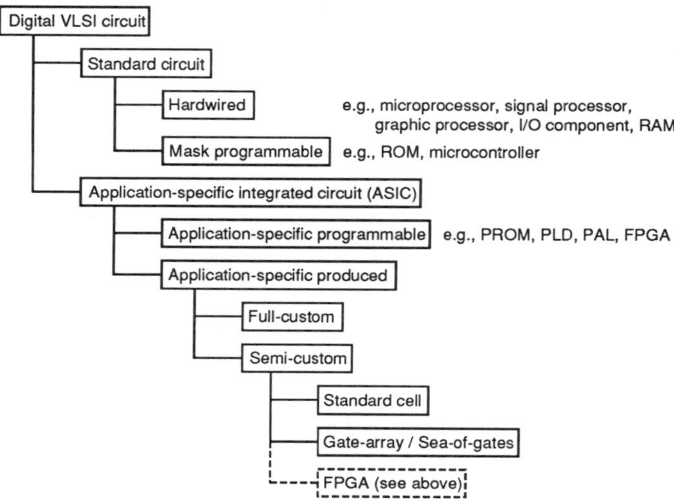

Figure 2.1 Classification of digital circuits

For *full-custom circuits*, design and production are fully controlled by the user. Figure 2.2 shows a CMOS inverter in space, as a *layout*, and as a composition of a p- and an n-transistor. Without a detailed understanding, it suffices for our purposes to realize that circuits are organized in *layers* and that a layout is a true-to-scale enlargement of the layers as manufactured by the silicon producer. In the spatial representation, the routing on the metal layer is only sketched symbolically. The full-custom designer specifies the transistors geometrically and hence electrically and places them geometrically in a spatially efficient way. A full-custom design thus allows optimal results, although the design effort is very high, normally too high for large circuits.

For the *semi-custom standard cell circuits* the production of all layers is still dependent upon the application. In the design method, however, only geometrically standardized library cells or standard cells are used, which afterwards are placed and routed efficiently on the chip by CAD tools. Instead of transistors and layouts, the designer faces only standard cells as the smallest units, which he composes logically, but not topologically, to larger circuits and which are verified before production by logic and timing simulation. For example, the designer need not know the internal transistor structure of a cell. Placement and routing tools group the standard cells of equal height to standard rows as in Figure 2.3a, the variable space between the rows being used for electrical connections. There are several standardizations and placing schemes for such standard cells, particularly as routing today takes place on two, three, or even more metal layers above the cells.

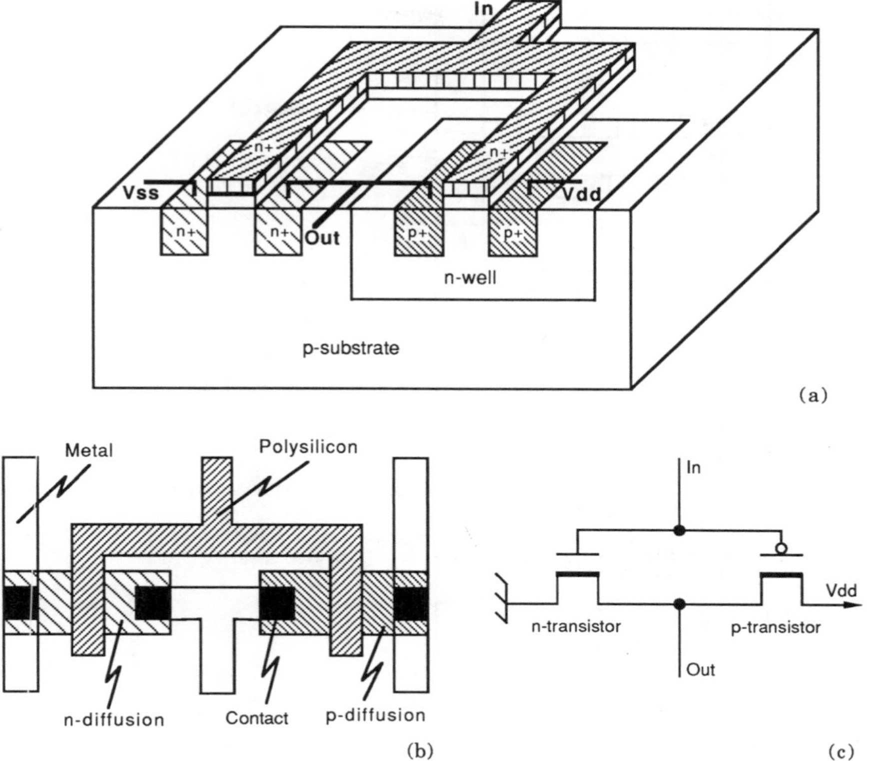

Figure 2.2 CMOS inverter (a) in space, (b) layout, (c) circuit

The design method for standard cells as the development of a simulated logic netlist of library cells can also be applied to *gate-arrays* and *sea-of-gates* circuits. The basic difference lies in the production, where regular arrays of transistors are preproduced and are only routed on two or three metal layers, dependent on application. Older gate-arrays with just one metal layer are placed in rows as in Figure 2.3b and are first composed locally to build library cells (Figure 2.4) and are then composed by routing channels of fixed width to form larger circuits. In contrast, several metal layers permit the chip area to be homogeneously occupied by transistors, over which the routing takes place. Such sea-of-gates are often also called gate-arrays.

The CAD tools for placement and routing can afterwards partition the chip area variably into actually used transistors and routing areas. The designer is again only interested in the function of given library cells, which he connects and simulates in time. Moreover, the dense transistor array permits a relatively easy inclusion of regular memory structures.

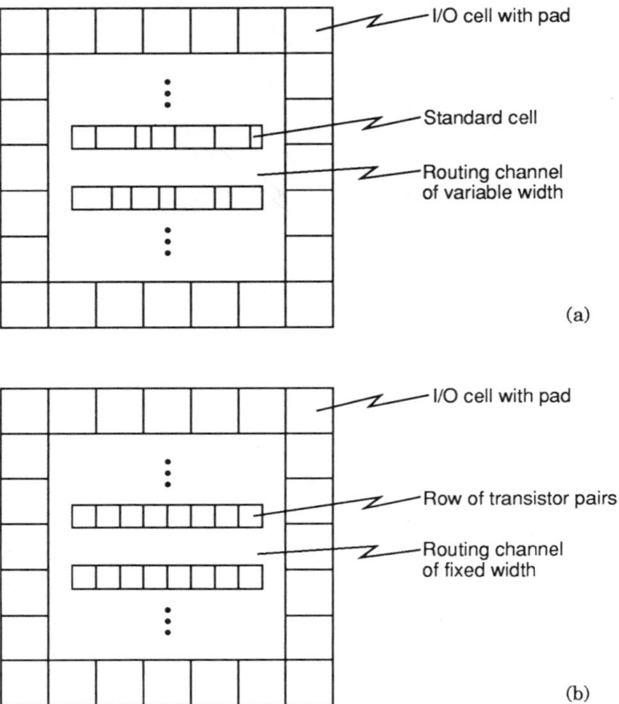

Figure 2.3 Examples of placing (a) standard cells, (b) gate-arrays

The size of a gate-array master is given in *gate equivalents* which are more or less useable due to routing. The processor TOOBSIE takes place on a master with 100 000 gate equivalents corresponding to 400 000 transistors, of which 53 000 gate equivalents are actually used.

The libraries of semi-custom design are offered by a silicon vendor and typically contain logic gates such as AND, NOR, or XOR, complex gates such as AND-OR-INVERT, drivers, latches and flipflops, input and output cells for pads, multiplexers, and simple arithmetic functions such as adders or counters. They vary with respect to driving force for output load, delay time, number of inputs, bits, and similar factors. Section 8.1 treats the LSI library as employed in our design. For every cell, there is a data sheet containing all necessary information, such as symbol and function, time behavior, input loads, driving force, gate equivalents, etc.

From the standpoint of production, also the application-specific programmable components are standard circuits (to be distinguished from standard cell circuits), but from the design standpoint they are personalized by the user. In particular, the FPGAs (field-programmable gate-arrays) constitute a fast

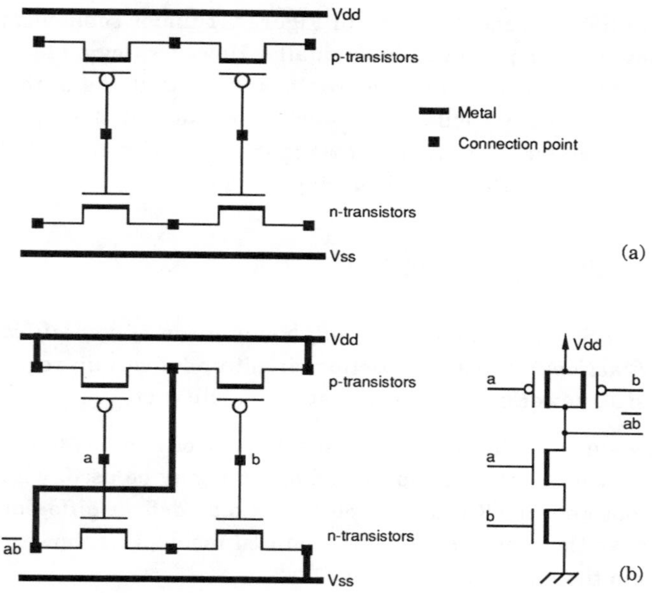

Figure 2.4 Transistor rows (a) gate-array master, (b) wired NAND

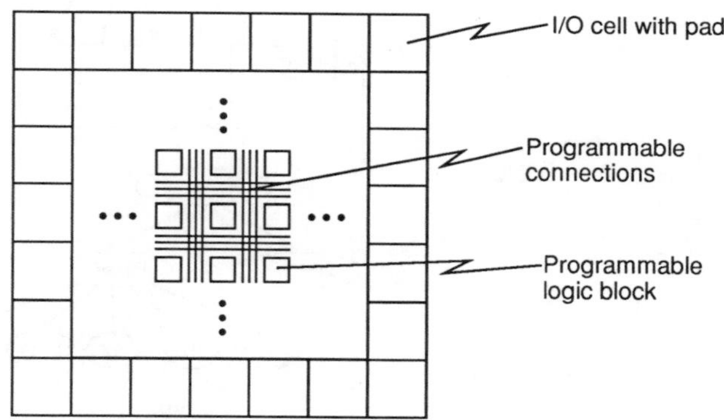

Figure 2.5 Typical structure of an FPGA

growing market today. As shown in Figure 2.5, a field of, say, 500 relatively simple logic blocks and a network of connection buses is given; both can be programmed by loading appropriate 0/1 patterns to obtain an individual net list of individual logic components.

When restricting the FPGA development to a simulated netlist, the design process is almost identical with that of standard cell and gate-array designs.

Therefore, we have repeated FPGAs in Figure 2.1 under semi-custom circuits, although they are not produced individually. However, logic blocks and their connecting buses involve serious restrictions, such that the automatic placement and routing often yields unsatisfactory results. If the logic blocks are restricted, for example, to nine inputs as is the case with the XILINX 4000, it makes sense to observe this already during design.

2.2 The Design Process

Designing a VLSI circuit means the *implementation* of a *specification* of the *behavior* or *function* of a not yet existing circuit under certain requirements on speed, chip size, power consumption, costs, reliability, etc.

To define behavior, we consider a circuit or part of it as a "black box" as in Figure 2.6a, of which only the inputs and outputs may be used, while the inner structure is not known. Of course, a black box may deliver different results for equal inputs, as there are usually states stored inside; this, however, can only be observed via the inputs and outputs.

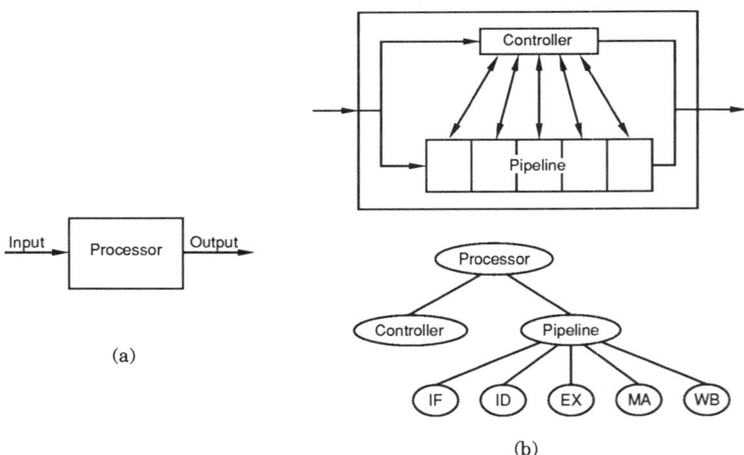

Figure 2.6 Circuit example (a) behavior, (b) structure

In many cases, the customer does not even know the behavior of the desired circuit precisely, it should therefore first of all be specified by the designer in cooperation with the customer. During subsequent implementation, the designer decomposes the problem into always finer structures, thus obtaining in semi-custom design as a solution a *hierarchical structure* of given library cells of a silicon producer, which has the desired behavior (Figure 2.6b).

In such a hierarchical decomposition, every node of the associated tree except for the leaves has a behavior that is structured by its successor nodes and is therefore implemented by a composition of several sub-behaviors. In this sense, the processor behavior in Figure 2.6 is implemented by a structure of controller and pipeline, the pipeline behavior in turn being decomposed into pipeline stages IF, ID, etc. It is the art of designing to decompose such problems by an interplay of behavior and structure in a *top-down* manner, a *bottom-up* manner, or a combination of both called *"yo-yo"* style.

Abstraction level	Smallest structures	Example
System level	Architecture blocks	Pipeline
Register transfer level (RTL)	Registers, combinational logic	d = a&c | d
Logic or gate level	Library cells	
Transistor level	Transistors	
Layout level	Geometries	

Figure 2.7 Abstraction hierarchy

From this *decomposition hierarchy*, we distinguish the *abstraction hierarchy* with the abstraction levels of Figure 2.7. Thus we will specify our RISC processor TOOBSIE first by a coarse structure and the instructions by an executable HDL interpreter model; on the *register transfer level* (*RTL level*), we will fix the data and control flow in detail in a "Coarse Structure Model" as a specification for a "Gate Model" on the *logic* or *gate level*.

All three models will have a hierarchical decomposition structure that is similar to the decomposition structure of other abstraction levels. Therefore, the behaviors of the various models have to be mutually *verified*, which usually is done by simulation of appropriate test programs. The *test* of a produced circuit is a task similar to verification.

Finally, there are the transistor and layout levels that are only needed in full-custom design and by place and route tools. As we will restrict our attention to semi-custom design, we do not augment behavior and structure ("what?" and "how?") by geometry ("where?").

Circuits with 100 000 transistors and more require not only a meaningful methodology of hierarchical design on various abstraction levels, but also a massive support by *CAD tools*, i.e., an environment of tuned software programs.

A *silicon compiler* translating every truly behavioral specification automatically into an efficient chip will for a long time remain a dream. Also *high level synthesis* starting from well structured models above the RTL level has not succeeded significantly in the professional domain in spite of intensive research. For dedicated problem classes, however, as in image processing, there are satisfactory synthesis tools. In a mature state are logic synthesis between RTL and logic level and the automatic placement and routing mapping to the layout level.

Of course, there are graphical and textual editors on all abstraction levels for the hierarchic capture and modification of models. Aside of many small special tools, *simulators* are at the center of modern chip design, predicting the behavior on all levels so precisely that normally the circuit has to be manufactured only once ("first time right").

As an input language for simulators and as a base of all design models, hardware description languages (HDL) mentioned in Chapter 1 have become most successful. We will summarize their main features in the following.

- An HDL is a "classical" higher programming language like C, extended by constructs for parallelism, time, and hardware related data structures.
- Especially, an HDL supports the hierarchical design method.
- HDL models can be executed or simulated.
- HDL models are precise and well-defined (which does not induce a unique circuit).
- HDL models constitute a precise documentation.
- HDL models serve as a base for a subsequent manual or automatic synthesis (the result possibly being another HDL model).
- An HDL can universally be applied from the top system level down to the bottom logic level.
- Also mixed-mode representations are efficiently possible, for example, by combining in just one model a controller as a pure behavioral algorithm with a pipeline stage being modelled on the gate level.
- Mixed-mode models avoid the (often too) high simulation effort of pure gate models and still enable the testing of detailed subcircuits.

Models in the HDL VERILOG are central in this book for designing a RISC processor. An additional overview on design methodology is given in [Cochlovius et al. 1993].

2.3 The Design Phases

Few things are harder to teach than the art (and embarrassment) of large project design, large software projects as well as large VLSI designs. It is certainly not sufficient to study small textbook examples in perfection and to hope that the transformation into the large will work out somehow. General rules, when given without large examples, often sound simplistic and obvious and are therefore not taken seriously enough.

The best training method, but also the most expensive one, is participation in a large design project or even its management. In doing so, one can experience (and suffer from) effects like time planning and misplanning, teamwork, group dynamics, difficulties in interface coordination, change of team members, and the often hopeless fight to keep documentation up-to-date.

As the second best method, we recommend studying a large project thoroughly. We have pointed out the difficulties to make the documents and details of such a large project available and the boredom that may arise when reading too many details. While we hesitate in this book to give untested theories, variants, and smart academic advice, we hope to give the reader a realistic impression and help in developing his or her own basic instinct.

Before a large project is performed, we recommend a smaller design for practice. One gets acquainted with the given CAD design environment, the library, and the process of the silicon producer. Experiences on special architectures may be sampled as on RISC architectures in our case. Ideally, the design team will practice cooperation. The training design, which we did for a smaller processor TOOBSIE1, may be "quick and informal"; the difficulties encountered increase the acceptance of a strict project organization and of conventions.

Similar to software engineering, we will now define project phases with documents and models. The following advantages can be expected.

- The design process is better structured;
- the models and documents at the end of a phase become more important;
- a "formalized group memory" increases the efficiency of team work, improves design safety, and makes decisions better understandable;
- design time can be controlled better.

On the other hand, a creative design process may be handicapped, as new and good ideas are hard to plan.

Phases known from software engineering are now adapted to hardware design and in particular to semi-custom design. The following phases are normally concluded by a processor model, at least a document. The sequential phase ordering might give a wrong impression. In practice, the phases may overlap: one part of the team may prepare a later phase, while another part finishes an early phase. An example is the preparation of the system and test environment, whose details do not yet exist (*hardware software codesign*).

Iterations of phases are to be expected, when errors discovered later or late improvements require the updating of early phases. The costs are higher, the further the design has come. Figure 2.8 summarizes the phases and documents planned for the design process.

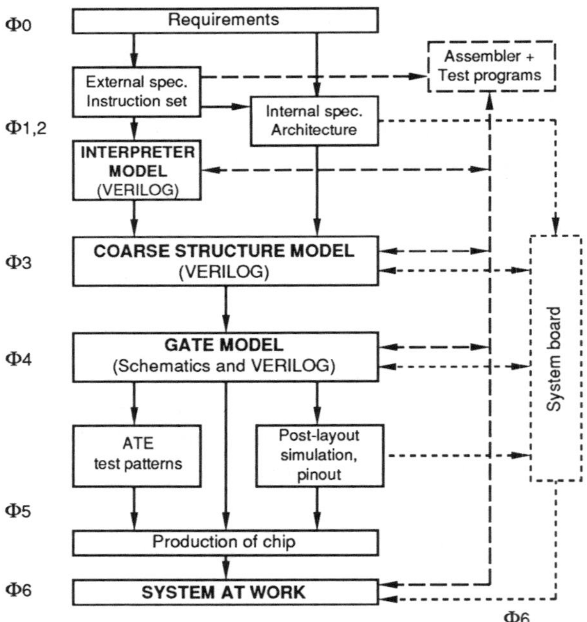

Figure 2.8 Design flow for processor TOOBSIE

Φ0 The Preliminary Phase

In this phase, ideas are sampled and discussed. Requirements on the processor and its architecture are stated, and the methodology and project organization is fixed. The preliminary phase is included in Chapters 2 and 3.

Φ1 The Phase of External Specification and the Interpreter Model

The processor behavior as visible for the outside user is specified. The behavior is mainly given by the instruction set.

In addition to a verbal explanation of the instructions, an interpreter for executing arbitrary programs of these instructions is produced. The interpreter will serve for later models as a reference or *golden device*. As the outer behavior is not connected with a particular inner structure, the interpreter can be realized in an arbitrary and abstract way.

Suitable test programs have to be developed for the interpreter. Large test programs will be generated by a compiler or at least an assembler. The assembler will also generate test patterns and simulation stimuli for all later models.

Φ2 The Phase of Internal Specification

As the internal specification, we consider the main architecture features of the RISC processor such as datapath, pipeline, registers and caches, main buses, interrupts, processor control, and timing. This specification should be detailed enough to sketch an implementation.

The specification is supported by considerations of efficiency, testability, and design plausibility. It depends on the given project whether the internal specification is the requirement of an experienced customer who has already decided on the main architectural features, or whether the internal specification is a solution to the general design task: implement the instruction set of Phase Φ1 with an efficiency of at least x with costs not more than y.

Φ3 The Phase of the Coarse Structure Model

In this phase, the internal specification is applied to build a model in the hardware description language VERILOG. It has an outer behavior as similar as possible to the Interpreter Model, but it contains already the main components of a later implementation on the gate level.

To verify the similarity with the Interpreter Model, the test programs of this model are again applied to the Coarse Structure Model and have to deliver the same results in the main points. The test programs, however, are usually extended in order to also test typical critical situations of the implemented pipeline.

In this phase, there is the important question of how detailed and close-to-hardware the model should be. This corresponds to the question of how many models between the first Interpreter Model and the last Gate Model are to be created. Obviously, also structures like the cache again have an outer behavior with easily understandable more abstract algorithms and a fine structure with registers, multiplexers, etc., that are harder to understand, but easier to implement.

More than that, there are arbitrary mixed-mode models representing some parts of the circuit by abstract behavior and others by a more detailed structure. These changes between behavior and structure constitute the actual *development* of a design.

We distinguish the more "official" models as milestones. As their mutual verification and consistency represent a major effort, there should not be too many models officially. In this sense, we have planned the Interpreter Model, the Coarse Structure Model, and the Gate Model, although in the original planning, there was at least one more model.

Φ4 The Phase of the Gate Model

The Coarse Structure Model is the starting point for the stepwise refinement into a netlist of gates and library components of the silicon producer LSI Logic.

On the one hand, it would be desirable to describe the Gate Model in the HDL VERILOG, as this language supports gate level descriptions well. For production, however, the "schematic entry" LSED from LSI is the mandatory input language. It has the advantage of a graphical representation that is better readable in detail, and it can be connected to earlier VERILOG models and be verified by an automatic translation of the LSED Gate Model into a VERILOG netlist. Thus we obtain two basically equivalent gate models: the normal one as a graphic netlist and the retranslated VERILOG model.

Also the simulation and verification of the Gate Model requires test programs, which again come from the programs of earlier models. In addition, the silicon producer expects test patterns for his *production test*, for the verification of the produced chip in an ATE (Automated Test Equipment). As the silicon vendor guarantees the conformance with these – and only these – test patterns, they are the key for a circuit that behaves as desired.

While in the general case, ATE test patterns have to be developed again at the gate level in a time-consuming manner, it suffices in our case of a RISC processor to extract ATE patterns from the existing functional test programs and to extend them by some additional patterns. A number of tester-specific restrictions have to be observed.

Moreover, the production test patterns are expected to have a high *fault coverage*. By this, we mean the percentage of faults discovered with respect to all faults of a fault model. The most common fault model is the stuck-at model assuming as faults all situations in which exactly one gate input or output constantly carries just one signal value, i.e., does not change appropriately. A fault simulator is used to compute the fault coverage.

Φ5 The Phase of Production

The Gate Model with ATE test patterns is sent to the silicon vendor for production. In a wider sense, this includes placement and routing of the gate netlist. The library elements are filled with the "flesh" of locally connected transistors (Figure 2.4) and are placed efficiently on the chip layout. This space saving placement serves as a base for subsequent short routing.

The wire length of the actually chosen routing constitutes an additional circuit time factor, which was not known before. These delays are sent to the customer and are "back-annotated" to his gate model. In a *post-layout simulation*, the correctness of the design is again studied carefully. Conservative rules during the earlier design of the Gate Model, however, make surprises at this late point relatively unlikely.

Finally, the placed and routed layout is manufactured, tested on the ATE and sent to the customer in a package (Figure 2.9).

Φ6 The Phase of Test and Application in a System Environment

The chip produced by the silicon vendor and tested in a production test is sent to us as the customer. If we have a tester (ATE) as well, we may test the circuit again and intensively. This, however, will normally only be done for first prototypes and not in volume production.

Such ATE tests are normally performed in slow motion, thus permitting only short test programs. Instead, we strive for a "real" test of the chip in a *system* or *testboard* similar to the later use in a real system. This is called a *system environment*.

Phase Φ6 of system test is strongly overlapping with earlier phases as is indicated in Figure 2.8. The development of test patterns and testboards can be started in parallel to Phase Φ1, even though many details have to remain open. The Coarse Structure Model, or the Gate Model at the latest, determine the timing and the interfaces of the board.

Conversely, the board imposes minimal requirements on the processor regarding driving strength, maximal load, and slew rate, which should conform with the parameters of the silicon vendor library. These data thus influence the Gate Model.

Figure 2.9 Manufactured prototype of the RISC processor TOOBSIE

Before the production in Phase Φ5, the package type and the *pinout* as the assignment of logical inputs and outputs to physical pins is determined. Only at this point can the processor socket, the routing, and the board be finished.

Every model depends upon the previous one. The Interpreter Model as the first one is derived from the semi-formal instruction set specification. Together with a consistent test strategy, we have the advantage that every model can be verified with respect to the previous one. Thus errors in the Coarse Structure Model will not come from the functionality of the instruction set.

We want to use existing and suitable CAD tools, in particular the HDL simulator VERILOG, the fault simulator VERIFAULT, and the design environment MDE of LSI Logic for logic simulation, placement and routing, and other tools.

Phase	Length
$\Phi 0$	4 weeks
$\Phi 1$	6 weeks
$\Phi 2$	8 weeks
$\Phi 3$	6 weeks
$\Phi 4$	8 weeks
$\Phi 5$	4 weeks
$\Phi 6$	no estimate

Table 2.10 Preliminary schedule

A preliminary schedule at the beginning is shown in Table 2.10. The design team consisted of four students with knowledge of VLSI design, processor architecture, and hardware description languages, as well as three permanently employed team members. Precise measurements of the actual work time needed, however, turned out to be difficult in a university environment, as the team members were also busy with different tasks.

3 RISC Architectures

RISC processors are simple and difficult at the same time. They are simple when regarding their instruction set as is indicated by the abbreviation RISC for *Reduced Instruction Set Computer*, there are significantly fewer special instructions and variants than with CISC computers (Complex Instruction Set Computer). They are difficult, because they have a higher degree of parallelism in implementations and they only become superior in connection with well tuned compilers.

In the introduction, we have emphasized that this is not meant as a special book on RISC processors like the outstanding work [Hennessy, Patterson 1990]. Rather, we design a RISC processor as an understandable and important example of a large VLSI design. We would like to encourage the reader: it suffices to have basic knowledge of the classical and well known von-Neumann computer with arithmetic unit, controller, registers, program counter, instruction and status register communicating with a main memory storing program and data, and with I/O periphery. After studying our RISC example, the reader will be acquainted with many features of modern RISC processors.

The following basic RISC features should be considered in parallel, as they all depend upon each other. Not all features are found in every RISC computer. Many of them are worked out in the following chapters.

1. *Few simple instructions*. This feature indicated by the name RISC allows efficient pipelining (features 4 and 6). Based on statistical analysis, only frequently needed instructions are implemented, the others will be synthesized by the compiler. This and the reduction of pipeline hazards (5) like data dependency or branch problems favor adapted compilers and special hardware. Simple instruction sets support simple instruction forwarding and are achieved by a restriction of memory operations to instructions load and store (3). CISC computers in turn have many complex instructions.

2. *Fixed and short format.* The simple instructions (1) basically have a constant length and fit into one processor word. They are restricted to few formats within a word. They support efficient fixed control and simple fast pipelines (4,6,7) as well as efficient caches and register files (8). The user, however, expects compilers offering the comfort of classical CISC computers with varying instruction word lengths and many complex formats (9).

3. *Load/store feature.* Main memory accesses are slow and expensive. RISC instructions only operate on registers of the processor chip (6,8), only the instructions load and store explicitly access memory. Besides, the instructions themselves are fetched from memory, but even these accesses can be reduced significantly by instruction caches (6,8). Instructions without slow memory access enable a smooth pipelining with high throughput (4,6). An efficient compiler achieves the reduction to load/store instructions only and avoids many pipeline hazards (5,9). CISC instructions, in contrast, combine memory contents directly and with registers.

4. *Pipelining.* An instruction is partitioned in tasks of equal length, for example, fetch, decode, and execute. In such a 3-stage pipeline, the first instruction is executed, while the second is decoded, and the third is fetched (Figure 3.1). While a particular instruction remains in the pipeline for three cycles, a well balanced pipeline achieves a throughput of CPI=1 (Cycles Per Instruction).

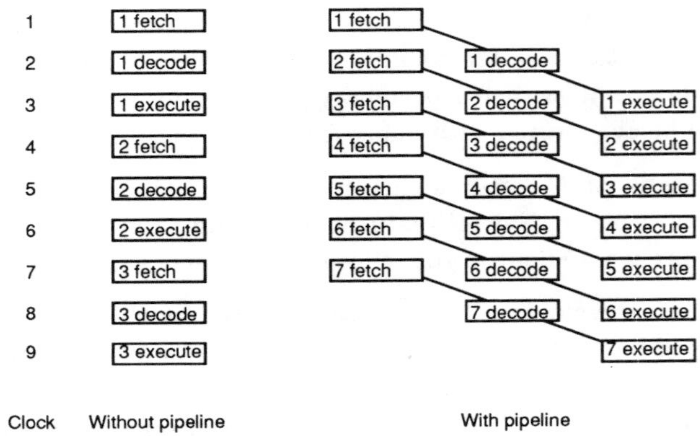

Figure 3.1 3-stage pipeline

This high throughput (6) is supported by simple and similar instructions with a simple format (1,2,3) that can be executed by a fixed control (7). Various pipeline hazards (5) tend to increase the CPI, but can be reduced by additional hardware (8) and intelligent compilers (9); even CPI<1 can be reached (6).

5. *Removal of pipeline hazards.* There is *data dependency* if, for instance, an instruction in pipeline stage 2 requires the contents of register R, while the previous instruction in the third stage writes its result back to R; data dependency can be avoided by a hardwired *forwarding* or by the compiler (9).

   Because a load instruction accesses main memory typically for longer than one cycle, the result cannot be used by the subsequent instruction. Such a *delayed load* can be avoided by the compiler (9).

   Taken branches disturb the quiet pipeline stream, as the subsequent (wrong) instruction has already entered the pipeline. A compiler optimized *delayed branch* (9) or even a cache for branch instructions (*branch-target cache,* 8) sustain the high pipeline throughput (4,6).

6. *High throughput.* By a smart combination of all features (1–5,7–9), a throughput of less than one machine cycle per instruction on average is the goal (CPI<1).

7. *No microprogramming.* The simple instructions with a fixed format permit a hardwired, simple, 1-stage decoding that saves time and chip area (1,2,6). An efficient compiler reduces complex instructions to efficient sequences of simple instructions and thus replaces microprogramming (9).

8. *Caches and registers.* Registers with more than one port and various caches as intermediate memory on-chip between main memory and processor (data, instruction, and branch caches) with suitable replacement strategies speed up the pipeline, help to avoid pipeline hazards and increase efficiency significantly (4,5,6). There is a relatively large array of multi-purpose registers – typically 32 or more – visible for the programmer or the compiler. Operations have three operands, the source operands are typically not replaced.

9. *Adapted compiler.* The high importance of an individually designed compiler in harmony with the selected special RISC architecture has become obvious when discussing the previous features (1–8). Nevertheless, we will just assume the existence of a suitable compiler in the following, as we want to focus on the actual VLSI design.

3.1 A Simple RISC Processor

After all that, we now become practical and sketch the simple RISC processor TOOBSIE1 with several of the features mentioned above. The large RISC processor TOOBSIE to be designed below in detail will be an extension of this "low-cost" processor. This section may serve for the reader as an exercise and a starting point; for the design team, TOOBSIE1 was developed for practice.

The architecture to be selected for the large processor in the next section will include the features of this small TOOBSIE1. The reader will so to speak catch up with the experiences of the design team. The following description is only meant as an overview, the functions and components will be explained in more detail in the specification of TOOBSIE.

TOOBSIE1 is a 32-bit RISC processor. It is characterized by a RISC-typical, uniform 32-bit instruction format. It has a load/store architecture, i.e., communication with main memory is only accomplished by instructions Load and Store. Operations will only be performed on registers, not on memory locations. The existing instructions are divided into the four classes of Table 3.2. In detail, TOOBSIE1 has the instructions of Table 3.3.

Class	Explanation
ALU	Arithmetic and logic operations for registers
LD/ST	Memory accesses (Load/Store)
CTR	Branches (control transfers) (conditional and unconditional)
Special	Special instructions for special registers like program counter PC

Table 3.2 Instruction classes of TOOBSIE1

The instruction set and the architecture of the low-cost processor TOOBSIE1 are restricted. There are no general shift instructions, but only shifts by one or two bits, and no hardware multiplication. The design has been implemented using approximately 16 000 gate equivalents of a gate-array.

Requirements for the system environment are low, as it is a classical von-Neumann architecture with just one common memory bus for instructions and data.

The processor executes instructions in one clock cycle except for LD/ST instructions. The bus protocol is designed for static RAMs. Such SRAM memories permit sufficiently fast memory accesses with a frequency of 25 MHz. This is necessary, because the processor has no intermediate memories (caches).

The datapath of TOOBSIE1 in Figure 3.4 is explained as follows.

- The *memory interface* contains a data register DATA for reading and writing and an address register ADDR.
- The *instruction register* IR holds the valid instruction.

Class	Instruction	Explanation
ALU	ADD	Add
	ADDC	Add with carry
	SUB	Subtract
	SUBC	Subtract with carry
	AND	And
	OR	Or
	XOR	Exclusive or
	LSL	Logical shift left
	LSR	Logical shift right
	ASR	Arithmetic shift right
	LDH	Load high
LD/ST	LD	Load (register from memory)
	ST	Store (register into memory)
CTR	BCC	Branch conditional
	CALL	Call (subroutine)
	HALT	Halt
Special	LRFS	Load register from special register
	SRIS	Store register into special register

Table 3.3 Instructions of TOOBSIE1

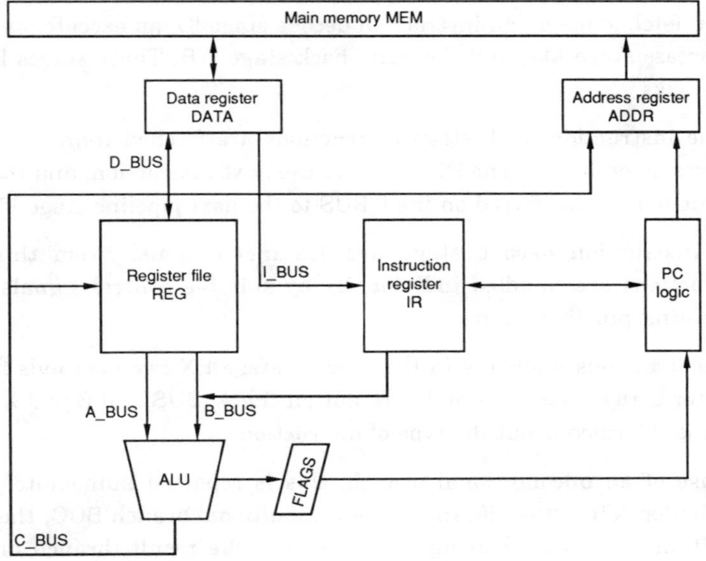

Figure 3.4 Datapath of TOOBSIE1

- The *register file* consists of 16 general-purpose registers of 32 bits. It is fully visible for the programmer. Register addresses are 5 bits (1 bit for future file extensions). The register file has a read/write port and an independent read port. Two accesses are possible per port per clock cycle.

- The *arithmetic logic unit* ALU is a simple and space saving Manchester Carry ALU in bit-slice technology. It consists of general function blocks and a carry chain. The function blocks permit shift operations by one or two bits. The ALU also computes addresses for LD/ST instructions.
- The *PC logic* computes addresses independently of the remaining datapath. An own adder for computing relative branch distances and an incrementer for increasing the program counter PC by 1 operate in parallel.

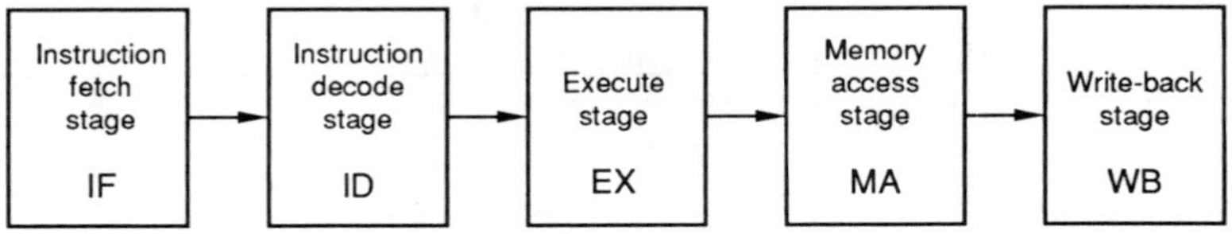

Figure 3.5 Pipeline of TOOBSIE1

The datapath as in Figure 3.5 is embedded in a 5-stage pipeline consisting of an instruction fetch stage IF, an instruction decode stage ID, an execute stage EX, a memory access stage MA, and the write-back stage WB. These stages have the following tasks.

IF In the instruction fetch stage instructions are fetched from the memory address given by PC. The PC points to the next instruction, and the loaded instruction is transferred on the I_BUS to the next pipeline stage ID.

ID The instruction decode stage decodes instructions. From this point, instructions are handled individually by suitable control signals for the remaining pipeline stages.

For instructions requiring in the execute stage EX two operands from the register array, these operands are put on the A_BUS and B_BUS. The EX stage is informed about the type of instruction.

In case of an unconditional branch, this is reported immediately to the instruction fetch stage IF. In case of a conditional branch BCC, the branch condition is evaluated using the flags, and the result (branch or not) is reported to the IF stage.

In case of instruction HALT, the pipeline must not accept new instructions, the first pipeline stages have to be stopped.

EX In the execute stage, the arithmetic logic unit ALU is located. Operands A_BUS and B_BUS are combined according to the control signals, and the result is put on C_BUS. If necessary, ALU flags are set.

MA The memory access stage either accesses memory, or it just forwards the result of the EX stage to the subsequent write-back stage WB. In case of an LD/ST instruction, the MA stage takes the address from the C_BUS and forwards it to the address register ADDR towards main memory. For instruction ST (Store), it transfers the data to be stored from D_BUS to data register DATA. For instruction LD (Load), it transfers data from main memory from DATA to C_BUS.

WB The write-back stage writes results from C_BUS into the register file.

For the pipeline, a *forwarding mechanism* makes sense, where, for example, an instruction Y needs the contents of register A, although instruction X preceding Y changes register A. Without forwarding, the new value of A would still be stuck in the pipeline. The forwarding fetches the result directly from the EX stage or the MA stage.

The processor supports a *delayed branch* by executing also the instruction following a CTR branch in the program independently of the branch being taken. This succeeding program position is called the *delay slot*, and the instruction in the delay slot is the *delay instruction*. In the pipeline, there is a one clock delay between the decision to take a branch and the fetching of a target instruction. During this delay, the delay instruction is loaded in any case. By executing the delay instruction, the pipeline remains better balanced.

3.2 Selection of a Processor Architecture

We are now in the preliminary Phase 0 of designing the RISC processor TOOBSIE, in which requirements of the architecture are specified (Section 2.3). Starting from the model TOOBSIE1 of the previous section with a 5-stage pipeline, we will first gather and evaluate possible architectural extensions, of which finally a reasonable subset will be selected.

At this point we would like to repeat that TOOBSIE is primarily an example of a large semi-custom design. If the focus was on computer architecture, particularly on the development of a maximally efficient new RISC processor, extensive research would be necessary at this point. For example, a suitable compiler would have to be developed and optimized, and extensive statistical simulations on the system level would be meaningful. We prefer to restrict ourselves to a relatively superficial, heuristic selection of some known RISC principles, which we will extend, however, at some places by new ideas. The following briefly sketched and evaluated architecture features require special knowledge; the inexperienced reader will be more extensively introduced in the design specification of Chapters 5 and 6 to the features actually selected.

3.2.1 Proposals for Architectural Extensions

The following list summarizes suggestions for additional architecture features extending the base model TOOBSIE1. It is not ordered regarding priorities or implementability.

1 Dynamic Register Blocks

"Multi-windows" [Scholz, Schäfers 1995] are based on a concept of [Quammen et al. 1989] called "threaded windows". Up to 1024 general-purpose registers are given in blocks of fixed size. The blocks are allocated dynamically at run time when needed. Without the fixed scheme of a ring buffer as in the Berkeley RISC [Katevenis 1985], the expensive saving and loading of registers can be reduced significantly. Other advantages include flexibility in process changes and interrupts. Disadvantages are a complex control logic and more chip area.

2 Pseudo-Harvard Architecture and Multi-Purpose Cache

We suggest having separate buses for instructions and data within the processor. Externally, however, the processor has just one 32-bit bus and a second one for memory addresses. For such a "Pseudo-Harvard" architecture, an on-chip instruction cache is meaningful. Advantages are a control logic simpler than for a data cache and an increased performance due to improved parallelism. A disadvantage could be a loss of performance, when the cache is too small due to cost limitations.

In a variant of such a cache, not every referenced address is stored, but only those instructions producing a deadlock with the IF stage due to an LD/ST access (Reduced Instruction Buffer, RIB-mode [Jove, Cortadella 1989]). When accessing such an instruction the next time, the IF stage need not wait. This feature is interesting from a research point of view, is relatively simple, and increases performance without additional prerequisites. A disadvantage is that the cache can only be used in a restricted way.

The combination of both modes is the *multi-purpose cache* MPC.

3 Branch-Target Cache

A cache at the address bus stores addresses of branch instructions and branch targets as well as delay instructions following a branch [Schäfers 1993, 1994]. When accessing such a branch again, the loading of the delay instruction can be omitted. The performance should increase, but a complex control logic is required.

4 Interrupts, Virtual Addressing, and Kernel/User Mode

The pipeline status has to be saved after an interrupt. There are various interrupt priorities. An interrupt mechanism should be implemented, because a "real" processor simply needs it. There are interesting questions concerning real-time interrupt delays. Expensive are the relatively high implementation effort and difficult testability as well as their understandability in a textbook.

This feature serves as a base for other useful concepts like *virtual addressing* or *kernel/user mode*. Virtual addresses generally require the keeping of virtual rather than physical addresses in the cache and an external memory management unit for memory tables and for triggering interrupts. These concepts require little additional effort, if an interrupt concept exists at all.

The kernel/user mode distinguishes between a kernel mode, where the whole instruction set is available, and a user mode, which allows, for example, only a restricted address space and offers no cache instructions. This is an important and relatively easy to implement concept for practical work.

5 Superscalar Pipeline and a More Efficient Memory Management

Modern memory components often have a fast burst mode increasing the average data transfer rate. This requires an efficient memory interface. It enables the loading of two instructions per cycle, which then should be executed in parallel by duplicated pipeline stages, e.g., parallel ALUs (superscalar system). Of course, the performance gain is positive, and there are interesting questions to be studied. A disadvantage is the need for a more complex or new compiler and a more complex hardware control.

6 More Efficient ALU

Aside from the instruction fetch stage, whose run time is mainly determined by memory access time, the ALU of TOOBSIE1 turned out to be a bottleneck.

Therefore, a faster ALU is desirable. One may also think of additional instructions for multiplication or division. Also a barrel shifter could be meaningful.

7 Asynchronous Pipeline

Execution time of one step of a pipeline stage varies not only from stage to stage, but also within a stage for different applications. Whereas a synchronous pipeline control has to wait for the slowest case, an asynchronous one, i.e., stages coupled in a clock-independent way, may gain performance. A disadvantage would be the known difficulties in the implementation and verification of such ideas.

3.2.2 Evaluation of Proposals

We begin with some basic thoughts on the evaluation of architecture features.

- One should balance the additional *chip area* of a feature and the *performance* gain. Such an analysis, however, can be time consuming.
- The expected additional *design time* should be considered.
- The expected *didactic benefit* of a feature should be considered. This may result in questions like: "What is the smallest meaningful superscalar extension (several parallel ALUs)?" or "What does a smallest meaningful branch-target cache look like?" The additional feature should in the case of failure not endanger the design as a whole, and it should therefore be possible to turn it off.
- The following basic consideration was discussed: should the processor have a high *real* or *potential* performance? A real performance is the one actually measured for TOOBSIE; as a potential performance of a feature, we consider the performance gain that would result when fully using the most modern technology, the maximum possible chip area, and no restrictions during design. For example, on a gate-array implementation, a cache with 16 entries might bring little real gain, but it prepares a large potential performance gain if later it is substituted by a full-custom cache with 256 entries.

  Real performance should be desired because performance values are testable and because under given restrictions, we strive for a maximum possible performance; we avoid "if-then promises".

  A potential performance should be desired because an interesting feature remains interesting, even if it is reduced, and it might allow a realistic extrapolation of performance.

In addition to the criteria mentioned above, Table 3.6 tries an evaluation of the suggested architecture features by a kind of election under pragmatic criteria. This table is partially speculative and not fully accepted in the team, but it gives some hints.

Architecture feature for TOOBSIE	General complexity (1 simple ... 6 complex)	Implementation effort (1 simple ... 6 hard)	Use (1 high ... 6 low)	Only meaningful ...	TOOBSIE1 fully (1) ... not at all (6) extended	Feature can be turned off	Further hints
1 Dynamic register blocks	4	4	2	–	2	yes	[Qua...89] [Scholz, Schä...95]
2 Pseudo-Harvard architecture, multi-purpose cache	1	2	2	if both are implemented	2	cache: yes	[Hill et al. 86]
3 Branch-target cache	3	3	3	–	2	yes	[Lee...84] [Man...93]
4 Interrupts, virtual addressing, kernel/user mode	4	4	1	with suitable operating system	3	yes	[Furber 89]
5 More efficient memory interface, duplicated pipeline stages	5	5	2	–	6	difficult	
6 More efficient ALU	2	2	1	–	2	no	
7 Asynchronous pipeline coupling	6	5	2-5	–	2-5	no	

Table 3.6 Evaluation of suggestions

The isolated consideration of features does not suffice, as also an efficient interplay between the components is important [AM29000 1988]. With an efficient memory interface, for example, supporting the fast burst mode of DRAM components, the use of a cache is smaller than with a less powerful memory control.

In a second evaluation phase, the single features are therefore compared pairwise (and even that is not fully sufficient). A + in Table 3.7 means a positive mutual support and dependency, a – means a negative one. Independence is marked by o. The diagonal contains further remarks. The table contains just very short hints as an additional stimulus for the expert.

Some suggestions were split into subfeatures due to internal dependencies, namely the fourth suggestion divided into subfeatures *interrupts, virtual addresses,* and *kernel / user mode*, and the fifth suggestion reduced to *more efficient memory interface*.

Some extensions have no direct impact on others and were therefore omitted in Table 3.7, such as the features *duplicated pipeline stages, more efficient ALU,* or *asynchronous pipeline coupling.* Instead, the new feature *extension of instruction set* is considered.

	1 Dynamic register blocks	2 Pseudo-Harvard architecture	3 Branch-target cache	4 Interrupts	5 More efficient memory interface	6 Extension of instruction set	7 Virtual addresses, kernel/user mode
1 Dynamic register blocks	too expensive (ineffic. gate-array implementation (--)						
2 Pseudo-Harvard architecture	1 supports procedure calls, but 2 requires small work. set (--)	multi-purpose cache to avoid pipeline hazards					
3 Branch-target cache	many procedure calls mean many branches (+)	1+3 large area (o)	good, if many branches				
4 Interrupts	1 supports independent register banks (++)	no problem, as cache does not belong to processor status (o)	3 set invalid (o)	external/internal signals cause context switch			
5 More efficient memory interface	1 good for large working set; this is also supported by 5 (++)	memory hierarchy not needed for fast memory (--)	3 always of advantage, no matter how fast memory (-)	fast memory good for saving and loading status (++)	1 cycle operations with SRAMs or in page mode		
6 Extension of instruction set	1 requires LD/ST instr. for blocks of registers, >1 cycle instructions! (o)	2 requires flush instr., >1 cycle instructions! (-)	3 set invalid (o)	additional instructions necessary	no influence	–	
7 Virtual addresses, kernel/user mode	process change expensive, as 1 means large status	external MMU, as otherw. TLB on-chip needed (--)	3 set invalid	access to interrupt instructions in kernel mode only (o)	7 requires translation and makes 5 more difficult (-)	additional instructions to select mode required	multitasking, multi-user, i.e., protected areas

Table 3.7 Dependencies of suggestions and further remarks

3.2.3 Summary of Extensions Accepted

After further research, the following architecture features were accepted for implementation in TOOBSIE.

- *Pseudo-Harvard architecture*: This is the central extension concerning performance and chip area. As data and instructions are loaded by the same memory bus, they may disturb each other. Therefore, a second processor memory path is implemented on the chip. It is supported by a multi-purpose cache MPC with a configurable load strategy.

In the normal mode, the MPC operates as a normal instruction cache. It is relatively small with about 16 lines of two entries each. It reduces pipeline hazards and increases performance even for slow memories. A small cache, however, can be worse than none at all. The replacement strategy plays a central role.

In the RIB mode, the MPC works as a reduced instruction buffer [Jove, Cortadella 1989]. Here, pipeline hazards are avoided directly. In contrast to the normal mode, 50–60% of pipeline hazards can be dissolved by the RIB mode [Mansfeld 1993]. A small RIB cache is not worse than none at all. A disadvantage is that for the about 70–80% of instructions not being load/store, another fast memory is required. For a fast processor with a slow memory, a normal instruction cache is therefore advantageous.

- *Branch-target cache (BTC):* This cache stores addresses of branch instructions with their branch targets and branch conditions as well as the succeeding delay instruction and history bits. It observes the address bus, catches memory accesses to branches, and replaces them by the branch target on the instruction bus. The branches themselves are suppressed in the pipeline thus increasing performance. Even a small cache with about 16 entries is very useful [Schäfers 1993, 1994]. The implementation, however, requires more complicated logic for the program counter.

- *Interrupts:* This feature is important for real processors and should be implemented as simply as possible. As variants, one may take a fixed vector base register or an interrupt address from the data bus. The main problem is saving the pipeline status.

  Virtual addresses are translated into physical ones not on the chip but externally.

- *Kernel/user mode:* This distinction is important for operating systems and security of multi-tasking.

- An *efficient ALU* increases throughput. A barrel shifter is not RISC-typical due to its high implementation costs. A complete shifter as a macro cell, however, as offered by the silicon vendor library, is acceptable.

- *Instruction set:* The existing instruction set of the first design is to be cleaned up. The additional features require some new instructions, such as a cache flush, interrupts, etc. We do not plan extensions for multiplication or division, but will instead implement these using software interrupts and software.

4 Short Introduction to VERILOG

This chapter will give the reader a first overview of the hardware description language VERILOG by several small examples. Together with the extensive introduction in Chapter 11, which can be used whenever needed in parallel to the remainder of the book, and with the training simulator VeriWell on the enclosed disk, all foundations and concepts for understanding the VERILOG models of the processor TOOBSIE are presented. We assume and recommend that the reader knows at least one structured programming language like Pascal, Modula-2, or C; in particular, VERILOG is very similar to C.

VERILOG allows both, structural descriptions as netlists of gates, components, and modules, and algorithmic behavioral models with variables, case selections (`if`, `case`), loops (`for`, `while`), and procedures (`function`, `task`) as well as arbitrary combinations of structure and behavior (Section 2.2).

```
module count;                          // this is a comment     // 00
integer I;                                                      // 01
                                                                // 02
initial                                                         // 03
begin                                                           // 04
  $display ("Starting simulation...");                          // 05
  for (I=1; I <= 3; I=I+1)                                      // 06
    $display ("run %d", I);                                     // 07
  $display ("Finished");                                        // 08
end                                                             // 09
endmodule                                                       // 10
```

Figure 4.1 A simple module

Modules are the basic units in VERILOG for gates, counters, CPUs, or complete computers. They can be nested hierarchically. Module `count` in Figure 4.1, enclosed by `module` and `endmodule`, outputs the numbers `1` to `3` on a display. In line 1, count variable `I` is defined. The compound statement following `initial` will be executed exactly once. The instruction `display` outputs a character string. As in C, `%d` outputs `I` as an integer. `//` starts a comment until the end of line. Like all reserved words, `begin` is written with small letters, and it is different from `Begin` and `BEGIN`. The instructions between `begin` and `end` are executed in sequential order. The simulator VERILOG-XL produces Figure 4.2 as result.

```
VERILOG-XL 2.0.1    Jun  7, 1995  13:50:32

. . .

Compiling source file "bsp1.v"
Highest level modules:
count

Starting simulation...
run           1
run           2
run           3
Finished
8 simulation events
CPU time: 0.1 secs to compile + 0.1 secs to link + 0.0 secs in simulation
End of VERILOG-XL 2.0.1    Jun  7, 1995  13:50:32
```

Figure 4.2 Ouput of Figure 4.1

Module `maximum` in Figure 4.3 computes the maximum of two numbers `A` and `B` and stores the result in `MAX`. The *parameter list* after the module name contains the variables coming from the outside of the module (`A` and `B`) and go to other modules (`MAX`). In addition, for every variable its direction `input` or `output` has to be declared; `inout` means both directions. In lines 4 to 6, the variable types are declared. Aside from `integer`, there are `wire`, `reg`, `real`, `event`, and `time`.

We will only explain the difference between `wire` and `reg`, the others are treated in Chapter 11. A *wire* of type `wire` represents a connection between several nodes of a circuit. In a *register* of type `reg`, binary values can be written and read. This is not possible for a wire only connecting two or more points in all directions.

`wire` and `reg` are *hardware oriented* data types; both represent words of several bits, where each bit may not only be `0` and `1`, but also `z` and `x`: `z` means the high impedance state, and `x` stands for unknown; when several sources drive a wire differently, the result is `x`. For both types, the bit width may be indicated by an interval in brackets before the variable definition. `A[31]` accesses bit 31 of `A`.

The statement `always` executes the following (compound) statement always again. When reaching condition

```
@ (A or B),
```

the simulator will only start a new loop, if at least one of the variables A or B has changed since the time the condition was reached by the simulator.

```
module maximum (A, B, MAX);          // determine maximum
input          A,
               B;
output         MAX;
wire   [31:0]  A,
               B;
reg    [31:0]  MAX;

always @(A or B)
begin
  if (A > B)
    MAX = A;
  else
    MAX = B;
  $display ("new maximum is %d", MAX);
end
endmodule
```

Figure 4.3 Interface, variable, always, and @

Figure 4.4 shows the module parallel_blocks. In contrast to normal programming languages with a sequential program flow, the components of a real circuit all work in parallel. For that, VERILOG offers several constructs.

```
module parallel_blocks;              // two parallel blocks
initial
begin
  $display ("yes");
  $display ("yes");
end

initial
begin
  $display ("no");
  $display ("no");
end

endmodule
```

Figure 4.4 Two parallel blocks

The two initial blocks in parallel_blocks are executed in parallel. This means that they are executed *in arbitrary order*, but only *sequentially*. The programmer cannot rely upon a specific order. When executing the same program several times, however, the same order is always chosen. Furthermore, it is assured that the instructions within a block are executed sequentially without a second block working in the meantime, until a *time control* is reached: @ (*condition*), # (*delay*), and wait.

```
module alu (OPCODE, A, B, RESULT); // ALU implementation
input         OPCODE,
              A,
              B;
output        RESULT;
wire   [2:0]  OPCODE;
wire  [31:0]  A,
              B;
reg   [31:0]  RESULT;

`define ADD    3'b000              // 0
`define MUL     'b001              // 1
`define AND    3'o2                // 2
`define LOGAND 3'h3                // 3
`define MOD       4                // 4
`define SHL    3'b101              // 5

`define SIMULATION_TIME 100

function [31:0] calculate_result;
input [2:0] OPCODE;
case (OPCODE)
  `ADD:    calculate_result = A + B;
  `MUL:    calculate_result = A * B;
  `AND:    calculate_result = A & B;
  `LOGAND: calculate_result = A && B;
  `MOD:    calculate_result = A % B;
  `SHL:    calculate_result = A << B;
  default: $display ("Unimplemented opcode: %d!", OPCODE);
endcase
endfunction

always  @ (OPCODE or A or B)
  RESULT = calculate_result(OPCODE);

initial                            // initial block equivalent
  forever                          // to always block
  begin
    @ (RESULT);
    $display ("Opcode= %d, A= %d, B= %d: RESULT= %d",
      OPCODE, A, B, RESULT);
  end

initial
begin
  $display ("Simulation starting");
  # `SIMULATION_TIME;              // end of simulation
  $display ("Simulation ending");
  $finish;
end
endmodule
```

Figure 4.5 A simple ALU

Possible simulation results are therefore

```
yes yes no no
```

or

```
no no yes yes    ,
```

but not

```
yes no no yes    ,
yes no yes no
```

and similar mixes. For a deeper understanding of this very fundamental notion of parallelism, we refer to Section 11.3.

Figure 4.5 shows a simple ALU (arithmetic logic unit) for the operations of addition, multiplication, AND, logical AND (which is true, iff in both, A and B, at least one bit is 1), modulo, and shift left. ALU inputs are the Opcode and both operands. After variable definition, some operation names are connected with bit combinations by `define. This corresponds to #define in C. Such replacements are valid until the end of source code, hence extend beyond the end of the module.

The general form of a constant is

<width> <base> <number> .

The width of a constant is optional, the smallest necessary value being the default. For the base, 'b (base 2), 'o (base 8), 'd (base 10), 'h (base 16), and 'B, 'O, 'D, and 'H are legal, the default being 10. For example, 'h12 represents a constant of width 5 bits.

The always and the two initial blocks of the ALU are executed in parallel in the sense explained before, i.e., the order of execution is arbitrary. The first initial block corresponds to an always block by containing an endless loop with forever. The second initial block terminates simulation by $finish after having waited for `SIMULATION_TIME units of time.

As soon as A, B, or OPCODE change, the always block calls the function calculate_result. Using the OPCODE of width 3, the case selects the function to be computed. It corresponds to switch in C; a break is not necessary. At most one alternative of case is executed. The function gives its result by its name. The result width may be declared before the function name.

The operations in Table 4.6 correspond to those in C. The difference between == and === and its negation will be explained later.

<table>
<tr><th>Operation group</th><th>Explanation</th></tr>
<tr><td>+, -, *, /, %</td><td>Arithmetic</td></tr>
<tr><td><, <=, >, >=</td><td>Compare</td></tr>
<tr><td>==, !=, ===, !==</td><td>Equality</td></tr>
<tr><td>!, &&, ||</td><td>Bit-wise operators</td></tr>
<tr><td>~, &, |, ^</td><td>Logic operators</td></tr>
<tr><td>?:</td><td>Selection</td></tr>
<tr><td><<, >></td><td>Shift</td></tr>
</table>

Table 4.6 Operations

A test of the ALU in Figure 4.5 would require a module with test values for A, B, and OPCODE. As an example, for A=3, B=2, and OPCODE=0 (`ADD), RESULT=5 would come up, with OPCODE=5 (`SHL), we would get RESULT=12.

The next example in Figure 4.7 instantiates submodules, generating a hierarchic structure of modules. There are two module types one_bit_adder and four_bit_adder. Signals CARRY_OUT and SUM are concatenated by { and } to form a new 2-bit variable. The sum of A, B, and CARRY_IN is assigned in an always loop to this composition as soon as one of the three variables changes. The four_bit_adder implements the addition of two 4-bit variables by four instances of the one_bit_adder. A result of width 5 is generated, and a flag is set, if the result is 0. In lines 30 and 31, another module nor is instantiated which is predefined in VERILOG. CARRY produces the carry bits.

```
module one_bit_adder (A, B, CARRY_IN, SUM, CARRY_OUT);               // 00
input             A,                                                 // 01
                  B,                                                 // 02
                  CARRY_IN;                                          // 03
output            SUM,                                               // 04
                  CARRY_OUT;                                         // 05
reg               SUM,                                               // 06
                  CARRY_OUT;                                         // 07
                                                                     // 08
always @ (A or B or CARRY_IN)                                        // 09
  {CARRY_OUT, SUM} = A + B + CARRY_IN;                               // 10
endmodule                                                            // 11
                                                                     // 12
                                                                     // 13
module four_bit_adder (A4, B4, SUM5, NULL_FLAG);                     // 14
input             A4,                                                // 15
                  B4;                                                // 16
output            SUM5,                                              // 17
                  NULL_FLAG;                                         // 18
                                                                     // 19
wire      [3:0]   A4,                                                // 20
                  B4;                                                // 21
wire      [4:0]   SUM5;                                              // 22
wire      [2:0]   CARRY;                                             // 23
                                                                     // 24
one_bit_adder Bit0 (A4[0], B4[0],     1'b0, SUM5[0], CARRY[0]);      // 25
one_bit_adder Bit1 (A4[1], B4[1], CARRY[0], SUM5[1], CARRY[1]);      // 26
one_bit_adder Bit2 (A4[2], B4[2], CARRY[1], SUM5[2], CARRY[2]);      // 27
one_bit_adder Bit3 (A4[3], B4[3], CARRY[2], SUM5[3],  SUM5[4]);      // 28
                                                                     // 29
nor nor_for_zeroflag (NULL_FLAG,                                     // 30
  SUM5[0], SUM5[1], SUM5[2], SUM5[3], SUM5[4]);                      // 31
endmodule                                                            // 32
```

Figure 4.7 Instantiation of submodules

The one_bit_adders are submodules of the four_bit_adder. Even completely separated modules without a common main module may be put side by side.

```
case (VALUE)
  3'b000: $display ("000");
  3'b001: $display ("001");
  3'b0?0: $display ("0?0");
  3'bz00: $display ("z00");
  default:$display ("undefined");
endcase

casez (VALUE)
  3'b000: $display ("000");
  3'b001: $display ("001");
  3'b0?0: $display ("0?0");
  3'bz00: $display ("z00");
  default:$display ("undefined");
endcase
```

Figure 4.8 case and casez

As a last example, we will explain the difference between `case` and `casez` (Figure 4.8). Both are *selection statements*. As mentioned before, wires and registers may assume at every bit position not only the usual values `0` and `1`, but also `x` (unknown) and `z` (high impedance). The high impedance `z` is used for tristate buses, for example, as a substitute for a disconnected wire.

`casez` differs from `case` only in the interpretation of `z` bits in the selection variable. If there is a `z`, `case` interprets this condition as true only if the select pattern has a `z` or a `?` at this position. In contrast, `casez` ignores this position and evaluates the remaining bits. The "wildcard" `?` stands for an arbitrary value except for `x`. The behavior of both select instructions is further clarified in Table 4.9.

Selection variable	Selection pattern	Compare with `case`	Compare with `casez`
3'b000	3'b000	1	1
3'b000	3'b001	0	0
3'b000	3'b00z	0	1
3'b000	3'b00?	0	1
3'b000	3'b00x	0	0
3'b00z	3'b000	0	1
3'b111	3'b1z1	0	1
3'b01z	3'b1z1	0	0
3'b01z	3'b01z	1	1
3'b???	3'b??x	0	1

Table 4.9 Evaluations with `case` and `casez`

A similar distinction is made by == and === or != and !==. The comparison with == is only 1 if on both sides, there is no `x` or `z` and if both sides are bit-wise equal. If one side contains an `x` or `z`, == yields value `x`. By the way, also !=

produces x in this case. In contrast, === compares both sides bit-wise, where x and z are compared literally. This behavior is explained in Table 4.10.

Left side	Right side	Compare with ==	!=	===	!==
1	1	1	0	1	0
0	1	0	1	0	1
1	x	x	x	0	1
0	x	x	x	0	1
x	x	x	x	1	0
z	x	x	x	0	1
z	1	x	x	0	1
z	z	x	x	1	0

Table 4.10 Comparisons

In the HDL models of the processor TOOBSIE, we have striven for a homogeneous VERILOG style and conventions for better readability. This is treated in Chapter 11. More discussions and interesting factors influencing modeling style are found in [Schäfers et al. 1993].

5 External Specification of Behavior

The RISC processor TOOBSIE is specified externally and internally. The external specification in this chapter is the processor view "from outside" as seen by an application programmer (or the compiler and the operating system). The external specification consists basically of the instruction set. The internal specification in Chapter 6 contains all important requirements and decisions concerning processor structure, architecture, and performance, and is therefore meant for the chip designer; but it is also of interest for the chip user as it explains seemingly arbitrary features of the external specification.

The external specification contains all details necessary for programming. This includes the meanings and results of all instructions (semantics). The programmer is informed about the interrupt mechanism and useful features for operating systems. In addition, there are implications of the planned architecture, such as a delay slot, processor mode, and the memory concept.

The internal specification describes the processor from the view of a designer and sketches a coarse design path. This includes requirements for the internal structure like caches, the implementation of the instruction set on a datapath, and the organization as a pipeline structure, as well as a description of processor control.

The result of the external specification is fixed in Section 5.3 by an interpreter acting as a *golden device* for the instruction semantics. The interpreter is written in the HDL (hardware description language) VERILOG, although at this high level, typical HDL features like parallelism are not yet required.

The internal specification of Chapter 6 is the base for a large design step in Chapters 7 and H4, where the specification is precisely fixed in an extensive HDL-based Coarse Structure Model and where numerous hardware aspects are included. The Coarse Structure Model heavily uses HDL properties.

While we separate external and internal specification theoretically, internal details influence the external specification at many points. Pragmatically, the designer knows already during external specification that there will be a pipeline, caches, etc.

5.1 The RISC Processor at Work

A system designer embeds the RISC processor in a system environment. This includes on the software side at least an assembler, later also an operating system and a compiler, on the hardware side preparations for the test on a tester, then on a testboard for a real-time test, and finally the full periphery.

Many implementation details of interest to the system designer, such as package, pin assignment, or precise timing are not yet fixed in the specification, as they strongly depend on the future processor implementation.

Nevertheless, it is meaningful in the sense of a *hardware software codesign*, to begin development of the system environment at this stage, in parallel to the processor design. This particularly includes an assembler and a testboard. As these are documented in [Mierse 1994] and Chapter 9, we only sketch them briefly here.

5.1.1 The Assembler

The training design of the first small RISC processor TOOBSIE1 has demonstrated how tedious the manual coding even of small test programs is. Therefore, the development and application of an assembler is meaningful already now. We plan to develop a configurable assembler for typical RISC architectures [Mierse 1994], which can be applied easily to many common RISC architectures. It has the following features.

- There is a well defined input grammar;
- specification of syntax and code are parametrized;
- target systems are VERILOG models and the processor itself;
- the assembler is independent of the system envionment.

The input format approximates known formats of other processors. Oriented to RISC typical aspects, it has a 3-operand scheme:

operation destination register, source register1, source register2 or

operation destination register, source register1, constant .

A configurable code generation is meaningful, as it may change. Not only the bit pattern but also syntactical rules should be easily modifiable. The experience with TOOBSIE1 shows, however, that instruction decoding in the processor is not a bottleneck and does not produce many costs. The reason lies in the simply structured RISC-typical instruction set. Therefore, encoding is not very critical and can be fixed at an early point in time.

The assembler is supposed to generate the code for several target systems. In the early design phases, it supports various VERILOG models like the Interpreter Model or the Coarse Structure Model with a commented ASCII input file. The later phases like the test of the Gate Model or the produced processor require uncommented binary code. It is an important part of the test strategy that both inputs come from the same assembler to exclude additional fault sources (Figure 2.8).

Furthermore, the assembler supports "synthetic" instructions defined additionally by the user. With these redundant instructions, the readability of assembler programs can be increased significantly.

5.1.2 The Testboard

A highlight of design is the demonstration of the correctly functioning chip. This is not done immediately in a complete system but on a testboard. This board can be designed in parallel to processor design (Chapter 9).

The testboard is a simple single-board computer with TOOBSIE as CPU. In addition, there are a PC interface and a static RAM system with memory logic. A PC is connected to the testboard to serve as a power supply and for memory initialization. After the program loading TOOBSIE is started. During and after its execution, the memory contents are read and evaluated by the PC.

The board is characterized by a flexible timing, a flexible memory protocol, and a not yet specified pin assignment of the processor chip.

5.2 The Instruction Set

In this section the RISC instruction set is specified. Instructions and their formats are presented. The instructions are divided into classes LD/ST, CTR, ALU, and Special. The complete description of all instructions in detail can be found in Chapter H2. The reader certainly has a basic understanding of such relatively simple instructions. We therefore concentrate on the details and exceptions.

Starting from the experiences of the first small RISC design, we now specify an instruction word length of 32 bits and a register file of 32 general-purpose registers also of 32 bits. According to [Huck, Flynn 1989], a set of about 8 registers is sufficient for a fairly well optimized allocation of local variables within procedures. In addition, mechanisms for register allocation may increase throughput (for example, register windows). An array of 32 registers typically permits a procedure nesting of depth 4. This covers a significant proportion of all programs [Katevenis 1985] and constitutes a good compromise between area and speed [Kane 1987].

We first define some logical instruction formats in Figure 5.1. The diversity of formats is intended only to ease understanding. During implementation, they will later be summarized to just a few RISC-typical formats.

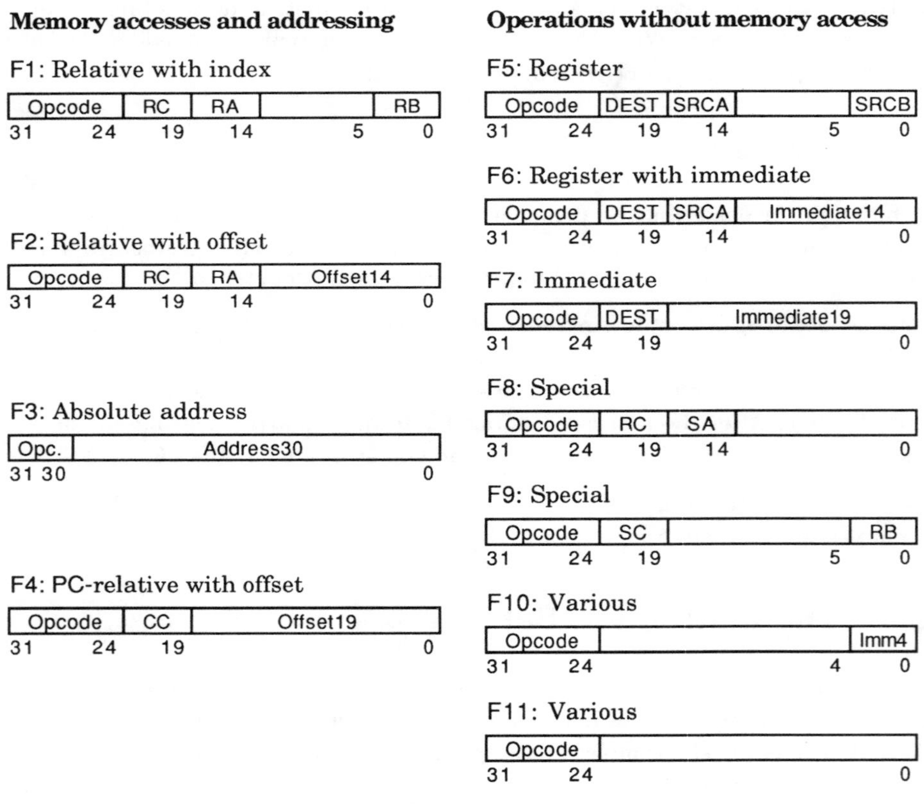

Figure 5.1 Instruction formats

The format names in Figure 5.1 have the following meaning, which is explained in detail later:

Opcode	Instruction code
RA, RB, RC	Addresses of general-purpose registers serving in memory accesses and special instructions as source, destination, memory address, or index
Offset n	Constant for address modification, target of a conditional branch, etc., n bits
Address30	Absolute address
CC	Code of a branch condition (condition code)
SRCA, SRCB, DEST	Addresses of source and destination registers for arithmetic-logic operations
Immediate n	Immediate constant in arithmetic-logic operations, for software interrupt, etc., n bits
Imm n	Short form of Immediate n
SA, SC	Addresses of special registers

In addition, we use:

REG	Register array (general-purpose registers)
rA, rC	Registers REG[RA], REG[RC]
rB	Register REG[RB] or Offset14 extended by 00, 01, 10, or 11 (Opcode dependent)
cc	Branch condition of CC
srcA, dest	Registers REG[SRCA], REG[DEST]
srcB	Register REG[SRCB] or Immediate14 (Opcode dependent)
sA, sC	Special registers for SA and SC
MEM[n]	External memory location n
N, Z, C, V	Status flags
SREG	Special register; alternatives are:
PC	Program counter
RPC	Return address
LPC	Last PC
SR	Status register
VBR	Vector base register
HWISR	Hardware interrupt status register
EXCSR	Exception status register
SWISR	Software interrupt status register
HWIRPC	Hardware interrupt return PC
EXCRPC	Exception return PC
SWIRPC	Software interrupt return PC
HWIADR	Hardware interrupt address
EXCADR	Exception address

Finally, we require some common operations on registers or memory locations A and B and an expression expr over registers:

A ← expr	Assignment
A ↔ B	Exchange
A>>B	Shift A by B positions right
A<<B	Shift A by B positions left
A>>>B	Rotate A by B positions right

{A,B}	Concatenation
A | B	Bit-wise logical OR
A & B	Bit-wise logical AND
A^B	Bit-wise logical XOR
~A	One's complement
A + B	Addition
A - B	Subtraction

When applying +, the usual difficulties are encountered as to whether the sign of operands of different width has to be extended.

5.2.1 Class LD/ST of Load and Store Instructions

In addition to being fetched, these instructions require a second memory access. They exchange data with the memory. A processor word is 32 bits (quad-byte Q), there are also 16-bit halfwords with two bytes (double-byte D) and 8-bit bytes (B).

Memory addresses for word accesses are always oriented at word limits, that is, the two least significant bits are 0. For halfword accesses, the least significant bit is 0. Special care is needed when, for reasons of efficiency, certain constants are stored without the least significant 00 and have therefore to be extended by 00 in the application.

LD/ST instructions use three address operands rA, rB, and rC. While rA and rC refer to register addresses RA and RC, rB means, depending on the Opcode, either a general-purpose register REG[RB] or a 14-bit constant Offset14 to be extended by 00, 01, 10, or 11.

Memory is addressed in four different kinds. Under the *relative addressing with index register* (format F1 in Figure 5.1), the memory address is determined as the sum of the general-purpose registers rA and rB serving as a base and an index. The *relative address with offset* (format F2) is the sum of register rA and the offset again denoted as rB. This mode permits simple array accesses, stack manipulations, and the management of local variables. For store instructions rC is the source register, for load accesses the destination. As we have a *delayed load* (Chapter 3), the destination register contains the new value only in the next step.

LDU instructions move words, halfwords, or bytes unsigned, LDS variants move values with sign. This is no difference for words, but for halfwords and bytes where the higher significant bits have to be set according to the sign. Table 5.2 specifies the LD/ST instructions. When a partial word is moved, its position in the memory word is determined by variants of the Opcode.

Mnem.	Name	Format	Explanation
LDU	Load unsigned	F1,2	rC ← MEM[rA+rB] (word)
LDU.D	Load unsigned double-byte	F1,2	rC ← MEM[rA+rB] (halfword)
LDU.B	Load unsigned byte	F1,2	rC ← MEM[rA+rB] (byte)
LDS	Load signed	F1,2	rC ← MEM[rA+rB] (word)
LDS.D	Load signed double-byte	F1,2	rC ← MEM[rA+rB] (halfword) most significant bits according to sign
LDS.B	Load signed byte	F1,2	rC ← MEM[rA+rB] (byte) most significant bits according to sign
ST	Store	F1,2	MEM[rA+rB] ← rC
ST.D	Store double-byte	F1,2	MEM[rA+rB] ← rC (least significant halfword)
ST.B	Store byte	F1,2	MEM[rA+rB] ← rC (least significant byte)
SWP	Swap	F1,2	rC ↔ MEM[rA+rB]

Table 5.2 Specification of instructions Load and Store of class LD/ST

5.2.2 Class CTR of Branch Instructions

CTR instructions (control transfers, branches) modify the control flow of a program by changing the program counter PC. Directly after a CTR instruction, there is a *delay instruction* in a *delay slot* to be executed before the branch, whether it is taken or not. In case of the ANNUL option .A, however, the delay instruction is ignored if the branch is not taken. *CTR instructions must not follow each other directly.*

Table 5.3 specifies the branches. The *absolute address* Address30 (format F3 in Figure 5.1) is only used by the CALL instruction. As only 32-bit words are targeted, the absolute address is extended by 00. This covers the whole range of 2^{30} memory words corresponding to an address space of 2^{32} bytes. As only CALL instruction use this address mode, two bits suffice for the Opcode.

For supporting high level programming languages, the *PC-relative addressing with offset* is important (format F4). Conditional branches (BCC instructions) contain a 19-bit constant Offset19, which is interpreted as a relative branch address. The distance is signed and extended by 00. Hereafter, it is added to the PC. This covers $\pm 2^{20}$ bytes.

Program traces [Huck, Flynn 1989, Mansfeld 1993] have shown that in more than 99% of all cases, PC-relative branches are within this distance. If a branch is outside, it can be substituted by an "inverse" branch and a CALL.

A subprogram is called by CALL and the return is accomplished by the *synthetic* CTR instruction RET (Return). It is called synthetic, because it does not belong to the RISC instruction set of the processor but summarizes existing instructions to obtain a more readable form. In that sense, RET as explained in more detail in Sections 5.2.4 and 5.2.5, stands for a special instruction SRIS

(Store register into special register) which copies the return address stored earlier somewhere else to the program counter PC.

As is typical for RISC, the return target after a CALL has to be saved by the user, and it is the address following the delay slot. This address is copied automatically during a CALL into the special register RPC (Return-PC), but then it has to be saved into an arbitrary general-purpose register Rb using the special instruction LRFS Rb, RPC (Load register from special register). Subprogram return takes place as mentioned before by using RET Rb.

Mnem.	Name	Format	if cc,	then
BGT	Branch on greater than	F4	~((N ^ V) | Z)	PC ← PC + {Offset19,00}
BLE	Branch on less or equal	F4	(N ^ V) | Z	PC ← PC + {Offset19,00}
BGE	Branch on greater or equal	F4	~(N ^ V) | Z	PC ← PC + {Offset19,00}
BLT	Branch on less than	F4	(N ^ V) & ~Z	PC ← PC + {Offset19,00}
BHI	Branch on higher	F4	~(C | Z)	PC ← PC + {Offset19,00}
BLS	Branch on lower or same	F4	C | Z	PC ← PC + {Offset19,00}
BPL	Branch on plus	F4	~N	PC ← PC + {Offset19,00}
BMI	Branch on minus	F4	N	PC ← PC + {Offset19,00}
BNE	Branch on not equal	F4	~Z	PC ← PC + {Offset19,00}
BEQ	Branch on equal	F4	Z	PC ← PC + {Offset19,00}
BVC	Branch on overflow clear	F4	~V	PC ← PC + {Offset19,00}
BVS	Branch on overflow set	F4	V	PC ← PC + {Offset19,00}
BCC	Branch on carry clear	F4	~C	PC ← PC + {Offset19,00}
BCS	Branch on carry set	F4	C	PC ← PC + {Offset19,00}
BT	Branch on true	F4	true	PC ← PC + {Offset19,00}
BF	Branch on false	F4	false	
XXX.A	.A-Option	F4		For all instructions above, the delay instruction is executed; with option .A, however, the delay instruction is not executed, if the branch is not taken
CALL	Call	F3		RPC ← PC, PC ← {Address30,00} execute delay instruction
JMP	Jump	F9		PC ← rB execute delay instruction (also synthetic instruction, Sections 5.2.4 and 5.2.5)
RET	Return	F9		PC ← rB execute delay instruction (also synthetic instruction)
SWI	Software interrupt	F10		PC ← VBR | {1,Imm4,000} save processor state
RETI	Return from interrupt	F11		Restore saved processor state
HALT	Halt	F11		Halt and wait for reset

Table 5.3 Specification of branches of class CTR

The synthetic CTR instruction JMP (Jump) permits branches to an address stored in a register (Section 5.2.5). Finally, there are two CTR instructions SWI and RETI for interrupts explained in Section 5.2.6 and the CTR instruction HALT.

We would like to summarize the various notions. The processor works with *instructions*. Special instructions are *branches* controlling the program flow as *control transfers*. Equivalent is the notion of *CTR (instruction)*.

A branch may be *conditional* and is then called a *BCC (instruction)*: BGT, BLE, etc. (Note that the BCC instruction Branch on carry clear is also abbreviated by BCC; as it is rarely used explicitly, confusions are unlikely.)

Unconditional branches consist of CALL, JMP, RET, SWI, RETI, and HALT. As JMP and RET are synthetic instructions reduced to the special instruction SRIS, we often speak of SRIS in the context of unconditional branches; however, SRIS is only a CTR instruction if it refers to the program counter: SRIS PC, Rb (Sections 5.2.4 and 5.2.5). HALT is not always mentioned explicitly, as it is not a very typical unconditional CTR.

5.2.3 Class ALU of Arithmetic and Logic Instructions

ALU instructions do not require memory. They use three operands srcA, srcB, and dest. While srcA and dest refer to register addresses SRCA and DEST, respectively, srcB is, depending on Opcode, either a general-purpose register REG[SRCB] or a 14-bit constant Immediate14. We therefore have operations with two source registers (format F5 in Figure 5.1) and operations with immediate and one register (F6). Finally, there is the exclusive immediate operand (F7).

Flag	Name	Computation	For ALU instructions with .F-option
N	Negative	dest[31]	all
Z	Zero	~(|dest[31,0])	all
C	Carry	dest[32] ~dest[32] srcA[srcB-1] 0 undefined	ADD, ADDC, LSL SUB, SUBC LSR, ASR, ROT, if srcB > 0 LSR, ASR, ROT, if srcB = 0, else
V	Overflow	Carry[32] ^ Carry[31] undefined	ADD, ADDC, SUB, SUBC else

Table 5.4 Computation of flags

Negative numbers are represented in two's complement. In the case of Immediate14, the remaining most significant bits are set according to the sign of the constant.

The logical operations are executed bit-wise on 32-bit data words. Shift and rotation distance is determined by REG[SRCB].

Except for the LDH instruction, all ALU instructions may use the .F-option, where the flags of the result are stored in the status word for subsequent branches. The four flags are computed according to Table 5.4 and the ALU instructions are specified in Table 5.5.

Mnem.	Name	Format	Explanation
ADD	Add	F5,6	dest ← srcA + srcB
ADDC	Add with carry	F5,6	dest ← srcA + srcB + C
SUB	Subtract	F5,6	dest ← srcA - srcB
SUBC	Subtract with carry	F5,6	dest ← srcA - srcB - C
AND	And	F5,6	dest ← srcA & srcB
OR	Or	F5,6	dest ← srcA | srcB
XOR	Exclusive or	F5,6	dest ← srcA ^ srcB
LSL	Logical shift left	F5,6	dest ← srcA << srcB
LSR	Logical shift right	F5,6	dest ← srcA >> srcB
ASR	Arithmetic shift right	F5,6	dest ← srcA >> srcB most significant bits according to sign
ROT	Rotate	F5,6	dest ← srcA >>> srcB
XXX.F	.F-option		for all instructions above, the flag register is set according to dest
LDH	Load high	F7	dest ← {Immediate19,0...0} most significant bits of dest are replaced by Immediate19

Table 5.5 Specification of ALU instructions

5.2.4 Instructions of Class Special

The Special instructions of Table 5.6 allow data exchange between general-purpose and special registers (formats F8 and F9 in Figure 5.1). The access to a special register depends on the kernel/user mode.

In processor mode KERNEL_MODE, all 13 special registers may be written and read. In USER_MODE, however, special registers PC, RPC, and LPC can be written and read, but the status register SR can only be read, write accesses are only permitted to the least significant bits SR[3..0]; write accesses to more significant bits remain without effect. The remaining special registers cannot be accessed in the USER_MODE. A prohibited access to a special register results in exception PRIVILEGE_VIOLATION.

Moreover, there is the control instruction CLC with the operand-less format F11 for clearing the caches.

Mnem.	Name	Format	Explanation
LRFS	Load register from special reg.	F8	rC ← sA rC general-purpose register, sA special register
SRIS	Store register into special reg.	F9	sC ← rB sC special register, rB general-purpose register (also as synthetic CTR instructions Jump and Return for sC=PC)
CLC	Clear cache	F11	Clear caches

Table 5.6 Instructions of class Special

5.2.5 Synthetic Instructions

The synthetic instructions are combinations of instructions already specified, which become a special and frequently needed meaning with certain operands and increase program readability. For example, instruction XOR R0, R0, R0 has no effect to the processor state and can thus be used as a NOP (no operation). In doing so, the RISC-typical feature is used that the general-purpose register R0 constantly contains value 0. Write accesses are permitted, but do not change R0.

The synthetic instructions Jump and Return were introduced in Section 5.2.2. Table 5.7 shows the reduction of standard instructions in assembler notation.

Mnem.	Name	Implementation
CLR	Clear	XOR Rd, R0, R0
NEG	Negate	SUB Rd, R0, Rb
NOP	No operation	XOR R0, R0, R0
NOT	Inversion bitwise	XOR Rd, Ra, -1
JMP	Jump	SRIS PC, Rb
RET	Return from subroutine	SRIS PC, Rb

Table 5.7 Synthetic instructions

5.2.6 External Specification of Interrupts

Interrupts in a normal instruction stream transfer control to an interrupt routine. After its execution, the processor returns to the old program. The execution of external interrupts has to be *transparent* in the sense that after rerunning the old program, the interrupt can no longer be recognized.

We use the term *rerun* to denote the continuation of the program before interrupt. For instance, the rerun point is pipeline stage ID, if the instruction in the ID stage before the interrupt request was aborted.

The processor status including the status register and the return address is saved in special registers and general-purpose registers R28 ... R31. Therefore, there are two additional *overlay sets of registers* for R28 ... R31 that are superimposed depending on the interrupt level.

There are *external* or *hardware interrupts* (Hwi) requested by another system component, and *internal* interrupts requested inside the processor. The latter divide into *exceptions* (Exc) and *software interrupts* (Swi). An exception is called automatically by an error in instruction execution (e.g., a CTR instruction in a delay slot or a Privilege Violation) and a software interrupt is called by the instruction SWI.

The software can distinguish the different meanings and priorities of interrupts by branching to appropriate interrupt routines. Hardware interrupts are identified by an individual interrupt number. Numbers of the remaining interrupts are either fixed or part of the opcode. From the interrupt number, the starting address of the interrupt routine can be computed.

A vector base register VBR permits fast assignment of the interrupt routine. This assignment can be programmed. A combination of interrupt number and VBR produces the interrupt routine address.

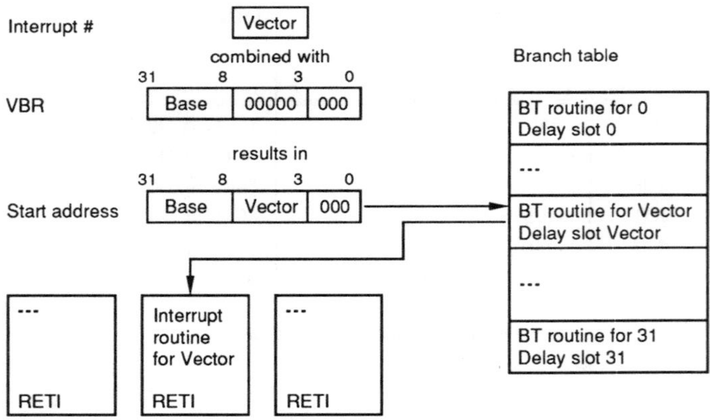

Figure 5.8 Branch target of an interrupt

The VBR contents or base give for every interrupt the starting address of a memory table. This table contains for each of the 32 interrupts the start of the interrupt routine consisting of a BT (Branch on true, always executed) with delay slot, hence two words or 8 bytes. Therefore, bits 0, 1, and 2 of VBR have constant value 0. The entry of an interrupt in the table is indexed by its number 0...31. This number is coded as a 5-bit vector, and it substitutes bits 3...7 of VBR resulting in the branch address (Figure 5.8).

The existing interrupts and their numbers are summarized in Table 5.9.

Type	Vector	Explanation
Hwi	00000	BUS_ERROR
00xxx	00001	PAGE_FAULT
	00010	MISS_ALIGN
	00011	Defined by operating system (OS)
	00100	Defined by OS
	00101	Defined by OS
	00110	Defined by OS
	00111	Defined by OS
Exc	01000	Delay instruction is CTR
01xxx	01001	PRIVILEGE_VIOLATION
	01010	ILLEGAL_INSTRUCTION
	01011	UNIMPLEMENTED_INSTRUCTION
	01100	Reserved
	01101	Reserved
	01110	Reserved
	01111	PANIC
Swi	1xxxx	Defined by OS
1xxxx		

Table 5.9 Interrupt numbers

The instructions SWI and RETI belong to class CTR and thus have a delay slot. Hardware interrupts and exceptions do not have a delay slot, but they are not instructions and do not have an opcode anyhow.

5.3 An Interpreter as a VERILOG HDL Model

For a precise specification of the instruction set, a model of the external processor behavior is developed as an interpreter. The behavior is a function transforming memory contents before execution of an application program into memory contents after its execution. This will be a coarse behavioral simulation neglecting all timing properties of the future processor. Figure 5.10 shows the role of this Interpreter Model as a reference (*golden device*).

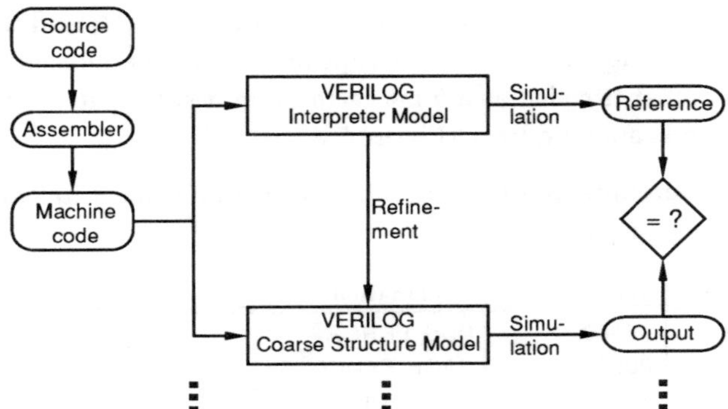

Figure 5.10 Interpreter Model as reference

The simulation results, however, are not equal as indicated in Figure 5.10, but only "similar" in an obvious way, as there are, for example, no caches modeled. Such differences are accepted for pragmatic reasons. This similarity will show from model to model, as a formal equality of results could only be achieved at the end of the design or even after production of the processor and would involve unacceptably high efforts. Rather, we will refine our models stepwise resulting also in finer simulation results.

Some peculiarities of the processor influencing its behavior are modeled already now, such as data dependency or a delay slot. These features appear at this point of time unmotivated and are modeled "artificially". Other features are still missing: not all special registers are implemented, the kernel/user mode is not supervised, and there are no overlay registers for software interrupts. The model was designed under the following aspects:

- abstract behavior (e.g., no timing and no hardware components);
- easy to modify;
- clear hierarchic organization;
- separation of processor and test environment.

The model is written in the hardware description language VERILOG. In the following, we first give an overview of the modularization and of typical design features, afterwards, we describe modules with their tasks and functions. An introduction to model applications with an example will follow. The model itself is on the disk in Chapter 💾2 and in the expert volume in H3.

5.3.1 Overview

The model is divided into the system module RISC2_System and the test module RISC2_Test on the highest level of hierarchy. The test module organizes processor input and output. These are the only modules, as the behavioral model does not contain hardware components. Figure 5.11 shows the tasks and functions employed.

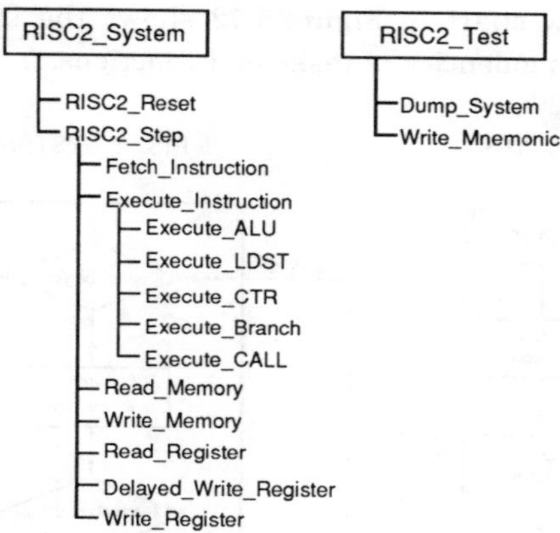

Figure 5.11 Modules, tasks, and functions of the Interpreter Model

The system module contains all tasks and functions for the simulation of the processor, the test module controls input and output and triggers a working step.

For the interpreter, there is no modeling of time behavior. A simple time behavior would differ too much from later models, and on the other hand, it would be unnecessarily difficult to simulate the future timing precisely, not to mention that this could not be predicted in this early design phase. Nevertheless, there is a "clock" whose unit is the execution of one instruction.

In the pipeline architecture planned and specified in the next chapter, there will be two special features that should be modeled already now, namely data dependency and delay slot.

Data dependency exists when a Load instruction with destination register R is followed by a second instruction with source R. For reasons explained later, such an instruction sequence is not permitted. To model this behavior, a FIFO memory is introduced into which the Load mentioned before writes its result. Only after the next instruction is this result copied from the FIFO into R.

The delay slot is generated artificially by replacing the single program counter PC by FPC (Fetch-PC) and NPC (Next-PC). These two registers are used as a FIFO: FPC contains the address of the present instruction, NPC that of the next one. After an instruction was fetched by FPC, the NPC is transferred to FPC, and NPC is increased by 1. Thus a future pipeline delay is modeled.

When a branch with delay instruction is executed, the NPC is not increased but set to the branch target. The delay instruction is then fetched from FPC, and the following instruction from NPC. An annulled delay instruction is handled analogously. The flow chart in Figure 5.12 shows the interpreter operation, Figure 5.13 shows dependencies of tasks and functions.

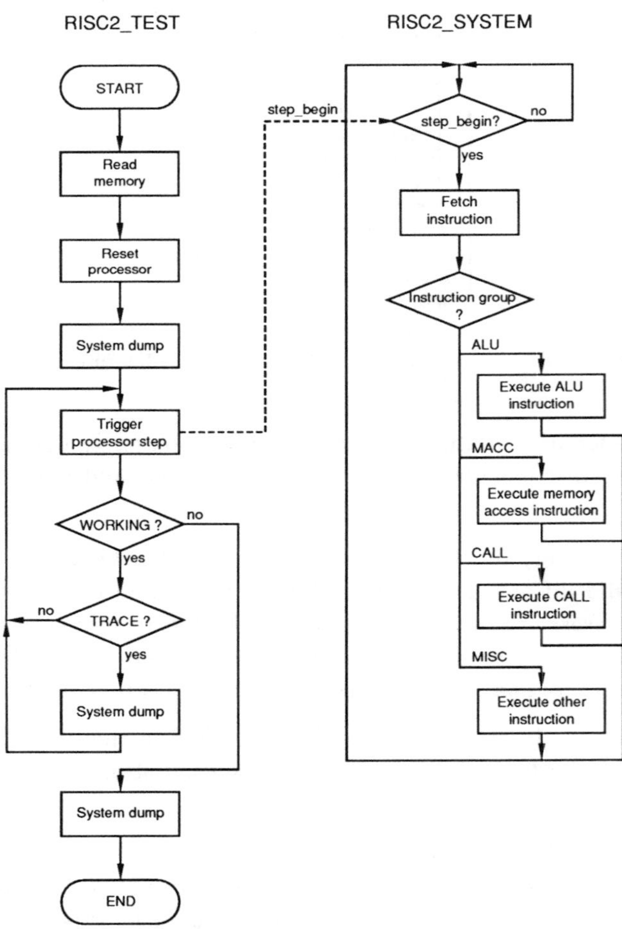

Figure 5.12 Flow chart of the interpreter

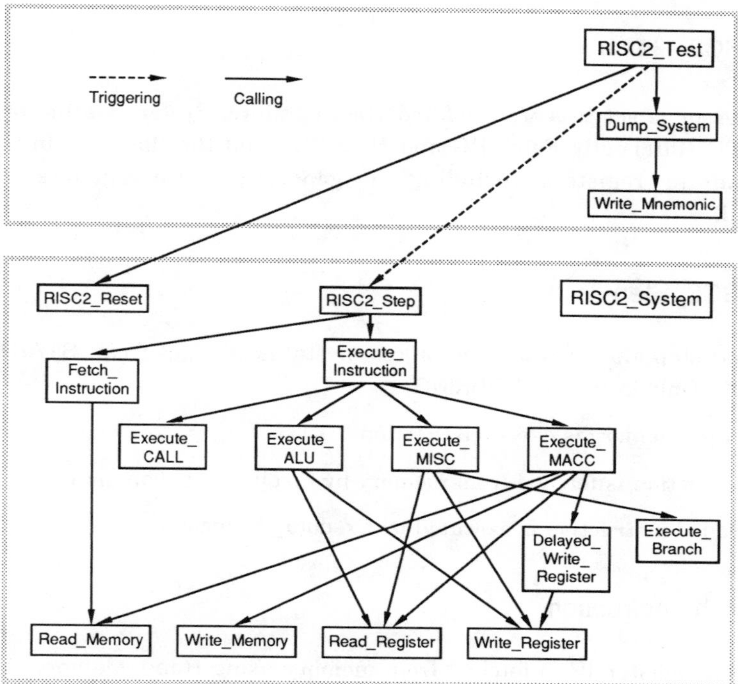

Figure 5.13 Calling graph of the interpreter

5.3.2 Components

In the system module RISC2_System, instructions are fetched, decoded, and executed. The instructions are divided into four groups ALU, MACC, MISC, and CALL. The ALU group contains arithmetic and logic instructions, the MACC group contains memory access instructions, the CALL group just instruction CALL, and in group MISC, there are all remaining instructions. These four groups are only used in the behavioral model and are determined by the two most significant bits of the opcode according to Table 5.14.

Bits 31	30	Group	Instructions
0	0	MACC	LDU, LDS, ST, SWP
0	1	ALU	ADD, SUB, ...
1	0	CALL	CALL
1	1	MISC	BGT, ..., SWI, RETI, HALT, LDH, LRFS, SRIS, CLC

Table 5.14 Encoding groups of the Interpreter Model

Task RISC2_Reset

The processor is set to a well defined starting state. System status, program counter PC (internally Fetch-PC and Next-PC), and the flags are initialized. The remaining registers, including the general-purpose registers, remain undefined.

Task RISC2_Step

In the first step after a reset, the processor status changes from `STARTED to `WORKING. Only in status `WORKING,

- the FIFO memory is executed (Section 5.3.1),
- an instruction is fetched from memory by Fetch_Instruction, and
- the loaded instruction is executed by Execute_Instruction.

Task Fetch_Instruction

Instruction register IR is fetched from memory using Read_Memory, and the fetch address is stored in LPC (Last-PC). FPC is set to NPC, from which the instruction will be fetched the next time. For a branch, this is not the address following FPC. Hereafter, NPC is incremented or set to the target of a taken branch.

Task Execute_Instruction

This task consists of a single case statement. Only the two most significant bits of the opcode distinguish the group. The four groups ALU, MACC, MISC, and CALL are decoded. Each group has its own task to which Execute_Instruction branches.

Task Execute_ALU

ALU instructions are executed. Data are fetched from registers and combined. Depending upon the opcode, the flags are set. Write_Register writes the result into the destination register. Data dependency need not be considered here, as there will be a forwarding.

Task Execute_MACC

First, source and destination address for memory access are computed. Data dependency is to be considered for Load and Swap operations by using Delayed_Write_Register instead of Write_Register.

Task Execute_MISC

In this task, BCC instructions and operations SWI, RETI, HALT, LDH, LRFS, SRIS, and CLC are executed. For a BCC instruction, it is transferred to task Execute_Branch. Instruction CLC is ignored as it has no influence on processor behavior at this level of abstraction.

Task Execute_Branch

Conditional branches are handled in this task. If a branch is taken, NPC is set to the address computed, otherwise it is checked whether the delay slot is to be annulled. In this case, the FPC is set to the old NPC, which then is incremented.

Task Execute_CALL

The CALL instruction is an unconditional branch, moreover, the NPC is written into RPC (Return-PC). By writing the branch address into NPC, also the CALL instruction has a delay slot.

Function Read_Memory

This function reads from the given memory address a byte, a halfword, or a word. First, a complete 32-bit word is fetched from memory ignoring the two least significant bits of the address. Then the required part of the 32-bit word is selected.

Task Write_Memory

This task proceeds analogously to Read_Memory. First, a complete 32-bit word is read. Then it is partially or completely substituted by the data to be written and written back to memory.

Function Read_Register

The contents of the indicated register are read. For R0, the result is always 0.

Task Delayed_Write_Register

For a Load instruction, the register writing has to be delayed. First, the register is set to an invalid state. Then data are written into the FIFO for modeling data dependency. In the next processor step, the contents are read from the FIFO and written into the final register. This phenomenon was explained in Section 5.3.1.

Task Write_Register

The given data are written into the appropriate register.

Test module RISC2_Test consists of an initialization routine and two tasks. In the initialization, an application program is first read into processor memory, the processor is reset, and memory as well as registers are output. Then a loop triggers a processor step by event RISC2_System.step_begin as long as no error occurs or the processor stops. With every step, memory and registers may be output.

Task Dump_System

This task outputs memory and processor registers. The degree of detail can be selected with switches (Section 5.3.3).

Task Write_Mnemonic

Because we do not want to output the mnemonics in the system module, another complete instruction decoding is performed in this task. This results in a clean separation of processor behavior from test and debug functions.

5.3.3 Application

Several switches control the output of a model simulation:

STEP	0	no break
	1	after each instruction, wait for user input

TRACE	0	dump after Halt
	1	dump after every instruction

Details of a dump may be controlled by the following switches:

MEMDUMP	0	no memory output
	1	memory output
REGDUMP	0	no output of processor registers
	1	output of processor registers
ACCDUMP	0	no output of memory accesses
	1	output of memory accesses

The memory range to be output in a dump may be set by MDUMPLO (memory dump low) and MDUMPHI (memory dump high). Furthermore, the file name PROGRAM of a machine program to be simulated is defined. MEMSIZE controls memory size in bytes.

The Interpreter Model is started by

```
verilog interpreter.v
```

The switch controlled output is explained in a small example. The program in Figure 5.15 triples a given positive integer.

```
            OR      R01, R00, 0         ; R01 = 0
            LDU.Q   R02, R00, input     ; R02 = *input
            NOP                         ; data dependency
loop:       SUB.F   R02, R02, 1         ; R02--
            BNE     loop                ; if (R02!=0) goto loop
            ADD     R01, R01, 3         ; R01+=3 (delayed)
            ST.Q    R01, R00, output    ; *output = R01
            HALT

input:      dc.q 2
output:     ds.b 4
```

Figure 5.15 Assembler program for tripling

A number is read from memory and counted down to zero. With every iteration, value 3 is added to a register. The NOP in the third line is important to ensure that the Load is not directly followed by a dependent ALU operation. Next, the assembler translates the program:

```
rasm -a -fh example.in example.exe
```

The assembler switches are not explained here. Figure 5.16 shows the assembler output serving as an input to the interpreter.

```
44080000 // 000           OR     R01, R00, 0       ; R01 = 0
0E100008 // 004           LDU.Q  R02, R00, input   ; R02 = *input
49000000 // 008           NOP                      ; data dependency
6A108001 // 00c loop:     SUB.F  R02, R02, 1       ; R02--
FC07FFFF // 010           BNE    loop              ; if (R02!=0) goto loop
60084003 // 014           ADD    R01, R01, 3       ; R01+=3 (delayed)
2E080009 // 018           ST.Q   R01, R00, output  ; *output = R01
FF000000 // 01c           HALT
         // 020
00000002 // 020 input:    dc.q 2
XXXXXXXX // 024 output:   ds.b 4
```

Figure 5.16 Machine code of Figure 5.15

```
`define STEP    0        // 0: no $stop, 1: $stop after every instruction
`define TRACE   1        // 0: dump after HALT, 1: dump after every instruction
`define MEMDUMP 0        // 0: no memory dump, 1: memory dump
`define REGDUMP 0        // 0: no register dump, 1: register dump
`define ACCDUMP 1        // 0: no access dump, 1: access dump
`define MEMSIZE 'h100_   // system memory size in bytes
```

Figure 5.17 Output parameters for a trace

```
Highest level modules:
RISC2_System
RISC2_Test

RISC2 Interpreter
Executing program: example.exe
RESET state
Step 1 completed
 -Memory Accesses
  ADDR: 00000000  DATA: 44080000   OR      instruction fetched
Step 2 completed
 -Memory Accesses
  ADDR: 00000004  DATA: 0e100008   LDU     instruction fetched
  ADDR: 00000020  DATA: 00000002   QBYTE   load initiated
Step 3 completed
 -Memory Accesses
  ADDR: 00000008  DATA: 49000000   XOR     instruction fetched
Step 4 completed
 -Memory Accesses
  ADDR: 0000000c  DATA: 6a108001   SUB.F   instruction fetched
Step 5 completed
 -Memory Accesses
  ADDR: 00000010  DATA: fc07ffff   BNE     instruction fetched
Step 6 completed
 -Memory Accesses
  ADDR: 00000014  DATA: 60084003   ADD     instruction fetched
Step 7 completed
 -Memory Accesses
  ADDR: 0000000c  DATA: 6a108001   SUB.F   instruction fetched
Step 8 completed
 -Memory Accesses
  ADDR: 00000010  DATA: fc07ffff   BNE     instruction fetched
Step 9 completed
 -Memory Accesses
  ADDR: 00000014  DATA: 60084003   ADD     instruction fetched
Step 10 completed
 -Memory Accesses
  ADDR: 00000018  DATA: 2e080009   ST      instruction fetched
  ADDR: 00000024  DATA: 00000006   QBYTE   stored
Step 11 completed
 -Memory Accesses
  ADDR: 0000001c  DATA: ff000000   HALT    instruction fetched
L875 "interpreter.v": $finish at simulation time 12
Data structure takes 183496 bytes of memory
1007 simulation events
CPU time: 0 secs to compile + 0 secs to link + 0 secs in simulation
```

Figure 5.18 Short simulation result for Figures 5.15 to 5.17

In the VERILOG program interpreter.v, the output parameters can now be set. First, only memory accesses are output in a trace. The configuration in Figure 5.17 produces a dump after every instruction and outputs no memory or registers, just memory accesses. With this configuration, one gets the result in Figure 5.18.

The correct result of 2 by 3 is written into address 24. A second program run with a much longer result and more information on model debugging is found in Chapter H3.

5.4 Specification of Test Strategy

We aim at a consistent test strategy by applying functional test programs to the Interpreter Model, to the Coarse Structure Model, to the Gate Model, and even to the manufactured chip (Figure 2.8). As models are refined, more test programs have to be added, for example, for testing the kernel/user mode which is not included in the Interpreter Model.

These test programs are small assembler programs translated by the TOOBSIE assembler into a machine code readable by the models or the chip itself. For each of the models, a main memory is simulated, from which the processor may read programs and data and into which it may write results. The processor chip will work correspondingly.

A consistent test strategy makes verification easier. The test programs have only to be checked against the Interpreter Model as a golden device. If there are errors in another model, this will not be due to a test program, thus restricting debugging to the given model. The consistent test strategy thus improves design safety and saves design time.

Such a functional test strategy, however, is not suited for the test of arbitrary integrated circuits. Even for microprocessors, it may happen that more complicated architectures have rare states not occurring in normal assembler programs (e.g., interrupts). Therefore, we will later have to check whether we have a sufficiently high fault coverage for the Coarse Structure Model or for production test or whether additional test patterns have to be developed.

Only very few internal signals can directly be observed at external processor pins. Therefore, we plan a signature analysis register, in which important internal signals like ALU results, flags, and register addresses are compressed and compared with a nominal value.

Signature analysis does not explain the type of error. As an additional test aid, a scanpath is provided connecting important registers. It is not used for production test, but allows the localization of faults.

Signature analysis and scanpath are implemented only in the Gate Model, as they require a knowledge of the final registers (Chapters 8, 9, and H5). Chapter 9 treats the areas of test and testability in detail.

5.5 Quantitative Specifications

In this section, all measurable data can be specified, such as cost, technology, chip size and gate count, pins, package, and most of all performance. These data are normally requested by the customer.

Realistic and implementable quantitative requirements exploiting the limits constitute an art, which requires a high degree of design experience. A general theory does not exist and will most likely never exist. Typically, the true data are only known after implementation, leading to iterations and new negotiations with the customer.

In the case of TOOBSIE, we have an example design with more freedom, for which, to be honest, the precise data became known only afterwards.

An important criterion in the development of every microprocessor is to achieve a high *performance*, which we want to discuss briefly. The performance should measure the ability of a processor to solve certain tasks in a certain time. As performance is hard to measure directly, one usually applies a relative performance. System A has a higher performance than system B if it solves the same problem in a shorter time or if it solves a larger problem in the same time. Questions about the notion of performance are discussed thoroughly in [Hennessy, Patterson 1990, Schäfers 1994].

The performance of a computer system is determined not only by the processor itself, but also by its disks, its memory components, the quality of its compiler, and the capabilities of its operating system. Because in the present project, the *design* of a microprocessor is at the center of interest, whereas the processor environment serves only to prove its correct functioning, we are mainly interested in processor performance.

The performance of a processor is mainly determined by:

1. the power of its instruction set and

2. the average execution time of an instruction.

The first point influences the performance, because a given problem can be described by a more powerful instruction set with fewer machine instructions. The faster an instruction is executed, the faster the problem is solved. This second point can further be divided into

2a. the average execution time of an instruction in cycles (CPI, cycles per instruction) and

2b. the cycle period or maximal clock frequency; this is determined by the critical path, i.e., the circuit part with the longest run time.

A performance estimation becomes difficult due to the mutual influence of all three factors. The more powerful an instruction, the longer will be its execution. The shorter a clock cycle, the more cycles the execution of an instruction will require.

Very roughly, we specify at this point that our processor should permit a maximal clock frequency of 20 – 30 MHz, that the CPI should be less or equal to 1, that 20 – 40 MIPS (million instructions per second) should be possible for the instruction set specified above, and that a sea-of-gates design with about 100 000 gates (used and unused) with a pin count of 150 – 200 is financially possible.

Of course, such requirements have strong implications for the internal architecture specification in the next chapter, like the necessity for a parallel pipeline, possibly even superscalar, like caches, or like requirements on memory components.

Changes of the internal specification may in turn result in changes of the external specification. For example, the delay slot property seems unmotivated in the external specification and is understandable only in the context of a pipeline.

The interplay between internal and external specification can even mean that the external processor behavior is not completely defined; for example, it is hard to predict when a cache memory will show a hit thus avoiding the slower fetching of an instruction from main memory. At least, however, the behavior should be *similar* and in a pragmatic sense correct.

6 Internal Specification of Coarse Structure

In the previous chapter, the RISC processor TOOBSIE was specified externally by defining its "outside" behavior, basically its instruction syntax and semantics, as seen by an application programmer. For reference purposes, the Interpreter Model was developed as a golden device in the HDL VERILOG.

The internal specification in this chapter sketches the coarse processor structure. By this, we mean important architecture features like data flow, timing, pipelines, buses, registers, caches, and interrupts. This will prepare a precise verification by a simulatable HDL model.

The internal coarse structure is together with the external specification the basic requirement for the VLSI designer. For a user of the processor, it is interesting from a pragmatic point of view.

External and internal specification indicate a design path beginning with a transformation of the coarse internal specification into a simulatable model – the *Coarse Structure Model* – which in contrast to the previous Interpreter Model makes intensive use of typical features of a hardware description language and which will reach the rather large amount of about 7 000 lines of code.

This Coarse Structure Model is treated in Chapter 7 and in H4. In turn, it is the specification for the next refinement, the Gate Model, being a hierarchical net list of gates and library elements.

Our internal coarse specification is already pretty detailed. It is neither easy nor relevant to decide whether this is still a design requirement or whether it constitutes an essential part of the design.

On the one hand, the coarse specification can be interpreted as the requirements of an experienced customer who already knows that he wants to implement a 32-bit RISC processor on a CMOS gate-array base with 30 MIPS efficiency by a 5-stage scan-testable pipeline with multi-purpose and branch-target cache and register forwarding. In this case, the subsequent design is restricted to routine engineering.

On the other hand, the requirements could only consist of an implementation of the given instruction set with best efficiency and lowest cost. In this case, a careful exploration of the coarse alternatives is necessary, and then this chapter contains important results of the design process.

In the given project, we chose more the first path with a rather detailed specification. One could also think of a shorter and more abstract specification with a shorter HDL model, which might be more pleasant to read in some respect. Then, however, an additional more physical HDL model would have to be developed before the Gate Model. To get by with few models, we have chosen a model rather close to implementation.

6.1 Data Flow

The data flow is given by a datapath of hardware units through which data are flowing during program execution. The distinction between data and control signals is not always unique. As data, we count operation codes, operands, memory addresses and contents, register addresses and contents, branch targets and constants, not, however, signals for controlling components, for timing, or for interrupt handling. These control signals will often be mentioned implicitly or verbally.

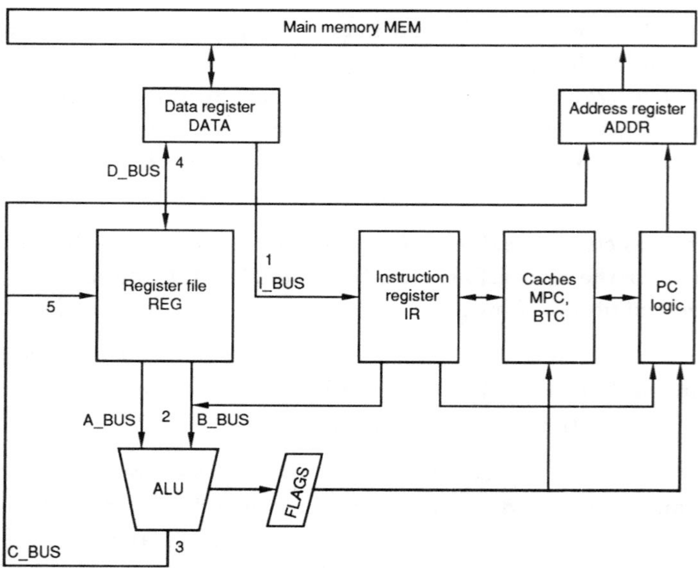

Figure 6.1 Datapath

6.1.1 Execution of Instructions in the Datapath

The basic execution of an instruction in the TOOBSIE datapath will first be explained. We only follow a single general instruction locally and do not say anything about the mutual influence of instructions when being executed in parallel.

A "general" instruction moves through the following stations in the datapath according to the numbers in Figure 6.1; this is only a first overview to be detailed later.

1 Instruction loading into instruction register IR: the instruction address is taken from the program counter PC. In the best case, the instruction comes from the instruction cache consisting of a branch-target cache BTC and a multi-purpose cache MPC, or in the adverse case from external memory. In more detail, the cache may be deactivated, there may be a valid entry (*hit*) for the given address, or the entry may be invalid or false (*miss*).

   Parallel to the cache access, several alternatives for the PC are prepared by an incrementation by 1, by adding a relative offset, or by loading a new branch target.

2 Decoding of instruction and preparation of operands: the register file is addressed and the result is put on buses A_BUS and B_BUS; possibly, a constant as part of the instruction is directly put on the B_BUS.

3 Instruction execution: from operands A_BUS and B_BUS, a result is computed and put on the C_BUS. If necessary, new flags are stored in the processor status.

4 Memory access: when needed, the access address is on the C_BUS and the data to be stored on the D_BUS, otherwise, the ALU result is only buffered on the C_BUS.

5 Saving of result: if necessary, the result is stored in the register file; this result may be a value of a data register (e.g., Load) or the buffered value of the C_BUS.

6.1.2 A Pipeline for the Datapath

To balance the hardware components of the datapath efficiently, several instructions will be executed in parallel, for example, by loading and decoding the next instruction, while the first one is being executed. We thus obtain a pipeline. The instruction set chosen is well suited for a pipeline structure due to its RISC character.

The datapath is embedded into a 5-stage pipeline with stages *Instruction Fetch* IF, *Instruction Decode* ID, *Execute* EX, *Memory Access* MA, and *Write-Back* WB, which all are described in the following sections. This partitioning is meaningful for the given instruction set, if the critical paths of all stages are of similar length. Ideally, there is no single stage slowing down the clock.

It is to be checked, whether other configurations would be better suited. A 3-stage pipeline (fetch, decode, execute) would also be possible. This scheme would increase the clock cycle, as for Load instructions, the execute stage would include the runtime for memory address computation, memory access, and for writing the loaded data into the register file. This 3-stage scheme is therefore badly balanced in its critical path.

With four stages, one might get the scheme fetch, decode, execute, and memory access. This would be unbalanced, too, as for Load instructions, the memory access stage would not only perform the memory access, but also write its result into the destination register. The critical path would then consist of a memory access followed by a register access. This would be longer than runtime of the execute stage and hence also unbalanced. A memory access in the execute stage would equally unbalance the paths.

We therefore separate memory access and register access and realize five stages: fetch instruction (IF), decode instruction and load register operands (ID), execute instruction in the ALU (EX), access memory (MA), and write back the result into a destination register (WB).

From this coarse distribution of tasks, we obtain a first partitioning of the pipeline datapath as follows.

- The IF stage contains the program counter PC, the caches MPC and BTC, and the memory interface DATA and ADDR.
- The ID stage contains the register file REG, the instruction register IR, and the processor status register with the flags.
- The EX stage contains the arithmetic logic unit ALU.
- The MA stage contains buffers and connections from ALU output to the WB stage and to the memory interface.
- The WB stage finally contains buffers and connections from the MA stage to the register file.

6.1.3 Pipeline Features Visible in Applications

The pipeline concept implies several clock cycles for execution of one instruction. For the application software, this means the undesired effects delayed branch, delayed load, and delayed software interrupt (Chapter 3). Delays of register accesses by the ALU, however, are avoided by a transparent forwarding mechanism.

Delayed branch means that a branch (control transfer, CTR) is only executed after the instruction following the CTR. Since the CTR property is only detected in the ID stage, the next instruction at the address following in the program text is already in the IF stage. This address is called *delay slot*. The instruction in the delay slot, the *delay instruction*, moves through the pipeline like a normal instruction.

The delay instruction is normally executed to avoid being loaded in vain, corresponding to the insertion of an empty step into the pipeline. In the example of Figure 6.2, the branch BNE is performed after the execution of ST.B. At five subsequent memory byte positions, an immediate 0 (contents of register R0) is written. In (4), ST.B is executed independently of the branch decision (3), such that there is always the execution sequence (2), (3), (4). The advantage of a delayed branch is an increased throughput.

```
        ADD     R1, R0, 5       ; (1)
loop:   SUB     R1, R1, 1       ; (2)
        BNE     loop            ; (3)
        ST.B    R0, R1, data    ; (4)
        ...
data:   DS.B    5
```

Figure 6.2 Delay instruction

The delayed branch is paid for with a slightly increased effort by the compiler, as program code has possibly to be sorted differently. If this is impossible, a NOP can be inserted. The software costs are small as compared to the gain, because the frequency of CTR instructions is 20–25% [Lee, Smith 1984], and more than 80% of all delay slots can be filled [Mansfeld, Schäfers 1993].

To further reduce costs, the delay slot of conditional branches can be annulled. This *ANNUL option* (.A-option) replaces the delay instruction by a NOP, if the branch is not taken. This often permits a meaningful use of delay slot, for example, with the first instruction of a loop [Lee, Smith 1984].

Two subsequent CTR instructions are prohibited, as they would result in an ambiguous branch target. The reaction to this case is an interrupt.

A *delayed load* is the property that a Load instruction for X is not followed by another instruction using X. The execution of LD/ST overlapping with other instructions, however, is permitted.

As the following example shows, a change of order of code is meaningful in some cases for a better pipeline balancing (Figure 6.3). Instruction ADD accesses register R1. This is loaded in step (1). Therefore, ADD can only be executed in step (3). For SUB, this holds analogously.

```
init:     LD      R1, R0, data1   ; (1)
          LD      R3, R0, data2   ; (2)
          ADD     R2, R1, 1       ; (3)
          SUB     R4, R3, 1       ; (4)
          ...
data1:    DC.W    hFF
data2:    DC.W    hAA
```

Figure 6.3 Delayed load

Also a *delayed software interrupt* is delayed, because they are treated as control transfers. The exact description of the interrupt mechanism can be found in Section 6.5.

Aside from these three effects, register operations become valid only two steps later in the destination register due to the delay between the EX and WB stages. Subsequent operations reading this destination produce data conflicts. To solve them and to achieve a good pipeline load, a *forwarding* is meaningful for both operands of the EX stage. This effect is invisible for the software. The forwarding requires additional buses extracting the new value at different pipeline points.

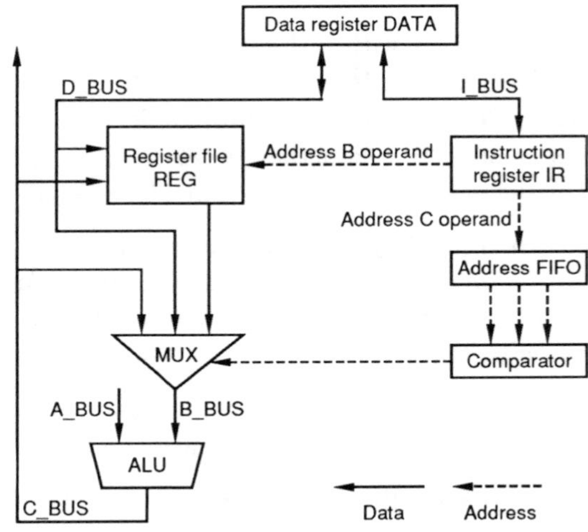

Figure 6.4 Forwarding of B-operand

Figure 6.4 shows a refined part of the datapath employing a forwarding of the ALU B-operand. It comes normally from the register file, when none of the two preceding instructions writes to the same register. If the direct predecessor instruction uses the register as destination, the present value is at the C_BUS being the ALU output. This is the second source for the B-operand. The third one is the MA output. A multiplexer MUX selects the proper source and puts it into the ALU input register. The decision is made by an address comparison of the present source register for the B-operands with the destinations of the last two instructions.

6.2 Timing

Based on the datapath and the coarse pipeline structure, time behavior and a clocking scheme (timing) have to be specified. From this, a suitable bus protocol is deduced.

6.2.1 A Simple Clocking Scheme

As a clocking scheme we employ a symmetrical external one-phase clock, the curve CP (clock pulse) in Figure 6.5. A *cycle* or *clock* is the base time unit of the processor and corresponds to the period between two rising edges of CP.

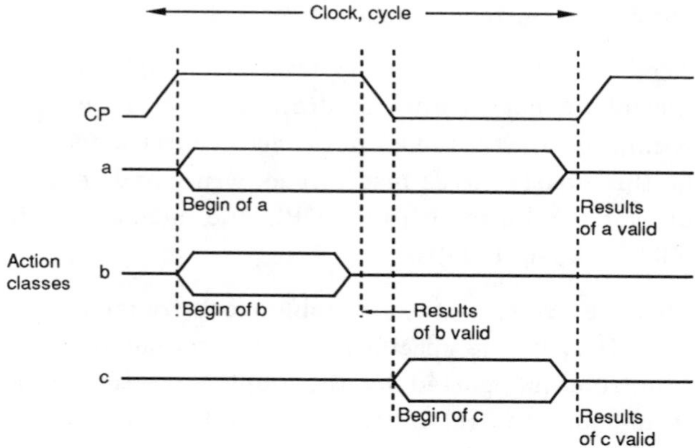

Figure 6.5 Clocking scheme and action classes

Per cycle, there are the events of the rising and falling CP edge, at which *actions* may be triggered synchronously in every pipeline stage. These actions can be divided into the following three classes of Figure 6.5.

a Actions starting with the rising edge and ending with the next rising edge;

b actions starting with the rising edge and ending with the next falling edge;

c actions starting with a falling edge and ending with the next rising one.

Real actions are mentioned during specification of the pipeline stages and are summarized in Section 6.3.7.

In addition to actions of one cycle, certain tasks may require several cycles. For example, memory accesses may last longer, in particular in the case of access faults. A *(pipeline) step* performs this task. Steps without memory access last one cycle, steps with memory access may last several cycles. Extremely difficult memory accesses may even consist of several steps. Per step, only one memory access is performed (instruction SWAP counting as a single memory access).

A step is started with an IO_READY signal with rising clock edge. At a beginning step, every pipeline stage accepts certain data from its predecesor stage with rising CP edge, the pipeline is "shifted".

6.2.2 The Bus Protocol

Based on the timing defined before, a bus protocol is now specified. The memory interface of the processor is the border to the system environment. Here, internal and external requirements meet.

We intend to keep the processor memory interface simple. The processor will not support special memory access modes, as they are offered by DRAM components for improved access (e.g., page mode, burst mode). The processor will support the three basic access modes read, write, and read-write. A small memory control logic is required between CPU and memory (Section 5.1.2 and [Stuckenberg 1992, Telkamp 1995]).

The processor will be driven with a variable clock frequency with an upper limit of about 25 MHz. In the specification, this cannot be finally fixed. An asynchronous interface supported by the implementation of a handshake protocol allows memory control independent of the clock frequency. Thus, different types of memory may be used.

The interface consists of signals nMRQ, nMHS, RnW, ACC_MODE, RMW, ADDR, and DATA. A leading n in the signal name means *active-low* (0=active) being useful for fast transitions from inactive to active. Table 6.6 groups memory interface signals as clock, handshake, mode, and bus signals.

Symbol	Name	Direction	Explanation
CP	Clock	in	One-phase clock
nMRQ	notMemoryRequest	out	No processor access request
nMHS	notMemoryHandshake	in	Memory ready
RnW	ReadNotWrite	out	Read / not write
ACC_MODE	AccessMode	out	Byte, halfword, or word access
RMW	ReadModifyWrite	out	Combined read-write access
ADDR	Address bus	tri	Access address
DATA	Data bus	tri	Access data

Table 6.6 Memory interface signals

Before we discuss the signals for the various access modes, we first consider some common factors. Every memory access starts with a rising clock edge by activating nMRQ. The preceding access has been completed. With nMRQ, also the three mode signals RnW, ACC_MODE, and RMW as well as the address are valid. The memory logic receives the access demand by the activation of nMHS and the end by its deactivation. The time depends upon the memory component and may be defined in the external control logic. The processor finishes the access by deactivating nMRQ. This concludes the pipeline step and leads to a new step with the next clock cycle. Table 6.7 summarizes the mode signals.

RMW	RnW	Access mode
inactive	inactive	Write
inactive	active	Read
active	inactive	Read-write access: write
active	active	Read-write access: read

Table 6.7 Memory access modes

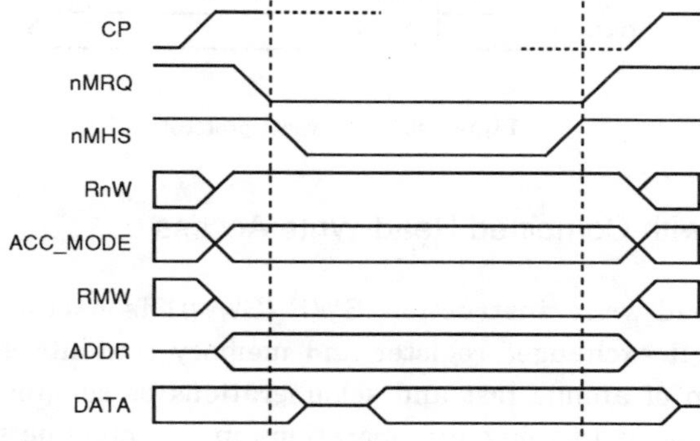

Figure 6.8 The read protocol

The Read Protocol

In the normal read cycle in Figure 6.8 (RnW active, RMW inactive), access mode ACC_MODE determines the width of data to be read. At the beginning, the address bus contains the memory address, and the end is signaled by deactivation of nMHS. This signal is interpreted by the processor as IO_READY, and the data bus is transferred into the data register.

The Write Protocol

In the normal write cycle (RnW and RMW inactive), access mode ACC_MODE determines the width and alignment of data to be written. At the beginning, the address bus contains the memory address and the data bus the value to be written, an active nMHS (nMHS=0) indicating a free bus. This prevents memory and processor simultaneously driving the data bus due to a previous read access. When free, the bus receives data from the processor. With the end of access (nMHS inactive), the memory has taken data, and the processor enables the data bus. Figure 6.9 shows the write protocol.

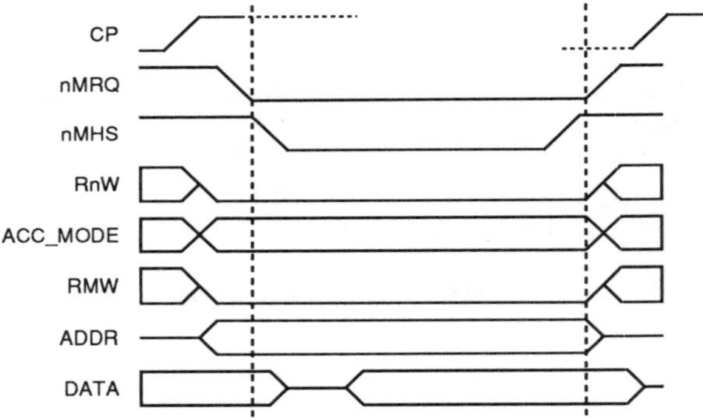

Figure 6.9 The write protocol

The Protocol with Combined Read-Write Access

The atomic read-write instruction SWP (Swap) is useful in multitasking environments. It exchanges register and memory contents and supports the implementation of atomic test and set operations or semaphores. The Swap instruction performs two memory operations in one pipeline step. If a special DRAM mode exists, this combined access may possibly be finished in one cycle.

When RMW is active, a read access is first performed with RnW active. The end of access is not acknowledged as usual by deactivation of nMRQ, but by a change of RnW. As a result, the memory control logic starts the write access by enabling nMHS using the same address as before. It is completed by deactivating nMHS and nMRQ. Figure 6.10 shows the protocol of a combined read-write access. Note that there are two memory operations, although nMRQ is activated only once. As before, the access mode ACC_MODE determines width and alignment of the data to be written.

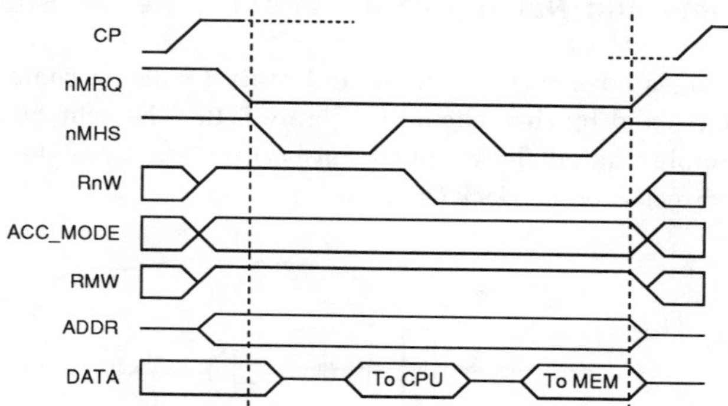

Figure 6.10 Protocol of combined read-write access

Abortion of Memory Access

The processor may start memory accesses in a speculative way, which need not to be completed. After a cache hit, for example, a memory access started before turns out to be unnecessary. It is aborted, unless it is already completed.

A pending access is aborted by deactivating nMRQ. Only read accesses may be aborted to ensure memory integrity.

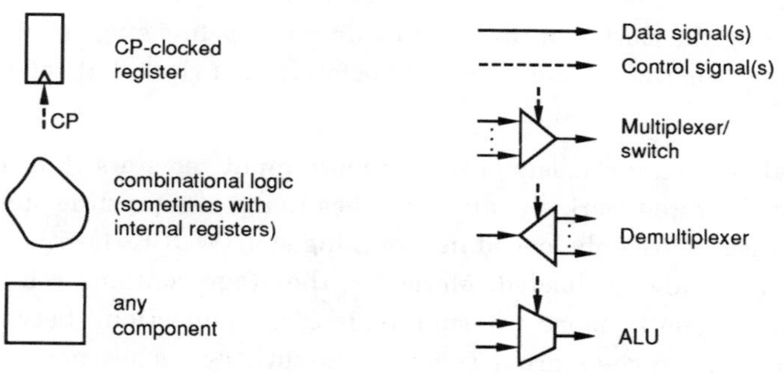

Figure 6.11 Symbols of block diagrams

6.3 Pipeline Stages

The various stages of the pipeline are now specified. First, a general scheme of a pipeline stage is presented. In the following figures and diagrams, we will use the symbols and arrows in Figure 6.11.

6.3.1 Scheme and Naming of a General Pipeline Stage

All pipeline stages have certain timing and control rules in common. They are basically constructed by the scheme in Figure 6.12. The scheme is simplified; later, for example, "gated clocks" must not be used, as a register must always be controlled directly by the clock CP.

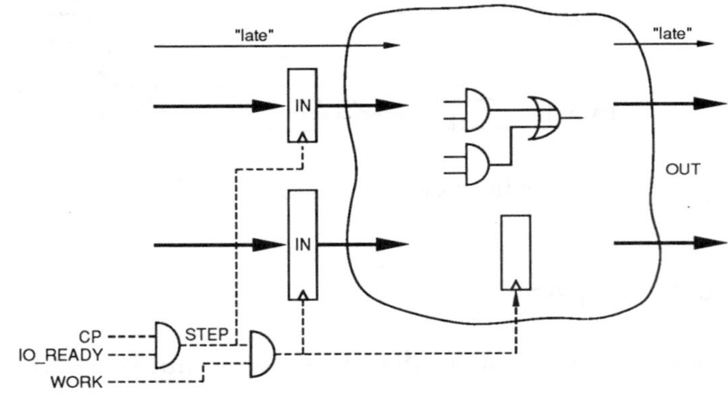

Figure 6.12 Basic idea of a pipeline stage

The interface of a stage consists of synchronous data and control signals on the input side, of a clock input CP and work signals IO_READY and WORK, as well as occasional *late* signals not arriving synchronously with the rising clock edge but later during the clock. On the output side, the pipeline stage generates data and control signals that usually are valid before end of clock, but sometimes are late.

The internal structure consists of one or more input registers that are loaded according to clock and work signals at the beginning of a pipeline step. Most of the input registers are only loaded in a working step (WORK=1), others serve as a buffer and are always loaded. Moreover, the stage contains combinational logic and occasionally more internal registers. Connections between these registers or with stage-external components such as caches may sometimes even lead to feedback loops. "Races", however, are excluded by the normally observed synchronous clocking scheme.

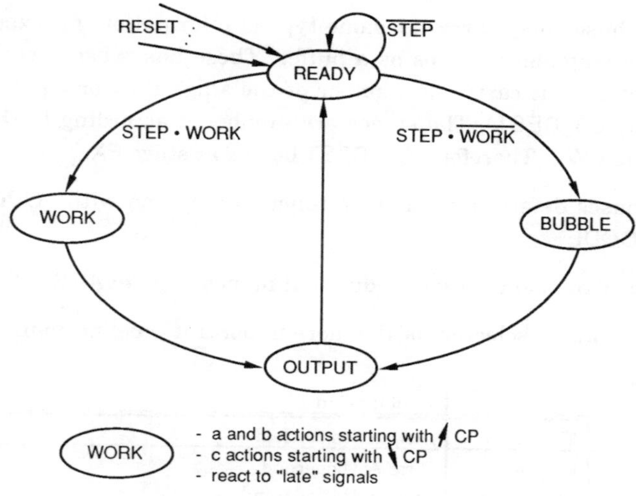

Figure 6.13 Behavior of a pipeline stage

Figure 6.13 shows certain "states" of a pipeline stage cycle. From any state, RESET leads to READY, which is only left in an active STEP (IO_READY at the rising CP edge). If WORK is inactive, the stage executes an empty step (bubble) in state BUBBLE. For example, this occurs when a BCC branch has reached the execute stage, but there are no actions to be executed. Only certain input buffers are loaded, shifting values unchanged to the next stage. When the output signals are valid, the stage reaches state OUTPUT and returns to starting state READY after a short delay.

When a pipeline step starts with an active control input WORK, the stage loads the input registers with the rising clock edge and combines them by combinational logic. These actions start immediately, if they are of type a or b (Figure 6.5), or with falling CP if of type c.

In addition to the synchronous signals, occasionally some late signals are processed, which nevertheless are sufficiently early to be stable before the end of the cycle.

To unify the names of connections between stages, we introduce the following nomenclature.

- Names of data buses of different function begin with a capital letter (e.g., A_BUS, B_BUS).
- A data bus and and its address bus begin with the same capital letter (e.g., C_BUS and C_DEST).

- Different buses may carry the same type of information, for example, when a pipeline stage only serves as a buffer. These buses begin with the same capital letter, but carry the number of the stage they originate from (e.g., C2_DEST, C3_DEST). The stages are numbered according to the sequence IF-ID-EX-MA-WB. Therefore, C3_DEST begins at stage EX.
- Control buses determining a stage function may end with _OPCODE (e.g., ALU_OPCODE).
- Several control signals carry individual names (e.g., FLAGS, MPC_MODE).

Table 6.14 contains a selection of the more important pipeline connections.

Name	from→ to	Explanation
I_BUS	IF → ID	Instruction fetched
A_BUS	ID → EX	First ALU operand
B_BUS	ID → EX	Second ALU operand
C3_BUS	EX → MA	Result of ALU operation
C4_BUS	MA → WB	Result of operation
C5_BUS	WB → RF	Write data for register file
C2_DEST	ID → EX	Destination address of operation
C3_DEST	EX → MA	Destination address of operation
C4_DEST	MA → WB	Destination address of operation
C5_DEST	WB → REG	Write address for register file
D2_BUS	ID → EX	Write data
D3_BUS	EX → MA	Write data

Table 6.14 Important pipeline connections

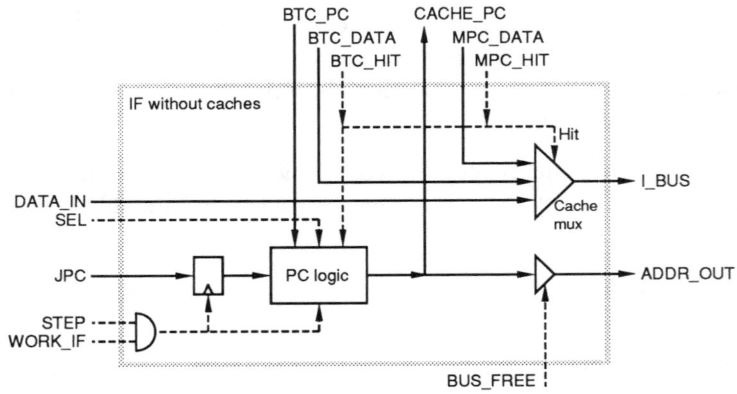

Figure 6.15 Instruction fetch stage IF

6.3.2 Instruction Fetch Stage IF

Pipeline stage IF loads an instruction from multi-purpose cache, branch-target cache, or memory. The IF stage contains the program counter PC, a PC adder independent of the ALU, and a PC incrementer as well as multiplexers for the instruction bus and PC. This stage is sketched in Figure 6.15.

The IF stage is closely connected with the two caches, whose ports can be seen at the upper border. As a deeper understanding of the caches is not needed at this point, they are discussed separately in Section 6.4. The interface and the more important components of the instruction fetch stage are summarized in Tables 6.16 and 6.17.

Signal	I/O	Explanation
DATA_IN	in	From external data bus
BTC_DATA	in	Data from branch-target cache BTC
MPC_DATA	in	Data from multi-purpose cache MPC
BTC_PC	in	PC from BTC
SEL	in	Other control signals for PC selection and for BTC control
JPC	in	PC of SRIS instruction
BTC_HIT	in	Hit or miss after BTC access
MPC_HIT	in	Hit or miss after MPC access
BUS_FREE	in	State of memory interface
STEP	in	Pipeline step
WORK_IF	in	IF stage active
ADDR_OUT	out	To external address bus
I_BUS	out	Instruction fetched
CACHE_PC	out	Address for caches

Table 6.16 Interface of the IF stage

Aside from these signals, the IF stage has internal signals for PC computation. PC+1 denotes the memory address following the present instruction. PC+2 skips PC+1, which is necessary in case of an untaken branch in the BTC, and LPC contains the address of the last instruction.

Component	Explanation
PC logic	Selection of next instruction address from internally generated or external choices
Cache MUX	Selection of correct instruction for I_BUS

Table 6.17 Components of stage IF

In an active instruction fetch stage, the PC logic offers the next instruction address to BTC, MPC, and memory. Only when both caches report a miss does a memory access become necessary. With an adder and an incrementer, the PC logic computes from the last address the next address and the branch target for conditional branches. The last PC value is stored in a register. Additional inputs give the branch target for absolute branches and the output BTC_PC of the BTC. Control signal SEL is stable for a sufficiently long time before the rising clock edge to ensure that the right alternative is selected.

If BUS_FREE is active, a memory access may be initiated. If the memory access stage, however, is already accessing memory, the access must be postponed. After a successful memory access, the new instruction can be transferred from DATA_IN to the I_BUS. In case of a cache hit, however, the multiplexer switches another value to the I_BUS. If the instruction comes from the BTC, the PC gets the branch target (Section 6.4).

Two important actions of the IF stage are summarized in Table 6.18, where the reference number containing action class a points to the summary in Table 6.36.

Reference number	Action
IF_a1	Cache access
IF_a2	Update PC

Table 6.18 Some actions of the IF stage

6.3.3 Instruction Decode Stage ID

Stage ID decodes instructions, which from then on are handled differently in the pipeline. Control signals for the following pipeline stages are generated according to these instructions, and necessary operands are fetched. This requires accesses to the register file REG as specified in Section 6.4.4. The ID stage contains the instruction register IR and the decoding logic, the processor status register for the flags, and the forwarding logic.

The forwarding logic does not necessarily belong to the ID stage, as it uses the outputs of execute, memory access, and the write-back stage. Figure 6.19 shows the structure of the ID stage. The interface and the more important components are summarized in Tables 6.20 and 6.21.

The activated ID stage loads an instruction to be decoded from the I_BUS into its instruction register IR. The decoding determines actions of the following pipeline stages including IF. The instruction code also contains operands or their addresses. The data addressed are loaded during the present cycle from the register file. For a Store instruction, for example, the register file is

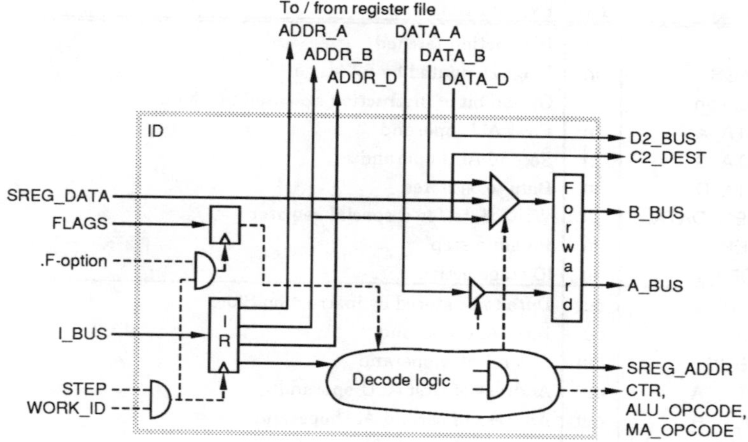

Figure 6.19 Instruction decode stage ID

addressed in the first half of the cycle by ADDR_D, and the data to be stored are read from DATA_D. In the second half of the cycle, two simultaneous read accesses are performed to the register file via DATA_A and DATA_B with addresses ADDR_A and ADDR_B for the ALU operands. According to instruction classes ALU, LD/ST, CTR, and Special (Section 5.2), the following cases can be distinguished.

Decoding of ALU Instructions

The operands required by the ALU are put onto the A_BUS and B_BUS, either directly as an Immediate constant or indirectly as contents from general-purpose registers. If register contents are to be loaded, the forwarding logic offers, if required, valid values except after a delayed load. The ALU is programmed by ALU_OPCODE. This code results directly from the corresponding instruction field (execute stage in Section 6.3.4). For the remaining instructions, the ALU is set to addition, which is sometimes necessary for non-ALU instructions.

Decoding of LD/ST Instructions

The memory address of an LD/ST access is computed by adding operands rA and rB (Section 5.2, formats F1 and F2) in the execute stage. Instructions Store and Swap require the data to be stored. These are sent to the memory access stage by a register access via D2_BUS. The ID stage sets control signals for the memory access mode (byte, halfword, or word access, direction).

Signal	I/O	Explanation
I_BUS	in	Instruction fetched
FLAGS	in	Flags computed by EX stage
.F-option	in	Option bit of instruction executed in EX stage
DATA_A	in	First ALU operand
DATA_B	in	Second ALU operand
DATA_D	in	Data to be stored
SREG_DATA	in	Write data for a special register
STEP	in	Pipeline step
WORK_ID	in	ID stage active
D2_BUS	out	Data to be stored by instruction Store
A_BUS	out	First ALU operand
B_BUS	out	Second ALU operand
ADDR_A	out	Address of first ALU operand
ADDR_B	out	Address of second ALU operand
ADDR_D	out	Address of data to be stored
C2_DEST	out	Destination address for operation result
SREG_ADDR	out	Corresponding address of special register
ALU_OPCODE	out	Operation to be executed by EX stage
MA_OPCODE	out	Operation to be executed by MA stage
CTR	out	Control transfer signals for selection of appropriate PC

Table 6.20 ID stage interface

Component	Explanation
Forward	Forwarding logic of address comparators and multiplexers
Decode logic	Decoding of instructions, generation of control signals
IR	Instruction register, containing the opcode of the instruction to be decoded
B MUX	Selection of data source for B bus independent of forwarding
FLAG register	Processor status

Table 6.21 Components of ID stage

After a cache miss, conflicts on the address and data bus may occur due to the von-Neumann architecture of the processor; these have to be recognized. The ID stage sends a disable signal in this case. Simultaneously, this signal reaches the IF stage, and the LD/ST instruction arrives at the MA stage. The stop signal prevents the IF stage from accessing the memory and delays it for one pipeline step (BUS_FREE signal in IF, Section 6.3.2). Also, it is prevented that the PC in IF changes and that an instruction gets lost.

Decoding of CTR Instructions

If a branch is unconditional (CALL, SWI, RETI, or the synthetic JMP and RET), this is reported to the IF stage by CTR signals. The remaining pipeline stages are not required for execution of this instruction and are therefore disabled for one step. The software interrupt SWI saves the processor status, which later will be restored by instruction RETI (details are given in Section 6.5).

If a branch is conditional (BCC instruction), the flags are first checked. If the branch condition is satisfied, ID behaves like for an unconditional branch. Otherwise, no CTR signal is sent.

If the ANNUL bit is set in the instruction code, the delay instruction must not be executed after an untaken branch. This is reported by signal ANNUL disabling the ID stage in the next pipeline step.

In case of a Halt instruction, no new instructions must be accepted. Then signal HALT will empty the ID and IF stage. Also the ALU will be disabled in the next step.

Decoding of Special Instructions

Special instructions are executed completely in the ID stage. This is possible, as the execute stage is not required for address computations. This is also necessary, as the return instruction SRIS PC, Rn belongs to class Special. This return is a control transfer and has a delay slot. Like the other CTR instructions, it has to be executed completely in the ID stage.

For SRIS, a register is addressed according to the operands, it is read, and in the second half of the clock, it is written into a special register. For LRFS, the data flow is inverted. As the destination is a general-purpose register, the data are written as usual by the write-back stage.

Parallel Decoding

The actions of the ID stage are not exclusive alternatives, but are mostly computed in parallel "just in case". Only at the end it is determined, which of the actions already executed are needed.

For example, for all instructions, the field from bits 19 to 23 is needed, sometimes as a Store destination RC, sometimes as an ALU destination DEST, sometimes as a branch condition CC, etc. (Figure 5.1). Therefore, this field is simultaneously evaluated as a register write address of a Store with a following register access as well as a branch condition with succeeding evaluation of status flags. Only hereafter it is decided, whether a Store or BCC instruction is given. In the first case, the branch decision is ignored, in the second case, the D2_BUS value is discarded.

This principle of one-stage decoding makes expensive PLAs for the control of multi-stage decoding unnecessary, as opposed to a CISC processor. This saves area, time, and costs. Two actions of the ID stage are summarized in Table 6.22, which take place in the first and second half of the clock (action classes a and c).

Reference number	Action
ID_a	Register accesses for Store, Swap
ID_c	Register accesses for ALU and others

Table 6.22 Some actions of the ID stage

6.3.4 Execute Stage EX

Pipeline stage EX executes arithmetic and logic operations. The structure of this stage is shown in Figure 6.23. The interface and the more important components are summarized in Tables 6.24 and 6.25.

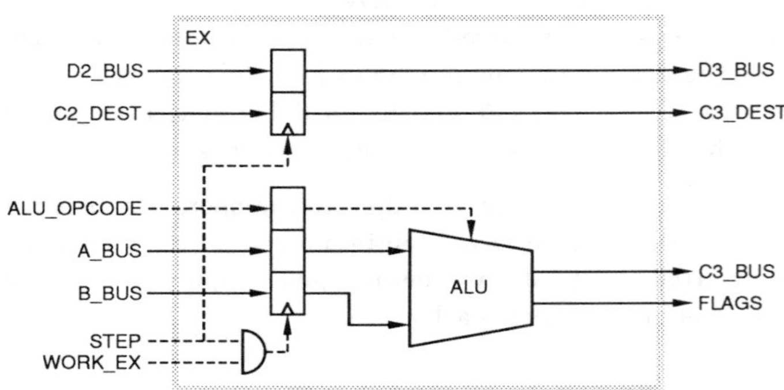

Figure 6.23 Execute stage EX

The ALU input register is divided into three separate registers for signals A_BUS, B_BUS, and ALU_OPCODE. The operands loaded by inputs A_BUS and B_BUS are transformed to results on C3_BUS and FLAGS according to the ALU_OPCODE. In parallel to the ALU, the buffers shift the destination address for the ALU result and the write data for Store. The design of an efficient ALU is an art, but the structure of the EX stage is simple at this point. Table 6.26 defines the ALU_OPCODE.

Signal	I/O	Explanation
A_BUS	in	First ALU operand
B_BUS	in	Second ALU operand
ALU_OPCODE	in	ALU operation
C2_DEST	in	Destination address for operation result
D2_BUS	in	Write data for Store
STEP	in	Pipeline step
WORK_EX	in	EX stage active
FLAGS	out	Flags of result
C3_DEST	out	Destination address for operation result
C3_BUS	out	Result of ALU operation
D3_BUS	out	Write data for Store

Table 6.24 EX stage interface

Component	Explanation
ALU	Logic combining operands and computing flags
ALU register	Input register for operands and ALU opcode
Address register	Input register for destination address of ALU result and write data for Store

Table 6.25 Components of EX stage

ALU_OPCODE	ALU instruction
1000	ADD
1001	ADDC
1010	SUB
1011	SUBC
0000	AND
0001	OR
0010	XOR
0110	ASR
0100	LSL
0101	LSR
0111	ROT

Table 6.26 ALU opcode

In a deactivated execute stage, the ALU is not working, but the buffers shift their data anyhow. Two actions of the EX stage are summarized in Table 6.27, the reference number pointing as before to the summary in Table 6.36.

Reference number	Action
EX_a1	Execute ALU operation
EX_a2	Compute ALU flags

Table 6.27 Some actions of stage EX

6.3.5 Memory Access Stage MA

Pipeline stage MA either performs a memory access or buffers the result from the execute stage. The structure of the stage is shown in Figure 6.28, the interface and more important components in Tables 6.29 and 6.30.

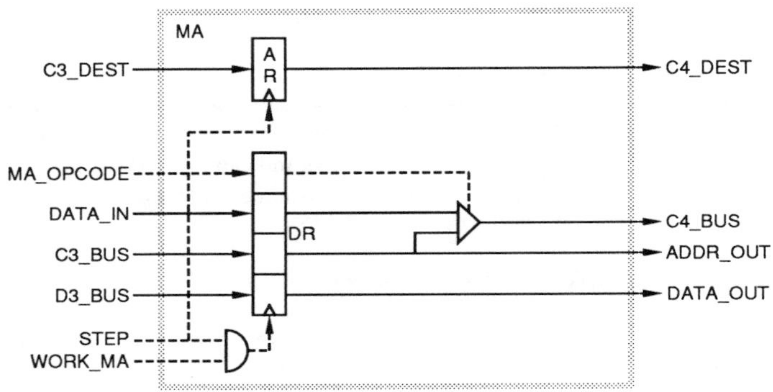

Figure 6.28 Memory access stage MA

Signal	I/O	Explanation
MA_OPCODE	in	MA operation
D3_BUS	in	Write data for Store
C3_DEST	in	Destination address for operation result
C3_BUS	in	Result of ALU operation
DATA_IN	in	Data after Load
STEP	in	Pipeline step
WORK_MA	in	MA stage active
C4_DEST	out	Destination address for operation result
C4_BUS	out	Result of operation
DATA_OUT	out	Write data for Store
ADDR_OUT	out	Memory address for LD/ST instructions

Table 6.29 MA stage interface

Component	Explanation
DR	Data register for operand loading and opcode
AR	Destination address register for result

Table 6.30 Components of stage MA

Input register DR is divided into separate registers for signals MA_OPCODE for an operation to be executed, DATA_IN for data to be read, C3_BUS for ALU result or memory access address, and D3_BUS for data to be written.

In most cases, no LD/ST instruction is given. With a beginning step, MA loads the C3_BUS into its data register DR and transfers it to output C4_BUS. If there is an LD/ST instruction, MA moves the memory access address from C3_BUS to ADDR_OUT. For a Store, write data are taken from D3_BUS to DATA_OUT, for a Load, MA moves data read from memory from DATA_IN to C4_BUS. Buffer AR for the destination address works independently of WORK_MA in every step.

Two actions of the MA stage are listed in Table 6.31.

Reference number	Action
MA_a1	Load operands
MA_a2	Wait for memory access and write result

Table 6.31 Some actions of stage MA

6.3.6 Write-Back Stage WB

Pipeline stage WB writes results into the register file. Its simple structure is shown in Figure 6.32. Tables 6.33 and 6.34 summarize the interface and two components.

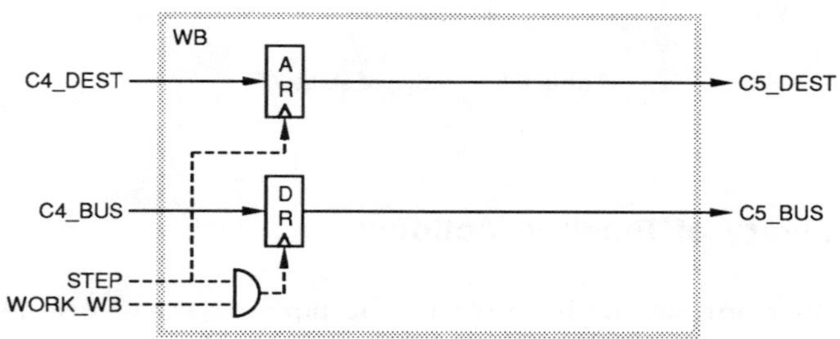

Figure 6.32 Write-back stage WB

Signal	I/O	Explanation
C4_DEST	in	Destination address for operation result
C4_BUS	in	Result of operation
STEP	in	Pipeline step
WORK_WB	in	WB stage active
C5_DEST	out	Write address for register file
C5_BUS	out	Write data for register file

Table 6.33 WB stage interface

Component	Explanation
DR	Write data register
AR	Destination address register

Table 6.34 Components of stage WB

An active write-back stage loads the write data from C4_BUS and their address from C4_DEST into input registers DR and AR and shifts them to outputs C5_BUS and C5_DEST, by which the data are written "back" into the register file in the first half of the clock. If the destination register is R0, the value is written from DR into this register, but in a later read access, this value is substituted by 0.

Store instructions are not meant to write into the register file. This is taken into account by destination address 0.

If this stage is inactive, no true actions take place. But input register AR is loaded and shifted to the output. The action in Table 6.35 belongs to class b and therefore takes place in the first half of the clock.

Reference number	Action
WB_b	Load operand and write

Table 6.35 Action of stage WB

6.3.7 Summary of Pipeline Actions

The more important actions initiated by the pipeline stages are now summarized. They belong to the three classes of Figure 6.5. Phrases such as "... signal X becomes valid ..." or "... signal X is computed ..." mean that the value of signal X is permanently computed by a combinational logic and is valid and stable long enough before the end of a half cycle.

a Actions lasting the whole cycle:

IF stage: The address of the instruction to be fetched is selected out of alternatives computed before. If the caches are turned off, the IF stage starts a memory access; otherwise, the caches are searched and, if necessary, a memory access is initiated. The alternatives for the next PC value are computed. At the end of a memory access, the value is put on the instruction bus. For CALL instructions, the branch target is stored.

ID stage: The instruction in the instruction register is decoded. Depending on the result, the pipeline control sets appropriate control signals. For Store instructions, the value to be stored is loaded from the register file in the first half cycle; in the second half cycle, the address operands are loaded. For BCC instructions, the flag evaluation has to be awaited (see c).

EX stage: Operands from ALU inputs A and B are combined. The evaluated flags are reported to the ID stage.

MA stage: According to control signals, a memory access is initiated, or a value is only buffered on the C_BUS. In case of a memory access, its end is awaited. If necessary, the loaded value is transferred to the input of stage WB.

b Actions in first half cycle:

WB stage: If necessary, a value on the C_BUS is written into a destination register.

c Actions in second half cycle:

IF stage: An initiated memory access turning out to be unnecessary is now aborted. Due to run time, valid control signals for selection of the next PC arrive only now.

ID stage: Two source registers of the operation are addressed, and two parallel read accesses to the register file are started. The forwarding logic selects for every operand one of its possible values (see above) and puts it to the inputs of stage EX. At the end of a cycle, the flags are valid. For BCC instructions, a branch decision is made and signaled to stage IF.

Table 6.36 summarizes the actions mentioned in the specification of every stage.

Class	Pipeline reference number	Action
a	IF_a1	Cache access
a	IF_a2	Update PC
a	ID_a	Register accesses for Store, Swap
c	ID_c	Register accesses for ALU and others
a	EX_a1	Execute ALU operation
a	EX_a2	Compute ALU flags
a	MA_a1	Transfer ALU result
a	MA_a2	Memory access
b	WB_b	Load operands and write

Table 6.36 Actions of pipeline stages

6.4 Caches and Register File

A cache saves data of frequently used addresses of the main memory in a small, fast, and local memory. Since a cache is usually integrated on the processor chip, it can be accessed faster than main memory. If the data in the cache are used more than once, the average access time for memory transactions is reduced.

A cache is small as compared to main memory, as cache RAMs are more expensive than the slower dynamic RAMs used for main memory. Therefore, only a small part of the memory can be buffered in the cache. The concept of a cache is based on the observation that computer programs tend to use at a given time just a small subset of memory (principle of "locality"). The efficiency of a cache is determined by the *hit rate*, i.e., the number of successful cache accesses divided by the total number of accesses. Typical hit rates are in the range 80 – 100%.

The pronounciation of "cache" as "cash" may suggest the analogy that data in a cache are like cash in the pocket, while data in main memory correspond to money in a bank: cash is accessible faster, but too much of it means loss of interest, while a bank account provides interest, but it takes longer to withdraw it.

An efficient cache strategy is vital: Which data should be stored in the cache, when, and how? As a RISC processor fetches an instruction from memory in every cycle, but only every fifth instruction is a data access, the fast fetching of instructions has priority.

This is the task of an *instruction cache* (IC) as opposed to a *data cache*. Also a combination of data and instruction cache is possible.

As data caches or combination caches are more complicated, TOOBSIE will only have an instruction cache. This decision is supported by the limited funds available thus restricting the cache size, while data caches pay only for larger caches. The cache concept, by the way, uses the fact that our programs are not self-modifying.

We will specify two instruction caches with very different strategies, a multi-purpose cache MPC and a branch-target cache BTC. The MPC holds arbitrary instructions, in a special RIB-mode, however, just those instructions causing delays due to a busy memory bus [Jove, Cortadella 1989].

The BTC tries to relieve the pipeline of conditional branches by recognizing branches used before by their program address and by predicting their branch behavior (to branch or not to branch) in a "speculative" manner.

As sources for the next instruction, we therefore have a memory and two caches. They are specified in Sections 6.4.1 and 6.4.2 and are integrated in Section 6.4.3 with the IF stage.

6.4.1 Multi-Purpose Cache MPC

As long as the external memory keeps pace with the processor, the problem of a single memory interface is predominant in a von-Neumann architecture, as the interface is occupied by LD/ST instructions preventing new instructions from being fetched.

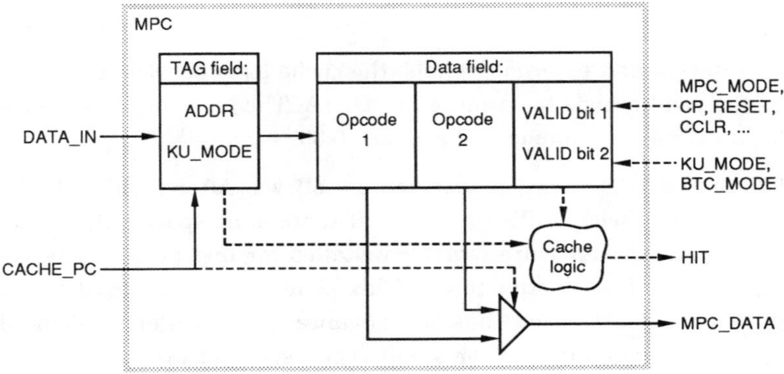

Figure 6.37 Multi-purpose cache MPC

In spite of the principle of locality, it is expensive to hold all instructions of a program section in a cache. In a RIB mode (reduced instruction buffer) as an alternative, we will therefore hold only those instructions in the cache which were required before when an LD/ST occupied the memory bus. In this way, the costs for an LD/ST operation reduce to one half in case of a cache hit.

The MPC in Figure 6.37 contains 16 lines with two entries each. One instruction is stored per entry. In addition, there is a TAG field for address and processor mode (KERNEL_MODE or USER_MODE) as well as a valid bit per instruction.

The MPC is fully associative. The TAG field contains the processor mode KU_MODE of the line and address bits 31 to 3. It thus requires 30 bits per line. Bits 1 and 0 are constantly 0 as instructions are oriented at word limits. As there are two subsequent instructions stored per line, bit 2 selects one of them.

The data section contains for every entry the 32-bit opcode and the associated bit VALID. The data section thus is 66 bits. The VALID bit is needed for the determination of the hit signal. If a global RESET is given or signal CCLR is active, all VALID bits are cleared. The format of a cache line is shown in Figure 6.38.

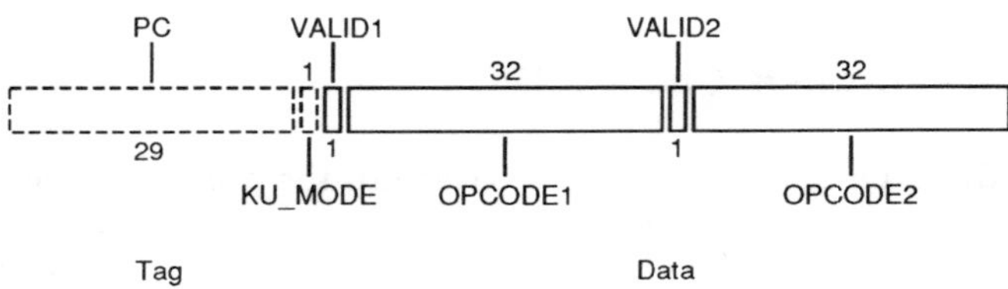

Figure 6.38 Line format of multi-purpose cache MPC

Based on internal and external signals, the cache logic decides if there is a hit and puts the valid opcode to output MPC_DATA. The more important signals of the MPC interface are summarized in Table 6.39.

The MPC replacing strategy is specified as follows. After a RESET or a CLC (Clear cache), the cache is filled in order. If there is no space left, replacement is done randomly. A signature register installed for test purposes serves as a random generator (see Section 9.3.3). This strategy as compared to an LRU strategy (least recently used) has the advantage of smaller implementation costs and of a higher hit rate for small cache sizes as are used here: if the processor working set does not fit completely into the cache, the LRU strategy results in a FIFO effect substituting the entries needed next.

6.4.2 Branch-Target Cache BTC

CTR instructions (control transfers) control the program flow. They include conditional (BCC) and unconditional branches (CALL). Hardware and software interrupts and exceptions also transfer control, but they are not of interest here.

Signal	I/O	Explanation	
DATA_IN	in	Opcode and processor mode of instruction to be stored	
CACHE_PC	in	Memory address of instruction searched in MPC, equal to the corresponding TAG field in case of a hit	
KU_MODE	in	Present kernel/user mode, coinciding with the corresponding TAG field in case of a hit	
MPC_MODE	in	Pin of processor chip setting the MPC mode:	
		IC mode	every instruction not in BTC is stored
		RIB mode	only those instructions not in BTC are stored, which are requested while memory bus is busy
MEM_ACC	in	Memory interface is occupied by stage MA; this case is relevant for RIB mode	
FETCH_MODE	in	Pin of processor chip setting the time at which stage IF fetches the next instruction from main memory after a miss of both caches:	
		serial fetch	the memory access is performed in the next step or later; it can only be initiated with an inactive MA stage; stage ID cannot work in the next step and has to be informed
		parallel fetch	with an inactive MA stage, memory access is initiated in parallel to cache access and is aborted in case of a hit (nMRQ set inactive); also in this case, a control signal is sent to ID, if there is a miss in both caches and the MA stage is active; a parallel fetch burdens the bus and is therefore less suited for multi-processor operation.
MPC_ACTIVE	in	Pin of processor chip enabling MPC; the deactivation of MPC is implemented by a combination of HIT with MPC_ACTIVE as a permanent miss	
CCLR, RESET	in	Set MPC to its initial state, in which all entries are invalid	
HIT	out	MPC contains the instruction searched	
MPC_DATA	out	Opcode after a cache hit	

Table 6.39 Interface of MPC

One tries to recognize a CTR instruction already in the IF stage by its program address. The cache strategy stores a CTR instruction in the cache after it was executed once; according to the principle of locality, the probability for a second execution is high. We use the fact that our instructions do not change addresses dynamically.

A CTR instruction is only in the ID stage really active, and the remaining pipeline stages are burdened unnecessarily as they do not execute any actions for the CTR.

Our goal is to free the pipeline by doubling all resources necessary, such that the CTR does not appear in the pipeline instruction stream any more and the branch target is directly substituted instead.

CTR Instructions for the BTC

For the BTC, only CTRs are of interest, as the execution of hardware and external interrupts is beyond processor control and cannot be predicted. The same holds for exceptions (Section 5.2.6).

A CTR enters the pipeline in stage IF, which puts the CTR address on the address bus and starts searching for the instruction. In the next cycle, the opcode of the instruction is decoded in the ID stage, while the IF loads another instruction, namely the delay instruction following the CTR. The CTR target has to be determined before the next pipeline step to finish execution of the CTR. In case of an ANNUL option, the delay instruction has to be suppressed, if the branch was not taken. This is done by disabling stage ID.

The idea is to solve the problem independently of the pipeline, as the later pipeline stages EX, MA, and WB are not required for the CTR. A CTR is uniquely assigned to its program address. In the simple case, the control transfer does not depend on further information (e.g., a CALL), but for BCC instructions, flags have to be evaluated. This is the more difficult case, therefore, BCC instructions are a main goal for optimization.

A distinction must be made between the unconditional instructions CALL, SWI, JMP, RET, RETI, and the BCC instructions. JMP, RET, and RETI are not suited for the BTC, as the return address may vary dynamically. The SWI instruction occurs too rarely and is therefore not considered, as it would reduce the hit rate. For a small BTC it has to be checked whether aside from BCCs, also CALLs should be included, which occur relatively rarely and will then reduce cache performance. We therefore introduce a BTC_MODE: in the BIG_MODE, BCC and CALL instructions are stored, in the SMALL_MODE only BCCs.

The Branch-Target Cache at Work

BCC and CALL instructions after being decoded in stage ID are stored in the BTC in the BTC_MODE. This includes the instruction address, the KU_MODE, the opcode of the delay instruction, the branch target, and the branch condition. The branch condition is always true for a CALL. After it is evaluated the *history bits* are updated. These two bits enable a heuristic branch prediction, as will be explained below.

If the address of an instruction searched by stage ID is found in the BTC, the branch logic indicates this by LOCAL_HIT. If the parallel access mode was chosen as FETCH_MODE, a possibly running fetch is aborted, and the delay instruction is transferred to the ID stage in the next step. If the branch is taken, the PC is set to the branch target, otherwise, the PC is incremented by 2, i.e., to the address following the delay slot.

This branch decision needs not to be final. In case of a BCC instruction, whose flags may be modified by the preceding instruction, a heuristic branch decision has to be made. This is not always correct and should therefore be correctable. Such a temporary situation is recognized by the pipeline control and is signaled to the BTC by NEW_FLAGS. In this case, the BTC uses the history bits for its branch decision.

History Bits for a Tempory Branch Decision

The two history bits HIBITS support a heuristic branch decision. They allow an inference from the past to the future. This is helpful when the final flags do not yet exist.

Each entry of the BTC has its own HIBITS with states N, N?, T?, and T, where N means the prediction that the branch will not be taken, T that it will be taken, and N? and T? weaken this prediction ("maybe"). If there are no valid flags, a temporary branch decision has to be made according to the HIBITS. Depending on the final decision, the HIBITS are updated.

With NEW_FLAGS active, the branch is temporarily not taken in states N and N?, and temporarily taken in states T and T? .

A false decision is corrected in the next pipeline step. The flags are now valid, as the preceding instruction is in the EX stage and the flags are computed until the end of the clock cycle. In case of a false decision, the already loaded instruction has to be discarded. It is in the IF stage and enters ID in the next step. Therefore, stage ID is disabled in the next step.

For a falsely taken branch with ANNUL option, the delay instruction in the ID stage possibly has to be discarded. Therefore, in the next step also stage EX is disabled. In both cases, only the appropriate WORK signal is reset and the PC is set properly. This is either the value of the old PC incremented by 2 or the branch target in the BTC.

Only after the final branch decision are the HIBITS updated. The update function is important for prediction quality. The function changes the states of HIBITS as in Figure 6.40, where inputs n and t of the state diagram refer to the final branch decision not taken or taken, respectively.

This heuristic is based on the principle of stability of conditional branches meaning that a BCC branch decision is either usually positive or usually negative. It changes rather rarely (Chapter 10, [Lee, Smith 1984, Schäfers 1994]). With the heuristic chosen, a hit rate of about 98% can be expected. Even an always changing branch decision will predict properly in about 50% of the cases. It must repeat at least twice to really change the HIBITS. In such a case, the BTC makes two false predictions.

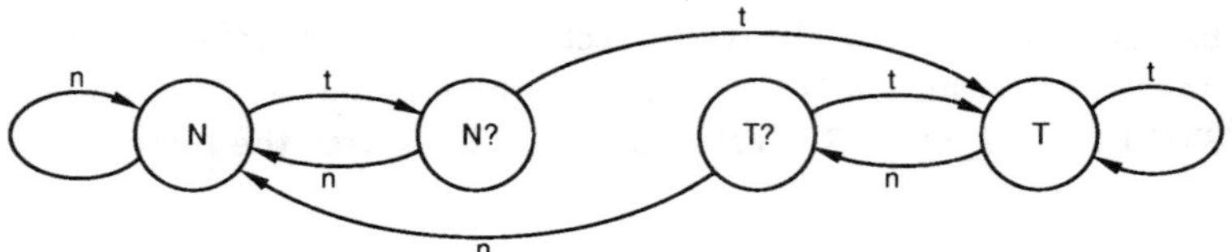

Figure 6.40 State diagram of history bits HIBITS

Replacing Strategy of the BTC

As with the MPC, the BTC is filled in order after a RESET or CLC (Clear cache) instruction. Afterwards, replacing is done randomly (Section 6.4.1). After every hit, the HIBITS are updated. After a miss, the CTR instruction is stored in the cache and its HIBITS are initialized with T? or N? For a CALL instruction, state T is set. New instructions will only be stored in the BTC after arriving in the ID stage, where they are decoded and recognized as BCC or CALL.

After an interrupt, the BTC is cleared. This can be done without harm, as it only reduces performance. Of course, the BTC must not contain false information and has therefore to be erased after a change of process.

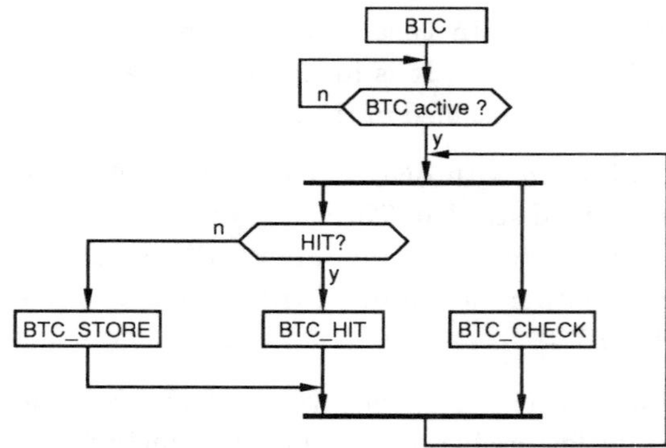

Figure 6.41 The BTC algorithm

The BTC Algorithm

Figure 6.41 sketches the BTC algorithm divided into two parallel tasks, namely on the one hand routine BTC_CHECK for heuristic branch prediction and its correction, and on the other hand, either routine BTC_HIT for hit rate evaluation or routine BTC_STORE for storing after a miss. The latter case was treated in the previous section, so we will now explain routine BTC_HIT in Figure 6.42.

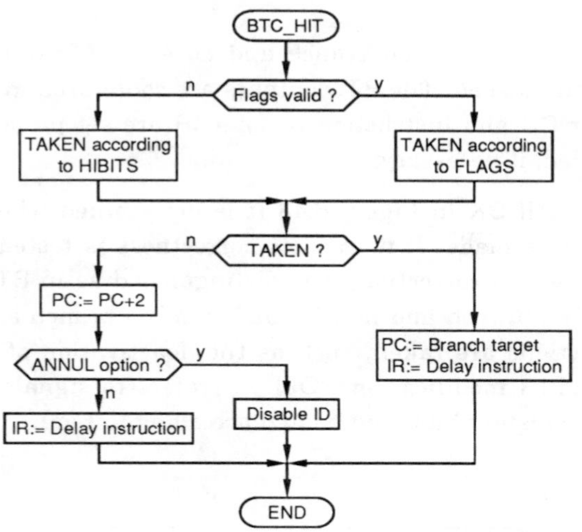

Figure 6.42 Routine BTC_HIT

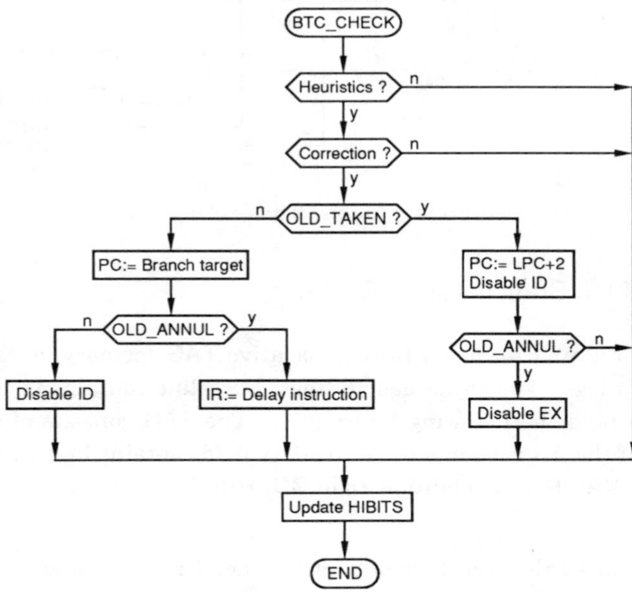

Figure 6.43 Routine BTC_CHECK

BTC_HIT provides the required data and changes the PC. It is tested whether the flags are valid or a heuristic branch prediction has to be made. If the decision is based on the HI_BITS, this must be remembered, such that the decision can be checked in the next step by routine BTC_CHECK and be corrected, if necessary.

Then three cases "branch", "no branch and no ANNUL", and "no branch and ANNUL" are distinguished. The BTC outputs are configured in such a way that program counter PC and instruction register IR are set properly and pipeline stages are disabled, if necessary.

In routine BTC_CHECK in Figure 6.43 it is determined whether a heuristic branch decision was made. If it was, its correctness is tested using the flags now valid. In case of a correction, it is distinguished as in BTC_HIT between cases "branch", "no branch and no ANNUL", and "no branch and ANNUL", and the necessary actions are taken, such as the deactivation of certain pipeline stages or PC and IR modification. "OLD..." refers to signals of the previous clock. Finally, the history bits are updated according to Figure 6.40.

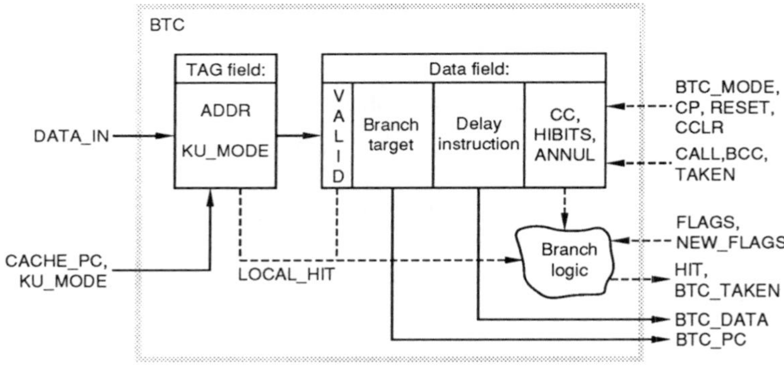

Figure 6.44 Structure of branch-target cache

Structure of the Branch-Target Cache

The BTC in Figure 6.44 has a fully associative TAG memory, a data memory, and a branch logic. The cache has 16 lines. Each line contains in its TAG field and its data field the following information. The TAG consists of address and KU_MODE of the instruction stored, the data field contains branch target, delay instruction, VALID bit, condition code CC, HIBITS, and a bit for the ANNUL option.

Figure 6.45 shows the structure of a cache line. The BTC interface is summarized in Table 6.46.

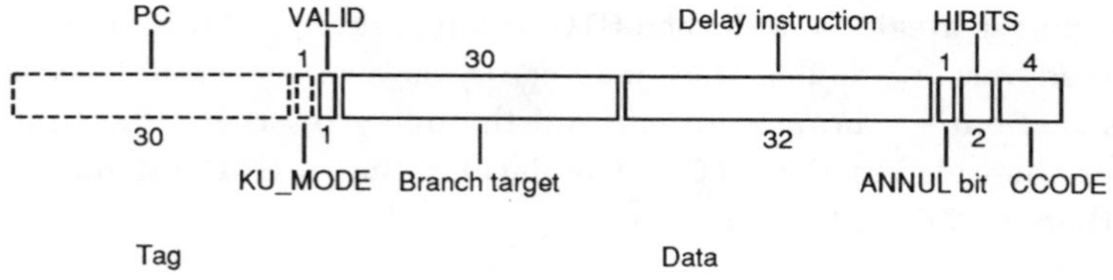

Figure 6.45 Line structure of the branch-target cache

Signal	I/O	Explanation
DATA_IN	in	Data to be stored for a BTC entry: processor mode, ANNUL bit, condition code, branch target, and delay instruction
CACHE_PC	in	Memory address of instruction searched in BTC, coinciding with appropriate TAG field in case of a hit
KU_MODE	in	Present kernel/user mode, coinciding with appropriate TAG field in case of a hit
BTC_MODE	in	Pin of processor chip setting BTC working mode:
		BIG_MODE BCC and CALL instructions are stored
		SMALL_MODE only BCC instructions are stored
CALL, BCC, TAKEN	in	By these signals, stage ID reports the decoding of a relevant CTR instruction; in case of a conditional branch, the BTC is told, whether it is taken;
NEW_FLAGS	in	Instruction will influence flags in the next cycle
BTC_ACTIVE	in	Pin of processor chip activating the whole BTC; the deactivation of BTC is implemented by a combination of HIT and BTC_ACTIVE resulting in a permanent miss
CCLR, RESET	in	Reset BTC to its starting state, in which all entries are invalid
BTC_TAKEN	out	Temporary or final branch decision
BTC_PC	out	Branch target of a cache hit
HIT	out	BTC contains instruction searched
BTC_DATA	out	Delay instruction of a cache hit

Table 6.46 Interface of BTC

6.4.3 Cooperation of MPC and BTC with the Pipeline

After their specification, the caches are integrated. For BTC and MPC, there are three states: deactivation, hit, and miss. The selection of an instruction is shown in Table 6.47.

BTC state	MPC state	Instruction from
Miss/off	Miss/off	Memory
Miss/off	Hit	MPC
Hit	Miss/off	BTC
Hit	Hit	BTC

Table 6.47 Sources for the instruction register

The replacing strategies of MPC and BTC usually prevent a hit in both caches at the same address. (A double-store may occur, however, when a delay slot of a CTR instruction is a branch target, and the delay instruction is first in the MPC, but then also in the BTC.) It is decided that a BTC hit has a higher priority than an MPC hit.

MPC mode	BTC mode	LD/ST class	BCC class	CALL	Other instructions
—	—	—	—	—	—
—	SMALL_MODE	—	BTC	—	—
—	BIG_MODE	—	BTC	BTC	—
IC_MODE	—	MPC	MPC	MPC	MPC
IC_MODE	BIG_MODE	MPC	BTC	BTC	MPC
IC_MODE	SMALL_MODE	MPC	BTC	MPC	MPC
RIB_MODE	—	MPC	—	—	—
RIB_MODE	BIG_MODE	MPC	BTC	BTC	—
RIB_MODE	SMALL_MODE	MPC	BTC	—	—

Table 6.48 Cache modes and instruction storing

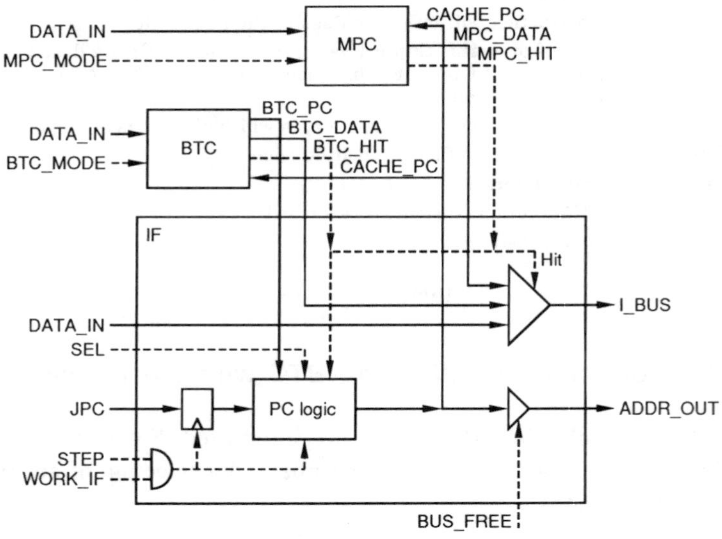

Figure 6.49 IF stage with caches

Storing depends as in Table 6.48 on the cache modes and the instruction class. For example, if the MPC is in the RIB_MODE and the BTC in the SMALL_MODE, an instruction colliding with an LD/ST instruction is stored in the MPC. To find the instruction class, an early decoding has to be performed in the IF stage; the simple instruction formats imply just a few gates for this task.

So far, IF stage and caches were specified almost independently. For a later implementation, additional aspects are to be considered. These include the interface complexity and aspects of an efficient placement and routing. Our silicon vendor requires that a functional modularization should also consider a desirable geometrical proximity. Therefore, the implementation in Chapter 7 combines the IF stage and the caches as in Figure 6.49.

6.4.4 The Register File

The register file REG consists of a RAM memory with 40 words of 32 bits, multiplexers, and additional access logic. The register file implements the general-purpose registers of the processor. Its structure is shown in Figure 6.50 and the interface is explained in Table 6.51.

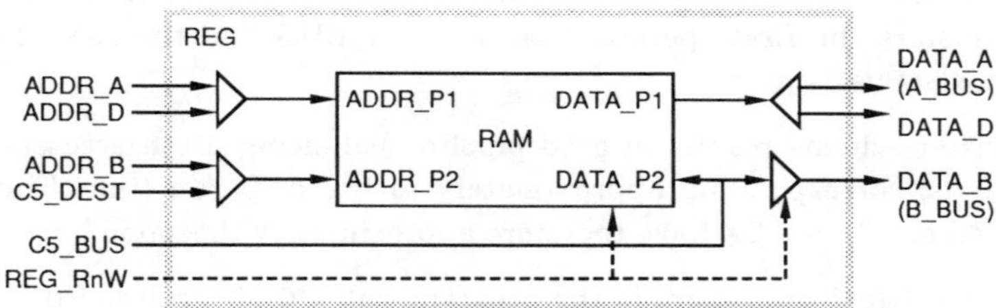

Figure 6.50 Structure of register file REG

Signal	I/O	Explanation
ADDR_A	in	Address of first ALU operand
ADDR_B	in	Address of second ALU operand
ADDR_D	in	Address of data to be stored
C5_DEST	in	Address of result to be written by WB stage
C5_BUS	in	Result to be written by WB stage
REG_RnW	in	Read/write selection of port P2
DATA_A	out	First ALU operand
DATA_B	out	Second ALU operand
DATA_D	out	Data to be stored

Table 6.51 Interface of the register file

The register file is accessed by stage ID for operand reading and by WB for writing results into main memory. The processor timing and the access scheme of ID and WB determine the register file control. When the pipeline is fully loaded, the file is accessed four times in every cycle. Three accesses are reading (for example, two address operands and data in Store instructions by WB) and one access is writing (for example, the ALU result by WB).

A four-port register file would require too much chip area, particularly in the context of a gate-array design. We therefore specify a two-port register file with a read-only port P1 and a write-read port P2. Both ports have address inputs ADDR_P1 and ADDR_P2, respectively. Port P1 has a data output DATA_P1, and P2 has a bidirectional data interface DATA_P2. Signal REG_RnW ensures that P2 operates in the first half of a cycle as a write port and in the second half as a read port. An additional pragmatic aspect comes from the cell library provided: the next larger register component has 6 ports and is thus too large. This supports the two-port solution chosen.

We require access times significantly less than half a cycle length of about 20 ns. This enables the distribution of four accesses sequentially to the two ports. In the first half of a clock cycle, the write-back stage performs a write access to port P2 connected with the C5_BUS, while the ID stage reads the Store data on port P1 and puts it onto the D_BUS. In the second half cycle, the ID stage transfers the first operand from P1 to A_BUS and the second operand from P2 to B_Bus.

This register scheme results in good pipeline balancing. Both accesses require about 40 ns, corresponding approximately to the ALU run time. The critical paths of stages ID and EX have therefore approximately the same length.

A feature of RISC processors is the constant value 0 of register R0. From the description of synthetic instructions (Section 5.2.5), it follows that this saves additional instructions. To implement this feature, a read access to R0 always delivers a 0 independently of the register contents.

In the array of 40 general-purpose registers, only 32 are visible for the user at a time; the remaining eight serve as a twofold set of overlay registers for registers 28 to 31. During an interrupt, an overlay set of registers superimposes these registers depending on the interrupt level. This supports an easy register saving.

6.5 Internal Specification of Interrupts

This section specifies the internal execution of interrupts and implications to the architecture.

For easy and efficient handling, interrupts are implemented by the pipeline similarly to a CALL instruction. The differences consist in the necessary saving of processor state and in a different computation of the branch target. These branch targets are the beginning of the interrupt routines and should be modifiable by the program, individually for every interrupt. Moreover, its computation has to be performed in one cycle. These requirements are satisfied with the vector base register (Section 5.2.6).

Interrupt execution has to be transparent in the sense that the processor state saved at the beginning is restored at the end of interrupt. This state contains therefore all information on a correctly running program before the interrupt occurred, which is necessary for a correct continuation. A *rerun* point determines for a given program, which instruction is executed last and completely in the pipeline, before it is branched to the interrupt routine.

The interrupt point is chosen between stages IF and ID. Therefore, the instruction in the ID stage at the begin of interrupt is moving through the pipeline as the last action. Directly after this instruction, the first instruction of the interrupt routine is executed, and the instruction in IF is discarded. After interrupt, IF starts with the discarded instruction.

In two special cases, it is more complicated to set the rerun point. These cases are interrupts caused by LD/ST instructions (I/O case) and interrupts following a CTR instruction (CTR case).

I/O case: an LD/ST instruction in stage MA may cause when accessing memory an interrupt PAGE_FAULT, a MISS_ALIGN, or a BUS_ERROR. In these cases, the rerun point must be between MA and WB, as there is no way to complete the running I/O operation successfully. After the removal of the interrupt cause, the I/O instruction is again executed by the interrupt routine, this time hopefully correctly.

CTR case: if an interrupt request which is itself a CTR arrives between a CTR and its delay instruction, this request must not be accepted immediately to avoid two subsequent control transfers, which were explicitly excluded. This case is recognized and solved by putting the rerun point before the CTR. Thus a CTR and its delay instruction are always removed together from the pipeline.

The two special cases may overlap, but even this results only in a shift of the rerun point.

In the design of TOOBSIE, the saving of some of the data is transferred to the system software in order to reduce hardware complexity. The hardware offers all status-relevant information by instructions LRFS and SRIS. For the interrupt routines, overlay registers superimpose the normal registers. As they are provided for this purpose only, they can save status information without changing the status.

Four additional registers are provided for this purpose. Theoretically, a single register would suffice, but four enable easier and more efficient saving. These registers overlay the normal registers R31,...,R28 and are accessible instead.

In addition to set R of R31,...,R28 in normal operations without interrupts, there are two additional sets RI and RE of overlay registers with addresses 31,...,28. RE serves for external interrupts (hardware interrupts Hwi), RI for internal interrupts consisting of software interrupts Swi and exceptions Exc.

Case	Interrupt sequence	Register set	Status saving
1	–	R	uncritical
2	Swi	RI	uncritical
3	Exc	RI	uncritical
4	Hwi	RE	uncritical
5	Swi Hwi	RE	uncritical
6	Exc Hwi	RE	uncritical
7a	Swi Exc	RI	poss. critical
7b	Swi Exc Hwi	RE	poss. critical
8	others	RI	critical (PANIC)

Table 6.52 Overlay registers

Table 6.52 shows all possible sequences of interrupts. An end of interrupt RETI removes the last entry of the corresponding interrupt sequence. For example, sequence Exc RETI Swi Hwi RETI finally results in case 2. In cases different from cases 1 to 7b, the processor state cannot be saved, and according to case 8, exception PANIC is requested, at least insuring a well defined processor state.

Case 7 is special, as in spite of additional and internal interrupts, no new set of internal overlay registers can be provided. This case is only meaningful in connection with certain routines of the operating system.

The pipeline control evaluates the interrupts, determines the rerun point, computes the new PC, and generates the necessary control signals. These are the WORK signals of the pipeline synchronization. In addition, we have the new PC value and an enable signal for stage IF.

7 Pipeline of the Coarse Structure Model

The RISC processor TOOBSIE was externally specified in Chapter 5 by a simulatable HDL behavior model. This *golden device* defines the instruction semantics. To implement this behavior, an internal architecture with a time behavior was specified in Chapter 6. Although these specifications were rather detailed and contained important design decisions, we have not yet proved that the specified parts fit together and do really generate the reference behavior.

This proof is now presented by a precise simulatable Coarse Structure Model in the hardware description language VERILOG. This second VERILOG model will afterwards serve as a specification for the Gate Model as a hierarchical composition of gate and library elements of the silicon vendor as a net list (*schematic*). Also this model will be precise and simulatable, and of course it has to produce essentially the same simulation results as the Interpreter Model and the Coarse Structure Model. It will precisely describe the future hardware to be produced except for the succeeding placement and routing, by which wire capacities may slightly change run time. This will have to be controlled in a post-layout simulation.

There is a conflict in designing the Coarse Structure Model. On the one hand, the model should be easily readable and understandable. It should therefore be rather abstract in the sense that it contains major structural components such as pipeline stages, caches, registers, etc., but that these are only modeled behaviorally like the Interpreter Model. On the other hand, the model should prepare the design and documentation of schematics, requiring a detailed and close-to-hardware design. For example, a signal code should coincide with the future code on the chip. Good readability is then only secondary.

Finally, there is a feature of our CAD design system which is not always ideal from a methodology point of view, namely that an efficient placement and routing can be expected if the design hierarchy coincides with the geometric layout component hierarchy to some extent.

The models are quite large and we do not want to build further models – also in the interest of the reader – so we developed the Coarse Structure Model as a compromise.

On the one hand, we shall consider pragmatic and physical-geometric aspects and will therefore not merely follow the logical decomposition into pipeline stages of the previous chapter.

On the other hand, we will strive for an understandable hierarchic structure, refining the units more and more, until on the bottom level, we have rather elementary behavior. It should be possible to understand the processor on various abstraction levels without studying the complete model.

We begin with an overview of major components of the Coarse Structure Model and their functions. Then we give hierarchically a more and more detailed description of all processor modules. The order of description corresponds to the VERILOG code in Chapter 🖫3 of the disk and H4.7. In Chapter 9, also the system and test environment of the processor model is treated, so that it can be intensively simulated and tested. Also the following block diagrams use the legend of Figure 6.11.

Starting from the five logical pipeline stages of the internal specification, the datapath of the Coarse Structure Model is modularized into the following *units: instruction fetch unit IFU*, *instruction decode unit IDU*, *arithmetic logic unit ALU*, *memory access unit MAU*, and *forwarding and register unit FRU*. The latter contains the write-back stage, the register file, and the forwarding logic.

In the process of modeling it turned out to be useful to move certain parts of units into other units. Guidelines were readability of model code or number and size of module interfaces, where we predicted an easier future transformation into an efficient Gate Model. For example, the branch decoding was moved from IDU to IFU.

Some functions concerning several stages, and most of all control functions, were concentrated in two separate units. This resulted in a *pipeline control unit PCU* and a *bus control unit BCU* implementing the interface to external memory and the bus protocol.

The description of the Coarse Structure Model is divided as follows. The datapath with the five-stage pipeline is commented in the present Chapter 7, the controllers PCU and BCU as well as the system environment with first simulation results are explained in the expert volume in Chapter H4. Equally, the somewhat complex comments on the implementation of the branch-target cache are postponed to H4.

The explanations are definitely only understandable in connection with the source code. This can be found on the disk in Chapter 🖫3 and is printed in

Section H4.7. The reader may explore the model using his own editor or may simulate it using an appropriate VERILOG simulator.

As we have decided on a complete presentation of our model, a large number of details is unavoidable. For the normally interested reader, we recommend, particularly in a first pass, not to try to understand every detail and rather focus on the *how*, namely the way certain features are modeled in an HDL.

Figure 7.1 shows the main connections of the seven units, whose major parts and tasks are now briefly presented.

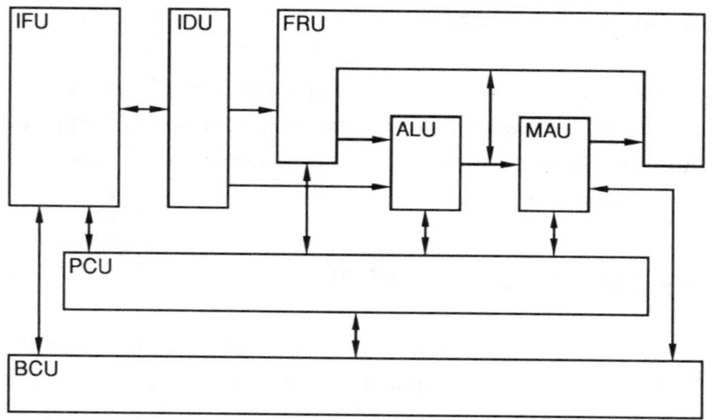

Figure 7.1 Processor units

The Instruction Fetch Unit IFU

The IFU contains the program counter PC, the branch decoding, the PC logic, the multi-purpose cache MPC, and the branch-target cache BTC. Certain branches with their delay instructions are stored in the BTC, all other instructions in the MPC. The IFU reads the next instruction from the caches or requests it from the BCU which in turn fetches it from main memory. Afterwards, the instruction is shifted to the IDU. Branches are recognized, and their branch target is computed.

The unit works in different modes: the FETCH_MODE selects between serial and parallel memory access, and the caches have various working modes or can be turned off completely.

The Instruction Decode Unit IDU

The IDU decodes the instructions of the IFU and generates control signals neccessary for their execution. It recognizes illegal or not implemented instructions and violations of the processor mode (PRIVILEGE_VIOLATION), and it reacts by requesting a suitable exception.

The Arithmetic Logic Unit ALU

The ALU computes the arithmetic and logic operations and performs rotation and shift operations. Moreover, it computes addresses for memory accesses of the memory access unit following next in the pipeline.

The Memory Access Unit MAU

The MAU accesses main memory. Write data are turned over to the bus control unit BCU, read data are taken from there. For instruction Swap, both are done in one pipeline step. When no memory access is executed, the unit serves only as a buffer in the pipeline.

The Forwarding and Register Unit FRU

The FRU contains the register file with the general-purpose registers, the forwarding logic, and the write-back pipeline stage. Due to the pipeline architecture, sometimes data are requested by a register which are written there only in the next step. This case is treated by a forwarding mechanism. The new data are read early and directly from an appropriate bus. The corresponding logic is completely contained in the FRU, such that other units do not know whether they receive data from a register or from the forwarding logic.

The Pipeline Control Unit PCU

The PCU controls the pipeline. It enables and disables pipeline stages, and provides all control signals for units IFU, IDU, MAU, FRU, and BCU. Furthermore, the PCU manages the externally requested or internally generated interrupts.

The Bus Control Unit BCU

The BCU supports chip communication with external memory. It implements an asynchronous and a synchronous bus protocol. Externally, it provides all signals for memory control. Internally, it provides a bus arbitration, such that IFU and MAU can safely share a common memory bus.

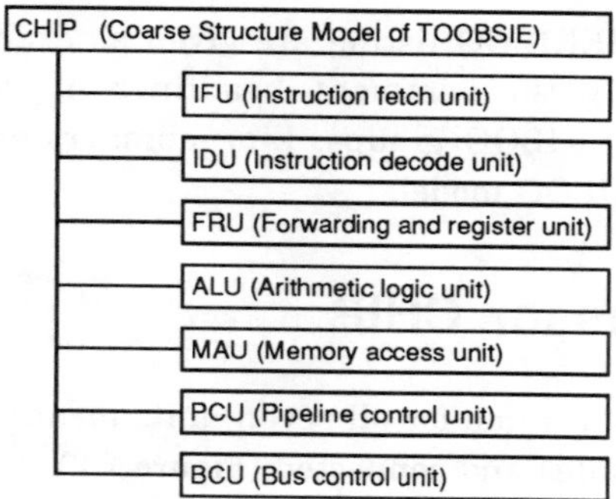

Figure 7.2 Module hierarchy of processor

The upper two levels of the module hierarchy of the processor are shown in Figure 7.2. While the top module SYSTEM containing the memory and the system and test environment of the processor is treated in Sections H4.5, 🖫3.9 and H4.7.9, we begin with the processor module CHIP itself which only instantiates all units and wires them (Sections 7.1, 🖫3.1, and H4.7.1). Next, the datapath units are explained in order in Sections 7.2 – 7.6 and the control units in H4.1 and H4.2; the VERILOG code is listed in 🖫3.2 – 🖫3.8 and H4.7.2 – H4.7.8, respectively.

The unit descriptions are structured similarly. The unit interface is given, usually by a table; its order corresponds to the parameter list of the VERILOG module. First, inputs are described, then the outputs. Both are sorted by signal width, such that address and data buses come first. To distinguish normal 1-active signals from low-active signals active at 0, the latter ones have a name beginning with n.

As in the VERILOG model, a unit is presented as a hierarchy of modules and groups. A *group* is a meaningful combination of one or more initial or always blocks. As parameter lists would be relatively long, a modeling of groups by modules seemed unfeasible. In figures showing a hierarchy like Figure 7.56, groups are distinguished from modules by rounded corners.

The order of components corresponds generally to that of the VERILOG listing. For complex units as the IFU, task and major components are briefly described, supported by a block diagram of the internal structure. This representation summarizes important signals and components of the units and connects them.

After the top level of a module description, the components are presented next. For complex components, this scheme is repeated.

Many extracts of the VERILOG listing are given as examples. These may be "skeletons" giving only the comment headlines of important groups or complete sections of VERILOG groups. Line numbers enable an easy orientation in the large VERILOG model.

7.1 The Processor CHIP

Module CHIP serves as a frame for all seven units mentioned before which are instantiated as submodules and connected (Figure 7.2). Also, the external chip signals are wired with the units. External signals may be inputs (in), outputs (out), or tri-state signals (tri).

The module interface with signal encoding is shown in Table 7.3. The corresponding VERILOG code is found in Section 🖫3.1 or H4.7.1.

Signal	I/O	Code	Explanation
CONFIG	in		Cache configuration
		0????	Parallel mode
		1????	Serial mode
		???00	BTC: off
		???01	BTC: BCC only
		???10	BTC: CALL only
		???11	BTC: BCC and CALL
		?00??	MPC: off
		?01??	MPC: RIB mode
		?10??	MPC: IC mode
IRQ_ID	in		Interrupt ID
		000	Bus error
		001	Page fault
		010	Misalign
CP	in		System clock
nRESET	in		RESET
		1	CPU working
		0	RESET
nIRQ	in		Interrupt request
		1	No request
		0	System requests interrupt
nMHS	in		Memory Handshake
		1→0	Begin of memory access
		0→1	End of memory access
nHLT	in		HALT
		1	CPU working
		0	CPU halts
BUS_PRO	in		Bus protocol
		1	Synchronous
		0	Asynchronous
ADDR_BUS	out		Memory address bus

ACC_MODE	out		Access mode for LD/ST instructions
		00	Byte
		01	Halfword
		10	Word
nIRA	out		Interrupt Acknowledge
		1 → 0	Received interrupt request
		0 → 1	Interrupt is executed
RnW	out		Memory Read not Write
		1	Read
		0	Write
nRMW	out		Read modify write
		0	Read-write access
		1	No read-write access
nMRQ	out		Memory Request
		0	Memory access
		1	no memory access
KU_MODE	out		Processor mode
		1	KERNEL_MODE
		0	USER_MODE
DATA_BUS	tri		Data bus

Table 7.3 Interface of module CHIP with signal encoding

To get an overview of the unit connections and a first impression of the module size, Table 7.4 contains all signals of module CHIP. It is grouped by modules, beginning with CHIP, and followed by unit modules in the order IFU, IDU, ALU, MAU, FRU, PCU, and BCU. For every model, the signals are listed in the same order as in the VERILOG model. An exception is the PCU. For a better readability, entries and exits are additionally ordered by destination and source. In any case, the order corresponds with the local tables of every unit presented later. Many details of this overview table are explained only in the special sections.

As a naming convention, actual parameters in the module CHIP normally are named by the formal parameters of the source and destination modules. They may, however, differ. An example is the actual parameter IF_KUMODE, whose formal name in IFU is KU_MODE. In column "signal", Table 7.4 contains the actual parameters. If the formal parameter of the source or destination differs, column "explanation" contains a hint of type IFU.KU_MODE.

Module	Signal	to/from	Explanation
CHIP	ADDR_BUS	← BCU	Memory address bus
	ACC_MODE	← BCU	Access mode for LD/ST instructions (BCU.ACMD)
	nIRA	← PCU	Interrupt acknowledge
	RnW	← BCU	Memory read not write
	nRMW	← BCU	Read modify write
	nMRQ	← BCU	Memory request
	FACC	← BCU	Fetch access
	KU_MODE	← PCU	Processor mode (PCU.SYS_KUMODE)
	DATA_BUS	↔ BCU	Data bus
	CONFIG	→ IFU	Cache configuration (IFU.CACHE_MODE)

	IRQ_ID	→ PCU	Interrupt ID
	CP	→ all	System clock
	nRESET	→ IFU, → IDU, → PCU	Processor reset
	nIRQ	→ PCU	Interrupt request
	nMHS	→ BCU	Memory handshake
	nHLT	→ BCU	HALT
	BUS_PRO	→ BCU	Bus protocol
IFU	I_BUS	→ IDU	Instruction
	IFU_ADDR_BUS	→ BCU	Address of next instruction to be fetched
	NPC_BUS	→ PCU	Return address of CALL (PCU.NPC)
	BREAK_MEM_ACC	→ BCU	Break memory access
	CALL_NOW	→ PCU	CALL instruction, NPC_BUS valid
	DIS_IDU	→ PCU	Deactivate IDU
	DIS_ALU	→ PCU	Deactivate ALU
	EXCEPT_CTR	→ IDU	Exception: CTR in delay slot of a branch (IFU.EXCEPT)
	DS_IN_IFU	→ PCU	Delay slot of a branch is executed (IFU.DS_NOW)
	IFU_FETCH_RQ	→ BCU	IFU intends to load (IFU.DO_FETCH)
	IFU_CORRECT	→ PCU	IFU correcting branch
	IFU_DATA_BUS	← BCU	Instruction from memory
	PC_BUS	← PCU	PC for branch request by PCU
	CONFIG	← extern.	Cache configuration (IFU.CACHE_MODE)
	IF_FLAGS	← PCU	Flags for BTC (IFU.FLAGS_IF)
	FD_FLAGS	← PCU	Flags for branch correction (IFU.FLAGS_FD)
	CP	← extern.	System clock
	WORK_IF	← PCU	IF enable
	WORK_FD	← PCU	FD enable
	CCLR	← IDU	Clear caches
	nRESET	← extern.	Processor reset
	IF_KU_MODE	← PCU	Processor mode (IFU.KU_MODE)
	USE_PCU_PC	← PCU	Branch request by PCU
	NEW_FLAGS	← IDU	Instruction in ALU changing flags
	LDST_ACC_NOW	← PCU	Memory bus busy
	EMERG_FETCH	← PCU	Branch request to be executed immediately
IDU	IMMEDIATE	→ FRU	Immediate operand B
	SWI_ID	→ PCU	SWI code
	EXCEPT_ID	→ PCU	Exception code
	ADDR_A	→ FRU	Address source register A
	ADDR_B	→ FRU	Address source register B
	ADDR_C	→ FRU	Address result register
	ADDR_D	→ FRU	Address write data register (FRU.ADDR_STORE_DATA)
	SREG_ADDR	→ PCU	Address special register (IDU.ADDR_SREG)
	ALU_OPCODE	→ ALU	ALU operation
	MAU_ACC_MODE2	→ PCU	MAU access width
	MAU_OPCODE2	→ PCU	MAU access mode
	USE_SREG_DATA	→ FRU	B operand is special register
	USE_IMMEDIATE	→ FRU	B operand is immediate
	SWI_RQ	→ PCU	SWI request
	EXCEPT_RQ	→ PCU	Exception request
	SREG_ACC_DIR	→ PCU	SREG access direction
	DO_RETI	→ PCU	Return from interrupt
	DO_HALT	→ PCU	Halt processor
	NEW_FLAGS	→ IFU, → PCU	ALU operation with .F option
	CCLR	→ IFU	Clear caches
	I_BUS	← IFU	Instruction
	CP	← extern.	System clock
	WORK_ID	← PCU	IDU enable
	STEP	← PCU	Pipeline enable
	KILL_IDU	← PCU	IDU disable
	nRESET	← extern.	Processor reset
	ID_KU_MODE	← PCU	Kernel/user mode (IDU.ID_KUMODE, PCU.ID_KUMODE)
	EXCEPT_CTR	← IFU	CTR exception (IFU.EXCEPT)

ALU	C3_BUS	→ FRU, → MAU	Result
	FLAGS_FROM_ALU	→ PCU	Result flags
	A_BUS	← FRU	Operand A
	B_BUS	← FRU	Operand B
	ALU_CARRY	← PCU	Carry operand
	ALU_OPCODE	← IDU	Opcode
	CP	← extern.	System clock
	WORK_EX	← PCU	EX enable
MAU	C4_BUS	→ FRU	Result data
	MAU_WRITE_DATA	→ BCU	Write data
	MAU_ADDR_BUS	→ BCU, → PCU	Memory access address
	D_BUS	← FRU	Data to be written (FRU.STORE_DATA)
	MAU_READ_DATA	← BCU	Data read
	C3_BUS	← ALU	Address or operand
	MAU_ACC_MODE3	← PCU	Access mode (MAU.MAU_ACC_MODE_3)
	MAU_OPCODE3	← PCU	Opcode (MAU.MAU_OPCODE_3)
	CP	← extern.	System clock
	WORK_MA	← PCU	MA enable
FRU	A_BUS	→ ALU	Data bus for operand A
	B_BUS	→ ALU	Data bus for operand B
	D_BUS	→ MAU	Delayed write data for MAU access (FRU.STORE_DATA)
	SREG_DATA	← PCU	Data from special register
	IMMEDIATE	← IDU	Immediate for data bus B
	C3_BUS	← ALU	Result for forwarding
	C4_BUS	← MAU	Result for forwarding
	ADDR_A	← IDU	Register address for data bus A
	ADDR_B	← IDU	Register address for data bus B
	ADDR_C	← IDU	Register address for result bus
	ADDR_D	← IDU	Register address for Store data (FRU.ADDR_STORE_DATA)
	INT_STATE	← PCU	Selection of interrupt overlay register set
	USE_IMMEDIATE	← IDU	Immediate bus valid
	CP	← extern.	System clock
	STEP	← PCU	Pipeline shift
	WORK_EX	← PCU	EX enable (FRU.WORK_ALU)
	WORK_MA	← PCU	MA enable (FRU.WORK_MAU)
	WORK_WB	← PCU	WB enable
	USE_SREG_DATA	← IDU	Take data from special register
PCU-PF -IF	LDST_ACC_NOW	→ IFU	MAU access
	EMERG_FETCH	→ IFU	Request new instruction fetch, invalidate last (interrupt)
	IF_FLAGS	→ IFU	Flags for IF (branch decision after BTC hit, IFU.FLAGS_IF)
	IF_KU_MODE	→ IFU	Kernel/user mode for fetch (IFU.KU_MODE)
	KILL_IDU	→ IDU	IDU disable
	PC_BUS	→ IFU	PC for IF
	USE_PCU_PC	→ IFU	IFU to use PC_BUS
	WORK_IF	→ IFU	IF enable
-ID	ALU_CARRY	→ ALU	Carry
	FD_FLAGS	→ IFU	Flags for FD (standard branch decision, branch correction, IFU.FLAGS_FD)
	ID_KU_MODE	→ IDU	Kernel/user mode for ID (IDU.ID_KUMODE)
	INT_STATE	→ FRU	Selection of interrupt overlay register set
	SREG_DATA	→ FRU	Data from special register
	WORK_FD	→ IFU	FD enable (decoding logic of IFU)
	WORK_ID	→ IDU	ID enable
	STEP	→ IDU	Pipeline shift
-EX	MAU_ACC_MODE3	→ MAU	Access width for MAU (MAU.MAU_ACC_MODE_3)
	MAU_OPCODE3	→ MAU	MAU opcode (MAU.MAU_OPCODE_3)
	WORK_EX	→ ALU, → FRU	EX enable (FRU.WORK_ALU)
-MA	WORK_MA	→ MAU,	MA enable (FRU.WORK_MAU)

		→ FRU	
-WB	WORK_WB	→ FRU	WB enable (write-back stage of FRU)
	STEP	→ FRU	Pipeline shift
-BCU	BCU_ACC_DIR	→ BCU	BCU access mode and direction
	BCU_ACC_MODE	→ BCU	BCU access unit (IFU/MAU) and access width
-extern.	nIRA	→ extern.	Acknowledge of HWI request
	KU_MODE	→ extern.	Kernel/user mode (PCU.SYS_KUMODE)
-IF	CALL_NOW	← IFU	CALL
	DIS_ALU	← IFU	EX disable
	DIS_IDU	← IFU	ID disable
	DS_IN_IFU	← IFU	CTR in ID and delay instruction in IF (IFU.DS_NOW)
	IFU_ADDR_BUS	← IFU	IFU memory address
	IFU_CORRECT	← IFU	Branch correction
	NPC_BUS	← IFU	Next PC in IFU (rerun after CALL and SWI, PCU.NPC)
-ID	B_BUS	← FRU	Operand from register file for SRIS
	DO_HALT	← IDU	HALT request
	DO_RETI	← IDU	RETI request
	EXCEPT_ID	← IDU	Exception ID
	EXCEPT_RQ	← IDU	Exception request
	MAU_ACC_MODE2	← IDU	Memory access width
	MAU_OPCODE2	← IDU	Opcode of memory access
	NEW_FLAGS	← IDU	Flag changing instruction in ID
	SREG_ACC_DIR	← IDU	Special register access direction
	SREG_ADDR	← IDU	Special register address (IDU.ADDR_SREG)
	SWI_ID	← IDU	SWI ID
	SWI_RQ	← IDU	SWI request
-EX	FLAGS_FROM_ALU	← ALU	Flags from ALU operation
-MA	MAU_ADDR_BUS	← MAU	MAU access address
-BCU	BCU_READY	← BCU	Memory access state
-extern.	CP	← extern.	System clock
	IRQ_ID	← extern.	HWI ID
	nIRQ	← extern.	HWI request
	nRESET	← extern.	Processor reset
BCU	MAU_READ_DATA	→ MAU	MAU read data, valid at end of step
	IFU_DATA_BUS	→ IFU	IFU read data, valid at end of step
	ADDR_BUS	→ extern.	External address bus
	ACC_MODE	→ extern.	External access mode for LD/ST instructions (BCU.ACMD)
	BCU_READY	→ PCU	BCU access done
	nMRQ	→ extern.	Memory access addresses valid
	FACC	→ extern.	Fetch access
	nRMW	→ extern.	Read-modify-write
	RnW	→ extern.	Read/write access
	DATA_BUS	↔ extern.	External data bus
	MAU_WRITE_DATA	← MAU	MAU write data
	IFU_ADDR_BUS	← IFU	IFU fetch address
	MAU_ADDR_BUS	← MAU	MAU access address
	CP	← extern.	System clock
	nRESET	← extern.	Processor reset
	BCU_ACC_MODE	← PCU	Access mode
	BCU_ACC_DIR	← PCU	Access direction
	BREAK_MEM_ACC	← IFU	Break memory access (cache hit)
	IFU_FETCH_RQ	← IFU	IFU fetch request (BCU.DO_FETCH)
	BUS_PRO	← extern.	Bus protocol
	nHLT	← extern.	Halt
	nMHS	← extern.	Memory handshake

Table 7.4 Wiring of module CHIP

To improve the connection between internal specification and Coarse Structure Model, Table 7.5 contains names of both processor descriptions. Of course, the Coarse Structure Model contains more names, and a unique correspondence is therefore quite impossible. This follows already from the different structure of the pipeline. The table helps one to find signals of the internal specification in the Coarse Structure Model. Only names differing in the Coarse Structure Model are mentioned. It may even happen that some signals of the internal specification no longer appear, for example, because the limits between pipeline stages have moved. This is not careless designing, but a typical feature of a design process.

Stage	Internal specification	Unit	Coarse Structure Model
IF	DATA_IN	IFU	IFU_DATA_BUS
	ADDR_OUT		IFU_ADDR_BUS
ID	A_BUS, B_BUS	FRU	A_BUS, B_BUS
	D_BUS		Internal
	DATA_A, B		A_BUS, B_BUS
	DATA_D		Internal
	D2_BUS		STORE_DATA
	SREG_DATA	PCU	B_BUS
	SREG_ADDR	IDU	SREG_ADDR
	MA_OPCODE		MAU_OPCODE2
	CTR	IFU	Internal
EX	C2_DEST	FRU	ADDR_C
	C3_DEST		Internal
	D2_BUS		STORE_DATA
	D3_BUS		Internal
	ALU	ALU	SHIFT, LOGIC, ARITHMETIC
MA	MA_OPCODE	MAU	MAU_OPCODE_3
	D3_BUS		D_BUS
	C3_DEST	FRU	Internal
	C4_DEST		Internal
	DATA_IN	MAU	MAU_READ_DATA
	DATA_OUT		MAU_WRITE_DATA
	ADDR_OUT		MAU_ADDR_BUS
WB	C4_DEST	FRU	Internal
	C5_DEST		Internal
	C4_BUS		C4_BUS
	C5_BUS		Internal

Table 7.5 From internal specification to Coarse Structure Model

7.2 The Instruction Fetch Unit IFU

The IFU implements mainly the functionality of the logical IF stage of the previous chapter with the task of reading instructions from memory and transferring them to the logical ID stage. A difference is that communication with external memory has been moved to the bus control unit BCU, while branch decoding originally in ID is now located here. The data flow context of the IFU is shown in Figure 7.1.

The IFU contains the program counter PC, the PC logic, the branch-target cache BTC, and the multi-purpose cache MPC. The IFU fetches an instruction via the BCU from memory and transfers it to the instruction decode unit IDU. When computing the next PC, it recognizes conditional and unconditional branches BCC and CALL. As this can only be done in the following step at the same time as decoding in the IDU, the IFU no longer fits exactly in the pipeline scheme "fetch → decode → execute → memory access → write-back", but includes the logical IF completely and parts of ID. To distinguish the decode stage of the IFU from the one in the IDU, it is denoted in the following as *fetch-decode stage* FD. Table 7.6 summarizes the external IFU signals.

Signal	from/to	Explanation
IFU_DATA_BUS	← BCU	Instruction from memory
PC_BUS	← PCU	PC for PCU branch request
CACHE_MODE	← ext.	Cache configuration
FLAGS_IF	← PCU	BTC flags
FLAGS_FD	← PCU	Flags for branch correction
CP	← ext.	System clock
WORK_IF	← PCU	IF enable
WORK_FD	← PCU	FD enable
CCLR	← IDU	Clear caches
nRESET	← ext.	Reset
KU_MODE	← PCU	Kernel/user mode
USE_PCU_PC	← PCU	PCU branch request
NEW_FLAGS	← IDU	Flag changing instruction
LDST_ACC_NOW	← PCU	Memory bus busy
EMERG_FETCH	← PCU	Immediate branch request
I_BUS	→ IDU	Instruction
IFU_ADDR_BUS	→ BCU	Address of instruction to be fetched
NPC_BUS	→ PCU	Return address of CALL
BREAK_MEM_ACC	→ BCU	Break memory access
CALL_NOW	→ PCU	CALL, NPC_BUS valid
DIS_IDU	→ PCU	Disable IDU
DIS_ALU	→ PCU	Disable ALU
EXCEPT	→ IDU	Exception: CTR in delay slot
DS_NOW	→ PCU	Delay slot of a branch
IFU_FETCH_RQ	→ BCU	IFU fetch request
IFU_CORRECT	→ PCU	IFU correcting branch

Table 7.6 IFU interface

Figure 7.7 shows the hierarchic structure of the IFU. In addition to the caches, there are several small modules.

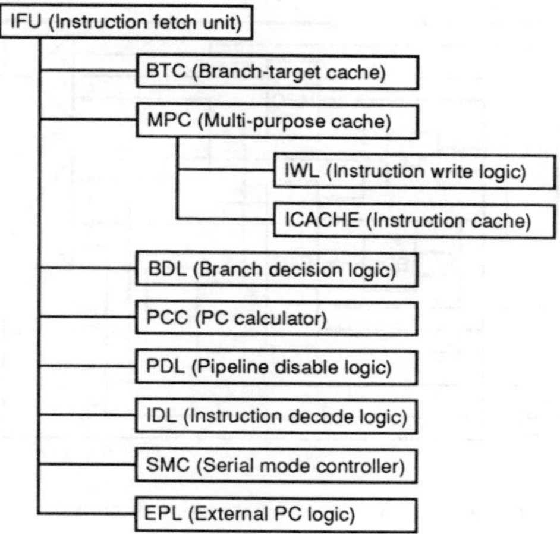

Figure 7.7 Hierarchic structure of module IFU

The branch decision logic BDL determines from the condition code of a branch instruction and the present flags whether the branch will be taken.

The program counter calculator PCC includes the PC and a register LPC for buffering the last PC. Additional offsets like PC+1, LPC+1, etc., are prepared.

The pipeline disable logic PDL controls the outputs DIS_IDU and DIS_ALU for disabling the instruction decode unit and the ALU. This deactivation becomes necessary when there is still no new instruction for the IDU or when a heuristic branch decision was falsely made.

The instruction decode logic IDL decodes an instruction. It signals the existence of a branch and offers information like condition code or branch distance.

A serial memory access is implemented by the serial mode controller SMC. It pretends a memory access to the remaining components of the IFU, while the instruction is searched only in the caches. Only after a cache miss, the instruction is really fetched from memory in the next cycle.

The external PC logic EPL has the following task. The PC is not only determined by the IFU, but can also be overwritten by the PCU with signal USE_PCU_PC. In this case, the delay instruction of a branch has first to be fetched, USE_PCU_PC has to be delayed and the PC has to be saved until the end of step. Modules BDL to EPL are explained in more detail from Section 7.2.6 on.

Aside from these submodules, there is some combinational logic and there are three multiplexers (partially in Figure 7.8). The I_BUS multiplexer selects the

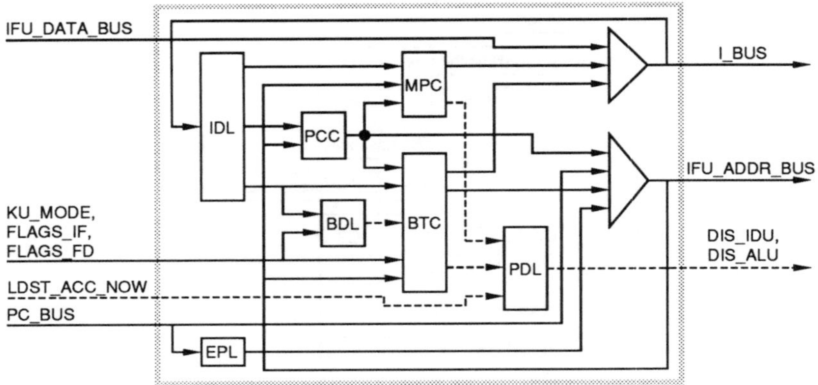

Figure 7.8 Structure of instruction fetch unit

appropriate instruction, the IFU_ADDR_BUS multiplexer forwards an appropriate memory address to the BCU, and the NPC_BUS multiplexer selects the correct alternative for the next value of register NPC, in which the return address for CALL instructions is saved. This depends on whether the last instruction comes from memory or cache. The contents of NPC are transferred from NPC_BUS to the PCU. Note that in Figure 7.8 there are feedbacks from I_BUS and IFU_ADDR_BUS.

The internal signal SHIFT is generated in the IFU and is used only there. If SHIFT is active with the rising clock edge, a new IFU step begins. This local step only relates to the processing within the IFU, not to the rest of the pipeline. SHIFT becomes active with active WORK_IF, if in addition in the last cycle, a memory access was possible, or if there is a cache hit or a branch correction or a branch request from the PCU to be executed immediately. A memory access is impossible, if the bus is busy for a data access by the memory access unit or if in the serial mode, only the caches are searched. An incomplete memory access is signaled by an inactive WORK_IF.

7.2.1 I_BUS Multiplexer

The I_BUS multiplexer selects the instruction for the IDU in the next clock. It depends on whether there is a cache hit or a memory access.

If there is a normal memory access, the instruction is transferred directly from IFU_DATA_BUS. If the BTC does not report a hit, but the MPC does, the instruction is taken from MPC. If the BTC reports a hit, the delay instruction from BTC is transferred to the IDU. In all remaining cases, the last instruction is taken again which comes from the instruction decode logic IDL.

Figure 7.9 shows the selection in the source code using a case statement. This description can easily be implemented in hardware.

```
// I_BUS multiplexer
//
// The instruction for the IDU in the next clock is selected.
// This depends on whether a branch has to be corrected,
// a cache hit did occur, no memory access was possible,
// or there was a normal fetch.
//
always @(BTC_HIT or MPC_HIT or NO_ACC
         or ID_INSTR or IFU_DATA_BUS or MPC_INSTR or BTC_DELAYSLOT) begin
  casez({BTC_HIT, MPC_HIT, NO_ACC})
    3'b000 : INSTR = IFU_DATA_BUS;          // normal fetch
    3'b001 : INSTR = ID_INSTR;              // no memory access
    3'b01? : INSTR = MPC_INSTR;             // MPC hit
    3'b1?? : INSTR = BTC_DELAYSLOT;         // BTC hit
    default : INSTR = ID_INSTR;
  endcase
end
```

Figure 7.9 Selection of appropriate instruction

7.2.2 IFU_ADDR_BUS Multiplexer

This multiplexer selects the address of the instruction to be fetched in the next clock. The selection depends on whether a new step begins, whether a PC value from the pipeline control unit PCU is to be taken, whether a branch has to be corrected, whether there is a BTC or an MPC hit, whether no memory access could be performed, or whether a branch was detected. For the next address, there are the following cases.

PC+1 — This is the normal case, where there is no branch or a conditional branch is not taken. Similarly, an MPC hit is treated. If there is no branch or an untaken one, the new address is PC+1. The program counter calculator PCC performs the incrementation.

JPC — If a branch to be taken was decoded, it is branched to the address JPC, if the last fetch was performed normally or if there is an MPC hit. The branch address is computed by the instruction decode logic IDL.

PC+2 — For a BTC hit without a branch to be taken, the new address is PC+2. It is computed by PCC.

BTC_PC — The address coming from the branch-target cache via BTC_PC is taken, if there was a hit and the branch is to be taken. If the branch is to be taken in a late branch correction, this address is also used. The BTC puts the corrected address on BTC_PC.

LPC+2 — If the BTC requests a branch correction, because a branch not to be taken was taken, the program has to continue with LPC+2. LPC+2 is offered by the program counter calculator PCC.

PC_BUS In case of an external branch request by the PCU, the corresponding target address comes from the PC_BUS.

LAST_PC_BUS In some cases, an external branch request is not to be executed immediately. In this case, the external address is saved by the external PC logic EPL and is offered as LAST_PC_BUS.

Figure 7.10 shows a part of the model.

```
// IFU_ADDR_BUS multiplexer
//
// The address for the next fetch is selected.
// This depends on whether a PC from PC_BUS is to be taken,
// a branch has to be corrected, there is a BTC hit or
// an MPC hit, whether no memory access was possible,
// or whether a branch was detected.
//
always @(SHIFT or USE_PCU_PC or LAST_USE_PCU_PC or BTC_CORRECT or BTC_HIT
         or MPC_HIT or NO_ACC or ID_BRANCH or BTC_TAKEN or BTC_USE_LAST
         or TAKEN
         or PC or PC_1 or JPC or PC_2 or BTC_PC or LPC_2
         or LAST_PC_BUS or PC_BUS) begin
  casez({SHIFT, USE_PCU_PC, LAST_USE_PCU_PC, BTC_CORRECT,
         BTC_HIT, MPC_HIT, NO_ACC, ID_BRANCH, BTC_TAKEN, BTC_USE_LAST,
         TAKEN})
    11'b0?????????? : NEW_PC = PC;            // keep old address
    11'b10000000??? : NEW_PC = PC_1;          // normal fetch
    11'b10000001??0 : NEW_PC = PC_1;          // branch not to be taken
    11'b100001?0??? : NEW_PC = PC_1;          // MPC hit, no branch
    11'b100001?1??0 : NEW_PC = PC_1;          // MPC hit, do not take branch
    11'b10000001??1 : NEW_PC = JPC;           // branch to be taken
    11'b100001?1??1 : NEW_PC = JPC;           // MPC hit, take branch
    11'b10001???0?? : NEW_PC = PC_2;          // BTC hit, do not take branch
    11'b10001???1?? : NEW_PC = BTC_PC;        // BTC hit, take branch
    11'b1001?????1? : NEW_PC = BTC_PC;        // branch correction
    11'b1001?????0? : NEW_PC = LPC_2;         // branch correction
    11'b101???????? : NEW_PC = LAST_PC_BUS;   // delayed external PC
    11'b11????????? : NEW_PC = PC_BUS;        // immediate external PC
    default         : NEW_PC = PC;
  endcase
end
```

Figure 7.10 Selection of appropriate address

7.2.3 NPC_BUS Multiplexer

The NPC_BUS delivers the return address for a CALL to the PCU. This is selected depending on a BTC hit and is buffered in the NPC register. Without a hit, it is LPC+2, and PC+2 otherwise.

7.2.4 Branch-Target Cache BTC

In the branch-target cache, branches are stored with their delay slot. If an address is found in cache, the delay instruction rather than the branch are transferred to the IDU saving one step. Branch-relevant flags have to be recomputed. Then the branch decision is made heuristically and is corrected in the next step, if necessary.

While this behavior of the branch-target cache and the corresponding algorithm were explained in the internal specification in Section 6.4.2, the details of the transformation into an HDL model close to the gate level is somewhat difficult. We have therefore postponed the commenting of the BTC coarse structure to Section H4.3. For a comprehension of the pipeline, a vague understanding of the extensive interface in Table 7.11 is sufficient.

Signal	I/O	Explanation
OPCODE	in	Present instruction, delay instruction to be stored
PC	in	Fetch address
JPC	in	Present branch target
LPC	in	Last fetch address
FLAGS_IF	in	Flags for branch decision
FLAGS_FD	in	Flags for branch correction
ID_CCODE	in	Present condition code
CONFIG	in	Cache mode
ID_ANNUL	in	Present ANNUL bit
BRANCH	in	Branch
TYPE	in	Branch type (0: BCC, 1: CALL)
TAKEN	in	Present branch taken
KU_MODE	in	Kernel/user mode
LAST_KU_MODE	in	Last kernel/user mode
IGNORE_HIT	in	Ignore last cache hit
CCLR	in	Clear cache
NEW_FLAGS	in	IDU instruction changes flags
NO_ACC	in	No memory access
WORK_IF	in	IFU enable
DO_IF	in	IFU was enabled
nRESET	in	Reset
CP	in	System clock
BTC_DELAYSLOT	out	Delay slot from cache
BTC_PC	out	Branch target from cache or address of branch correction
BTC_HIT	out	Cache hit
BTC_CORRECT	out	Branch correction
BTC_USE_LAST	out	Take last fetch address in branch correction
BTC_DIS_IDU	out	BTC requesting IDU disable
BTC_DIS_ALU	out	BTC requesting ALU disable
BTC_TAKEN	out	Branch to be taken after hit
BTC_TYPE	out	Branch type (0: BCC, 1: CALL)

Table 7.11 Interface of branch-target cache BTC

7.2.5 Multi-Purpose Cache MPC

In the multi-purpose cache, all those instructions are stored in the working mode IC_MODE (instruction cache) which are not stored in BTC. In the RIB_MODE (reduced instruction buffer), only those instructions are stored which could not be fetched due to a busy memory bus. The storing is delayed to the second half of the clock following the fetch step. Table 7.12 gives an overview of the MPC interface.

Signal	I/O	Explanation
INSTR	in	Last instruction
PC	in	Instruction address to be searched
LPC	in	Last PC
CONFIG	in	Cache configuration
CCLR	in	Clear cache
BRANCH	in	Branch
LAST_LDST	in	Memory access was impossible
LAST_HIT	in	Last was hit
KU_MODE	in	Kernel/user mode
LAST_KU_MODE	in	Last kernel/user mode
LAST_NO_ACC	in	No memory access was performed
LAST_CORRECTION	in	Last branch was corrected
WORK_IF	in	IFU enable
DO_IF	in	IFU was enabled
nRESET	in	Reset
CP	in	System clock
MPC_INSTR	out	Instruction from cache
MPC_HIT	out	Cache hit

Table 7.12 Interface of multi-purpose cache MPC

According to Figure 7.13, the MPC contains a write-read logic IWL (instruction write logic) and the instruction cache ICACHE as its core.

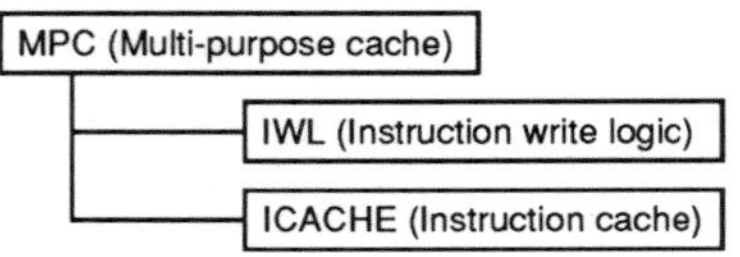

Figure 7.13 Module hierarchy of MPC

7.2.5.1 Instruction Write Logic IWL

The first half of a clock is the reading phase, the second the writing phase. An instruction is written into MPC, if all of the following conditions are satisfied:

- The MPC is in RIB_MODE, with no memory access possible in the previous step, or in IC_MODE.
- It is not a branch for BTC.

- In the last clock, no hit was reported, but a memory access was performed, and no branch correction is necessary.

Then the cache is triggered to write by WnR. The source code in Figure 7.14 shows the modeling by two separated always blocks being triggered with a negative and positive clock edge.

```
// Write phase
//
always @(negedge CP) begin
  if (DO_IF) begin
    if (~((LAST_LDST & CONFIG==2'b01) | (CONFIG==2'b10))
          & ~BRANCH & ~LAST_HIT & ~LAST_NO_ACC & ~LAST_CORRECTION)
         WnR = 1'b1;
    else WnR = 1'b0;
  end
end

//
// Read phase
//
always @(posedge CP)  WnR = 1'b0;
```

Figure 7.14 The instruction write logic IWL

7.2.5.2 Instruction Cache ICACHE

The core of the MPC contains 16 lines with a TAG field and two entries (Figure 7.15). Each entry stores one instruction. As in the BTC, the TAG is fully associative and contains the 29 address bits 31...3 as well as a bit for the processor mode KU_MODE. The TAG therefore requires 30 bits per line.

Only successive instructions can be stored in one line in such a way that the instruction with the odd address is stored in the first entry. For both instructions, address bits 31...3 are identical. Bit 2 of the address selects one of the two instructions of the line. Its bits 1 and 0 are not required, as instructions may only be at addresses divisible by four.

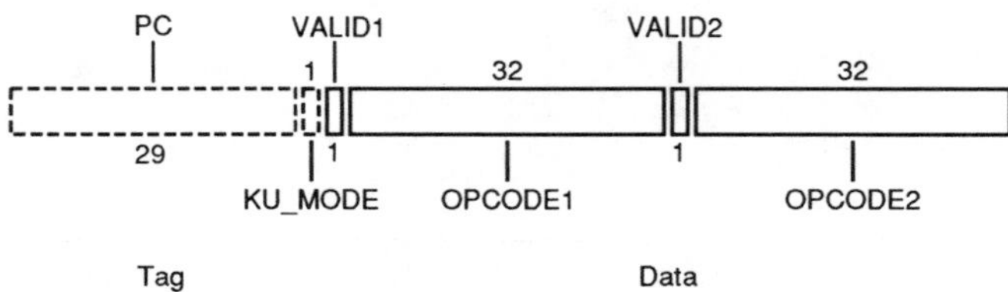

Figure 7.15 One line in multi-purpose cache

The data section contains for every entry 32 bits for the Opcode and the VALID bit. It is therefore 66 bits and the whole line is 96 bits. As every entry has its own VALID bit, entries can be used independently. After a reset or a cache clear signal CCLR, activated by instruction CLC, all VALID bits are set to 0. As an additional design safeguard, the other entries of the model are set undefined.

With an active WnR, a new cache entry is executed. While the write-read logic is in the IWL, the replacing strategy is implemented directly in the instruction cache. If a line with appropriate PC and processor mode already exists, the instruction is stored at this location. Otherwise, an invalid line is selected, if possible. A line is invalid, if both entries are invalid. Otherwise, it is searched for a line with a different KU_MODE. If this is unsuccessful, too, the entry is put in any line. In the first case above, the VALID bit of the second entry of a line remains unchanged, in all other cases it is set to 0.

With an inactive WnR, an entry is read, if there is a hit and the VALID bit is set. Otherwise, the outputs are set undefined.

The associativity of the TAG RAM is modeled by a parallel search. As with the BTC, a line is selected randomly by a register that is incremented by 3 with every rising WnR edge. This may later be implemented differently.

Signal	I/O	Explanation
FLAGS	in	Flags
CCODE	in	Condition code
BDL_TAKEN	out	Branch taken

Table 7.16 Interface of module BDL

```
always @(FLAGS or CCODE) begin
  case(CCODE)
    `MISC_BCC_GT: BDL_TAKEN = (~((NFLAG ^ VFLAG) |  ZFLAG));
    `MISC_BCC_LE: BDL_TAKEN = ( ((NFLAG ^ VFLAG) |  ZFLAG));
    `MISC_BCC_GE: BDL_TAKEN = ( ~(NFLAG ^ VFLAG) |  ZFLAG);
    `MISC_BCC_LT: BDL_TAKEN = (   (NFLAG ^ VFLAG) & ~ZFLAG);
    `MISC_BCC_HI: BDL_TAKEN =  (~(CFLAG | ZFLAG));
    `MISC_BCC_LS: BDL_TAKEN =     (CFLAG | ZFLAG);
    `MISC_BCC_PL: BDL_TAKEN =    (~NFLAG);
    `MISC_BCC_MI: BDL_TAKEN =    ( NFLAG);
    `MISC_BCC_NE: BDL_TAKEN =    (~ZFLAG);
    `MISC_BCC_EQ: BDL_TAKEN =    ( ZFLAG);
    `MISC_BCC_VC: BDL_TAKEN =    (~VFLAG);
    `MISC_BCC_VS: BDL_TAKEN =    ( VFLAG);
    `MISC_BCC_CC: BDL_TAKEN =    (~CFLAG);
    `MISC_BCC_CS: BDL_TAKEN =    ( CFLAG);
    `MISC_BCC_T:  BDL_TAKEN = 1'b1;
    `MISC_BCC_F:  BDL_TAKEN = 1'b0;
    default:      BDL_TAKEN = 1'b0;
  endcase
end
```

Figure 7.17 Branch evaluation

7.2.6 Branch Decision Logic BDL

Module BDL is instantiated by the IFU and the BTC and models a branch decision whether given flags satisfy a given condition. Its interface is shown in Table 7.16. The VERILOG modeling by a case statement is shown in

Figure 7.17. This case statement can be found in the same form in the source code of the Interpreter Model.

7.2.7 Program Counter Calculator PCC

The PCC contains the present and last program address PC and LPC. Based on these addresses, various offsets are computed: PC+1, PC+2, and LPC+2. Moreover, the target address of a branch is calculated here. Table 7.18 summarizes the interface of the PCC. Figure 7.19 shows its structure.

Signal	I/O	Explanation
NEW_PC	in	New fetch address
CPC	in	CALL target
DIST	in	BCC branch distance
TYPE	in	Branch type (0: BCC; 1: CALL)
SHIFT	in	Shift pipeline
CP	in	System clock
PC	out	Fetch address
LPC	out	Fetch address of last step
JPC	out	Branch target address
PC_1	out	PC + 1
PC_2	out	PC + 2
LPC_2	out	LPC + 2

Table 7.18 Interface of program counter calculator PCC

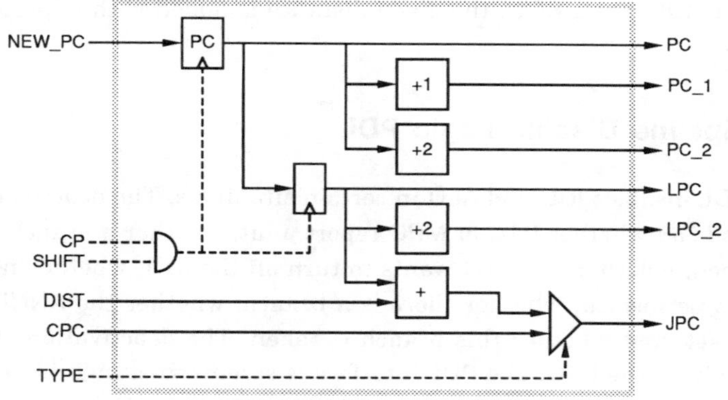

Figure 7.19 Structure of module PCC

After a reset, all PC registers are set undefined, because in this case, the starting address of the processor is determined by the PCU transferring this address as a branch request to the IFU. With the rising clock, fetch address NEW_PC for the present cycle is taken into the PC register. This is only done, if the SHIFT signal is set and hence the last step is completed. At the same time, the old address of PC is assigned to LPC.

The computation of the different values is shown in the source code of Figure 7.20. Depending on triggering conditions, the computations are done in parallel.

```
always @(posedge CP) begin
  if (SHIFT) begin
    fork
      LPC = #`DELTA PC;
      PC  = #`DELTA NEW_PC;
    join
  end
end

always @(PC) begin
  fork
    PC_1 = #`DELTA PC + 30'b01;
    PC_2 = #`DELTA PC + 30'b10;
  join
end

always @(LPC) LPC_2 = #`DELTA LPC + 30'b10;

always @(TYPE or CPC or LPC or DIST) begin
  JPC = (TYPE ? CPC : LPC + {{11{DIST[18]}}, DIST});
end
```

Figure 7.20 PC evaluations

With every change of PC, offsets PC+1 and PC+2 are recomputed. The same holds for the LPC offset LPC+2. If the present branch or the LPC change, the branch target is updated. For a CALL, this is the address from the instruction decode logic IDL. For a BCC, the given distance is added with appropriate sign to LPC.

7.2.8 Pipeline Disable Logic PDL

Module PDL disables IDU and ALU in certain situations. The deactivation of the IDU depends on whether BTC or MPC report a hit, whether a branch correction is performed, whether the BTC wants to turn off the IDU, whether no memory access was performed, whether there is a branch, whether the ANNUL bit of a branch is set, and whether this branch is taken. The deactivation of the ALU depends only on the BTC. The PDL interface is summarized in Table 7.21.

The ALU disable signal is directly taken from BTC. The IDU is disabled in the following five situations.

1 BTC reports no hit and no branch correction, a memory access was performed, there is a branch, the ANNUL bit is set, and the branch is not taken.

Signal	I/O	Explanation
MPC_HIT	in	MPC hit
BTC_HIT	in	BTC hit
BTC_CORRECT	in	BTC requesting branch correction
BTC_DIS_IDU	in	BTC requesting IDU disable
BTC_DIS_ALU	in	BTC requesting ALU disable
NO_ACC	in	No memory access
BRANCH	in	Branch
ANNUL	in	ANNUL bit
TAKEN	in	Branch taken
DIS_IDU	out	Disable IDU
DIS_ALU	out	Disable ALU

Table 7.21 Interface of module PDL

2 BTC reports no hit and no branch correction, no memory access was performed, but MPC reports a hit, there is a branch, the ANNUL bit is set, and the branch is not taken.

3 BTC and MPC report no hit, no branch correction is to be performed, and there is no memory access by the IFU.

4 The BTC wants to correct a branch and to disable the IDU.

5 The BTC reports a hit, there is no branch correction, and the BTC wants to disable the IDU because of a hit.

In all remaining cases, the IDU is not turned off by the IFU.

7.2.9 Instruction Decode Logic IDL

After a fetch, the instruction is decoded to detect a branch (BCC or CALL). Module IDL determines instruction, target of a CALL, branch distance, condition code, and ANNUL bit of a BCC. It also informs about the branch type (BCC or CALL). Furthermore, it is reported whether the last decoded instruction was a branch, as this is necessary to detect branches in the delay slot and to request an exception. Any CTR instruction is considered as a branch (CALL, BCC, SWI, RETI, and SRIS PC).

Table 7.22 summarizes the IDL interface. Figure 7.23 shows its structure.

ID_LAST_BRANCH and ID_LAST_CTR together with ID_BRANCH and ID_CTR serve to recognize branches in the delay slot of a branch. An exception is requested, if two branches follow each other. For this purpose, ID_BRANCH and ID_CTR are transferred to ID_LAST_BRANCH and ID_LAST_CTR with the beginning of a new step.

Signal	I/O	Explanation
INSTR	in	Instruction
EMERG_FETCH	in	Externally requested branch
SHIFT	in	Shift
WORK_IF	in	IFU enable
WORK_FD	in	IDU enable
nRESET	in	Reset
CP	in	System clock
ID_INSTR	out	Last instruction
ID_CPC	out	CALL branch target
ID_DIST	out	BCC branch distance
ID_CCODE	out	BCC condition code
ID_ANNUL	out	BCC ANNUL bit
ID_BRANCH	out	Branch (BCC or CALL)
ID_LAST_BRANCH	out	Last was branch (BCC or CALL)
ID_TYPE	out	Branch type (0: BCC; 1: CALL)
ID_CTR	out	SWI, RETI, or SRIS PC
ID_LAST_CTR	out	Last was SWI, RETI, or SRIS PC

Table 7.22 Interface of instruction decode logic IDL

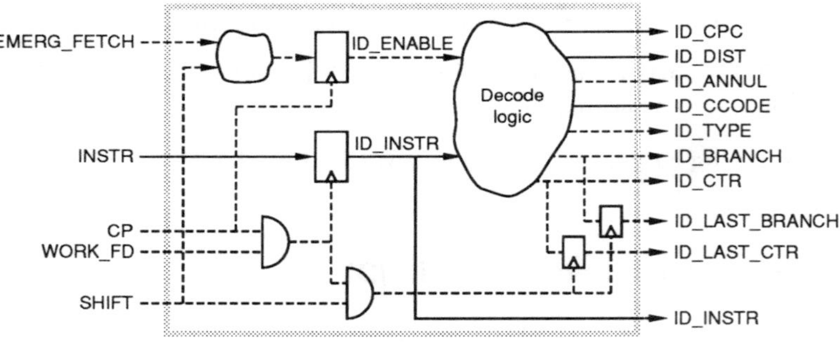

Figure 7.23 Structure of module IDL

In case of a processor reset, signals ID_BRANCH, ID_LAST_BRANCH, ID_CTR, and ID_LAST_CTR are set inactive to avoid an unwanted exception. ID_ENABLE is also deactivated, and the decoding is thus turned off.

With the rising clock edge, the instruction is taken from the external data bus into the internal register ID_INSTR to ensure a stable decoding during the whole cycle.

Signal ID_ENABLE is explained as follows. An emergency fetch, i.e., a PCU branch request to be executed immediately, may also occur in the delay slot of a branch. In this case, the IDL has to be disabled, because after an interrupt, it has to be continued with this branch. The IDL may only be enabled again, if SHIFT is set meaning that the first instruction after the branch requested by PCU was loaded. Otherwise, the PC_BUS multiplexer would recognize the reported branch and would transfer to the branch address. Practically, the IDL is disabled, when EMERG_FETCH is active. It is turned on with EMERG_FETCH inactive and SHIFT set.

As soon as the instruction stored in the internal register changes, it is decoded again. Existence and type of a branch are detected. ID_BRANCH is activated for a CALL or BCC, ID_TYPE becomes active for a CALL and inactive for a BCC. Furthermore, condition code, ANNUL bit, branch distance, and branch address are computed in case of a CALL. ID_CTR is set active, if the CTR instruction is not a BCC or CALL, but a software interrupt SWI, a return from interrupt RETI, or an instruction to write the program counter (SRIS PC).

7.2.10 Serial-Mode Controller SMC

The IFU operates in parallel or serial access mode, referring to the order of cache and memory access. In the parallel mode, cache and memory are accessed simultaneously, and after a cache hit the memory access is aborted by BREAK_MEM_ACC. This bus load is avoided in the serial mode, where the cache is first searched for the required instruction. After a miss, the memory access is initiated in the next cycle.

As the behavior of the IFU with respect to the memory coincides in case of a cache-only access with the behavior in the case where the memory bus is occupied by the memory access unit MAU, exactly this case is simulated by signal NO_FETCH. This signal has to be observed by MPC in the RIB_MODE, as the instruction may only be stored if the memory lock was not modeled artificially.

A cache access is followed by a memory access in the next cycle, if there is no hit. Otherwise, the cache is accessed again in the next cycle. The interface of module SMC is summarized in Table 7.24.

Signal	I/O	Explanation
HIT	in	BTC or MPC hit
SERIAL_MODE	in	Serial mode
WORK_IF	in	IFU enable
nRESET	in	Reset
CP	in	System clock
NO_FETCH	out	No IFU fetch

Table 7.24 Interface of module SMC

7.2.11 External PC Logic EPL

The pipeline control unit PCU may request IFU by USE_PCU_PC to transfer directly to address PC_BUS. This is, for instance, necessary in case of a SRIS instruction with target register PC, or in case of an interrupt or a RETI instruction. If in case of a serial access mode or an access by MAU, the access could not be completed, the branch of a SRIS cannot be executed immediately. The address has therefore to be stored until the end of the step. If in this case, there is a second branch request to be delayed or to be executed immediately, the old saved address is overwritten in the first case and discarded in the second.

Signal	I/O	Explanation
PC_BUS	in	PCU PC
USE_PCU_PC	in	Use PCU PC
SHIFT	in	Shift
WORK_IF	in	IFU enable
nRESET	in	Reset
CP	in	System clock
LAST_PC_BUS	out	Last PCU PC
LAST_USE_PCU_PC	out	Use last PCU PC

Table 7.25 Interface of module EPL

With the rising clock edge of an active IFU it is checked whether the step is completed. In this case, the signal to use the buffered instruction is cleared. Otherwise, a branch request is buffered. The interface of module EPL is summarized in Table 7.25. The modeling by an always block is shown in Figure 7.26.

```
always @(posedge CP) begin
  if (WORK_IF) begin
    if (SHIFT) LAST_USE_PCU_PC = #`DELTA 1'b0;
    else begin
      if (USE_PCU_PC) begin
        fork
          LAST_USE_PCU_PC = #`DELTA 1'b1;
          LAST_PC_BUS     = #`DELTA PC_BUS;
        join
      end
    end
  end
end
```

Figure 7.26 External PC logic EPL

To encourage the reader, we mention that the IFU is the most difficult and longest unit of the VERILOG model. The pipeline units following now are easier to understand.

7.3 The Instruction Decode Unit IDU

The instruction decode unit models the logical ID stage except for branch decoding which is now in the IFU, and the forwarding logic now in the FRU. In the data flow, IDU is located between IFU, ALU, and FRU (Figure 7.1).

The IDU generates control signals to execute the present instruction. This includes register addresses for ALU operands ADDR_A and ADDR_B, the ALU_OPCODE, mode and opcode for the memory access unit MAU, control signals for special register access, and the clear cache signal CCLR. Moreover, exceptions are requested by the pipeline control unit PCU initiating interrupts. Table 7.27 summarizes the external signals of the IDU.

Signal	from/to	Explanation
I_BUS	← IFU	Instruction
CP	← ext.	System clock
WORK_ID	← PCU	IDU enable
STEP	← PCU	Pipeline enable
KILL_IDU	← PCU	IDU disable
nRESET	← ext.	Reset
ID_KUMODE	← PCU	Kernel/user mode
EXCEPT_CTR	← IFU	CTR exception
IMMEDIATE	→ FRU	Immediate operand B
SWI_ID	→ PCU	SWI ID
EXCEPT_ID	→ PCU	Exception ID
ADDR_A	→ FRU	Address source register A
ADDR_B	→ FRU	Address source register B
ADDR_C	→ FRU	Address result register C
ADDR_D	→ FRU	Address write data register D
ADDR_SREG	→ PCU	Address special register
ALU_OPCODE	→ ALU	ALU operation
MAU_ACC_MODE2	→ PCU	MAU access width
MAU_OPCODE2	→ PCU	MAU access opcode
USE_SREG_DATA	→ PCU	Operand B is special register
USE_IMMEDIATE	→ PCU	Operand B is immediate
SWI_RQ	→ PCU	SWI request
EXCEPT_RQ	→ PCU	Exception request
SREG_ACC_DIR	→ PCU	SREG access direction
DO_RETI	→ PCU	Return from interrupt
DO_HALT	→ PCU	HALT
NEW_FLAGS	→ IFU, → PCU	ALU operation with .F option
CCLR	→ IFU	Clear caches

Table 7.27 Interface of instruction decode unit

Instruction decoding of the IDU is divided into six groups generating signals for equal control and data wires. Module IDU therefore contains the six subgroups DG1 to DG6 of Figure 7.28.

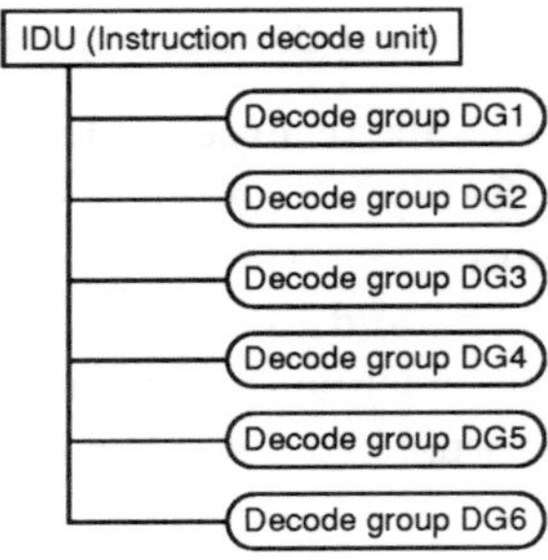

Figure 7.28 Hierarchic structure of module IDU

In the first group DG1, all signals are generated depending only upon the instruction register I_REG. Group DG2 decodes signals depending only on the instruction register and the exception request state EXCEPT_RQ. DG3 generates all signals depending on instruction register, decode enable, and exception request state. DG4 decodes signals depending on instruction and decode enable. DG5 concerns signals depending on instruction, decode enable, and processor mode ID_KUMODE. Finally, DG6 determines the exception request EXCEPT_RQ depending on instruction, decode disable, and EXCEPT_CTR. Figure 7.29 shows these dependencies.

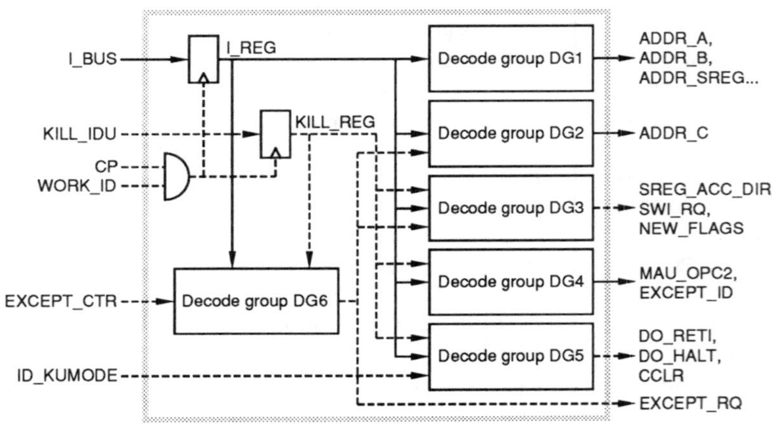

Figure 7.29 Structure of instruction decode unit

Aside from a work enable WORK_ID, the IDU has a decode disable input KILL_IDU. With an active WORK_ID at rising clock edge, inputs are loaded synchronously. If there is no work enable, input registers hold their values. This keeps decoding and its outputs stable, which is necessary while the processor waits for memory. But there are also cases in which the instruction in the IDU has to become invalid, for instance, when the pipeline is cleared in case of an interrupt or when the IDU is disabled. It would be insufficient to only deactivate the IDU by a work disable. If the decode disable KILL_IDU is active, the decoding of critical signals is prevented. Table 7.30 summarizes the critical states of the outputs signals.

Signal	Value	Explanation
SREG_ACC_DIR	1	Write access to special register
SWI_RQ	1	Software interrupt request
NEW_FLAGS	1	New flags
MAU_OPCODE2	0??	Request MAU memory access from BCU
EXCEPT_ID		IDU exception, IFU request considered
CCLR	1	Clear caches
DO_RETI	1	Return from interrupt
DO_HALT	1	HALT
EXCEPT_RQ	1	Request exception from PCU

Table 7.30 Critical states of IDU output signals

When a KERNEL_MODE operation is executed in USER_MODE, decoding is not completed, but rather, an exception is requested from the pipeline control unit PCU. The following instructions are only admitted in KERNEL_MODE: CLC, RETI, HALT, LRFS (if the source is not PC, RPC, LPC, or SR), and SRIS (if destination is not PC, RPC, LPC, or SR).

The IDU may request the following exceptions:

- Delayed_CTR exception, if IFU requests an exception;
- Unimplemented_Instruction exception for ALU instructions MUL and DIV;
- Privilege_Violation exception, if a user attempts a KERNEL_MODE instruction;
- Illegal_Instruction exception for undefined instructions.

7.3.1 Decode Group DG1

In the first group, all signals are generated depending only on the contents of the instruction register with no restrictions (Table 7.31).

Signal	Explanation
ADDR_A	Address operand A
ADDR_B	Address operand B
ADDR_D	Register address for ST or SWP
ALU_OPCODE	ALU opcode
IMMEDIATE	Immediate
MAU_ACC_MODE	MAU access mode
SWI_ID	SWI ID
USE_IMMEDIATE	Immediate valid
USE_SREG_DATA	Special register valid

Table 7.31 Decode group DG1

The VERILOG skeleton in Figure 7.32 gives an overview of decode group DG1.

```
// Decode group DG1
//
// Update all outputs depending
// on instruction register

always @(IDU_IREG) begin : DG1

  // Update ADDR_B, ADDR_D, SWI_ID,
  // and MAU_ACC_MODE2

  // Update IMMEDIATE depending on instruction class;
  // for MACC instructions, bit 0 is determined from the lowest bit
  // of access mode in case of a byte access, and bit 1 from the
  // middle bit in case of no word access (byte or halfword access)

  // Update ADDR_A depending on bit 31 of instruction
  // (upper bit of instruction class)

  // Update ADDR_SREG depending on bit 24 of instruction

  // Update ALU_OPCODE depending on instruction class

  // Update USE_SREG_DATA depending on instruction

  // Update USE_IMMEDIATE depending on instruction

end
```

Figure 7.32 VERILOG skeleton of decode group DG1

7.3.2 Decode Group DG2

In the second group, address ADDR_C of the destination register is decoded depending on the instruction and the exception request state. The source code in Figure 7.33 shows the address generation.

The address is set to 0 for all instructions not writing into the general-purpose register file. If the instruction causes an exception request, the address is also set to 0, as this instruction continues to move through the pipeline, although the register file must not be written.

```
// Decode group DG2
//
// When instruction register or exception request change,
// update all relevant outputs

always @(IDU_IREG or EXCEPT_RQ)  begin : DG2

  // Update ADDR_C depending on instruction
  // and exception request
  //
  casez({EXCEPT_RQ, IDU_IREG[31:24]})
    9'b1????????: ADDR_C = 5'b0;              // exception
    9'b00010????: ADDR_C = 5'b0;              // STORE
    9'b010??????: ADDR_C = 5'b0;              // CALL
    9'b0111111??: ADDR_C = 5'b0;              // RETI, SWI, HALT, and BRANCH
    9'b011100111: ADDR_C = 5'b0;              // CLC
    9'b011101011: ADDR_C = 5'b0;              // SRIS
    default:      ADDR_C = IDU_IREG[23:19];  // else
  endcase

end
```

Figure 7.33 Generation of destination address ADDR_C

7.3.3 Decode Group DG3

The third group decodes signals depending on instruction register, decode enable, and exception request state (Table 7.34).

Signal	Explanation
NEW_FLAGS	Flag changing ALU instruction
SREG_ACC_DIR	Special register access direction (0=read, 1=write)
SWI_RQ	SWI request

Table 7.34 Decode group DG3

With decode disable, these signals are also inactive, as there is no valid instruction in the ID. There is neither a write access to a special register nor an SWI request.

The deactivation occurs also if the IDU requests an exception, because in the case of an Unimplemented_Instruction exception, the status flags must not be changed, in the case of a Privilege_Violation exception, no write access to a special register may occur, and in the case of a Delayed_CTR exception, a software interrupt is invalid.

The VERILOG skeleton in Figure 7.35 gives an overview of decode group DG3.

```
// Decode group DG3
//
// With changing instruction register,
// enable register, or exception,
// update all relevant outputs

always @(IDU_IREG or IDU_DEREG or EXCEPT_RQ) begin : DG3

  // Update SREG_ACC_DIR depending on instruction,
  // enable state, and exception request

  // Update SWI_RQ depending on instruction,
  // enable state, and exception request

  // Update NEW_FLAGS depending on instruction class,
  // enable state, and exception request

end
```

Figure 7.35 VERILOG skeleton of decode group DG3

7.3.4 Decode Group DG4

The fourth group decodes the signals in Table 7.36 depending on the instruction and decode enable.

Signal	Explanation
EXCEPT_ID	Exception ID
MAU_OPCODE	MAU opcode

Table 7.36 Decode group DG4

An overview of decode group DG4 shows the VERILOG skeleton in Figure 7.37.

```
// Decode group DG4
//
// When instruction register or enable state change,
// update all relevant outputs

always @(IDU_IREG or IDU_DEREG) begin : DG4

  // Update MAU_OPCODE2 depending on
  // instruction class and enable state

  // Update EXCEPT_ID depending on
  // instruction and enable state
  //
  // Exception code:  000 delayed CTR instruction (requested by IFU)
  //                  001 privilege violation
  //                  010 illegal instruction
  //                  011 unimplemented instruction

end
```

Figure 7.37 VERILOG skeleton of decode group DG4

Normally, the code is set according to the only possible exception for this instruction. However, if decoding of the IDU is disabled or there is no instruction possibly requesting an exception, an exception can only be requested by signal EXCEPT_CTR by the IFU. In these cases, EXCEPT_ID is set to exception code Delayed_CTR.

The MAU opcode is not only delayed and transferred from PCU to MAU, but is also used by the MAU to perform a bus arbitration between IFU and MAU. For MAU instructions enabled for decoding, signal MAU_OPCODE2 may therefore be set to a value resulting in a MAU memory access. Possible exception codes for EXCEPT_ID and their interpretation are shown in Table 7.38.

ID	Explanation
000	Delayed CTR
001	Privilege violation
010	Illegal instruction
011	Unimplemented instruction

Table 7.38 Exception codes for signal EXCEPT_ID

7.3.5 Decode Group DG5

In the fifth group, the signals of Table 7.39 are decoded depending on instruction, decode disable, and processor mode and may only be enabled if the activating instruction in KERNEL_MODE is permitted for decoding.

Signal	Explanation
CCLR	Clear caches
DO_HALT	HALT
DO_RETI	Return from interrupt

Table 7.39 Decode group DG5

The VERILOG skeleton in Figure 7.40 gives an overview of decode group DG5.

```
// Decode group DG5
//
// When instruction register, enable state,
// or processor mode change,
// update all relevant outputs

always @(IDU_IREG or IDU_DEREG or ID_KUMODE) begin : DG5

  // Set CCLR depending on instruction,
  // enable state, and processor mode

  // Set DO_RETI depending on instruction,
  // enable state, and processor mode

  // Set DO_HALT depending on instruction,
  // enable state, and processor mode

end
```

Figure 7.40 VERILOG skeleton of decode group DG5

7.3.6 Decode Group DG6

In the sixth group, finally, exception request EXCEPT_RQ is determined depending on instruction, decode enable, Delayed_CTR request (EXCEPT_CTR), processor mode, and address of a special register. By EXCEPT_RQ, the IDU requests an exception from the PCU. There are three alternatives: EXCEPT_RQ active, inactive, or equal to the EXCEPT_CTR request by the IFU. The exception request occurs if at least one of the following conditions exists:

- there is one of the following instructions not permitted for decoding in USER_MODE: CLC, HALT, RETI, or LRFS/SRIS to a privileged register;
- there is a MUL or DIV instruction or an illegal instruction code not permitted for decoding;
- a Delayed_CTR exception is requested by the IFU.

These alternatives are handled in Figure 7.41.

```
// Decode group DG6
//
// When instruction register, enable state,
// input of exception request, processor mode,
// or special register address change,
// update all relevant outputs

always @(IDU_IREG or IDU_DEREG or
         EXCEPT_CTR or ID_KUMODE or ADDR_SREG) begin : DG6

  // Update EXCEPT_RQ depending on instruction,
  // enable state, input of exception request,
  // processor mode, and special register address
  //
  casez({IDU_DEREG, IDU_IREG[31:24], ID_KUMODE, (|ADDR_SREG[3:2])})
    11'b100????????: EXCEPT_RQ = 1'b0;          // MACC
    11'b101000?????: EXCEPT_RQ = 1'b0;          // ALU (AND, OR)
    11'b1010010????: EXCEPT_RQ = 1'b0;          // ALU (XOR)
    11'b10101??????: EXCEPT_RQ = 1'b0;          // ALU (LSL, LSR, ASR, ROT)
    11'b10110??????: EXCEPT_RQ = 1'b0;          // ALU (ADD, ADDC, SUB, SUBC)
    11'b101111?????: EXCEPT_RQ = 1'b1;          // ALU (MUL, DIV): unimplemented
    11'b110????????: EXCEPT_RQ = EXCEPT_CTR;   // CALL
    11'b111111100??: EXCEPT_RQ = EXCEPT_CTR;   // MISC (BRANCH)
    11'b111111101??: EXCEPT_RQ = EXCEPT_CTR;   // MISC (SWI)
    11'b11111111?0?: EXCEPT_RQ = 1'b1;          // MISC (RETI, HALT): PV
    11'b11111111?1?: EXCEPT_RQ = EXCEPT_CTR;   // MISC (RETI, HALT)
    11'b111100000??: EXCEPT_RQ = 1'b0;          // MISC (LDH)
    11'b1111001110?: EXCEPT_RQ = 1'b1;          // MISC (CLC): PV
    11'b1111001111?: EXCEPT_RQ = 1'b0;          // MISC (CLC)
    11'b11110101?00: EXCEPT_RQ = EXCEPT_CTR;   // MISC (LRFS, SRIS)
    11'b11110101?01: EXCEPT_RQ = 1'b1;          // MISC (LRFS, SRIS): PV
    11'b11110101?1?: EXCEPT_RQ = EXCEPT_CTR;   // MISC (LRFS, SRIS)
    11'b0??????????: EXCEPT_RQ = EXCEPT_CTR;   // disable
    default:         EXCEPT_RQ = 1'b1;          // illegal instructions
  endcase

end
```

Figure 7.41 Generation of signal EXCEPT_RQ

The privileged registers (kernel registers) include all special registers except PC, RPC, LPC, SR, i.e., all registers with a number > 3.

During the active nRESET, the instruction register is loaded with instruction XOR R0,R0,R0 (synthetic NOP), to initialize the pipeline with a valid instruction register. Otherwise, the contents of the instruction register would be undefined, and the processor would immediately face an illegal instruction exception.

7.4 The Arithmetic Logic Unit ALU

This unit corresponds to the logical EX stage of the specification. In the data flow, it is located as in Figure 7.1 between the instruction decode unit and the forwarding and register unit on the one side and the memory access unit on the other side. The opcode comes from the IDU, the operands from the FRU.

The ALU performs arithmetic and logic operations as well as rotations and shifts by a variable distance. Aside from the execution of ALU instructions, it is also used for address computations for memory accesses by unit MAU. Table 7.42 lists external signals of the ALU.

Signal	from/to	Explanation
A_BUS	← FRU	Operand A
B_BUS	← FRU	Operand B
ALU_CARRY	← PCU	Carry operand
ALU_OPCODE	← IDU	Opcode
CP	← ext.	System clock
WORK_EX	← PCU	EX enable
C3_BUS	→ FRU, → MAU	Result
FLAGS_FROM_ALU	→ PCU	Result flags

Table 7.42 ALU interface

The arithmetic logic unit contains three submodules, ARITHMETIC, LOGIC, and SHIFT (Figure 7.43).

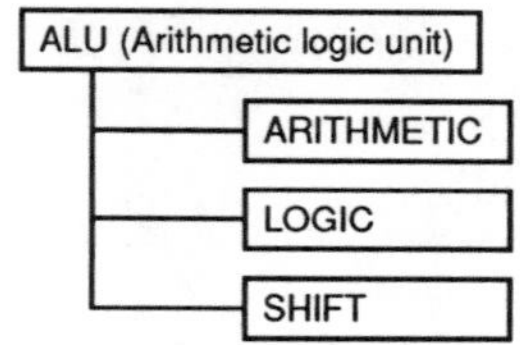

Figure 7.43 Hierarchic structure of module ALU

In module ARITHMETIC, additive ALU operations are computed including the arithmetic carry and overflow flags. Module LOGIC performs logical operations. In SHIFT, rotation and shift operations are executed and the shift carry flag is computed. Figure 7.44 shows the ALU structure. An orientation is given in Figure 7.45.

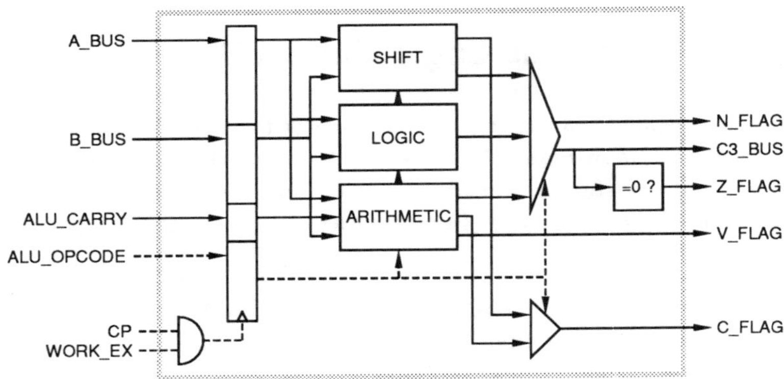

Figure 7.44 Structure of arithmetic logic unit

```
// ALU: module of arithmetic logic unit

module alu (
    C3_BUS, FLAGS_FROM_ALU,
    A_BUS, B_BUS, ALU_CARRY, ALU_OPCODE,
    CP, WORK_EX
  );

  // Read inputs with rising clock edge,
  // if work enable

  // Select result according to opcode;
  // update negative flag and zero flag

  // Update overflow flag

  // Select carry flag according to opcode
  // (logic operations do not generate a carry)

endmodule // alu

// arithmetic: execution of arithmetic operations

module arithmetic (
    RESULT, C_OUT, V_OUT,
    A_IN, B_IN, C_IN, OP_IN
  );

  // Operand B to be added effectively
  // ADD, ADDC:  B_IN
  // SUB, SUBC: -B_IN-1 (one's complement)

  // Carry operand to be added effectively
  // ADD:   0
  // ADDC:  C_IN
  // SUB:   1     (=> adding two's complement of B_IN)
  // SUBC: ~C_IN (=> adding one's complement of B_IN, if carry)

  // Add depending on A_IN, B_EFF, and C_EFF

  // Carry to bit 31 (2^31)

  // Carry from bit 31

  // Carry bit for operation executed
```

```
  // ADD, ADDC:  C_32
  // SUB, SUBC: ~C_32 (carry inverted due to complement addition)

  // Overflow bit

endmodule // arithmetic

// logic: execution of logic operations

module logic (
     RESULT,
     A_IN, B_IN, OP_IN
  );

endmodule // logic

// shift: execute shift operations

module shift (
    RESULT, C_OUT,
    A_IN, B_IN, OP_IN
  );

  // Left rotation value for barrel shifter rotating left only
  // left shift: B_IN
  // right shift and rotation: 32-B_IN (= -B_IN for 5 bit encoding)

  // Output of left rotating barrel shifter

  // Carry bit for operation executed
  // left shift:                bit 0  of rotation result
  // right shift and rotation: bit 31 of rotation result
  // no shift (B_IN is 0):      0

  // Pattern of filter mask for deletion of
  // rotated bits in left shifts and pattern of
  // sign mask for sign maintaining right shift

  // Set filter mask in rotation or 0-shifts to full transmission;
  // take from pattern directly for left shifts
  // and inverted for right shifts;
  //
  // take sign mask from pattern only for
  // sign maintaining right shift and
  // shift not equal 0, otherwise, erase

  // Compute result of shifter from barrel shifter result
  // by combination with filter mask and sign mask

endmodule // shift
```

Figure 7.45 VERILOG skeleton of arithmetic logic unit

With WORK_EX active, ALU input registers are loaded with the rising clock edge, otherwise, they keep their values. For high performance, the ALU has a parallel structure with its own computational path for every instruction group. The actually needed results are selected afterwards (Figure 7.46). Moreover, the flags are set.

```
  // Select result according to opcode;
  // update negative flag and zero flag
  //
  always @(ARITH_RES or LOGIC_RES or SHIFT_RES or ALU_OREG) begin
    case(ALU_OREG[3:2])
      2'b00: C3_BUS = LOGIC_RES;          // logic operations
      2'b01: C3_BUS = SHIFT_RES;          // shift operations
      2'b10: C3_BUS = ARITH_RES;          // arithmetic operations
    endcase
    FLAGS_FROM_ALU[3] = C3_BUS[31];       // negative flag
    FLAGS_FROM_ALU[2] = ~(|C3_BUS[31:0]); // zero flag
  end
```

Figure 7.46 Result selection for C3_BUS

The computation of flags ZERO and NEGATIVE is valid for all operations. The operations implemented, the opcode, and the corresponding instruction are shown in Table 7.47.

Operation	Code	Instruction	Class	Explanation
C3 = A AND B	0000	AND[.F]	Logic	AND
C3 = A OR B	0001	OR[.F]	Logic	OR
C3 = A XOR B	0010	XOR[.F]	Logic	Exclusive OR
C3 = A << B	0100	LSL[.F]	Shift	Shift left
C3 = A >> B	0101	LSR[.F]	Shift	Shift right (unsigned)
C3 = A >> B	0110	ASR[.F]	Shift	Shift right (signed)
C3 = A >>> B	0111	ROT[.F]	Shift	Rotate right
C3 = A+B	1000	ADD[.F]	Arithmetic	Add
C3 = A+B+CARRY	1001	ADDC[.F]	Arithmetic	Add with carry
C3 = A-B	1010	SUB[.F]	Arithmetic	Subtract
C3 = A-B-CARRY	1011	SUBC[.F]	Arithmetic	Subtract with carry

Table 7.47 ALU operations implemented

Operations for multiplication and division are not implemented in hardware. Their execution is achieved by exception Unimplemented_Instruction and software routines of the operating system. Aside from the 32-bit result, the ALU also generates four status bits in signal FLAGS_FROM_ALU (Figure 7.46, Table 7.48, and Figure 7.49).

Bit	Flag	Explanation
Bit 0	CARRY	Carry (arithmetic and shift)
Bit 1	OVERFLOW	Overflow (arithmetic)
Bit 2	ZERO	Result 0
Bit 3	NEGATIVE	Result negative

Table 7.48 ALU flags

```
// Update overflow flag
//
always @(ARITH_VFG)
  FLAGS_FROM_ALU[1] = ARITH_VFG;

//
// Select carry flag according to opcode
// (logic operations do not generate a carry)
//
always @(ARITH_CFG or SHIFT_CFG or ALU_OREG) begin
  case(ALU_OREG[3])
    2'b0: FLAGS_FROM_ALU[0] = SHIFT_CFG;  // shift operations
    2'b1: FLAGS_FROM_ALU[0] = ARITH_CFG;  // arithmetic operations
  endcase
end
```

Figure 7.49 Computation of flags

7.4.1 Module ARITHMETIC

In this part, the additive ALU operations are performed and the arithemtic flags CARRY and OVERFLOW are computed. A 32-bit adder with carry-in and carry-out is used, whose second operand and carry input receive values according to Table 7.50.

Operation	Second operand	Carry input
ADD	B	0
ADDC	B	CARRY
SUB	~B	1
SUBC	~B	~CARRY

Table 7.50 Selection of second operand and carry input

Subtraction from B without carry is implemented by adding the two's complement of B to A by computing

$$A + (\sim B) + 1 = A + (\sim B+1) = A - B .$$

When considering also the carry, the subtraction is done due to ~C=1-C according to

$$A + (\sim B) + (\sim C) = A + (\sim B) + 1 - C = A - B - C .$$

Carry out to the ALU is inverted for subtraction, as a carry is indicated by 0.

The overflow flag, indicating whether the result of operations with sign is outside the 32-bit range, is computed by a XOR of carry-out and the carry to the most significant position of the adder. For this purpose, computation is extended to a 33-bit representation with sign. A difference of the two most significant result bits then means extension beyond the 32-bit range.

```
always @(A_IN or B_IN or OP_IN) begin
  case(OP_IN)
    2'b00: RESULT = A_IN & B_IN;    // AND
    2'b01: RESULT = A_IN | B_IN;    // OR
    2'b10: RESULT = A_IN ^ B_IN;    // XOR
  endcase
end
```

Figure 7.51 Computation of output RESULT

7.4.2 Module LOGIC

In this module, logical operations AND, OR, and XOR are performed. Figure 7.51 shows the computation of RESULT.

7.4.3 Module SHIFT

In this module, rotation and shift operations are performed, and the shift carry flag CARRY is computed. This is done by a 32-bit barrel shifter executing left rotations up to a distance of 31 bits. Two bit masks are applied to the result, the first one filtering the rotated bits for shift operations, and the second one performing sign extension for right rotations with sign. For registers of 32 bits, the left rotation by k corresponds to a right rotation by 32–k, and 32–k is equivalent to –k for a 5-bit binary encoding. Thus the barrel shifter can execute all necessary rotations, where the distance for right rotations and right shifts is in two's complement.

Shift flag CARRY is determined from the first bit that is shifted out of the word. This occurs for a distance different from 0, hence in true rotations. If the distance is 0, CARRY is set to 0.

7.5 The Memory Access Unit MAU

The memory access unit corresponds mainly to the logical MA stage. As a difference, memory communication by a bus protocol is moved to the bus control unit BCU. In the data flow in Figure 7.1, the MAU is located between ALU and FRU.

In the memory access unit, data to be written are transferred to the bus control unit BCU, and data to be read are taken from this unit. If there is no memory access, the module only buffers the data. Table 7.52 summarizes the external MAU signals.

The functionality of the MAU is so simple that a further structuring is unnecessary. Figure 7.53 shows components and main connections.

With active WORK_MA, input registers are loaded with the rising system clock, otherwise, they keep their values. There are the operations and access modes of Table 7.54 (MAU_OPCODE_3 and MAU_ACC_MODE_3).

As for all memory access operations except SWAP, also halfword and byte accesses are possible, the data to be read or written are adapted in their bit positions. This is done by two multiplexers after reading or writing.

Signal	from/to	Explanation
D_BUS	← FRU	Write data
MAU_READ_DATA	← BCU	Read data
C3_BUS	← ALU	Address or operand
MAU_ACC_MODE_3	← PCU	Access mode
MAU_OPCODE_3	← PCU	Opcode
CP	← ext.	System clock
WORK_MA	← PCU	MA enable
C4_BUS	→ FRU	Result
MAU_WRITE_DATA	→ BCU	Write data
MAU_ADDR_BUS	→ BCU, → PCU	Memory access address

Table 7.52 Interface of MAU

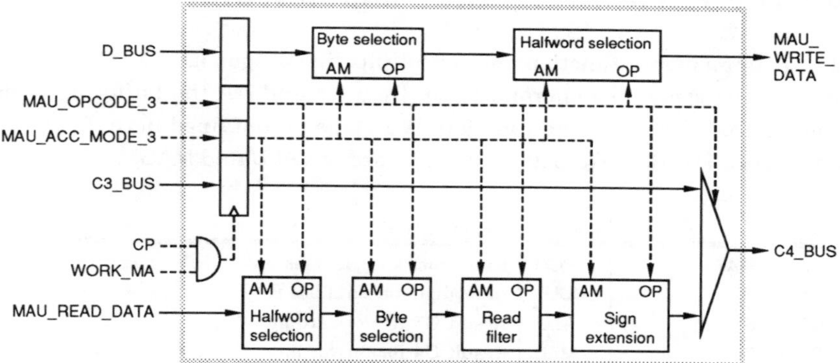

Figure 7.53 Structure of memory access unit

Opcode	Access	Explanation
000	0??	Read byte
000	1?0	Read halfword
000	1?1	Read word
001	0??	Read byte with sign extension
001	1?0	Read halfword with sign extension
001	1?1	Read word
010	0??	Store byte
010	1?0	Store halfword
010	1?1	Store word
011	???	Exchange words (SWAP) (read MAU_READ_DATA, write D_BUS)
1??	???	Buffer (transfer data to WB stage)

Table 7.54 MAU operations implemented

The multiplexers for selection of bytes and halfwords are controlled by the two least significant bits of the access address and by the access type. These are given by MAU_ADDR_BUS and MAU_ACC_MODE_3. The four bytes in a read word have to be brought into the range of bits 7...0. This is done in two steps by first selecting the halfword and then the bytes. For writing, byte selection is done before halfword selection to ensure that bits 7...0 can be brought to any position.

After the multiplexers, read data are cut to the width required by setting irrelevant bits to 0. If a read operation with sign extension of halfwords or bytes is executed, the bits outside the data width are set to the value of the most significant data bit.

7.6 The Forwarding and Register Unit FRU

This unit implements functions of logical pipeline stages ID, EX, MA, and WB. From stage ID comes the operand fetch, from EX and MA the buffering of data and addresses. Moreover, the complete WB stage is contained here. In the data flow of Figure 7.1, the FRU acts as a frame around ALU and MAU.

Signal	from/to	Explanation
SREG_DATA	← PCU	Data from special register
IMMEDIATE	← IDU	Immediate for data bus B
C3_BUS	← ALU	Result C3 for forwarding
C4_BUS	← MAU	Result C4 for forwarding
ADDR_A	← IDU	Register address for A
ADDR_B	← IDU	Register address for B
ADDR_C	← IDU	Register address for result C
ADDR_D	← IDU	Register address for store data D
INT_STATE	← PCU	Interrupt overlay register set
USE_IMMEDIATE	← IDU	Immediate valid
CP	← ext.	System clock
STEP	← PCU	Shift pipeline
WORK_EX	← PCU	EX enable
WORK_MA	← PCU	MA enable
WORK_WB	← PCU	WB enable
USE_SREG_DATA	← IDU	Use data from special register
A_BUS	→ ALU	Data for operand A
B_BUS	→ ALU	Data for operand B
STORE_DATA	→ MAU	Delayed write data for MAU access

Table 7.55 FRU interface

The module also contains the register file of general-purpose registers. Due to the pipeline structure, a look-ahead to future register contents or *forwarding* is required. Some registers are only accessible under certain conditions like an interrupt. To access the proper registers, there is an address converter. Special data have to be transferred to subsequent pipeline stages. They have to be buffered. Table 7.55 summarizes external FRU signals.

The forwarding and register unit FRU consists basically of a converter for register addresses, a forwarding logic for address comparison, and a register access logic (Figure 7.56). A modeling overview is given in Figure 7.57.

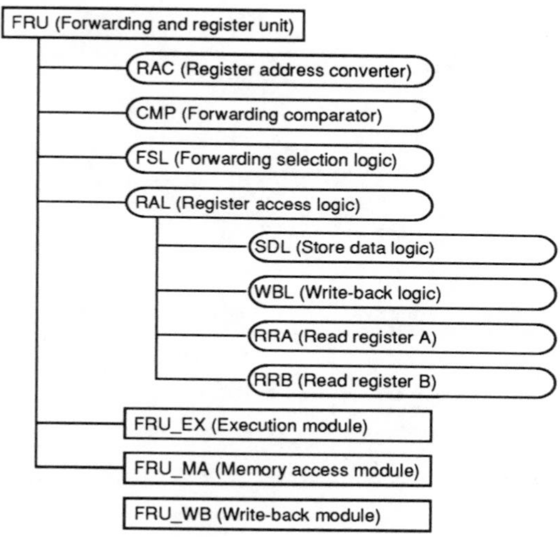

Figure 7.56 Hierarchic structure of module FRU

The register address converter RAC generates an address for the register file. In a forwarding comparator CMP, the converted address is compared with the addresses currently in the pipeline. The forwarding selection logic FSL contains three multiplexers putting the required data onto suitable buses. In the store data logic SDL, data for the MAU are read from the register file. The write-back logic WBL writes data to the register file. Components RRA (read register A) and RRB (read register B) read ALU operands A and B from the array.

To underline that some buffering elements of FRU belong to the logical pipeline stages EX and MA, these functional units are encapsuled in separate FRU modules (Section 7.6.5). Figure 7.58 shows the FRU structure. Module FRU_EX works in parallel to the ALU and shifts data and register addresses in the pipeline. Module FRU_MA works in parallel to the MAU and shifts the write-back register address to the next pipeline stage. Module FRU_WB corresponds to the write-back stage of the pipeline.

```
module fru (
    A_BUS, B_BUS, STORE_DATA,
    SREG_DATA, IMMEDIATE, C3_BUS, C4_BUS,
    ADDR_A, ADDR_B, ADDR_C, ADDR_STORE_DATA,
    INT_STATE, USE_IMMEDIATE,
    CP, STEP, WORK_ALU,
    WORK_MAU, WORK_WB, USE_SREG_DATA
  );

  // Take inputs synchronously

  // RAC (register address converter)
  //
  // Register addresses are transformed depending on the
  // interrupt status. Two comparators and some wiring
  // suffice to generate the address for the register
  // file. This is necessary, as for every interrupt
  // status, the upper four registers are private
  // and to be superimposed correspondingly.
  // The generated addresses are REG_XXX and are
  // further used by the forwarding comparators
  // and for register accesses.
  // These addresses are shifted in the pipeline.

  // CMP (forwarding comparator)
  //
  // The transformed register address is
  // compared with the corresponding address
  // presently in some pipeline stage.
  // When coinciding, output multiplexer SEL_X is switched
  // to the corresponding stage. Earlier pipeline stages
  // are preferred. Only pipeline stages with valid
  // work signal are considered for a forwarding.
  // Register 0 is not forwarded.

  // FSL (forwarding selection logic)
  //
  // This multiplexer puts correct values to A_BUS, B_BUS,
  // and STORE_DATA depending on the forwarding logic.

  // RAL (register access logic)
  //
  // Only registers different from register 0 are
  // accessed. A partition in first and second
  // half of the clock was chosen considering a
  // future realization with a two-port RAM.
  // Precise timing is required, as this is
  // not the normal register transfer logic.

endmodule // fru


// FRU_EX (execution module)
//
// Operating in parallel to ALU;
// shifts data and register addresses in the pipeline

module fru_ex (STORE_DATA2, REG_ADDR_C, CP, WORK_ALU, STORE_DATA, REG_ADDR_C3);

endmodule // fru_ex


// FRU_MA (memory access module)
//
// Operating in parallel to MAU;
// shifts register address for write-back to next pipeline stage

module fru_ma (REG_ADDR_C3, CP, WORK_MAU, REG_ADDR_C4);

endmodule // fru_ma


// FRU_WB (write back module)
//
// Module declaration for write-back unit (WB);
// stores write-back address REG_ADDR_C5 and C_BUS

module fru_wb (C4_BUS, REG_ADDR_C4, WORK_WB, CP, C5_BUS, REG_ADDR_C5);

endmodule // fru_wb
```

Figure 7.57 VERILOG skeleton of forwarding and register unit FRU

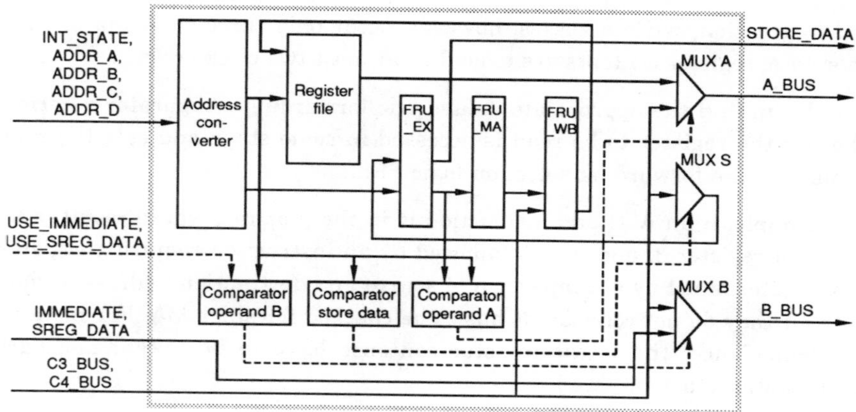

Figure 7.58 Structure of forwarding and register unit

7.6.1 Register Address Converter RAC

The forwarding and register unit contains 32 general-purpose registers. The top four registers exist three times. These register sets are switched according to interrupt status. For example, after a software interrupt, only the four registers for a software interrupt are visible in addition to the normal registers R0...R27, but not the other two register sets.

This behavior is achieved by a register address converter switching the upper four registers depending on interrupt status. The lower 28 registers are used in all modes. The transformed addresses are used in the whole module, in the forwarding comparison as well as for the WB stage. In Figure 7.59, the transformation of register addresses is shown for ADDR_A.

```
// Register address transformation  ADDR_A -> REG_ADDR_A
//
casez ({INT_STATE,ADDR_A})
  7'b01111??:              // internal interrupt, upper registers
    REG_ADDR_A = {4'b1000,ADDR_A[1:0]};
  7'b1?111??:              // hardware interrupt, upper registers
    REG_ADDR_A = {4'b1001,ADDR_A[1:0]};
  default:                 // lower registers
    REG_ADDR_A = {1'b0,ADDR_A};
endcase
```

Figure 7.59 Transformation of register addresses

7.6.2 Forwarding Comparator CMP

One write access is possible per pipeline step. This is done together with a read access in the first half of a cycle. Register read accesses happen due to some

IDU instruction; write accesses, however, occur only three stages later in WB. Therefore, register contents are too old by at most two clock cycles.

In order to find the appropriate values, the forwarding comparator determines whether the register to be read is accessed in some stage and sets the control signals for the forwarding selection logic FSL.

For example, if an ALU add instruction is in the pipeline, whose result is to be stored in register 3, and if it is followed by an instruction requiring register 3, this is determined by a comparison of source and destination address of the EX stage. If they do not coincide, it has to be checked for stage MA. For more than one coincidence, the latest register contents have to be taken, i.e., earlier pipeline stages are prefered.

For this look-ahead it has to be known which destination register is assigned to each item in every pipeline stage. Therefore, there is a pipeline in the FRU parallel to stages EX, MA, and WB, in which the destination register of every stage is contained. According to their logical counterparts, these signals are called ADDR_C2 (ID stage), ADDR_C3 (EX stage), and ADDR_C4 (MA stage).

For this forwarding, read addresses are compared with destination registers of other stages. For ALU instructions, this is done for ALU operands A and B, and for STORE instructions, for the write data of MAU. The FRU receives information from the decoding unit, whether data for operand B are contained in an immediate instruction by an active USE_IMMEDIATE. If data from a special register are to be used, USE_SREG_DATA is active. These signals are also considered below when determining control signals for the output multiplexers.

An additional necessary condition for forwarding is that the data of a stage are valid at all. This is indicated by a corresponding WORK signal. If it is inactive, the stage performs a bubble step, its data are invalid in this case and are not used. Moreover, register R0 has to be excluded from a comparison.

We now list all forwarding cases relevant for all registers read. The corresponding addresses are ADDR_A, ADDR_B, and ADDR_D. These are abbreviated for simplicity by ADDR_read. We assume a read access at register address L (ADDR_read = L).

Case 1 The destination register of an ALU operation has address L (ADDR_C3 = ADDR_read = L), and the ALU executes a valid operation (WORK_EX=1). Then it is loaded from C3_BUS.

Case 2 The ALU destination register has address M. The MAU destination has address L, WORK_MAU is set. We thus have ADDR_read = ADDR_C4. Therefore, data are loaded from MAU output C4_BUS.

Case 3 WORK_WB is set. The ALU destination has address N, the MAU destination has address M. The destination of the write-back operation is L. As data for STORE_DATA are read in the same step, in which a register is written, forwarding has to be activated in this case, too: ADDR_read = ADDR_C5. Nevertheless, there is no forwarding in this case. According to the specification, it need not be implemented, as the write access occurs in the first half of the clock and the read access in the second half. Therefore, the correct value is read from the register.

7.6.3 Forwarding Selection Logic FSL

The forwarding selection logic selects the correct data according to the forwarding comparator. It contains three multiplexers for buses A_BUS, B_BUS, and STORE_DATA.

The output multiplexers also have the task of replacing register values by IMMEDIATE from the IDU or special register SREG_DATA from PCU and to put it to output B_BUS. Forwarding comparators detect this case. The selection signals are called SEL_A, SEL_B, and SEL_S. This selection is shown in Figure 7.60.

```
// FSL (forwarding selection logic)
//
// This multiplexer puts correct values to A_BUS, B_BUS,
// and STORE_DATA depending on the forwarding logic.

always @(SEL_A or SEL_B or SEL_S or READ_A or READ_B or READ_STORE_DATA or
         C3_BUS or C4_BUS or IMMEDIATE or SREG_DATA)
begin: FSL

  //
  // ALU operand A (MUX_A)
  //
  case(SEL_A)
    `TAKE2_ADDR: A_BUS = READ_A;
    `TAKE2_C3:   A_BUS = C3_BUS;
    `TAKE2_C4:   A_BUS = C4_BUS;
  endcase

  //
  // ALU operand B (MUX_B)
  //
  case (SEL_B)
    `TAKE3_ADDR: B_BUS = READ_B;
    `TAKE3_C3:   B_BUS = C3_BUS;
    `TAKE3_C4:   B_BUS = C4_BUS;
    `TAKE3_IMM:  B_BUS = IMMEDIATE;
    `TAKE3_SREG: B_BUS = SREG_DATA;
  endcase

  //
  // Store data (MUX_S)
  //
  case (SEL_S)
    `TAKE2_ADDR: STORE_DATA2 = READ_STORE_DATA;
    `TAKE2_C3:   STORE_DATA2 = C3_BUS;
    `TAKE2_C4:   STORE_DATA2 = C4_BUS;
  endcase
end
```

Figure 7.60 Forwarding selection logic

MUX_A selects ALU operand A. It is taken from a register, or there is a forwarding from C3_BUS or C4_BUS. MUX_B selects ALU operand B, coming as a direct value from IDU, or from a register or special register from PCU. There may also be a forwarding from C3_BUS or C4_BUS. The value for STORE_DATA is selected by MUX_S from a register or as a forwarding from C3_BUS or C4_BUS.

7.6.4 Register Access Logic RAL

The register access logic consists of the store data logic SDL, the write-back logic WBL, the read register A (RRA), and the read register B (RRB). These groups represent the four access cases to the register file.

Reading and writing of a register is done in one pipeline step, as there is combinational logic with an execution time of less than half a period. Read accesses take place within the decoding phase and thus belong logically to stage ID.

Reading write data for a STORE instruction from the register file is done in the store data logic SDL. Writing data into the register file is done by the write-back logic WBL. Write accesses to register R0 are ignored. Reading ALU operands A and B is done in RRA and RRB. If register R0 is the source, value 0 is always returned. The reason is in the RISC-typical interpretation of R0 as a constant value.

```
// FRU_WB (write back module)
//
// Module declaration for write-back unit (WB);
// stores write-back address REG_ADDR_C5 and C_BUS

module fru_wb (C4_BUS, REG_ADDR_C4, WORK_WB, CP, C5_BUS, REG_ADDR_C5);
  input  [31:0] C4_BUS;
  input  [ 5:0] REG_ADDR_C4;
  input         WORK_WB,
                CP;
  output [31:0] C5_BUS;
  output [ 5:0] REG_ADDR_C5;

  wire   [31:0] C4_BUS;
  wire   [ 5:0] REG_ADDR_C4;
  wire          WORK_WB,
                CP;
  reg    [31:0] C5_BUS;
  reg    [ 5:0] REG_ADDR_C5;

  always @(posedge CP)  if (WORK_WB)  REG_ADDR_C5 = #`DELTA REG_ADDR_C4;
  always @(posedge CP)  if (WORK_WB)  C5_BUS      = #`DELTA C4_BUS;

endmodule // fru_wb
```

Figure 7.61 Pipeline stage FRU_WB

7.6.5 Data and Address Pipeline

The forwarding and register unit works in parallel to three logical pipeline stages. It needs to know which register is in which stage. An internal pipeline modeled by three modules FRU_EX, FRU_MA, and FRU_WB saves the register address for each stage. In case of stage FRU_EX, also the write data for the MAU have to be buffered. The FRU_WB stage also holds the value from C4_BUS of the processor pipeline. As an example, the FRU_WB stage in Figure 7.61 is shown.

7.7 Building a Complete Processor

We have so far constructed the datapath of the RISC processor and have practiced modeling in the hardware description language VERILOG. The extension to a complete Coarse Structure Model with a system environment is contained as an HDL description on the disk in Chapter 🖫3. Due to the extent of the material, only Chapter H4 of the expert volume comments the many parts of the pipeline control in the general control PCU and the memory bus control BCU, the branch-target cache BTC, interrupt execution, the system environment, and first simulation experiments.

We now turn to the transformation of such an HDL model into a net of cells of a gate library.

8 Synthesis of Gate Model

In this chapter, we come pretty close to the actual hardware on the chip. For this purpose, the Coarse Structure Model developed before in the hardware description language VERILOG is transformed to a Gate Model or *synthesized*. The given library of the silicon producer consisting of logic gates, flip-flops, drivers, adders, etc. serves as a base. We will develop a hierarchic model with the higher modules corresponding exactly to the modules of the Coarse Structure Model. Synthesis of this model is partially done manually, partially automatically. The Gate Model is so extensive that in the present volume the reader is introduced to the design method only by examples, and the wealth of technical details is hidden in the expert volume (Chapter H5).

After the presentation of the library of the silicon vendor, we manually transform the HDL model in Section 8.2 using examples. In the next section, tools for logic synthesis are used. In Section 8.4, a larger example will follow. After some general remarks, Section 8.7 treats dynamic simulation of the Gate Model. This will verify the coincidence with the corresponding VERILOG components of the Coarse Structure Model. After the functional correctness is verified, the electrical and timing behavior is checked and corrected, if necessary. For example, we will try to shorten critical paths and thus overall runtime.

Already when constructing the Coarse Structure Model, we tried to prepare a simple transition to a gate netlist, partially by reducing algorithmic readability. We now try to achieve a coincidence of both models as good as possible also with respect to the hierarchic structure, the names, and the function of modules and signals. Objects with equal names in both models will usually have a corresponding meaning. Obviously however, the Gate Model will contain considerably more objects than the Coarse Structure Model, a unique (one-to-one) correspondence can therefore not be expected. Differences will also occur on lower model levels, as not all parts of the HDL model are structure oriented. Very rarely, there are naming conflicts due to the silicon vendor, for example, when the reserved name BTC requires a renaming of the branch-target cache to BTIC.

8.1 The Library of the Silicon Vendor

The cells of the silicon vendor LSI Logic are characterized in detail on proprietory data sheets. We will restrict ourselves to a general summary, assuming logic components like AND or flip-flops as known. Aside from gates, storing devices, and drivers, there are larger cells, called *megafunctions* such as adders, shifters, or RAMs. We have left out library cells not required in our design and have extended the library with some cells of our own. In the names, a suffix P means an increased driving force, Xn an n-fold parallelization.

8.1.1 Gates

The cells of this group divide into basic logic operations like AND and OR with a varying number of inputs, into cells with frequent combinations like a 3-input NOR with a preceeding AND at one input (AO1), and into special functions like adders and multiplexers.

AN2	2-Input AND	
AN3	3-Input AND	
AN4	4-Input AND	
AO1	2-AND into 3-NOR	
AO2	2 2-AND into 2-NOR	
AO3	2-OR into 3-NAND	
AO4	2 2-OR into 2-NAND	
AO6	2-AND into 2-NOR	
AO7	2-OR into 2-NAND	
EN	2-Input Exclusive NOR:	XOR with output inverted (XNOR)
EO	2-Input Exclusive OR	
EO3	3-input Exclusive OR	
EON1	2-OR, 2-NAND into 2-NAND	
FA1	Full Adder	
FA1A	Full Adder	
HA1	Half Adder	
MUX21CBM	Transfer Gate MUX for Booth Multiplying: 2 MUX21L cells in series; first multiplexer controlling second	
MUX21H	Non-Inverting Gate MUX	
MUX21L	Inverting Gate MUX:	output inverted for reasons of run time
MUX24P	4-Bit 2-to-1 MUX, Non-Inverting: 4 parallel MUX21H for two 4-bit buses	
MUX31L	3-Bit Inverting MUX	
MUX41	4-Bit Non-Inverting MUX	
MUX51H	Non-Inverting 5-to-1 MUX	
MUX81	8-Bit Non-Inverting MUX	
ND2	2-Input NAND	
ND3	3-Input NAND	
ND4	4-Input NAND	
ND5	5-Input NAND	
ND6	6-Input NAND	

ND8	8-Input NAND
NR2	2-Input NOR
NR3	3-Input NOR
NR4	4-Input NOR
NR6	6-Input NOR
NR16	16-Input NOR
OR2	2-Input OR
OR3	3-Input OR
OR4	4-Input OR

8.1.2 Internal Buffers

Internal buffers are not static registers, but signal delays by a short defined runtime, inverting at the same time.

B4I	4 Parallel Inverters: four parallel inverters IV for high driving force
B5I	5 Parallel Inverters
DELAY3	Internal Buffer with 3 ns Nominal Delay: this cell delays the input by 3 ns; this, for example, ensures setup and hold times when controlling registers
DELAY5	Internal Buffer with 5 ns Nominal Delay
IV	Inverter
IVA	Inverter with Parallel P Transistors
IVDA	Inverter into Inverter

8.1.3 Flip-Flops

Although there are many different flip-flops, most of them can be considered as variants of the edge-triggered D-flip-flop FD1. There are the following variations. Load is an additional control input for loading the flip-flop. Scan denotes flip-flops, which can be part of a scanpath (Section 9.3.2). They have additional ports to control the scan mode and to shift data within the scanpath. Clear is an additional control input for asynchronous reset of a flip-flop. Enable means for cells with Scan the existence of a Load input. Set will set the contents of a flip-flop asynchronously to 1. The control input Synchronous Clear will erase the flip-flop synchronously.

FD1	D Flip-Flop
FD1SLP	D Flip-Flop with Enable, Scan
FD2	D Flip-Flop with Clear
FD2S	D Flip-Flop with Clear, Scan
FD2SL2	D Flip-Flop with Clear, Scan, Load
FD4	D Flip-Flop with Set
FD4S	D Flip-Flop with Set, Scan
FD2X4L	4 D Flip-Flop, low CP Load
FDN1	D Flip-Flop
FDN2	D Flip-Flop with Clear
FDS2SLP	D Flip-Flop with Enable, Synchronous Clear, Scan
FD1SLQPX2	Dual D Flip-Flop with Scan
FDS2SLQPX2	Dual D Flip-Flop with Scan, Synchronous Clear
FJK2	JK Flip-Flop with Clear

8.1.4 Latches

While flip-flops take signals edge triggered and synchronously with a clock, latches are level-driven static registers without clock.

LD1	D Latch
LD1X4	4 LD1 in Parallel with Common Gates

8.1.5 Input Clock Drivers

According to the design rules of the producer, the clock signal must only come from special input clock drivers with a high driving force. They are located at the top level of the Gate Model to achieve a simple balancing of the clock tree. A Schmitt trigger in cell DRVSC will correct dirty input edges.

DRVSC	Clock Driver with CMOS Schmitt Trigger Input

8.1.6 Input Buffers

Input buffer cells connect the circuit with input pads. External signals should have a CMOS level. For critical signals such as nMHS, a Schmitt trigger will correct dirty edges.

IBUF	CMOS Input Buffer
IBUFN	Inverted CMOS Input Buffer
ICPTNU	Input Buffer for TN
SCHMITC	Schmitt Trigger Input Buffer

8.1.7 Unidirectional Output Buffers

Output buffer cells connect the circuit with output pads in one direction with varying driving force.

B1	1 mA Unidirect Output Buffer
B2	2 mA Unidirect Output Buffer
B4	4 mA Unidirect Output Buffer

8.1.8 Bidirectional Tristate Output Buffers

Cell BD4 can be switched to input, output, or high impedance. As output, it offers 4 mA driving force.

BD4	4 mA Bidirectional 3-State Output Buffer

8.1.9 Test Cell as a Megafunction

This large library cell offers varying delays. After production, doping density and etch parameters and thus runtimes of the whole chip can be estimated.

PROCMON	Process Monitor

8.1.10 Adder as a Megafunction

These cells add two 16 or 32-bit operands and a carry-in with carry-select.

CFB0220B	16-Bit Carry Select Adder
CFB0230B	32-Bit Carry Select Adder

8.1.11 Shifter as a Megafunction

A 32-bit operand is rotated by at most 31 bit positions left. Right rotations can be simulated by a negative rotation constant. True shifts for instructions LSL, LSR, and ASR can be implemented by erasing corresponding bit positions afterwards.

CFC1020B	32-Bit Barrel Shifter

8.1.12 Custom-Specific RAM Library as a Megafunction

The register file or groups of several registers are not composed of single flip-flops, but rather use generated RAM banks. These are located on the top model level for reasons of placement and routing. They differ in width and number of registers and in type and number of ports for accesses. They were developed individually by the silicon vendor for the requirements of TOOBSIE by using a RAM compiler.

RR40X32	2 Read-, 1 Write-Port RAM, 40 Word x 32 Bit
RR32X32	1 Read-, 1 Write-Port RAM, 32 Word x 32 Bit
RR16X32	1 Read-, 1 Write-Port RAM, 16 Word x 32 Bit
RR16X30	1 Read-, 1 Write-Port RAM, 16 Word x 30 Bit
RR16X5	1 Read-, 1 Write-Port RAM, 16 Word x 5 Bit

8.1.13 Internal Buffers as Self-Developed Library Cells

The buffers distribute a 1-bit signal to a 30, 32, or 107-bit output by a tree of inverters.

BUF30	30-Bit Buffer
BUF32	32-Bit Buffer
BUF107	107-Bit Buffer
IV32	32-Bit Inverter: inverting BUF32

8.1.14 Flip-Flops as Self-Developed Library Cells

Given flip-flops are augmented by further ones. They usually are an n-fold parallelization of given cells for storing n-bit signals. The naming conventions above apply here as well.

FD1SLPX3	3 D Flip-Flop	with Load, Scan
FD1SLPX4	4 D Flip-Flop	with Load, Scan
FD1SLPX32	32 D Flip-Flop	with Load, Scan
FD1SLQPX6	6 D Flip-Flop	with Load, Scan, no Qn-output
FD1SLQPX8	8 D Flip-Flop	with Load, Scan, no Qn-output
FD1SLQPX30	30 D Flip-Flop	with Load, Scan, no Qn-output
FD1SLQPX32	32 D Flip-Flop	with Load, Scan, no Qn-output
FD2S2LX4	4 D Flip-Flop	with Clear, Scan, 2 Load
FD2SLPX30	30 D Flip-Flop	with Clear, Scan, Load
FD2SLPX32	32 D Flip-Flop	with Clear, Scan, Load
FD2SLX3	3 D Flip-Flop	with Clear, Scan, Load
FD4S2LPX4	4 D Flip-Flop	with Set, Scan, 2 Load
FD4SL	D Flip-Flop	with Scan, Load, Asynchronous Set
FD4SLP	D Flip-Flop	with Scan, Load, Asynchronous Set
FD4SLX4	4 D Flip-Flop	with Scan, Load, Asynchronous Set
FDS2SLQPX8	8 D Flip-Flop	with Scan, Synchronous Clear, Load, no Qn-output
FDS2SLQPX24	24 D Flip-Flop	with Scan, Synchronous Clear, Load, no Qn-output
FDS2SLQPX30	30 D Flip-Flop	with Scan, Synchronous Clear, Load, no Qn-output
FDS2SLQPX32	32 D Flip-Flop	with Scan, Synchronous Clear, Load, no Qn-output

8.1.15 Multiplexers as Self-Developed Library Cells

As with flip-flops, we have composed our own multiplexer arrays, usually as an n-fold parallelization of given cells selecting n-bit signals. The naming conventions above apply here, too.

MUX21HPX8	8-Bit	Non-Inverting	2-to-1 MUX
MUX21HPX8B1	8-Bit	Non-Inverting	2-to-1 MUX, 1-Bit B-Input
MUX21HX4	4-Bit	Non-Inverting	2-to-1 MUX
MUX21HX5	5-Bit	Non-Inverting	2-to-1 MUX
MUX21HX6	6-Bit	Non-Inverting	2-to-1 MUX
MUX21HX10	10-Bit	Non-Inverting	2-to-1 MUX
MUX21LPX4	4-Bit	Inverting	2-to-1 MUX
MUX21LPX8	8-Bit	Inverting	2-to-1 MUX
MUX21LPX8B1	8-Bit	Inverting	2-to-1 MUX, 1 Bit B-Input
MUX21LX16	16-Bit	Inverting	2-to-1 MUX
MUX24HX2	8-Bit	Non-Inverting	2-to-1 MUX (two MUX24P)
MUX31HX8	8-Bit	Non-Inverting	3-to-1 MUX
MUX31HX10	10-Bit	Non-Inverting	3-to-1 MUX
MUX31LX16	16-Bit	Inverting	3-to-1 MUX
MUX41X8	8-Bit	Inverting	4-to-1 MUX
MUX51HPX8	8-Bit	Non-Inverting	5-to-1 MUX
MUX51HPX10	10-Bit	Non-Inverting	5-to-1 MUX
MUX51HX8	8-Bit	Non-Inverting	5-to-1 MUX
MUX51HX10	10-Bit	Non-Inverting	5-to-1 MUX
MUX81X10	10-Bit	Non-Inverting	8-to-1 MUX

8.2 Manual Synthesis

In this section we demonstrate manual transformation of typical VERILOG parts of the Coarse Structure Model to *schematics* of library cells; in the next section, we will apply suitable synthesis tools. In practice, we have mixed both methods, for example, by synthesizing certain parts of combinational logic automatically and composing them manually afterwards.

When transforming VERILOG groups into schematics, there are frequent directly transformable situations such as synchronous transfer, register block with combinational logic, register pipeline, multiplexer for data selection, as well as constant and variable assignment. They are treated in the following Sections 8.2.1 – 8.2.6.

8.2.1 Synchronous Data Transfer

At the beginning of a new cycle, information has to be transferred and kept for the whole cycle. Examples are the WORK signals that are only valid with the positive clock edge. As they are needed in the forwarding and register unit FRU during the whole cycle, they have to be stored synchronously in registers.

Figure 8.1 shows an extract of the VERILOG FRU model with three always blocks triggered with the positive clock edge. The value of the WORK signal is taken into a register if a new step begins with this clock.

```
// Take inputs synchronously                                        e0123
//                                                                  e0124
always @(posedge CP) if (STEP) DO_ALU  = #`DELTA WORK_ALU;          e0125
always @(posedge CP) if (STEP) DO_MAU  = #`DELTA WORK_MAU;          e0126
always @(posedge CP) if (STEP) DO_WB   = #`DELTA WORK_WB;           e0127
```

Figure 8.1 Synchronous transfer to FRU

The corresponding schematic FRU_DO in Figure 8.2 contains three 1-bit registers of type FD1SLP with names U0...U2. The appropriate WORK signal is connected with data input D, the clock with input CP. The flip-flop takes the data input with the positive edge of CP if load input LD is set. Connecting STEP with LD implements the if instruction. Output Q takes input D with a short delay modeled by #`DELTA in the Coarse Structure Model.

In addition, the flip-flops have scan inputs TE and TI, output Q is also the scan output connected with the scan input of the next register. Thus a scanpath is implemented (Section 9.3.2).

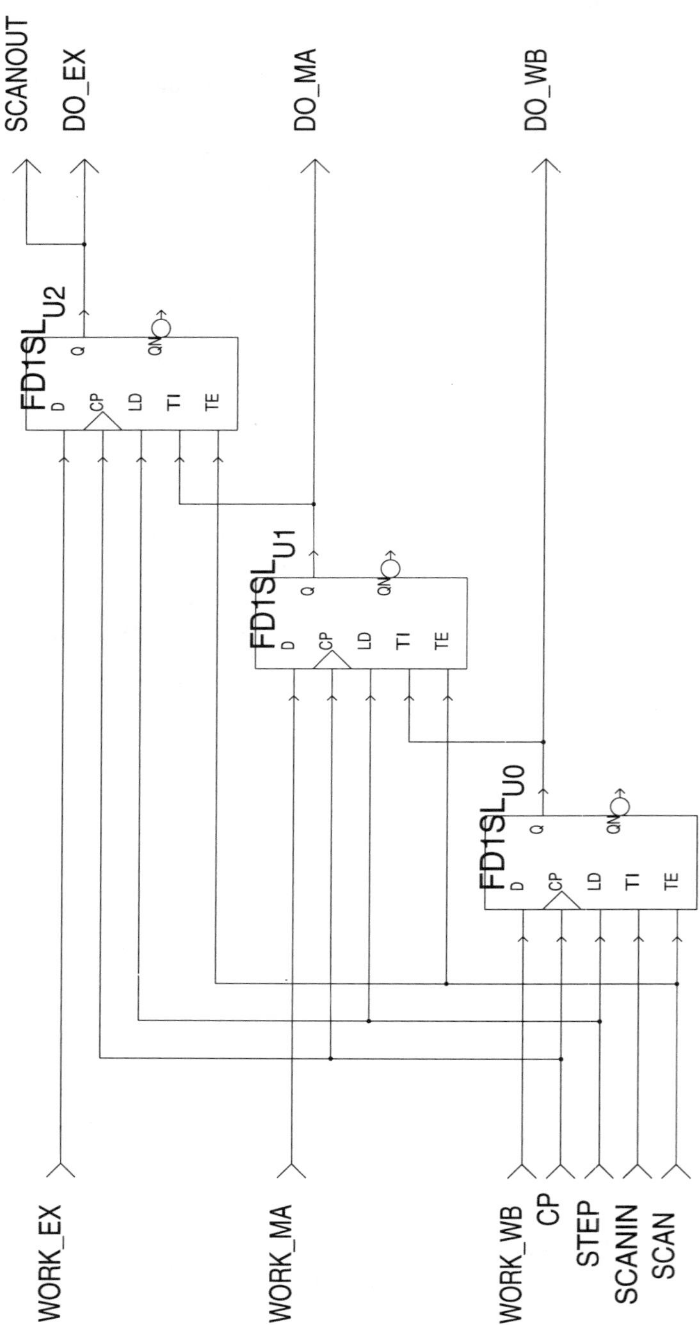

Figure 8.2 Signal register FRU_DO

8.2.2 Registers with Combinational Logic

The synchonous transfer is extended in this section by combinational logic. Register inputs are connected with combinational operations of other signals. An example is the memory access stage in the status pipeline of the pipeline control unit in Figure 8.3. In the first block (lines f0870...f0878), there are three registers combined by fork and join with the same load signal STEP. The value of MAU_USES_BUS results in ~MAU_OPCODE3[2] & WORK_MA.

```
f0857 // Status pipeline: MA stage
f0858 //
f0859 // MA memory access status for instruction
f0860 // taken into MA (MAU_USES_BUS);
f0861 // delay slot status of MA instruction taken from EX;
f0862 // PC and status bits for MA

f0867   // Memory access status, delay slot status,
f0868   // and status bits for MA instruction
f0869   //
f0870   always @(posedge CP) begin
f0871     if (STEP) begin
f0872       fork
f0873         MAU_USES_BUS = #`DELTA ~MAU_OPCODE3[2] & WORK_MA;
f0874         DS_IN_MAU    = #`DELTA DS_IN_ALU;
f0875         MA_STATUS    = #`DELTA EX_STATUS;
f0876       join
f0877     end
f0878   end
f0879
f0880   //
f0881   // PC for MA instruction
f0882   //
f0883   always @(posedge CP)
f0884     if (WORK_MA) PC_MA = #`DELTA PC_EX;
```

Figure 8.3 Register block with combinational logic in PCU

In the corresponding schematic STAP_MA in Figure 8.4, signal MAU_OPCODE3[2] is first extracted from MAU_OPCODE3 and afterwards inverted by inverter U0. Then there is an AND connection with signal WORK_MA by AND gate U1 for the input of register U5.

Flip-flops FD2SL2 (U4) and FD2SL2P (U5) come from the vendor library, FD2SLX8 (U3) and FD1SLQPX30 (U2) are our own library cells with 8 or 30 flip-flops. The scanpath leads internally through all flip-flops in such a way that bit 0 is the last one in the path and scan output of the register. For example, bit 0 leads from the output of FD1SLPQX30 to scan input of FD2SLX8.

8.2.3 Register Pipeline

Several register blocks with combinational logic result in a register pipeline as in the WORK_UNIT of the pipeline control unit in Figure 8.5 to generate the work signals for the pipeline stages.

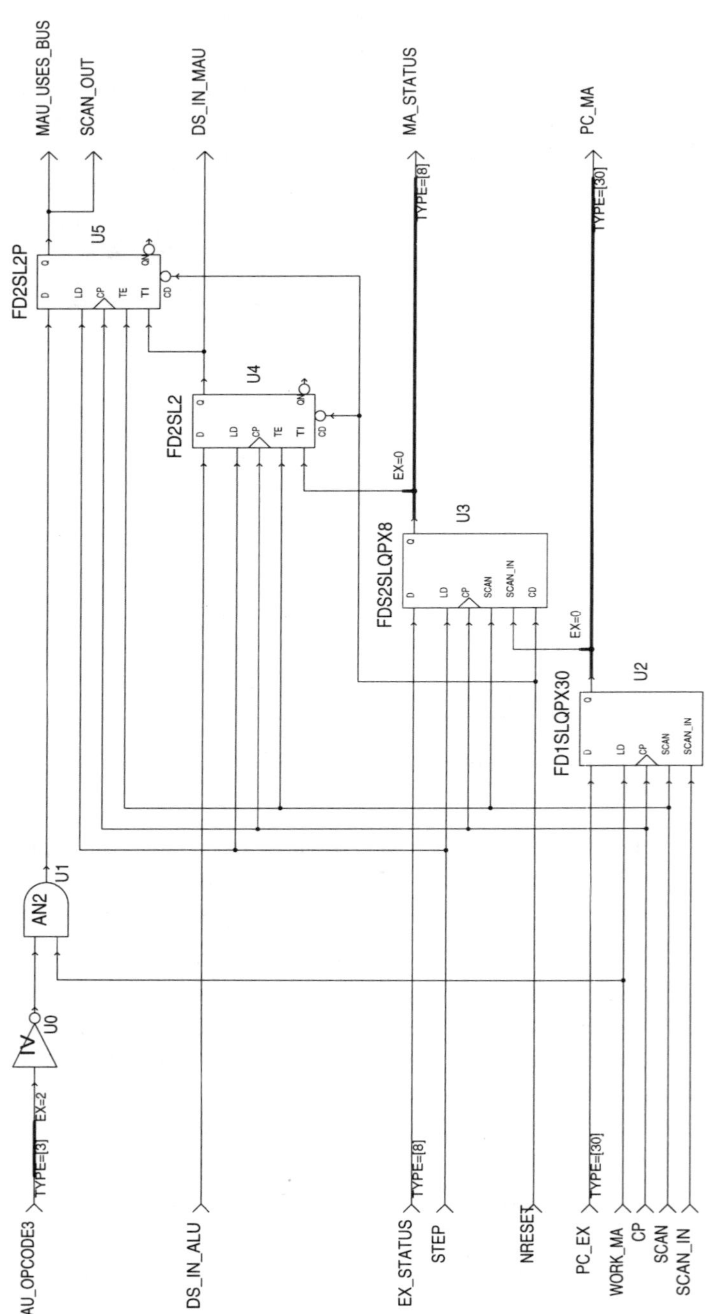

Figure 8.4 Status pipeline STAP_MA

```
// Wires for inputs
wire    CP,                 // system clock
        nRESET,             // reset
        STEP,               // pipeline enable
        DIS_IDU,            // turn off IDU
        KILL_ALU,           // turn off ALU
        RERUN_MA,           // clear pipeline stages MA and WB
        FLUSH_PIPE,         // clear all pipeline stages from ID to WB
        NO_DELAY,           // ignore HWI and EXC delay instruction
        DO_HALT;            // processor disable

// Pipeline active (source of 1's of WORK FIFO)
reg     ACTIVE;

// WORK FIFO
reg     WORKFF_IF,          // instruction fetch stage
        WORKFF_ID,          // instruction decode stage
        WORKFF_EX,          // execute stage
        WORKFF_MA,          // memory access stage
        WORKFF_WB;          // write back stage

// Assignments for outputs
wire    WORK_IF;            // instruction fetch stage
wire    WORK_FD;            // instruction fetch/decode stage
wire    WORK_ID;            // instruction decode stage
wire    WORK_EX;            // execute stage
wire    WORK_MA;            // memory access stage
wire    WORK_WB;            // write-back stage

assign WORK_IF = WORKFF_IF & STEP    & nRESET;
assign WORK_FD = WORKFF_ID & STEP    & ~FLUSH_PIPE & ~NO_DELAY & ACTIVE;
assign WORK_ID = WORKFF_ID & WORK_FD & ~DIS_IDU;
assign WORK_EX = WORKFF_EX & STEP    & ~KILL_ALU   & ACTIVE;
assign WORK_MA = WORKFF_MA & STEP    & ~FLUSH_PIPE & ~RERUN_MA;
assign WORK_WB = WORKFF_WB & STEP    & ~FLUSH_PIPE & ~RERUN_MA;


//
// Asynchronously reset registers
// ACTIVE and WORK FIFO
//
always @(nRESET) begin
  while (~nRESET) begin
    ACTIVE    = 1'b1;
    WORKFF_IF = 1'b1;
    WORKFF_ID = 1'b0;
    WORKFF_EX = 1'b0;
    WORKFF_MA = 1'b0;
    WORKFF_WB = 1'b0;
    #1;
  end
end

//
// Clear ACTIVE when valid HALT request
//
always @(posedge CP) if (STEP) begin
  if (~KILL_ALU & DO_HALT) ACTIVE = #`DELTA 1'b0;
end

//
// Shift WORK FIFO at rising
// clock edge when pipeline enable;
// initialize WORK FIFO, when reset
//
always @(posedge CP) begin
  if (STEP) begin
    fork
      WORKFF_IF = #`DELTA ACTIVE;
      WORKFF_ID = #`DELTA WORK_IF;
      WORKFF_EX = #`DELTA WORK_ID;
      WORKFF_MA = #`DELTA WORK_EX;
      WORKFF_WB = #`DELTA WORK_MA;
    join
  end
end
```

Figure 8.5 Register pipeline in the PCU

The main components of the corresponding schematic WORK_UNIT in Figure 8.6 are the five registers U8, U13, U18, U23, and U29. They correspond

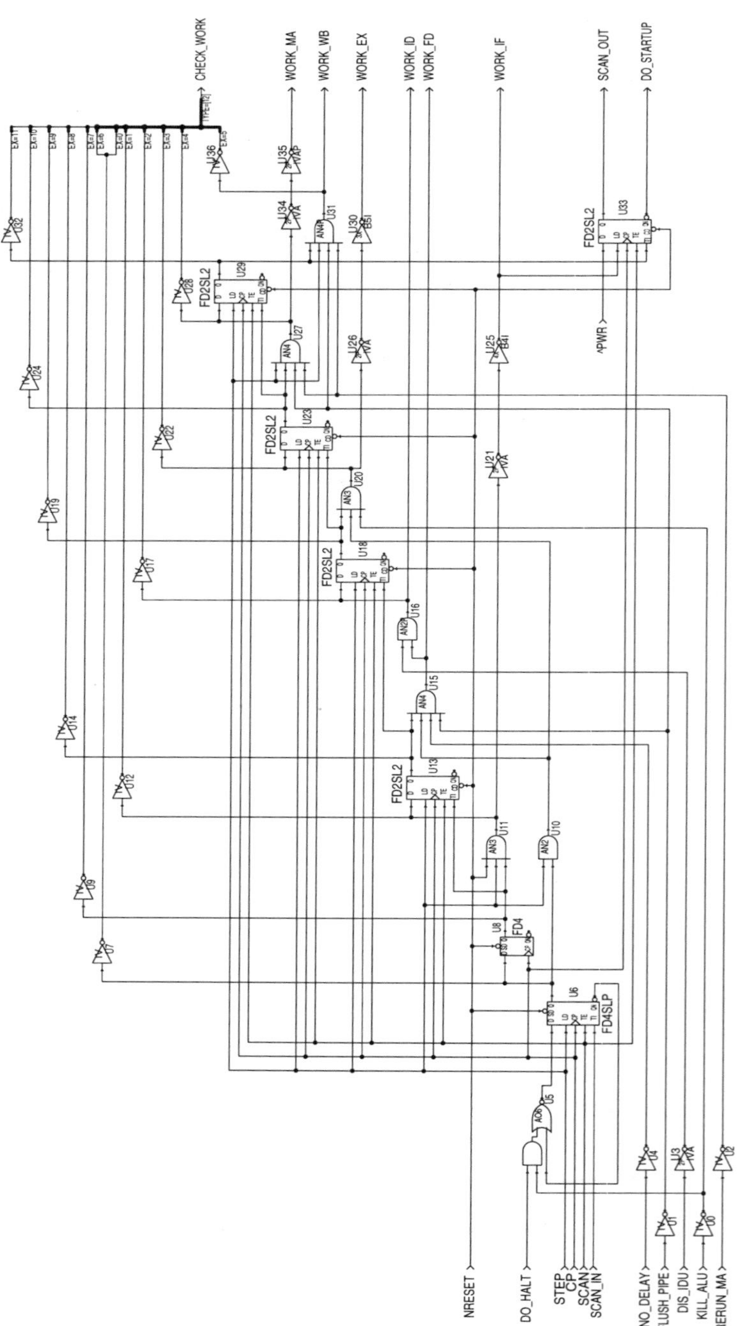

Figure 8.6 WORK_UNIT of pipeline control

to registers WORKFF_IF, WORKFF_ID, WORKFF_EX, WORKFF_MA, and WORKFF_WB of the Coarse Structure Model. According to lines f1238...f1248, the input signals are taken with the positive clock edge, when STEP is set.

Flip-flop U6 models register ACTIVE of the VERILOG model. The feedback ensures that the contents are preserved. The flip-flop is set by NRESET, it is reset by the logic U0/U5 corresponding to ~KILL_ALU & DO_HALT.

The logic between the pipeline registers in lines f1202...f1207 can easily be found in the schematic. For example, WORK_IF is generated by AND gate U11 from NRESET, STEP, and WORKFF_IF. The two inverters U21 and U25 serve as drivers for the relatively large load behind WORK_IF. WORK_IF is also the input to register U13 corresponding to WORKFF_ID following WORKFF_IF in the pipeline.

8.2.4 Multiplexers for Data Selection

Signals have frequently to be extracted from data buses or composed to form new buses. An example is the write data selection of the memory access unit in Figure 8.7. Here the write data are extracted from a 32-bit bus and are composed according to access width and access address to form a new 32-bit bus.

```
d0132 // Write data selection
d0133 //
d0134 // Put data to be written to MAU_WRITE_DATA
d0135 // according to access width and address

d0139   //
d0140   // Byte selection in write data
d0141   //
d0142   always @(MAU_DBREG or MAPPING[0]) begin
d0143     case(MAPPING[0])
d0144       1'b0: ST_MAPP08 = {MAU_DBREG[31:16], MAU_DBREG[15:8], MAU_DBREG[7:0]};
d0145       1'b1: ST_MAPP08 = {MAU_DBREG[31:16], MAU_DBREG[ 7:0], MAU_DBREG[7:0]};
d0146     endcase
d0147   end
d0148
d0149   //
d0150   // Halfword selection in write data
d0151   //
d0152   always @(ST_MAPP08 or MAPPING[1]) begin
d0153     case(MAPPING[1])
d0154       1'b0: ST_MAPP16 = {ST_MAPP08[31:16], ST_MAPP08[15:0]};
d0155       1'b1: ST_MAPP16 = {ST_MAPP08[15: 0], ST_MAPP08[15:0]};
d0156     endcase
d0157   end
d0158
d0159   //
d0160   // Put write data to MAU_WRITE_DATA
d0161   //
d0162   always @(ST_MAPP16)
d0163     MAU_WRITE_DATA = ST_MAPP16;
```

Figure 8.7 Multiplexers for data selection in the MAU

In the first always block (d0149...d0154), bits 15...8 are assigned the original bits 7...0 or bits 15...8 depending on MAPPING[0]. This selection is accomplished in

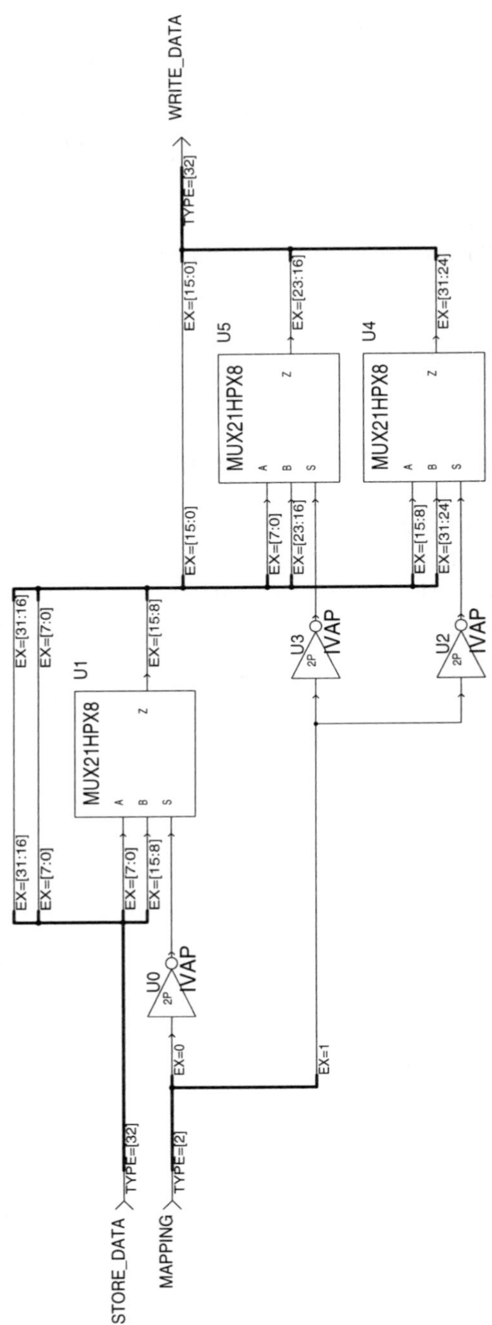

Figure 8.8 Module SELWD (select write data)

the schematic of Figure 8.8 by multiplexer U1 assigning input A to output Z if selection input S is not set, and input B otherwise.

As it is an 8-bit multiplexer, selection signal MAPPING[0] has to be enhanced by inverter IVAP (U0). Analogously, inputs A and B have to be exchanged: A receives bits 7...0 from STORE_DATA, B bits 15...8. For MAPPING[0]=0, S is set thus connecting input B with output Z. This corresponds to line d0144 in the VERILOG model. The remaining two multiplexers U4 and U5 generate the upper 16 bits correspondingly. Two multiplexers of 8 bits each are used.

8.2.5 Constant Assignment

Frequently, constants are assigned to a signal depending on other signals. In the example of the pipeline disable logic, this is modeled in Figure 8.9 by a casez statement. DIS_IDU is set depending on MPC_HIT, BTC_HIT, BTC_CORRECT, BTC_DIS_IDU, NO_ACC, BRANCH, ANNUL, and TAKEN.

```
always @(MPC_HIT or BTC_HIT or BTC_CORRECT or BTC_DIS_IDU or NO_ACC
         or BRANCH or ANNUL or TAKEN) begin
  casez({MPC_HIT, BTC_HIT, BTC_CORRECT, BTC_DIS_IDU, NO_ACC,
         BRANCH, ANNUL, TAKEN})
    8'b000?00?? : DIS_IDU = 1'b0;    // normal instruction
    8'b000?010? : DIS_IDU = 1'b0;    // branch, ANNUL not set
    8'b000?0110 : DIS_IDU = 1'b1;    // branch not taken, ANNUL
    8'b000?0111 : DIS_IDU = 1'b0;    // branch taken, ANNUL
    8'b000?1??? : DIS_IDU = 1'b1;    // memory access impossible
    8'b100??0?? : DIS_IDU = 1'b0;    // MPC hit
    8'b100??10? : DIS_IDU = 1'b0;    // MPC hit, branch, no ANNUL
    8'b100??110 : DIS_IDU = 1'b1;    // MPC hit, branch not taken, ANNUL
    8'b100??111 : DIS_IDU = 1'b0;    // MPC hit, branch taken, ANNUL
    8'b??10???? : DIS_IDU = 1'b0;    // BTC corrects branch
    8'b??11???? : DIS_IDU = 1'b1;    // BTC corrects branch
    8'b?100???? : DIS_IDU = 1'b0;    // BTC hit
    8'b?101???? : DIS_IDU = 1'b1;    // BTC hit
    default     : DIS_IDU = 1'b0;
  endcase
end
```

Figure 8.9 Constant assignment in the IFU

When synthesizing schematic PDL in Figure 8.10, the casez statement changes to the multiplexer logic U4 and U5. A gate solution would be slower. Signal BTC_DIS_IDU belongs to the critical path, therefore, emphasis is here put on speed. Inverter U6 serves as a driver. The inversion is compensated by another inverting multiplexer U5 of type MUX21LP.

8.2.6 Variable Assignment

Depending on various input signals, an output signal may have a variable assigned. This is the case, for example, in the forwarding and register unit in Figure 8.11, where depending on control bus SEL_A, one of the inputs READ_A, C3_BUS, or C4_BUS is connected with output A_BUS.

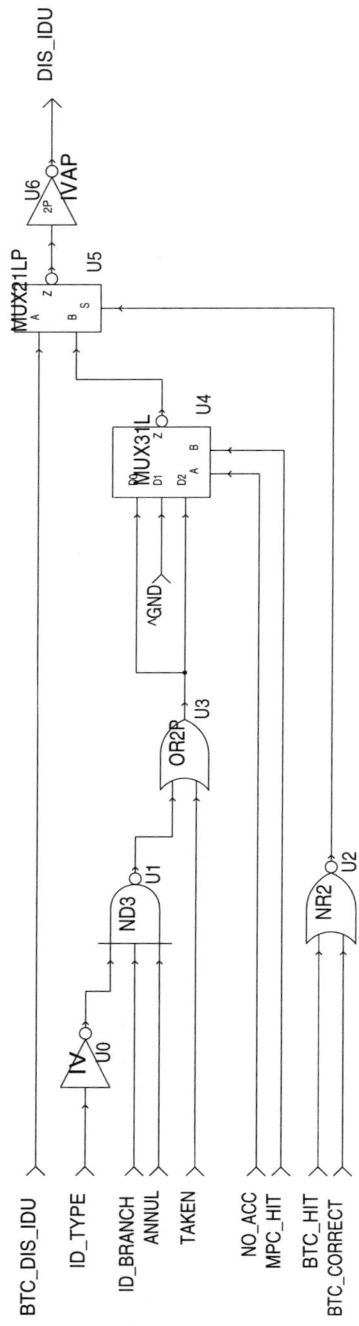

Figure 8.10 Pipeline disable logic PDL

```
// FSL (forwarding selection logic)
//
// This multiplexer puts correct values to A_BUS, B_BUS,
// and STORE_DATA depending on the forwarding logic.

always @(SEL_A or SEL_B or SEL_S or READ_A or READ_B or READ_STORE_DATA or
         C3_BUS or C4_BUS or IMMEDIATE or SREG_DATA)
begin: FSL

  //
  // ALU operand A (MUX_A)
  //
  case(SEL_A)
    `TAKE2_ADDR: A_BUS = READ_A;
    `TAKE2_C3:   A_BUS = C3_BUS;
    `TAKE2_C4:   A_BUS = C4_BUS;
  endcase

  //
  // ALU operand B (MUX_B)
  //
  case (SEL_B)
    `TAKE3_ADDR: B_BUS = READ_B;
    `TAKE3_C3:   B_BUS = C3_BUS;
    `TAKE3_C4:   B_BUS = C4_BUS;
    `TAKE3_IMM:  B_BUS = IMMEDIATE;
    `TAKE3_SREG: B_BUS = SREG_DATA;
  endcase

  //
  // Store data (MUX_S)
  //
  case (SEL_S)
    `TAKE2_ADDR: STORE_DATA2 = READ_STORE_DATA;
    `TAKE2_C3:   STORE_DATA2 = C3_BUS;
    `TAKE2_C4:   STORE_DATA2 = C4_BUS;
  endcase
end
```

Figure 8.11 Variable assignment in the FRU

In the corresponding schematic MUX_A in Figure 8.12, four 2-to-1 multiplexers of 8 bits of type MUX31HPX8 (U8–U11) are connected to form a 32-bit multiplexer by splitting a bus and extracting four buses of eight bits each and recomposing them after the multiplexer. Inverters U2 to U7 drive the multiplexers. The selection is done by SEL_A. The XOR gate U0 and the inverter U1 encode the selection signal.

8.2.7 Indirect Synthesis of Behavioral Parts

When modeling in the Coarse Structure Model is relatively behavior oriented, it has to be synthesized indirectly. The difficulty depends on the special case. VERILOG code and schematic are only connected by equal functionality, which can only be demonstrated by thorough simulations. There are no rules for an implicit synthesis at this point. We have tried to avoid such cases.

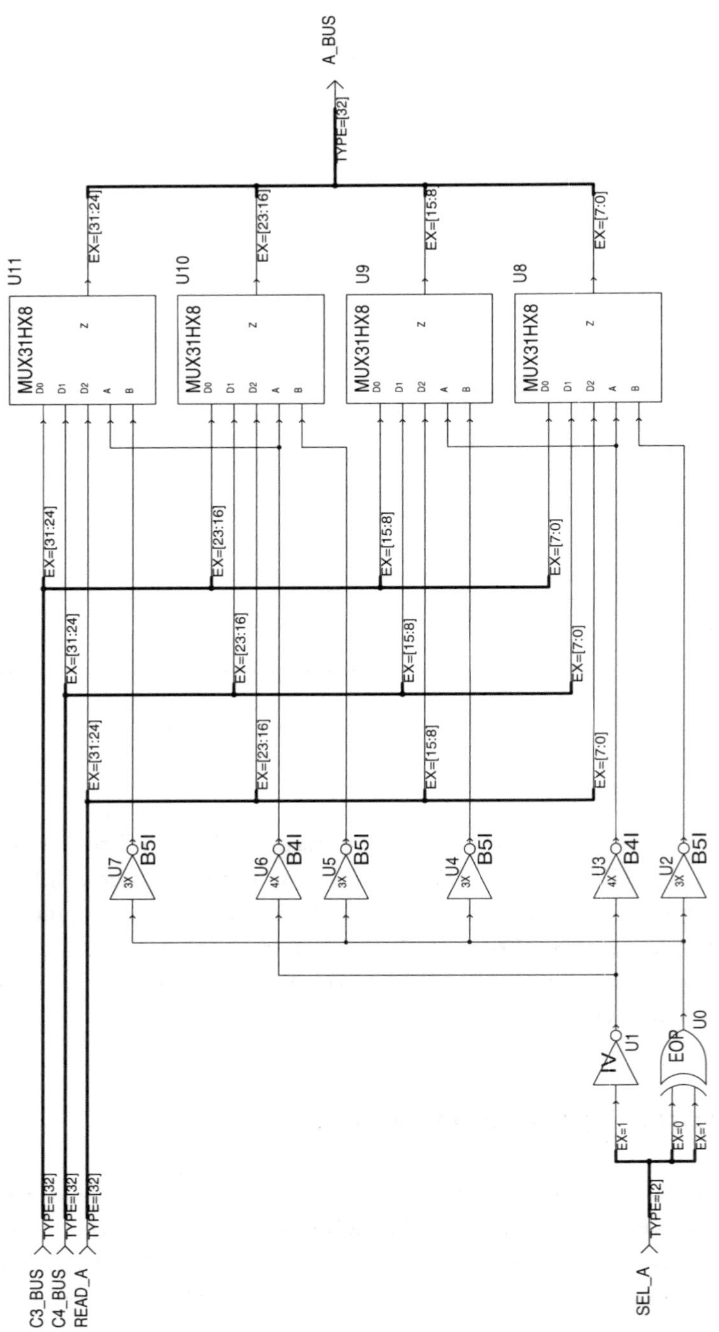

Figure 8.12 Multiplexer MUX_A

8.3 Support by Logic Synthesis

The Coarse Structure Model contains many combinational logic blocks, for which an automatic synthesis with appropriate tools is well suited. Errors are avoided that occur easily in manual synthesis. The number of gates employed can be optimized. However, the blocks synthesized should not be very time critical.

8.3.1 Synthesis Tools

We use the synthesis programs BDSYN and MIS II of the system OCTTOOLS from the University of Berkeley. BDSYN compiles the hardware description language BDS into format BLIF (Berkeley Logic Intermediate Format), afterwards, program MIS II synthesizes the BLIF description by using a library resulting in a gate netlist in format BDNET. There are various choices for optimization.

Unfortunately, our VERILOG descriptions first have to be converted to BDS inputs, and at the end, the BDNET result has to be translated to LSI schematics. This appears to be impractical, but in our case it did not mean many difficulties as the following example shows.

8.3.2 Example of a Logic Synthesis

In the VERILOG Coarse Structure Model, we want to synthesize the history update logic HUL of the branch-target cache BTC, in which the history bits NEW_HIBITS are computed. The transition function in Figure 8.13 uses signals LAST_HIBITS and TAKEN.

Figure 8.14 shows adaptation to the BDS format, which is documented in connection with the OCTTOOLS. After variable declaration, the control structure SELECT...FROM... selects like the VERILOG case statement an alternative depending on ltake & lhibits.

BDSYN compiles the BDS input into the intermediate format BLIF in Figure 8.15 serving as a starting point for gate synthesis by MIS II. The center of the BLIF representation are the truth tables for logic variables (.names), a "–" representing a "don't care". MIS II also requires a library with the gates of the target technology in order to generate a logic as small as possible in a BDNET netlist while considering various given operations (Figure 8.16).

First, input and output variables are declared, where the second is the name in the netlist. [n] denotes an internal connection. For example, [18414] connects output O of the AND-OR gate AO2 with input b of the NOR gate NR2.

```
// HUL (history update logic)
//
// The following state transition function
// determines new history bits from the
// old ones and the branch decision:
//
//          LAST_HIBITS      ~TAKEN       TAKEN
//          ---------------------------------
//          N  (00)          N  (00)      N? (01)
//          N? (01)          N  (00)      T  (10)
//          T? (11)          N  (00)      T  (10)
//          T  (10)          T? (11)      T  (10)

module hul (NEW_HIBITS, LAST_HIBITS, TAKEN);
  output [1:0]  NEW_HIBITS;          // new history bits
  input [1:0]   LAST_HIBITS;         // old history bits
  input         TAKEN;               // branch taken

  // Outputs
  reg [1:0]     NEW_HIBITS;          // new history bits

  // Inputs
  wire [1:0]    LAST_HIBITS;         // old history bits
  wire          TAKEN;               // branch taken

  always @(TAKEN or LAST_HIBITS) begin
    casez({TAKEN, LAST_HIBITS})
      3'b00? : NEW_HIBITS = 2'b00;              // N: N->N & N?->N
      3'b010 : NEW_HIBITS = 2'b11;              // N: T->T?
      3'b011 : NEW_HIBITS = 2'b00;              // N: T?->N
      3'b100 : NEW_HIBITS = 2'b01;              // T: N->N?
      3'b101 : NEW_HIBITS = 2'b10;              // T: N?->T
      3'b11? : NEW_HIBITS = 2'b10;              // T: T->T & T?->T
    endcase
  end
endmodule // hul
```

Figure 8.13 History update logic HUL to be synthesized

```
! BDSYN model
! CHIP:IFU:BTCHUL
! New history bits depending on
! old history bits and branch decision
!
MODEL nhibits
  nhibits<1:0> =      ! new history bits
  lhibits<1:0>,       ! old history bits
  ltake<0>;           ! branch decision
 ROUTINE calc;
  SELECT (ltake & lhibits) FROM
    [000#2]: nhibits = 00#2;
    [001#2]: nhibits = 00#2;
    [010#2]: nhibits = 11#2;
    [011#2]: nhibits = 00#2;
    [100#2]: nhibits = 01#2;
    [101#2]: nhibits = 10#2;
    [110#2]: nhibits = 10#2;
    [111#2]: nhibits = 10#2;
  ENDSELECT;
 ENDROUTINE;
ENDMODEL;
```

Figure 8.14 History update logic in BDS format

The transformation into an LSI schematic in Figure 8.17 is a routine task, which certainly could be automated, too. For example, output nhibits<1> coincides with netlist node [18357] and hence with the ouput of complex gate AO7.

```
.model nhibits
.inputs lhibits<1> lhibits<0> ltake<0>
.outputs nhibits<1> nhibits<0>
.names lhibits<0> ltake<0> lhibits<1> $$COND2<0>0.1
001 1
.names lhibits<0> lhibits<1> ltake<0> $$COND4<0>0.1
001 1
.names lhibits<1> lhibits<0> ltake<0> $$COND5<0>0.1
011 1
.names lhibits<0> lhibits<1> ltake<0> $$COND6<0>0.1
011 1
.names lhibits<0> lhibits<1> ltake<0> $$COND7<0>0.1
111 1
.names $$COND8<0>0.1
.names $$COND2<0>0.1 $$COND4<0>0.1 nhibits<0>
1- 1
-1 1
.names $$COND2<0>0.1 $$COND5<0>0.1 $$COND6<0>0.1 $$COND7<0>0.1 nhibits<1>
1--- 1
-1-- 1
--1- 1
---1 1
.end
```

Figure 8.15 Intermediate format BLIF

```
MODEL "nhibits";

INPUT
        "lhibits<1>" :   "lhibits<1>"
        "lhibits<0>" :   "lhibits<0>"
        "ltake<0>"   :   "ltake<0>";

OUTPUT
        "nhibits<1>" :   "[18357]"
        "nhibits<0>" :   "[18417]";

INSTANCE "IVA":"physical"
        "a"          :   "lhibits<1>";
        "O"          :   "[18373]";

INSTANCE "IVA":"physical"
        "a"          :   "ltake<0>";
        "O"          :   "[18372]";

INSTANCE "IV":"physical"
        "a"          :   "[18417]";
        "O"          :   "[18387]";

INSTANCE "ND2":"physical"
        "a"          :   "[18387]";
        "b"          :   "ltake<0>";
        "O"          :   "[18392]";

INSTANCE "AO7":"physical"
        "a"          :   "lhibits<0>";
        "b"          :   "[18373]";
        "c"          :   "[18392]";
        "O"          :   "[18357]";

INSTANCE "AO2":"physical"
        "a"          :   "[18372]";
        "b"          :   "lhibits<1>";
        "c"          :   "[18373]";
        "d"          :   "ltake<0>";
        "O"          :   "[18414]";

INSTANCE "NR2":"physical"
        "a"          :   "lhibits<0>";
        "b"          :   "[18414]";
        "O"          :   "[18417]";

ENDMODEL;
```

Figure 8.16 Synthesis result as a BDNET netlist

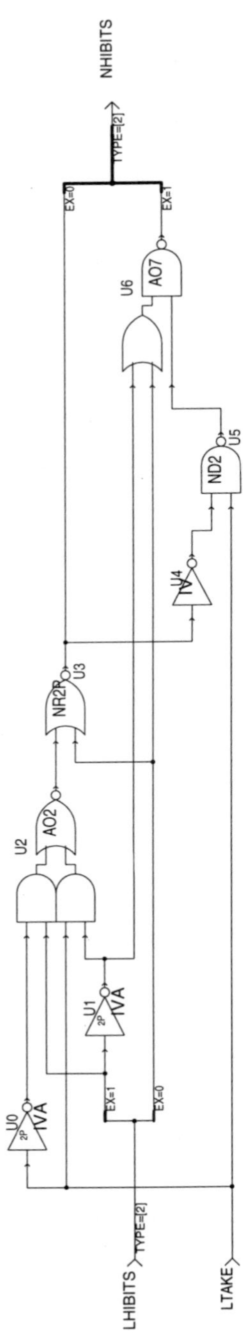

Figure 8.17 Schematic BTC_HUL

8.4 A Larger Example

In the following synthesis of the memory access unit MAU, we will apply several techniques of the previous sections, namely direct and indirect manual synthesis, but also logic synthesis.

8.4.1 Synchronous Data Transfer

```
d0085 // Read inputs with rising clock edge,
d0086 // if work enable
d0087 //
d0088 always @(posedge CP) begin
d0089   if (WORK_MA) begin
d0090     fork
d0091       MAU_C3REG = #`DELTA C3_BUS;
d0092       MAU_DBREG = #`DELTA D_BUS;
d0093       MAU_AMREG = #`DELTA MAU_ACC_MODE_3;
d0094       MAU_OPREG = #`DELTA MAU_OPCODE_3;
d0095     join
d0096   end
d0097 end
```

Figure 8.18 Synchronous data transfer in the MAU

In the VERILOG extract of Figure 8.18, data are taken with a rising clock edge and WORK_MA set and are held during the whole cycle. For example, input C3_BUS is transferred into register MAU_C3REG. Synthesis of the schematic in Figure 8.19 is done as in Section 8.2.1. The registers are implemented by flip-flops. As destination of the 32-bit buses C3_BUS and D_BUS, we use a flip-flop bank FD1SLPX32 (U0, U1), as destination of the 3-bit control signals MAU_ACC_MODE_3 and MAU_OPCODE_3, we take a cell FD1SLPX3 (U2, U3). The clock is CP, as a load signal, we connect WORK_MA with register input LD to model the if statement of line d0089.

The scanpath can easily be detected: scan input SCAN is connected to all flip-flops, SCAN_IN of the module with the first register U0. Scan output of U0 is the least significant bit of the data output. It is taken by an extractor and connected with the scan input of the second flip-flop U1. In the same way, the path leads to the fourth flip-flop U3. There, the least significant bit of the inverted data output is used as scan output, and it is inverted again at U8, before it reaches the scan output of the module.

In Figure 8.20, module output MAU_ADDR_BUS is permanently updated; as soon as MAU_C3REG changes, the new value is assigned to module output MAU_ADDR_BUS. For the implementation in the schematic of Figure 8.19, it suffices to connect register MAU_C3REG (U0) with module output MAU_ADDR corresponding to the module output MAU_ADDR_BUS.

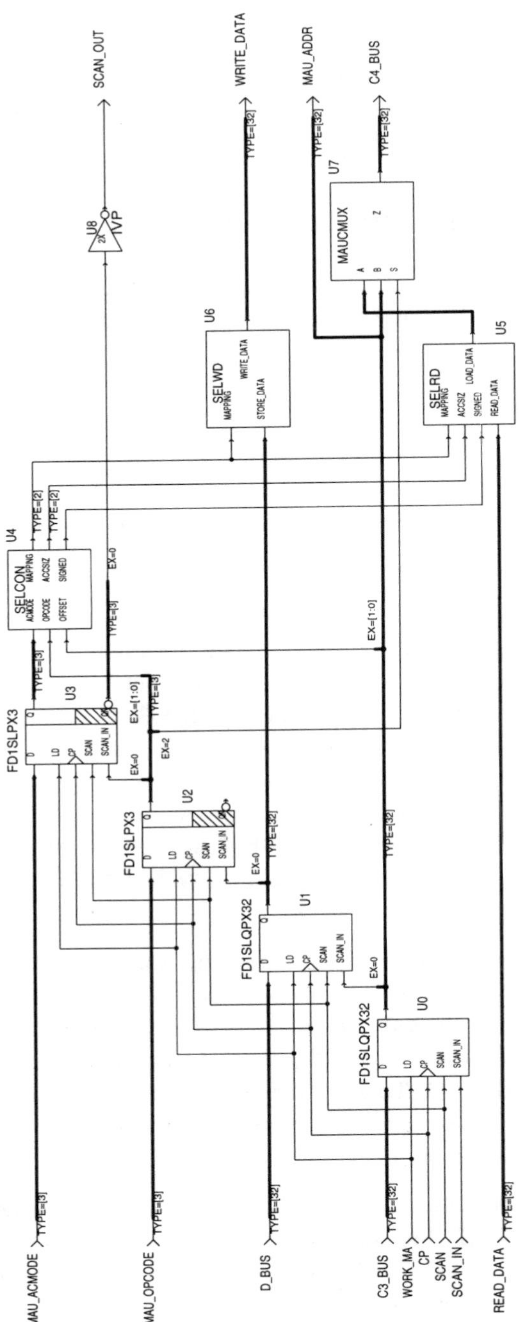

Figure 8.19 Memory access unit MAU

```
// Update MAU_ADDR_BUS
//
always @(MAU_C3REG)
  MAU_ADDR_BUS = MAU_C3REG;
```

Figure 8.20 Updating a module output in MAU

8.4.2 Combinational Logic

The determination of access width and of byte and halfword selection is accomplished in Figure 8.21 using combinational logic.

```
// Access width
// ACCSIZ: 00: swap, read, or write access to a word
//         01: read or write access to a byte
//         10: read or write access to a halfword
//
always @(MAU_OPREG or MAU_AMREG) begin
  ACCSIZ[0] = ~(&MAU_OPREG[1:0]) & ~MAU_AMREG[2];
  ACCSIZ[1] = ~(&MAU_OPREG[1:0]) & ~MAU_AMREG[0] & MAU_AMREG[2];
end

//
// Byte and halfword selection for read/write accesses using
// access address bits 0,1 (position in data word)
//
// MAPPING: X0: map bits 0-7  from/to bits  0- 7
//          X1: map bits 0-7  from/to bits  8-15
//          0X: map bits 0-15 from/to bits  0-15
//          1X: map bits 0-15 from/to bits 16-31
//
always @(MAU_C3REG or ACCSIZ) begin
  MAPPING[0] = MAU_C3REG[0] & ACCSIZ[0];
  MAPPING[1] = MAU_C3REG[1] & (|ACCSIZ);
end
```

Figure 8.21 Combinational logic in MAU

To avoid an overloading of schematic MAU, this logic is contained in a separate submodule SELCON in Figure 8.22. Input signals ACMODE, OPCODE, and OFFSET correspond to the variables of Table 8.23 in the Coarse Structure Model.

Signals ACCSIZ[0,1] and MAPPING [0,1] can be substituted and transformed as follows and then be directly translated into schematics SELCON.

$$\begin{aligned} ACCSIZ_0 &= \sim(\&\ MAU\_OPREG_{1:0}) \ \&\ \sim MAU\_AMREG_2 \\ &= \sim(OPCODE_0 \ \&\ OPCODE_1) \ \&\ \sim ACMODE_2 \\ &= \sim((OPCODE_0 \ \&\ OPCODE_1) \ | \ ACMODE_2) \end{aligned}$$

$$\begin{aligned} ACCSIZ_1 &= \sim(\&\ MAU\_OPREG_{1:0}) \ \&\ \sim MAU\_AMREG_0 \ \&\ MAU\_AMREG_2 \\ &= \sim(OPCODE_0 \ \&\ OPCODE_1) \ \&\ \sim ACMODE_0 \ \&\ ACMODE_2 \\ &= \sim((OPCODE_0 \ \&\ OPCODE_1) \ | \ ACMODE_0 \ | \ \sim ACMODE_2) \end{aligned}$$

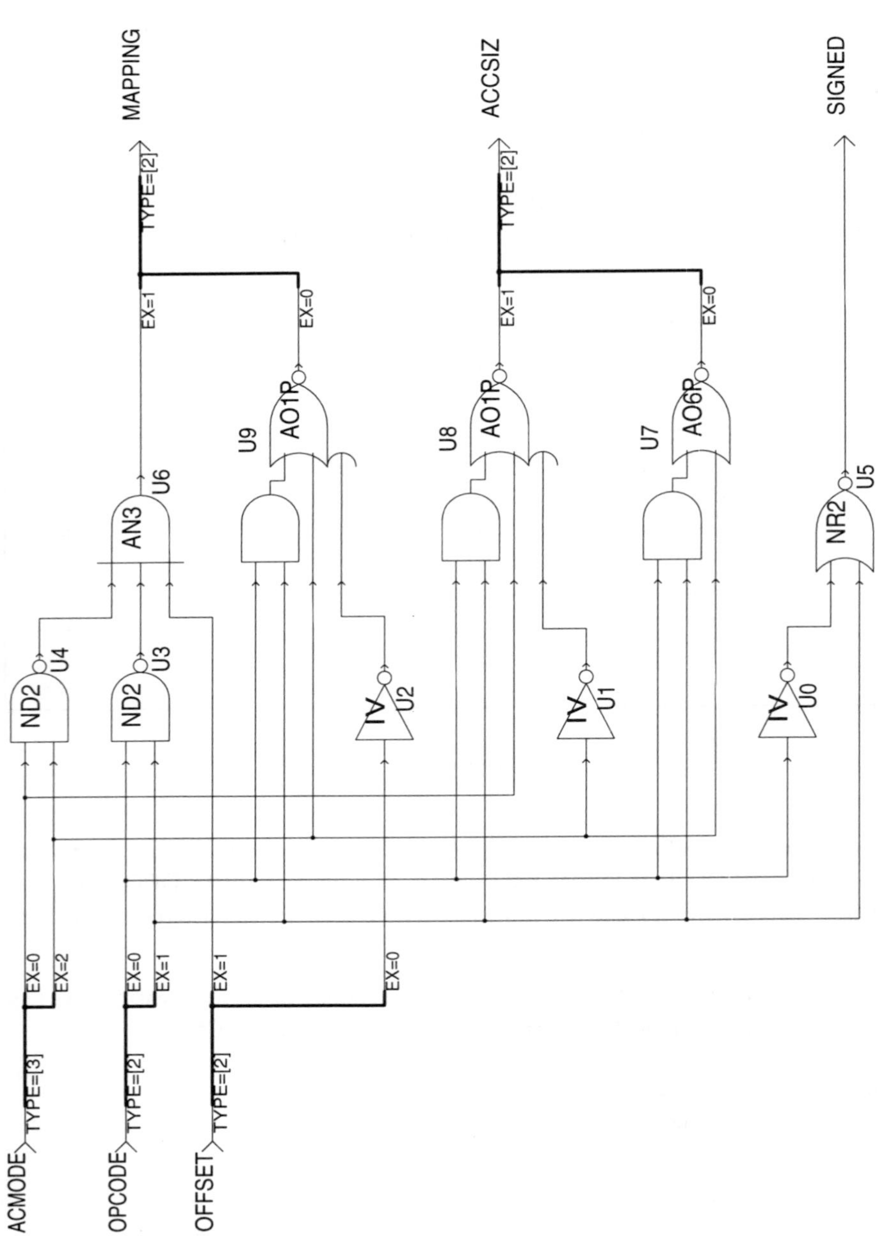

Figure 8.22 Selection controller SELCON

MAPPING$_0$ = MAU_C3REG$_0$ & ACCSIZ$_0$
= OFFSET$_0$ & ~ ((OPCODE$_0$ & OPCODE$_1$) | ACMODE$_2$)
= ~ ((~ OFFSET$_0$ | (OPCODE$_0$ & OPCODE$_1$)) | ACMODE$_2$)

MAPPING$_1$ = MAU_C3REG$_1$ & (| ACCSIZ)
= OFFSET$_1$ & (~ ((OPCODE$_0$ & OPCODE$_1$) | ACMODE$_2$)
| ~ ((OPCODE$_0$ & OPCODE$_1$) | ACMODE$_0$ | ~ ACMODE$_2$))
= OFFSET$_1$ & (~ (OPCODE$_0$ & OPCODE$_1$) & ~ ACMODE$_2$
| ~ (OPCODE$_0$ & OPCODE$_1$) & ~ ACMODE$_0$ & ACMODE$_2$)
= OFFSET$_1$ & (~ (OPCODE$_0$ & OPCODE$_1$)
& (~ ACMODE$_2$ | ~ ACMODE$_0$ & ACMODE$_2$))
= OFFSET$_1$ & ~ (OPCODE$_0$ & OPCODE$_1$)
& ~ (ACMODE$_2$ & (ACMODE$_0$ | ~ ACMODE$_2$))
= OFFSET$_1$ & ~ (OPCODE$_0$ & OPCODE$_1$)
& ~ ((ACMODE$_2$ & ACMODE$_0$)
| (ACMODE$_2$ & ~ ACMODE$_2$))
= OFFSET$_1$ & ~ (OPCODE$_0$ & OPCODE$_1$)
& ~ (ACMODE$_0$ & ACMODE$_2$)

Coarse Structure Model	Schematic SELCON
MAU_AMREG	ACMODE
MAU_OPREG[1:0]	OPCODE
MAU_C3REG[1:0]	OFFSET

Table 8.23 Correspondence of inputs of the MAU selection controller

8.4.3 Multiplexers for Data Selection

The data to be written or read by the memory access unit have to be put on bus MAU_WRITE_DATA or extracted from MAU_READ_DATA according to access width and access address (Figure 8.24).

The selection of data is achieved as in Section 8.2.4 using multiplexers. The write data are selected in submodule SELWD (select write data, Figure 8.8). The selection is done in two steps.

In the first step, bits 8...15 are replaced by bits 0...7 according to MAPPING[0]. The corresponding always block is found in lines d0142...d0147. The schematic is synthesized by a 2-to-1 multiplexer U1. The write data in register MAU_DBREG are at input STORE_DATA of submodule SELWD. They are 32 bits and are first split using extractors. Bits 0...7 and 16...31 remain unchanged and become the corresponding bits of the new write data. The remaining bits 8...15 are taken from the output of multiplexer U1. There, input A or B is selected by select input S. This depends on MAPPING[0] according to line d0143.

```
d0132 // Write data selection
d0133 //
d0134 // Put data to be written to MAU_WRITE_DATA
d0135 // according to access width and address

d0139   //
d0140   // Byte selection in write data
d0141   //
d0142   always @(MAU_DBREG or MAPPING[0]) begin
d0143     case(MAPPING[0])
d0144       1'b0: ST_MAPP08 = {MAU_DBREG[31:16], MAU_DBREG[15:8], MAU_DBREG[7:0]};
d0145       1'b1: ST_MAPP08 = {MAU_DBREG[31:16], MAU_DBREG[ 7:0], MAU_DBREG[7:0]};
d0146     endcase
d0147   end
d0148
d0149   //
d0150   // Halfword selection in write data
d0151   //
d0152   always @(ST_MAPP08 or MAPPING[1]) begin
d0153     case(MAPPING[1])
d0154       1'b0: ST_MAPP16 = {ST_MAPP08[31:16], ST_MAPP08[15:0]};
d0155       1'b1: ST_MAPP16 = {ST_MAPP08[15: 0], ST_MAPP08[15:0]};
d0156     endcase
d0157   end
d0158
d0159   //
d0160   // Put write data to MAU_WRITE_DATA
d0161   //
d0162   always @(ST_MAPP16)
d0163     MAU_WRITE_DATA = ST_MAPP16;
```

Figure 8.24 Selection of write data in MAU

In the second step, the upper halfword is replaced by the lower one depending on MAPPING[1]. The converting always block is in lines d0152...d0157. The synthesis is done by two multiplexers U4 and U5. After passing or bypassing the first multiplexer U1, the data are composed to a 32-bit word using extractors. The lower halfword with bits 0...15 leads directly to the output. Bits 16...23 of the write data are generated by multiplexer U5, bits 24...31 by multiplexer U4.

The selection depends on MAPPING[1] as in line d0153. This also requires inverters U2 and U3 for driving. If MAPPING[1] is set, selection inputs S of multiplexers U4 and U5 are reset thus connecting inputs A with outputs Z. As in line d0155, bits 0...15 have therefore to be put to inputs A and for the reverse case, bits 16...31 to inputs B of the multiplexers.

The output of the multiplexers and the directly taken 16 least significant bits are then composed by extractors to a 32-bit word and put to output WRITE_DATA according to line d0163. The selection of data to be written is now finished.

The read data are filtered in the VERILOG group of Figure 8.25.

Selection of read data is delegated to submodule SELRD (select read data) in Figure 8.26. The filtering is accomplished in three steps: first a halfword selection, next a byte selection, and finally, restriction of access width and sign extension.

The first part is modeled in the always block of lines d0177...d0182. The lower halfword is replaced by the upper one, if MAPPING[1] is set, the upper halfword

```
d0167 // Read data selection
d0168 //
d0169 // Filter data to be read from MAU_READ_DATA
d0170 // according to access width and address

d0175   // Halfword selection in read data
d0176   //
d0177   always @(MAU_READ_DATA or MAPPING[1]) begin
d0178     case(MAPPING[1])
d0179       1'b0: LD_MAPP16 = {MAU_READ_DATA[31:16], MAU_READ_DATA[15: 0]};
d0180       1'b1: LD_MAPP16 = {MAU_READ_DATA[31:16], MAU_READ_DATA[31:16]};
d0181     endcase
d0182   end
d0183
d0184   //
d0185   // Byte selection in read data
d0186   //
d0187   always @(LD_MAPP16 or MAPPING[0]) begin
d0188     case(MAPPING[0])
d0189       1'b0: LD_MAPP08 = {LD_MAPP16[31:16], LD_MAPP16[15:8], LD_MAPP16[ 7:0]};
d0190       1'b1: LD_MAPP08 = {LD_MAPP16[31:16], LD_MAPP16[15:8], LD_MAPP16[15:8]};
d0191     endcase
d0192   end
```

Figure 8.25 Selection of read data in MAU

remains unchanged. Synthesis is again done by multiplexers. The 16 bits are selected by two 8-bit inverting 2-to-1 multiplexers U3 and U4. Selection of bits 0...7 is done by multiplexer U3, of bits 8...15 by U4. Signal MAPPING[1] has to be enhanced by inverters U1 and U2, bits 0...15 are put to inputs B, bits 16...31 to A.

The second part of filtering is modeled in the always block of lines d0187...d0192. The 8 least significant bits 0...7 are replaced by 8...15, if MAPPING[0] is set. The most significant bits 8...31 remain unchanged.

Multiplexer U5 is used for selection. U3 produces bits 0...7, U4 produces 8...15. The selection is accomplished by MAPPING[0] enhanced by U0. If this is set, multiplexer input S is reset. Then bits 8...15 have to be selected according to line d0190. Input A has therefore to be connected with the output of U4, input B with the output of U3.

At the output of multiplexer U5, there are now the 8 least significant bits of the selected data, bits 8...15 come inverted from multiplexer U4, bits 16...31 directly from input READ_DATA.

The third part is described in the following section.

8.4.4 Indirect Synthesis

Restriction to access width and sign extension are this time done indirectly. Figure 8.27 shows the VERILOG model extract. After selection, the read data are first filtered, i.e., the bits outside the access width are set to zero. In parallel, mask SIGNMASK for sign extension is determined. The data are combined with this mask in line d0221.

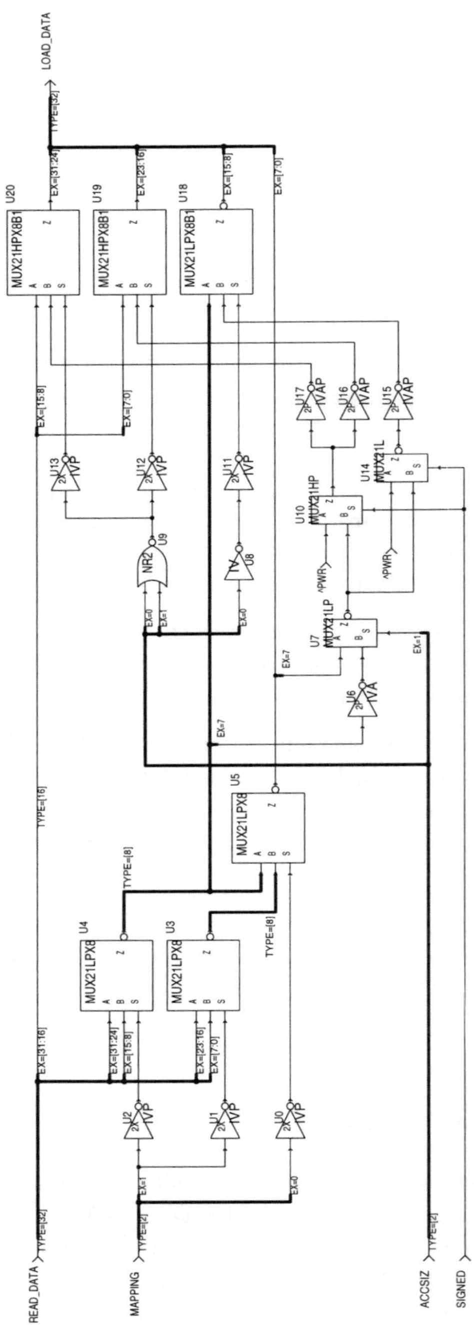

Figure 8.26 Schematic SELRD (select read data)

```
  // Filter read data
  // (set bits outside access width to 0)
  //
  always @(LD_MAPP08 or ACCSIZ) begin
    FILTERED = LD_MAPP08 & {{16{~(|ACCSIZ)}}, {8{~ACCSIZ[0]}}, {8{1'b1}}};
  end

//
// Sign extension mask
//
always @(LD_MAPP08 or ACCSIZ) begin
  case(ACCSIZ)
    2'b01:    SIGNMASK = {{24{LD_MAPP08[ 7]}}, {8{1'b0}}};  // byte
    2'b10:    SIGNMASK = {{16{LD_MAPP08[15]}}, {16{1'b0}}}; // halfword
    default: SIGNMASK = 32'b0;                              // word
  endcase
end

//
// In access operations, combine filtered read data with
// sign mask (only if 'load signed' active) and put to C4_BUS;
//
// when buffering, transfer C3 input register to C4_BUS
//
always @(MAU_OPREG or MAU_C3REG or FILTERED or SIGNMASK) begin
  case(MAU_OPREG[2])
    1'b0: C4_BUS = FILTERED | (SIGNMASK & {32{MAU_OPREG[0]}});
    1'b1: C4_BUS = MAU_C3REG;
  endcase
end
```

Figure 8.27 Filtering and sign extension of read data in MAU

In synthesis, we proceed differently. First, the sign is determined. Depending on the access width, this is either bit 7 or bit 15. Then it is decided depending on SIGNED, which was computed in SELCON, whether this sign bit or 0 is used for filling. Finally, the selection, whether it is filled or whether the bytes are taken directly, again depends on the access width.

The sign is computed by multiplexer U7 using ACCSIZ[1]. If this is set, bit 15 is selected, which was gained before from the inverted representation using inverter U6; if ACCSIZ[1] is reset, bit 7 is selected. Because a MUX21LP was used, the sign at the output is inverted.

When accessing with sign, it has to be filled with the sign bit, otherwise with value 0. The access mode SIGNED was generated in the selection controller. The selection is achieved by two multiplexers U10 and U14. These have the same inversion as the multiplexers controlled by them. This results in a correct sign.

If SIGNED is set, inputs B of multiplexers U10 and U14 are selected having the inverted sign. Inputs A must therefore have value 1. The outputs of the multiplexers are enhanced by inverters U15, U16, and U17. The outputs of U16 and U17 now carry the correct bit for filling, the output of U15 is inverted.

In the last step it is selected, which bytes have to filled or taken. Bits 0...7 are always taken and come directly from multiplexer U5. Bits 8...15 are filled, if ACCSIZ[0] is set, otherwise, they are taken from multiplexer U4. Signal ACCSIZ[0] is enhanced by inverters U8 and U11.

For selection, a multiplexer MUX21LPX8B1 is used with an input A being 8 bit, but input B just 1 bit. B is duplicated internally to 8 bits. For bits 8...15, the output has to be inverted, because the byte comes inverted from multiplexer U4.

The upper halfword is filled with bits 16...31, if ACCSIZ[0] or ACCSIZ[1] (halfword access) is set. Inverters U12 and U13 serve as amplifiers. The selection is done by multiplexers U19 and U20 (MUX21LPX8B1). The bit to be filled with comes from inverters U16 or U17, the original halfword can directly be taken from input READ_DATA.

Now the outputs of the multiplexers are composed to form a complete word using extractors and are connected to output LOAD_DATA.

8.4.5 Variable Assignment

When the memory access unit works only as a shift stage as in Figure 8.28, input register MAU_C3REG is connected with C4_BUS, otherwise the data read are taken.

```
// In access operations, combine filtered read data with
// sign mask (only if 'load signed' active) and put to C4_BUS;
//
// when buffering, transfer C3 input register to C4_BUS
//
always @(MAU_OPREG or MAU_C3REG or FILTERED or SIGNMASK) begin
  case(MAU_OPREG[2])
    1'b0: C4_BUS = FILTERED | (SIGNMASK & {32{MAU_OPREG[0]}});
    1'b1: C4_BUS = MAU_C3REG;
  endcase
end
```

Figure 8.28 Variable assignment in MAU

Expression FILTERED | (SIGNMASK & {32{MAU_OPREG[0]}}) comes from module SELRD of the previous section. The selection is done by multiplexer MAUCMUX in Figure 8.29. This is a multiplexer with two data inputs and one output. The ports are 32 bits. If selection input S is set, the output is connected with input B, otherwise with input A. After dividing the inputs into bytes, a byte selection is done with four multiplexers, whose outputs are afterwards recomposed.

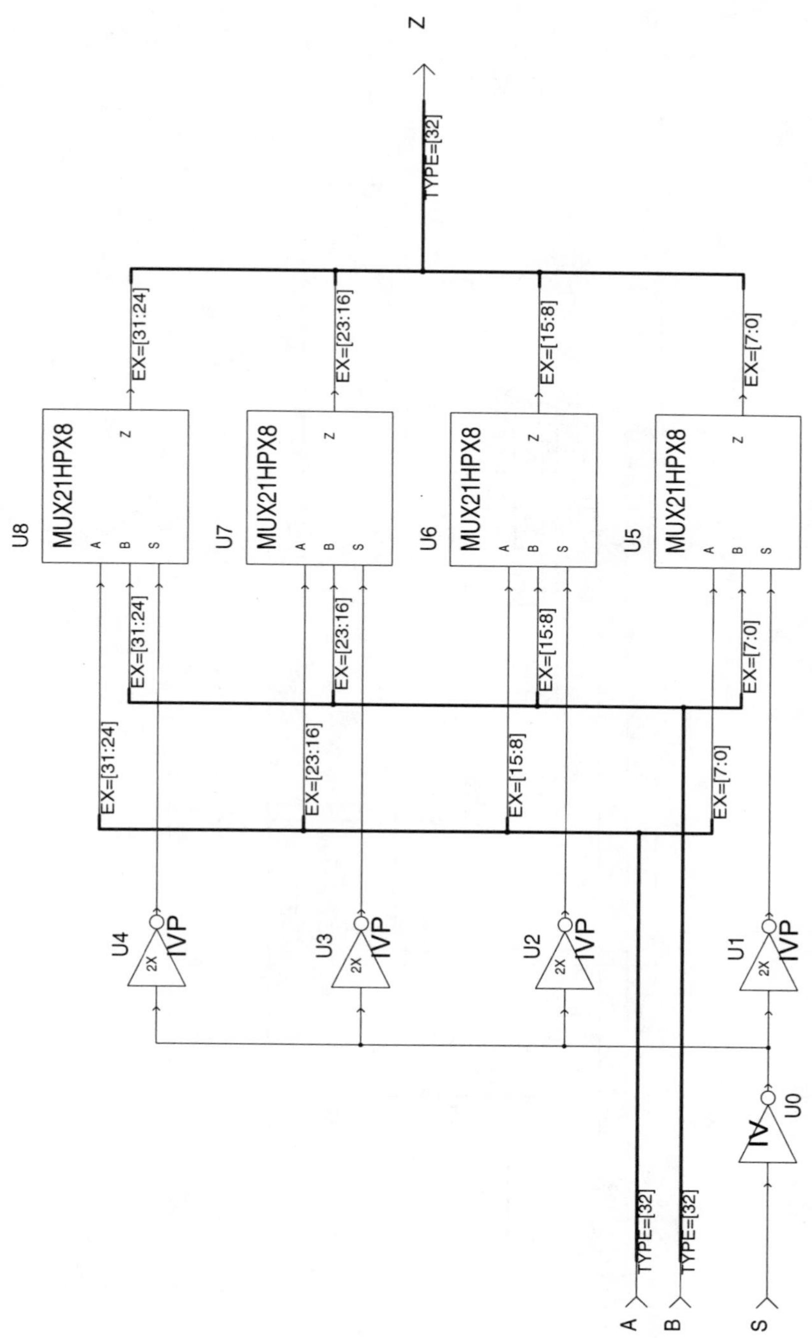

Figure 8.29 Multiplexer MAUCMUX

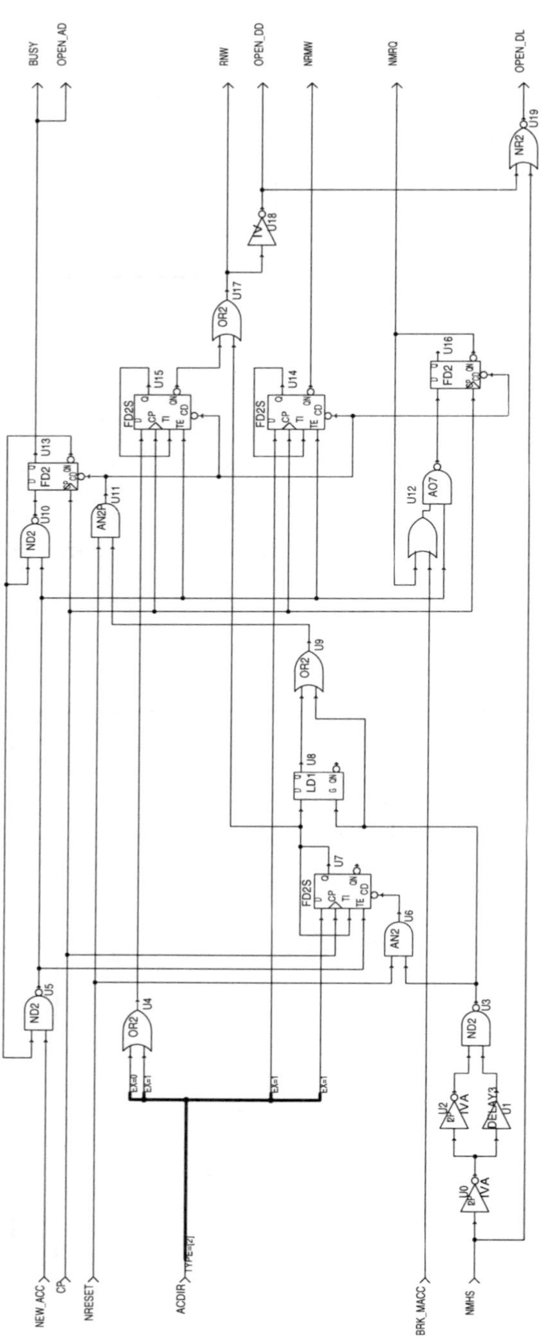

Figure 8.30 Schematic BCUASM (BCU asynchronous state machine)

8.5 The Asynchronous Bus Protocol as a Special Case

So far we have synthesized synchronous register transfers with time independent combinational functions in between by taking values with the edge of a central clock into registers.

While an implementation presents few problems, there is the disadvantage of the clock frequency depending on the slowest path. To lose no synchronization time in memory accesses, the asynchronous bus protocol of Figure 6.10 is implemented. Only the begin of a memory access is clock dependent; its further conduction depends only on the memory handshake signal nMHS.

Aside from normal accesses, the SWAP access (Section 5.2.1) exchanges the contents of a processor register and a memory location by first reading a value from memory and then writing a value to this memory location. A register transfer logic is to be developed, which is initialized synchronously with clock and afterwards goes through states Read, Write, and Ready (schematic BCUASM in Figure 8.30).

The registers for these states must be written with the rising edge of nMHS. For this purpose, an edge detector is constructed with modules U0...U3, which for a positive nMHS edge generates a low pulse of few nanoseconds by purposely using a signal race. This pulse is used to control the asynchronous clear direct input CD of registers U7, U13, U14, and U16.

The delay component for pulse detection should on the one hand produce a sufficiently long clear pulse, and on the other hand should not disturb the protocol. In state Ready, the component should be ready for initialization as soon as possible. To prevent in case of a SWAP two changes of state from Read to Ready by a clear pulse, a latch suppresses the clear signal for other registers in a transition from Read to Write.

It should be emphasized that asynchronous logic as compared with the synchronous case requires a high design and simulation effort. Moreover, the design becomes dependent on special timing properties of a particular production process.

8.6 Statistics and Experiences

After synthesizing schematics from VERILOG groups, we now want to give some general data and experiences.

The chip of TOOBSIE consists of about 50 000 gates actually used. Figure 8.31 indicates that about half of the gates are used for regular structures like caches, CAM cells, or the register RAM. Partially regular structures require another 25% of area, in particular the remaining registers like the 30-bit PC. Of the irregular structures, about every fifth was synthesized automatically.

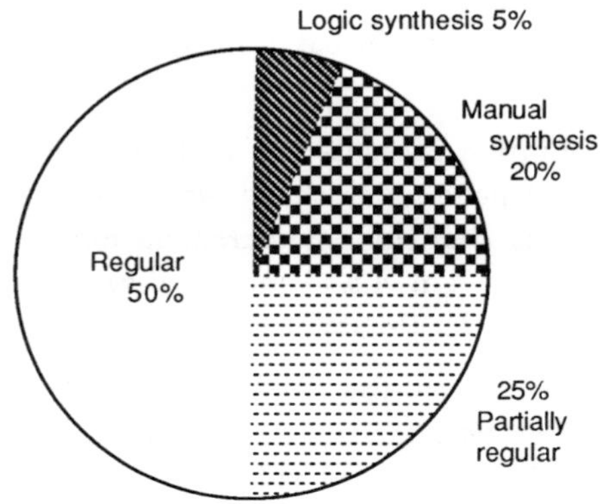

Figure 8.31 Chip area by design style

The large portion of regular structures is described very briefly in the VERILOG Coarse Structure Model. Had there been more chip area, this regular portion would even increase, as then the caches would have been enlarged.

It is not meaningful to estimate the synthesis effort or the required number of gates from the amount of VERILOG code. On the one hand, register declaration as for a cache may require little space in VERILOG, but will lead to a large amount of chip area. On the other hand, a lot of VERILOG code for irregular structures may lead to just a few gates. In particular, it is difficult to evaluate indirect synthesis. Here the result may be very compact as with the asynchronous bus protocol of the previous section, but also very complex as with the control logic for the caches.

For the transformation of VERILOG groups, automatic logic synthesis has turned out to be a useful tool. Its application depends, however, in particular on the question of whether the group is time critical and contains regular structures. For example, for a `case` statement containing a few lines assigning different constants to a register, the following cases may be distinguished.

- The group is not time critical, and there is no regularity. In this case, manual and automatic synthesis may result in an equal effort of two to three hours.
- The group is not time critical, but there are regular structures. In this case, one might synthesize the regular core automatically and duplicate it

manually afterwards. The effort may again be in the range of two to three hours.

- The group is time critical. In such cases, manual design is preferred as automatic logic synthesis usually gives suboptimal results. The effort of transformation is hard to estimate and may be quite high.

The indirect transformation may require maximal effort, as there are few learning effects. Overall it may be better to invest more time in an HDL model that is easily translatable into schematics. The reasons are obvious: HDL is more flexible in simulation and verification. Errors can be found more easily as compared to schematics.

The following statement may be taken as a modeling guideline. It may pay off to develop an HDL model – possibly an additional one – that is close to a future gate implementation; the additional time may be less than the effort in translating a difficult HDL model into schematics.

8.7 Simulation and Optimization of the Gate Model

In the previous sections we have learned to synthesize graphic schematics from small groups of the VERILOG Coarse Structure Model and to compose them to a hierarchically structured Gate Model. Also this model can be simulated in all phases of its design. In addition to a *logic simulation* as was performed with the Coarse Structure Model, namely the verification of results synchronously with a rather abstract clock CP, there is now also a true *timing simulation*. The library cells of the silicon producer offer for the first time real and realistic delays. These delays will only be modified by a future placement and routing and resulting layout wires, which again has to be checked in a *post-layout simulation*.

Also the Gate Model could have been developed completely in VERILOG, which also offers constructs for gates and their delays. Thinking in graphic schematics, however, has the following advantages.

- The design of small schematics is easier, as a graphic representation corresponds to the imagination of the designer.

- At least in small schematics, functional properties and signal flow at the gate level are better understandable; larger schematics, however, require a hierarchic structure, whose understanding is more related to HDL thinking.

- Simulation, analysis, and optimization can often be better displayed for schematics, for instance, by graphically indicating signals at netlist nodes or by highlighting time critical paths.

A major justification of schematics lies also in the fact that they can be *retranslated* into VERILOG easily. Thus arbitrary schematics can be embedded into the original Coarse Structure Model by exchanging them with corresponding modules or groups.

8.7.1 Verification

In addition to the direct check of one or several schematics, verification with respect to the counterpart in the Coarse Structure Model is even more important. Figure 8.32 shows a conical extract of the hierarchy tree of the Gate Model. The top module CHIP contains among others submodules IDU, ALU, and MAU. The ALU again contains, among others, the units ARITHMETIC, SHIFT, and LOGIC, where SHIFT divides into ROLVAL, PATTERN, etc. The complete tree, by the way, can be found in Section H5.1 of the expert volume.

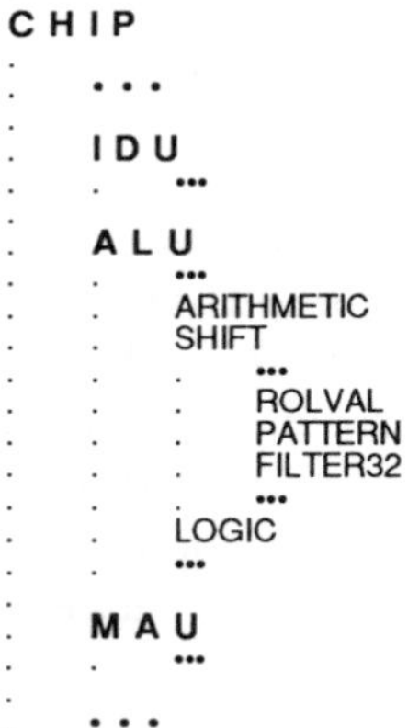

Figure 8.32 Conical extract of the Gate Model hierarchy

As mentioned before, every module and every partial tree can be retranslated into VERILOG. This enables numerous verifications. First of all, for small units like SHIFT, a small VERILOG test frame can be constructed, in which both module SHIFT of the Coarse Structure Model and the retranslated schematic SHIFT are embedded and tested for equal results. Only very small units like ROLVAL have no explicit counterpart in the Coarse Structure Model.

But we may also simulate a large part of the Coarse Structure Model, even the model itself, with a fixed test program and then exchange small units like

SHIFT or larger partial trees like the ALU, until finally the complete retranslated Gate Model has to produce the same results in the VERILOG system environment (although this is quite computation intensive). Suitable programs evaluate and compare corresponding simulation results. By the way, CHIP is the top module of the Gate Model, because a model of the system environment is not meaningful at the gate level.

8.7.2 Optimization

After logic verification, or even in parallel with it, the design is further optimized. We try to reduce the number of gates and runtime. Both criteria were, of course, considered already before.

We can now determine the output load of various gates and choose suitable drivers. Flip-flops can be combined for a reduction of clock load. Appropriate tools may balance signal delays and find critical paths.

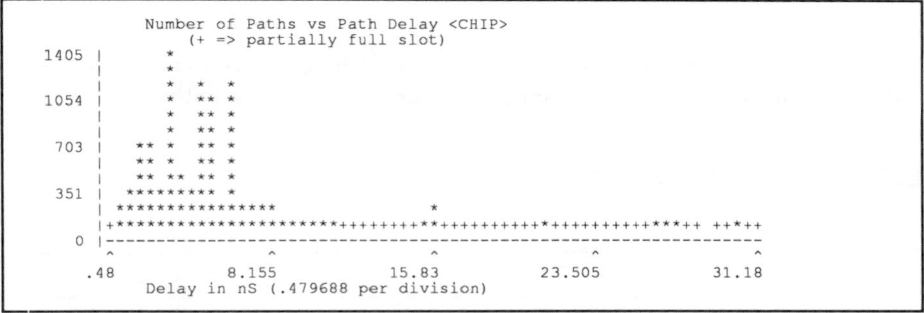

Figure 8.33 Balance of delays

In the example of Figure 8.33, the number of paths of module CHIP is shown against delay. One may recognize quite a few short paths, but also some longer ones that are distributed relatively evenly up to the maximal delay. An optimization of the longest paths would require a lot of effort. Only if the longest paths were just a small group separated from the next paths by a large gap, would their optimization pay off.

Interesting paths may also be listed in detail as in Figure 8.34. Every line describes a cell of the critical path. In the first column, there are the cells from the library cell to the root of the tree, the second column shows port names, the third the cell name. Rise and fall time are given in parentheses as the sum from the beginning up to the present instance.

```
U31/U0/U4.1                Q      FD1SLP      (1.30/1.12)
U31/U4/U0/U0.1             A      IVAP
U31/U4/U0/U0.1             Z      IVAP        (1.74/2.02)
U31/U4/U0/U6               B      AN4P
U31/U4/U0/U6               Z      AN4P        (2.80/2.91)
U31/U4/U0/U7               A      MUX21LP
U31/U4/U0/U7               Z      MUX21LP     (3.36/3.36)
U31/U4/U0/U12.3            A      MUX21LP
U31/U4/U0/U12.3            Z      MUX21LP     (4.09/4.23)
U31/U4/U1                  S16    CFC1020B
U31/U4/U1                  ZN31   CFC1020B    (9.41/10.25)
U31/U4/U4/U14/U0.7/U4      D      MUX21CBM
U31/U4/U4/U14/U0.7/U4      Z      MUX21CBM    (10.64/9.89)
U31/U7/U5/U0.1             D13    MUX24P
U31/U7/U5/U0.1             Z3     MUX24P      (11.34/10.69)
U31/U9/U8/U0.7             B      MUX21HP
U31/U9/U8/U0.7             Z      MUX21HP     (12.59/12.36)

[...]

U14/U14/U5                 A      MUX21LP
U14/U14/U5                 Z      MUX21LP     (25.95/25.94)
U14/U14/U6                 A      IVAP
U14/U14/U6                 Z      IVAP        (26.44/26.54)
U28/U2/U3                  A      IVA
U28/U2/U3                  Z      IVA         (26.79/26.78)
U28/U2/U16                 A      AN2P
U28/U2/U16                 Z      AN2P        (27.88/27.74)
U22/U1/U1                  A      IVAP
U22/U1/U1                  Z      IVAP        (28.88/29.13)
U22/U1/U2/U2               A      MUX21LP
U22/U1/U2/U2               Z      MUX21LP     (29.67/29.53)
U22/U1/U2/U4               TE     FD2SLP      (31.17/31.18)
```

Figure 8.34 Example of a critical path

Using several such lists, common subpaths of long paths may be detected, whose optimization may simultaneously shorten many long paths.

8.7.3 Timing Simulation

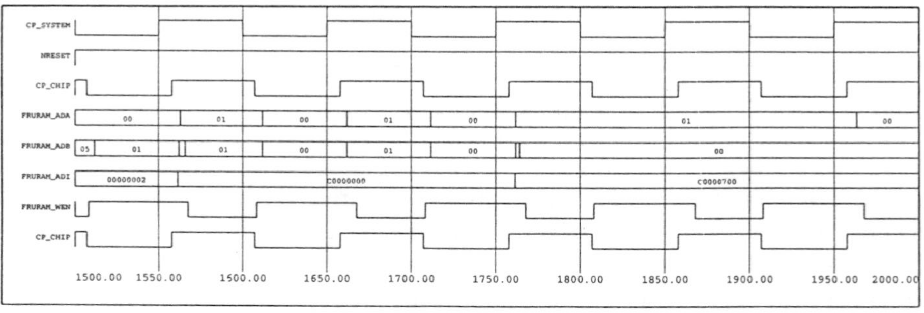

Figure 8.35 Timing analysis of write access of module FRU

Realistic time behavior of signals can be represented graphically. One can verify the timing at critical points. Figure 8.35 shows the signal behavior for accesses to the register file of the forwarding and register unit FRU. The first signal CP_SYSTEM shows the system clock external to the model. Due to the necessary input buffers, the signal appears in the model as a delayed CP_CHIP.

The FRU register file has two read ports and one write port. The latter one has an address bus FRURAM_ADA, its data bus is called FRURAM_ADI. FRURAM_WEN is the low-active write enable signal.

One can see that the negative edge of FRURAM_WEN is delayed as compared to CP_CHIP. The reason is a delay component, which has to be dimensioned properly. The timing is correct if FRURAM_ADA remains stable during the complete low phase of the write enable signal. One can check in Figure 8.35 that this condition holds.

9 Testing, Testability, Tester, and Testboard

The highlight (or bottom) of our design is without doubt the production of prototypes and their successful (or failed) *test*. As we intend to check our chip with test programs that are as good as possible, we introduce in Section 9.1 the notion of *fault coverage* as a criterion. Not only at the silicon producer, but also in our lab, the circuit is analyzed in a tester (automated test equipment, *ATE*, Section 9.2). A successful test depends not only on good test programs but also on well *testable* circuits. In Section 9.3, we explain *design for testability* as a set of structures like *scanpath*, an intelligent "checksum" called *signature analysis*, test circuits for memories and pad drivers, as well as test units for process parameters permitting estimations of circuit speed.

Especially in the case of our microprocessor, for which we have worked out several HDL models, it makes sense to extract from former simulations functional test patterns as part of a consistent test strategy (Section 9.4). The approximately 34 000 test patterns can obviously not be listed in Section 9.5, but we will explain the basic procedure and the practical transformation into suitable test data.

Conducting the test in an automated tester and the results to be obtained are summarized in Section 9.6 – these results are, of course, not disclosed here. For the Coarse Structure Model of TOOBSIE, about 3 instructions per second can be simulated on a workstation. Thus a program of only 30 seconds on a 25 MIPS machine would result in a simulation time of about eight years. Therefore, benchmarks with several billions of instructions can only be performed on the real processor. In Sections 9.7 and 9.8, a real action on the testboard is treated.

This chapter is based on [Blinzer 1994, Telkamp 1995] as well as on [Stuckenberg 1992].

9.1 Fault Models and Fault Coverage

We want to develop *good* test programs discovering every potential *production fault*. A production fault exists, if the chip differs from its nominal behavior. Even though a designer is always interested in *design faults* – and large designs always contain logical faults – we will only consider circuit faults after production at this point. We also exclude *temporary* faults, as they can only be approximated with intensive statistical tests. Dynamic faults, for example run time problems, will be considered later. We now focus on permanent static oberservable faults.

On the one hand, the wealth of possible technical reasons is quite large, and we do not know the technological details of the silicon producer, his transistors, masks, dimensions, chemical processes, etc. On the other hand, the behavior of a large chip is far too complex to be tested completely. However, if we test somehow incompletely, we do not know *how* incomplete or good our test was.

Therefore, we now consider abstract faults or fault models that are separated from the transistor level and the given technology on the one hand, and can easily be computed from logical circuit functions on the other hand. A fault model produces finitely many abstract faults for every circuit in a unique way, we may therefore define the quality of a test program as its *fault coverage*: it is the percentage of actually observable faults related to all possible faults. A set of test vectors (test stimuli with nominal results) has a fault coverage of 70%, if for 100 possible faults of the fault model, 70 can be found by application of the test vectors.

In practical work, mainly the first of the following two fault models has turned out to be applicable and sufficient:

- the *stuck-at fault model*: a stuck-at fault at 0 (*stuck-at-0*) exists, if an input or output of a gate permanently has value 0; in the same way, stuck-at-1 is defined;
- the *bridging fault model*: two signal wires are permanently connected.

Stuck-at faults can easily be considered in a simulation. By this model, for instance, bridges between signal wires and supply voltages are detected. In many cases, the disconnection of a signal produces a similar fault, therefore, these faults are usually also covered. Signal disconnections, however, may lead in redundant circuits to dynamic faults, although the circuit remains statically correct.

In contrast, bridging faults are hard to consider in simulations. To analyze the implications of a bridging between two neighboring wires, we need to know not only the employed gates and their connections, but also the precise routing of all signals. We first have to determine the directly neighboring signals and group them pairwise, before a simulation makes sense. A bridging will only result in a fault if the signals of a group differ; therefore, two simulations are necessary for every group.

It may be difficult to obtain the information on the layout routing, as the exact position of the gates and their real wiring usually are computed only by the silicon producer. Therefore, this fault model is usually not considered by fault simulators and test pattern generators.

We can now manually or automatically develop test data to detect the modeled faults. In assuming a single such fault, input data have to be determined which drive the faulty connection with a value not possible in the fault case. This procedure can be demonstrated for stuck-at-0 faults using the two NAND gates of Figure 9.1.

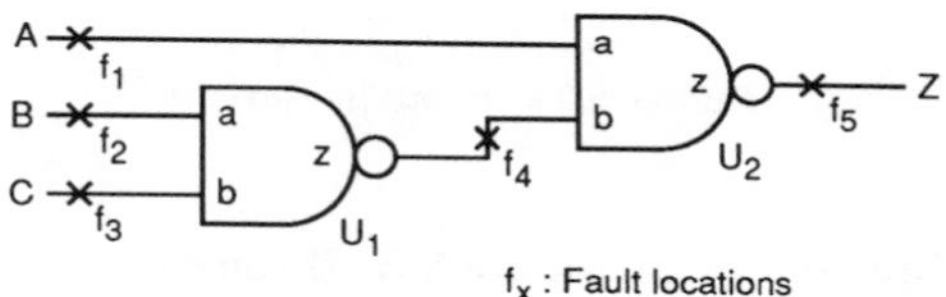

Figure 9.1 Possible stuck-at faults

To detect stuck-at fault f1, on the one hand, values 0 and 1 have to be fed to input A and on the other hand, B or C have to receive a 0, in order to observe the change of A at Z. The test of fault f1 includes a test of f5, as Z will reach states 1 and 0 in the fault-free case. For a test of f2 and f3, input A has to be brought to state 1 and B and C must be 0 and 1, while C or B are kept at 1. The tests of f2 and f3 include the test of f4, as the state of Z depends on the result computed by U1 and has to reach values 0 and 1. For a complete test of all stuck-at faults of this circuit, the five test vectors of Table 9.2 are therefore sufficient.

Test vector				Faults detected				
A	B	C	Z	f_1	f_2	f_3	f_4	f_5
0	0	0	1	sa1				sa0
1	0	0	0	sa0				sa1
1	0	1	0		sa1		sa0	sa1
1	1	1	1		sa0	sa0	sa1	sa0
1	1	0	0			sa1	sa0	sa1

sa0: stuck-at-0 sa1: stuck-at-1

Table 9.2 Test vectors for the circuit of Figure 9.1

For a complete functional test (exhaustive test), the three given inputs would result in $2^3=8$ test vectors, but no additional faults could be detected this way.

Although bridging faults between neighboring wires are hard to simulate, we want to consider this fault type. With the simplifying assumption that this fault type occurs mainly in signal buses running usually in parallel in the layout, the development of test data is relatively simple. The signal bus is tested with a 01-vector 010101... and a 10-vector 1010101... . Thus all bridges between neighboring wires can be detected, which are ordered by the layout according to their bits.

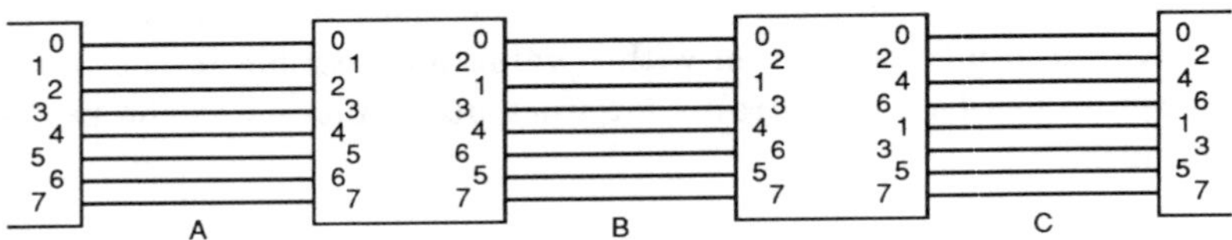

Figure 9.3 Various bus layouts

For different bus layouts as in Figure 9.3, these patterns are not suited. As opposed to bus section A, the wires in B and C are not in order, therefore, the 01/10-vectors detect in B only three of seven possible bridges, in C just one. To detect all bridging faults of a bus independently of the bus layout, the test vectors should not only put every wire to states 0 and 1, but they should also produce for every bus wire a difference to all other bus signals.

An obvious possibility is to use diagonal patterns that always put a particular bus wire to a state different from all others. If the stimuli are sorted by bit position of the distinguished signal in a matrix, they form a diagonal. This is called a *walking zero test* or *walking one test*. A disadvantage is the high number of test vectors necessary. For theoreticians, a different possibility is an extension of 01/10 patterns by elements of the formal languages

$$\{ (02^n\ 12^n)^+ : n=1,2,\ldots\} \quad \text{and} \quad \{ (12^n\ 02^n)^+ : n=1,2,\ldots\}$$

For a bus of m signals, the additional patterns correspond to language elements with $n < \log_2 m$ assigning values to all bus signals (exceeding digits being ignored). The resulting patterns test the bus for bridging faults in groups of 2n bits and do recognize the same faults as diagonal patterns. As opposed to m diagonal vectors, only at most $2+\log_2 m$ vectors are required in this case. The logarithmic order of magnitude makes this pattern type interesting for large signal buses. The reduction of test vectors is paid for by an information loss on the exact fault position. For a bridging test of an arbitrary 8-bit bus, the test patterns of Table 9.4 are suited.

Diagonal patterns	$10 / 0^{2^n} 1^{2^n}$	$01 / 1^{2^n} 0^{2^n}$
1 0 0 0 0 0 0 0	1 0 1 0 1 0 1 0	0 1 0 1 0 1 0 1
0 1 0 0 0 0 0 0	0 1 0 1 0 1 0 1	1 0 1 0 1 0 1 0
0 0 1 0 0 0 0 0	0 0 1 1 0 0 1 1	1 1 0 0 1 1 0 0
0 0 0 1 0 0 0 0	0 0 0 0 1 1 1 1	1 1 1 1 0 0 0 0
0 0 0 0 1 0 0 0		
0 0 0 0 0 1 0 0		
0 0 0 0 0 0 1 0		
0 0 0 0 0 0 0 1		

Table 9.4 Layout independent test patterns for bridging faults

Test programs developed for fault models with a good fault coverage are *structure oriented* tests as they consider the gate level structure. They do not consider the circuit specification, in contrast to *function oriented* tests ("the processor executes a machine program correctly"). For instance, a non-required gate may be detected in a structural test as a fault but not in a functional test. Conversely, a functional fault is possibly not detected even under a fault coverage of 100% in a structural test.

This does not exclude functional tests from a design simulation producing important parts of a structure oriented test program. This, however, depends on the circuit type. In the case of our RISC processor, this strategy has turned out to be of advantage (Sections 9.4 and 9.5).

9.2 Automated Tester (ATE)

A tester applies test patterns to a chip and observes its reactions. It can also measure various chip data like maximal clock frequency, current requirement, and slew rate. Parameters such as voltage stability or electro-magnetic stability may also be of interest, but are not considered here.

A tester (*automated test equipment, ATE*) is a sensitive device. In general, it works by the *stored-response principal*. The test patterns are divided in phases of equal length (*test cycles*). In every test cycle, the inputs of the circuit to be tested (device under test, *DUT*) are assigned *input test patterns*, and the outputs are compared at strobe times with nominal values (*output test patterns*). "Stored" refers to the output test patterns stored in the ATE, which are compared with the circuit "response".

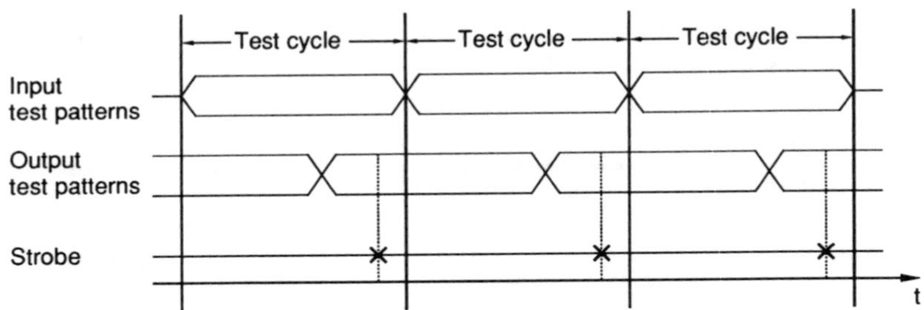

Figure 9.5 Test cycles of stored-response tester

Figure 9.5 shows three test cycles with three strobe points. The coarse resolution of the test cycles basically distinguishes ATE testing from logic design simulation, where every level change may always be observed at any circuit node. More than one level change within one test cycle cannot be detected directly by a stored-response ATE.

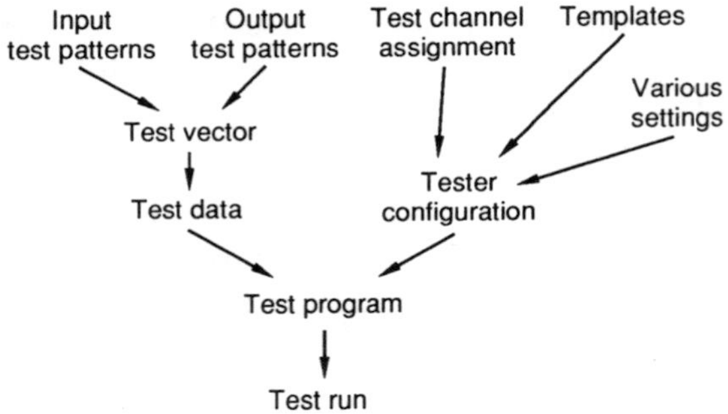

Figure 9.6 Development of a test run

According to Figure 9.6, all input and output test patterns are composed in every test cycle to form a *test vector*. Many subsequent test vectors constitute the *test data*, which in connection with a *tester configuration* described below result in the actual *test program*. Its application is denoted as a *test run*.

9.2.1 Set-up and Operation of Tester

Figure 9.7 shows a simplified block diagram of a typical stored-response tester. For the test of processor TOOBSIE, we have used an LV512 of Tektronix. The tester includes controller, clock generator, format generators, a test vector memory, a comparator logic, a DUT interface, and a power supply. Peripherals such as terminal, disc, hard disc, Ethernet, and RS-232 interface enable input and storage of test patterns.

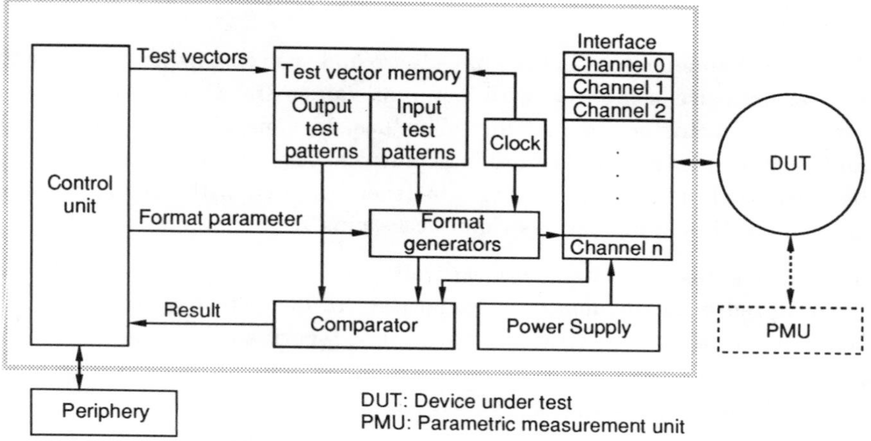

Figure 9.7 Structure of stored-response tester

The circuit to be tested is connected with the ATE interface by a test socket using a special board (DUT card). For different chips, several DUT cards are required, which can easily be exchanged.

The interface offers up to 256 test channels depending on the ATE version. Each test channel is connected with the test pattern memory and the comparator logic and can be configured as input or output. Moreover, the DUT power supply can be taken from additional interface ports.

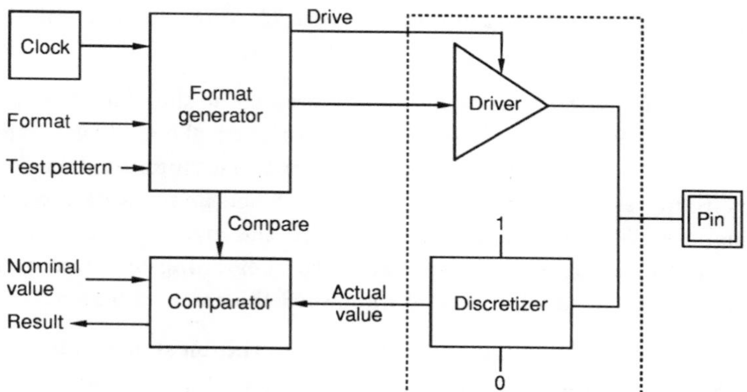

Figure 9.8 Structure of a test channel

Figure 9.8 shows the schematic structure of a test channel. It can be applied in modes *force*, *compare*, or *mask*. If the driver of a test channel is turned on, the connected DUT input is supplied with patterns from the test pattern memory (mode force).

If the test channel output is high impedance and the comparator logic is active, chip outputs are compared with nominal values (mode compare). Analog voltages are transformed into digital values. In general, a threshhold value can be defined: voltages below are interpreted as logic-0, voltages above as 1. In the third mode mask, the circuit is neither supplied with test patterns nor compared with nominal values ("don't care pins").

The various test channels are controlled by *format generators* that are synchronized by a common clock generator. To every test channel, one of at most 16 format generators can be assigned permanently, which activate drivers or comparator logic by a programmed scheme. The assignment is static and holds for a complete test run.

A meaningful extension of the tester is a parametric measurement unit (PMU). This component permits high precision measurement of current requirement of the complete circuit or of particular pins. The PMU is an important tool for chip testing. A significant deviation in current requirement indicates a production fault. Many faulty chips can thus be detected in advance.

9.2.2 Formats and Templates

ATE channels are connected with the DUT pins on the DUT card. As a considerable simplification, names can be assigned to test channels in an ATE program. For bus structures, test channels may be grouped, and octal or hexadecimal values may be assigned to these groups. This makes test patterns more readable. The pin assignment of test channels is part of the tester configuration.

As not all actions within one test cycle take place at the same time, a stored-response tester offers format generators mentioned above. These components not only control the test channel functions but also support delay or modification of input test patterns. Moreover, the strobe point is defined, at which output signals of the chip are compared with the given output test patterns. Input test patterns are usually applied at the beginning of a test cycle, while output comparison normally takes place toward the end of a test cycle.

Format generators offer various format types, the most frequent ones being summarized in Figures 9.9 and 9.10. Input test patterns usually have format NRZ (non-return to zero). These are applied to DUT inputs at the beginning of a test cycle without delay and remain constant during the complete cycle. If signals are to be delayed, there is format DNRZ (delayed non-return to zero). With an additional format parameter, delay time can be set for every clock generator individually.

Symbol	Name	Explanation	Pattern	Signal
NRZ	Non-return to zero	Pattern at begin of test cycle	0 1	
DNRZ	Delayed non-return to zero	Pattern delayed after begin of test cycle	0 1	
RTZ	Return to zero	Pattern returns to zero	0 1	
RTO	Return to one	Pattern returns to one	0 1	

Figure 9.9 Formats for input test patterns

Symbol	Name	Explanation	Pattern	Signal
C	Compare	Output compared with nominal value at one time	0 1	
WC	Window compare	Output compared with nominal value during time interval	0 1	

Figure 9.10 Formats for output test patterns

Formats RTZ (return to zero) and RTO (return to one) enable, for example, a simple clock generation avoiding two test vectors per cycle. This would reduce the maximal test frequency by one half. After a preset delay time, the format generator applies the input test pattern under RTZ to a desired test channel and resets it after a given amount of time to zero.

For the circuit outputs, there are two formats (Figure 9.10) controlling the comparator logic. It compares the output signals either at a defined strobe point or during a defined time interval. With the latter option, certain hazards can be detected (here: short and unwanted signal pulses resulting from asynchronous switching).

The combined set of formats of all signals of a test cycle is denoted as a *template*. A template thus determines the configuration of all format generators in a test cycle by the format parameters. If some signals require different formats (for instance, bidirectional pins), several templates have to be applied.

For the test program, one of the predefined templates is first of all assigned to every test vector. This configures the test channels at the beginning of a test cycle. They are part of the tester configuration also including channel assignment and other parameters like clock frequency, threshold voltage, power voltage, and maximal current consumption.

If the test of a circuit is repeated with changing format parameters, this is called a *parametric test* (not to be confused with the parameter tests of the PMU). For example, the strobe point could move step by step. The earliest value still testing the chip successfully indicates a minimal run time delay. Some test devices also permit the stepwise change of two parameters within a certain interval and the graphic output as a *Schmoo plot*. For instance, the maximal run time delay depending on power voltage can be determined.

9.3 Design for Testability

Even excellent test patterns are of little value if components inside of a circuit are difficult to reach or inaccessible. The components of a processor are generally not directly reachable via input and output pins of the chip, but indirectly by instruction sequences. Depending on the number of required instructions, quite long sequences of test vectors may result. For example, in a cache test based only on processor instructions, the number of actually used test vectors would not justify the large number of preparing vectors.

A waste of test vectors is unacceptable in a production test, as every vector consumes test time and test program length is quite limited. The *testability* of a circuit somehow measures the effort necessary to test components. There is the question, which actions make circuits better testable (design for testability).

Our processor TOOBSIE was equipped with additional test circuits simplifying its test considerably. Moreover, it contains test circuits according to rules of the silicon producer, which test parameters like input and output driver sensitivity and general circuit speed. There are the following six test circuits.

- test multiplexers for direct RAM and CAM access;
- a scanpath for serial access of all remaining registers;
- a signature analysis register for observation of internal control signals;
- a NAND tree for the test of input driver sensitivity;
- a central tristate enable for the test of tristate drivers;
- a process monitor PROCMON to determine process parameters and general switching speed.

Task and function of these test circuits are briefly described in the following. As they were only used in the phase of the Gate Model, they do not occur in the specification of Chapters 5–7.

Test multiplexers for memory tests and scanpath logic directly modify the gate implementation, while the other circuits operate in parallel to the processor and only observe its signals.

9.3.1 Multiplexers for Memory Test

For a direct memory test, the memory control leads completely through multiplexers switching between normal and test mode. To save test pins, input data for memory tests use the data bus, and the resulting output data use the address bus as well as a test output bus. Control is achieved by signals RTSEL, RTWEN, RTE, RTADRA, and RTADRB, whose function is explained in Table 9.11; positions X mean arbitrary bits (details in Chapter H5).

Signal	Name	Value	Function
RTADRA	RAM Test Address A	XXXXXX	Read address for RAMs RR16x5, RR16x30, RR16x32, RR32x32, and RR40x32 (Port A) Write address for RAM RR40x32 (Port A) and CAMs
RTADRB	RAM Test Address B	XXXXXX	Read address for RAM RR40x32 (Port B) Write address forRAMs RR16x5, RR16x30, RR16x32, and RR32x32
RTE	RAM Test Enable	0	Normal operation
		1	Memory test operation
RTSEL	RAM Test Select	000	ADDR_BUS = RR32x32 [RTADRA] RTOUTB = RR16x5 [RTADRA]
		001	ADDR_BUS = RR16x30 [RTADRA] RTOUTB = RR16x5 [RTADRA]
		01X	ADDR_BUS = RR40x32 [RTADRA] RTOUTB = RR16x5 [RTADRA]
		100	ADDR_BUS = RR16x32 [RTADRA] RTOUTB = RR40x32 [RTADRB]
		101	ADDR_BUS = {BTCCAM, MPCCAM} RTOUTB = RR40x32 [RTADRB]
		11X	ADDR_BUS = RR40x32 [RTADRA] RTOUTB = RR40x32 [RTADRB]
RTWEN	RAM Test Write Enable Negative	0	Write accesses
		1	Read accesses

Table 9.11 Signals of memory tests

Note that write accesses to memory RR40x32 take only place during CP=1, write accesses to the remaining memories only during CP=0. The combination with multiplexers for memory test is shown in Figure 9.12.

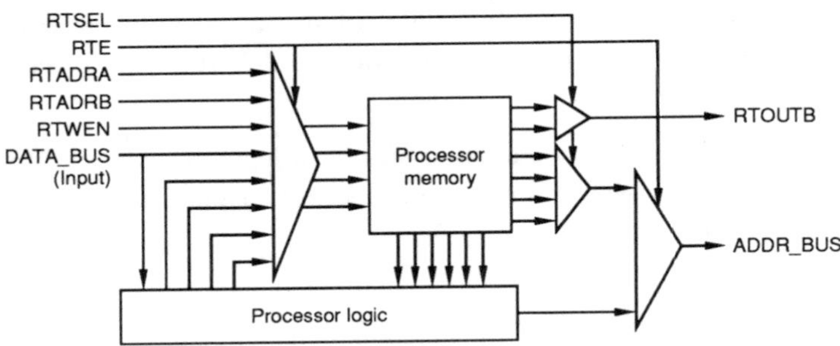

Figure 9.12 Test multiplexers

9.3.2 Scanpath

Access to registers outside RAMs or CAMs is supported by a scanpath as the second test circuit. A scanpath is one of the most efficient test circuits of all.

The inputs of the registers concerned, in our case D-registers, are switched by 2-to-1 multiplexers between normal and test mode. These multiplexers are integrated in scannable D-registers. In normal mode, the registers operate as usual as buffers and drivers between combinational logic (Section 11.4). In test mode, the registers are switched to form a long shift register in such a way that, aside from signal SCAN for the test mode, only two additional test pins are required for input SCANIN and output SCANOUT of the shift register.

In our case, the scanpath is 944 bits long and therefore not well suited for production test, because in the test mode, the complete scanpath has to be loaded serially. One might split this long scanpath into several parallel parts, but in our case, this turned out to be unnecessary, because the registers can relatively easy be controlled by instruction sequences. The scanpath is useful for reading and changing the complete internal processor state when searching for faults. If in spite of a successful production test, the behavior turned out to be faulty, the scanpath would help in searching for the reason. The structure of a scanpath and its operation modes are explained in Figure 9.13.

9.3.3 Signature Analysis

Signature analysis as the third test circuit of TOOBSIE supports a permanent indirect observation of internal processor control signals. Foundations of signature analysis are explained in [Wojtkowiak 1988], for example.

In our case, signature analysis is implemented by a 107-bit shift register corresponding to the primitive polynomial

$$x^{107} + x^7 + x^5 + x^3 + x^2 + x + 1$$

of binary arithmetic. In every cycle, the control signals to be observed are combined with the bits of the shift register by an addition modulo 2 (XOR). As compared with check sum methods, the probability of detecting faults of more than one bit is significantly increased.

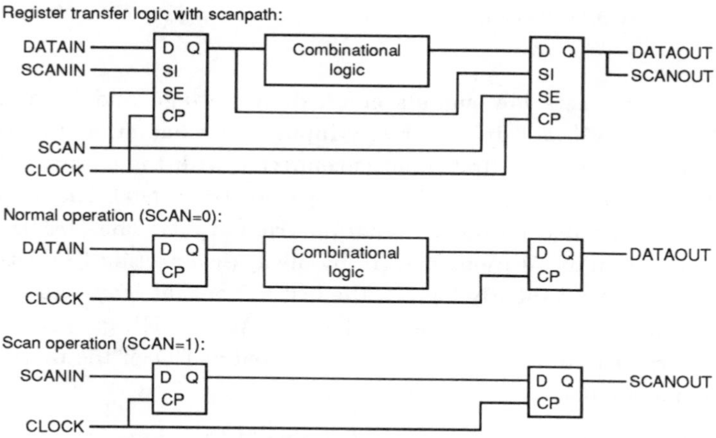

Figure 9.13 Operation modes of a scanpath

Aside from a normal operation mode, a signature register has a scan mode activated by signature scan enable SIGSE and permitting as for a scanpath a serial access to register contents by input SIGSI (signature scan in) and output SIGSO (signature scan out). In both modes, the output is connected with the least significant bit 0 of the signature register, such that the signature may be controlled in the normal and in the test mode. The signals monitored include register addresses of instructions, C4_BUS, WORK signals of pipeline stages, status of stages IF and ID, as well as cache hit signals.

The circuit also supports the principle of pseudo-random generation [Wojtkowiak 1988]. In addition to test information, it generates random numbers for replacing lines in the caches. Figure 9.14 sketches the structure of the signature register and the implementation of the polynomial.

9.3.4 Test Circuits of the Silicon Vendor

The remaining three test circuits, NAND tree, central tristate enable, and process monitor do not work completely independently and are given by the producer LSI Logic [LSI 1989]. They basically test the electrical specifications.

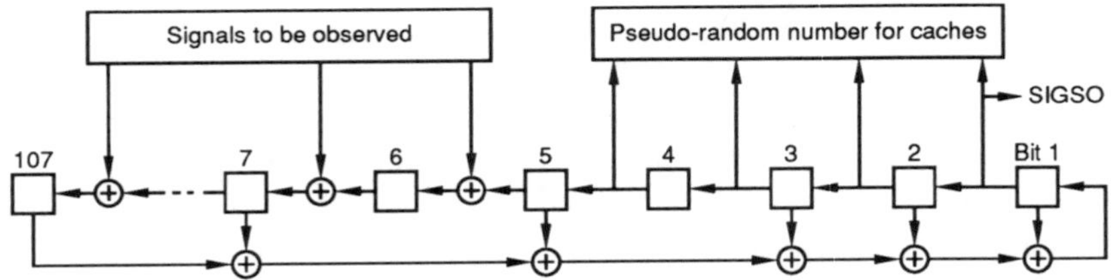

Figure 9.14 Simplified structure of the signature register of TOOBSIE

The NAND tree tests low signals of maximal voltage and high signals of minimal voltage of input drivers. Every input driver has an additional NAND gate with two inputs. The first input is connected with the output of the input driver, the second one is the test input PI (parametric input). The output of the NAND gate is the test output PO (parametric output). The NAND tree is a serial combination of all input drivers by always connecting PO with PI. The first PI input is permanently logic-1, the last PO output leads via the process monitor PROCMON to a test output of the chip. As a NAND gate either outputs a 1, if the driver is 0, or the value of PI inverted at PO, if the driver is 1, an observation of a particular driver is possible.

The PI input of every driver to be tested should thus have value 1, which is always the case for the first driver and is achieved for the remainig drivers by a 0 at the output of the preceding driver. Furthermore, the outputs of the following drivers in the NAND tree have to be 1. Under these conditions, a logical change of the observed input is shifted to the test output.

For circuits with bidirectional drivers, their input components are included in the NAND tree like the other inputs. Here it is necessary to set the output components of the drivers to tristate to avoid conflicts betweeen input and output data. This is accomplished by a special input for central tristate enable controlling all tristate drivers (TN in our case). This input is implemented by driver type ICPTNU that moves input data inverted to the test NAND but is not included in the NAND tree (Section 8.1).

A 0 at this input sets the connected output drivers to high impedance. This input is also used for the tristate test checking, whether all tristate outputs can be brought to a high impedance state. The PO output of the ICPTNU driver controls the process monitor PROCMON. The PI input of the ICPTNU driver is 1, such that the input data do not appear at the PO output.

Test circuit PROCMON has four inputs A, E, N, and S, an output Z and three operation modes. In the first mode activated by S=0, which is not used in our case, input N is transferred unchanged to Z. Outside the parametric test operation, the output can thus carry other signals. For TOOBSIE, inputs S and N of PROCMON are permanently 1.

In the second operation mode (S=1, E=0), input A is delayed and inverted by a chain of 90 NOR3/IVAP gates and moved to output Z (Section 8.1). As E is controlled by output PO of the ICPTNU driver, the NAND tree test is active in this operation mode. The 90 gates delay determines the speed of PMOS and NMOS transistors. Rising and falling signal edges in the NOR3/IVAP gates pass various serial and parallel circuits of NMOS and PMOS transistors resulting in different delays in PROCMON.

The third operation mode of PROCMON is basically a variation of the second one and is active for 1 at inputs S and E. Two different delays of input A are XORed at output Z. The first delay comes from the 90 NOR3/IVAP gates used above, the second from a serial chain of 30 standard inverters IV. Due to the shorter signal delay of the inverter chain, changes of input A result in pulses at output Z allowing the estimation of switching speed.

Figure 9.15 summarizes NAND tree, tristate enable, and process monitor.

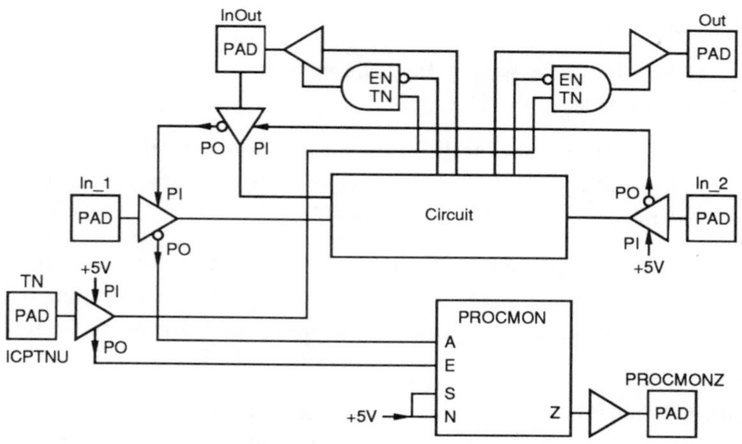

Figure 9.15 Test circuits of the silicon producer

The NAND tree starts at the input driver of pad In_2, leads via the input components of the bidirectional driver of pad InOut to the input driver of In_1 and ends at input A of PROCMON. The input driver of pad TN (ICPTNU) leads signal TN to the PROCMON circuits and to the TN inputs of the tristate drivers of pads InOut and Out. The results leave the circuit at the output driver of pad PROCMONZ.

9.4 Functional Test

From fault models, we obtain simplified logic faults, which on the one hand are abstracted enough from the mostly unknown physical reality, but on the other hand permit the development of sufficient structure oriented test programs (Section 9.1). In a tester (ATE) for circuits after production, test stimuli and observation points are restricted as compared to a simulator (Section 9.2). In a design for testability, we create a well testable circuit with components like scanpath, memory test, or signature analysis (Section 9.3). Before we turn in the next sections to the practical creation of test patterns and finally to the real test, we want to consider and repeat function oriented tests.

A function oriented test by simulation is meant to verify the circuit function before production. After production, the circuit structure is tested for production faults in a tester, which basically is independent of the circuit function. For ATE test after production, we may further distinguish between

- ATE test or production test at the silicon producer, testing – especially in mass production – every chip with as few as possible test patterns in the shortest time possible, and
- ATE test in our lab as a step towards system test, in which the circuit is embedded in a system environment.

In the first case, there are additional restrictions by the silicon producer discussed in the next section. In the second case, we are also interested in functional testing, run times, and similar things.

In our case of a microprocessor, function and structure test are related; an important fraction of test patterns can be deducted from functional tests. For test pattern development, there are various possibilities as indicated in Figure 9.16.

First of all, test patterns can be generated manually by using the specification (1). With increasing circuit complexity and particularly for pipeline based RISC processors, this method is too fault sensitive. Many operations are only executed several clock cycles after they were fetched, leading to a reduced transparency of data and address bus.

As we have stepwise refined circuit models from Interpreter Model to Coarse Structure Model to Gate Model, it is easily possible for every circuit to develop only the input test patterns and to determine the output test patterns by simulation (2) by monitoring the levels of all pins in every cycle.

Input test patterns for microprocessors are mainly based on short typical machine programs. To convert these into input test patterns, the processor models must include main memory with a program (3).

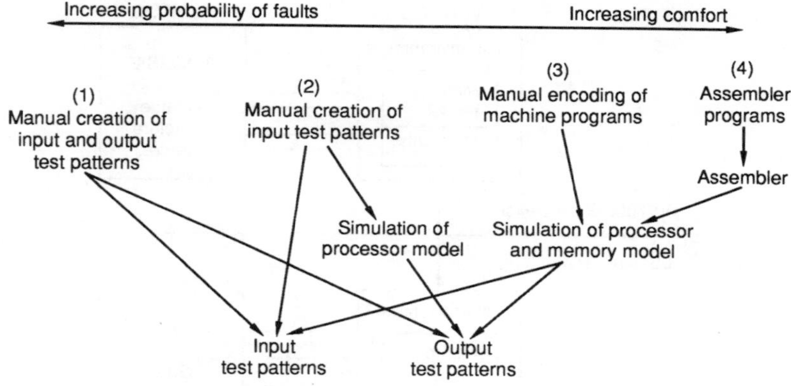

Figure 9.16 Alternatives of test pattern generation

The extension of this method consists of the inclusion of a suitable assembler producing equal or similar input test patterns for Interpreter Model, Coarse Structure Model, Gate Model, and ATE. We call this a (function oriented) *consistent test strategy*.

Each successive model and the chip itself, however, are more detailed and more powerful than its predecessor model, resulting in additional test patterns. For example, the Coarse Structure Model also contains caches, the Gate Model also a scanpath, and the chip has actual electrical and physical properties.

These models and their simulations are presented in Chapters 5, 🖫2, and H3 for the Interpreter, in Chapters 7, 🖫3, and H4 for the Coarse Structure Model, and in 8 and H5 for the Gate Model.

With Gate Model simulation, also parameters like operation voltage or temperature may be considered. With limited precision, also the maximal clock frequency to be expected can be determined. Once the circuit is placed and routed, there are wire lengths and capacitive loads for particular gates influencing the post-layout simulation, which permits a more exact timing prediction.

In almost every CAD environment for the development of real large circuits, there are hurdles and detours. In the given case, there was a change from the Coarse Structure Model in the HDL VERILOG to the Gate Model with a simulation environment of the silicon producer. In principle, it would be no problem to design also this part in VERILOG, but the silicon vendor has good legal and practical reasons to insist on his reference simulator.

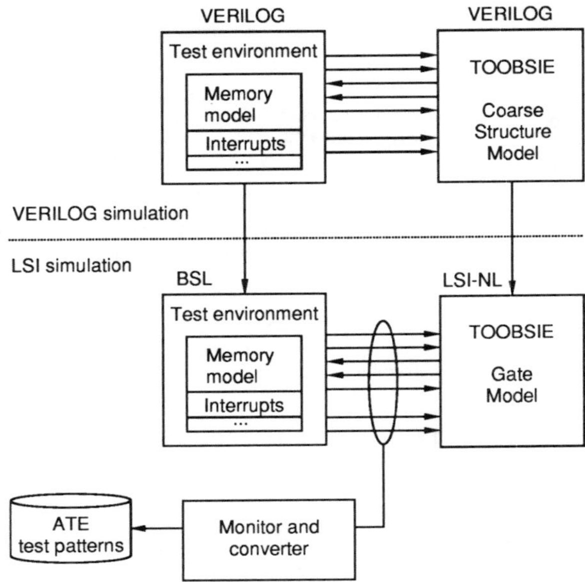

Figure 9.17 Extraction of ATE test patterns

```
*   N                                      N N I   N B          S S S S   R
*   R DATA                                 M I R   H U          C C I I R T
*C  S 33222222222222111111111110000000000  H R I   L S CONFIG   A I S S T W                         T
*P  T 10987654321098765432109876543210     S Q D   T P 43210    N N E I E N RTS RTADRA RTADRB N
*-----------------------------------------------------------------------------------------------------
  1 0 zzzzzzzzzzzzzzzzzzzzzzzzzzzzzzzz 1 1 000 1 0 00000  0 0 0 0 0 1 000 000000 000000 1
  1 0 zzzzzzzzzzzzzzzzzzzzzzzzzzzzzzzz 1 1 000 1 0 00000  0 0 0 0 0 1 000 000000 000000 1
  1 0 zzzzzzzzzzzzzzzzzzzzzzzzzzzzzzzz 1 1 000 1 0 00000  0 0 0 0 0 1 000 000000 000000 1
  1 0 zzzzzzzzzzzzzzzzzzzzzzzzzzzzzzzz 1 1 000 1 0 00000  0 0 0 0 0 1 000 000000 000000 1
  1 0 zzzzzzzzzzzzzzzzzzzzzzzzzzzzzzzz 1 1 000 1 0 00000  0 0 0 0 0 1 000 000000 000000 1
* It follows the first VOS instruction
  1 1 10110000000000000000000000000010 0 1 000 1 0 00000  0 0 0 0 0 1 000 000000 000000 1
  1 1 10110000000000000000000000000010 0 1 000 1 0 00000  0 0 0 0 0 1 000 000000 000000 1
  1 1 10110000000000000000000000000010 1 1 000 1 0 00000  0 0 0 0 0 1 000 000000 000000 1
  1 1 11100000000011100000000000000000 0 1 000 1 0 00000  0 0 0 0 0 1 000 000000 000000 1
*...
* OR instruction
  1 1 01000100000001000000000000000000 0 1 000 1 0 00000  0 0 0 0 0 1 000 000000 000000 1
  1 1 01000100000001000000000000000000 0 1 000 1 0 00000  0 0 0 0 0 1 000 000000 000000 1
  1 1 01000100000001000000000000000000 1 1 000 1 0 00000  0 0 0 0 0 1 000 000000 000000 1
  1 1 00001110000010000000000000001000 0 1 000 1 0 00000  0 0 0 0 0 1 000 000000 000000 1
  1 1 00001110000010000000000000001000 0 1 000 1 0 00000  0 0 0 0 0 1 000 000000 000000 1
*...
* HALT instruction
  1 1 11111111000000000000000000000000 1 1 000 1 0 00000  0 0 0 0 0 1 000 000000 000000 1
  1 1 00000000000000000000000000000000 0 1 000 1 0 00000  0 0 0 0 0 1 000 000000 000000 1
  1 1 00000000000000000000000000000000 0 1 000 1 0 00000  0 0 0 0 0 1 000 000000 000000 1
  1 1 00000000000000000000000000000000 1 1 000 1 0 00000  0 0 0 0 0 1 000 000000 000000 1
  1 1 11111111000000000000000000000000 0 1 000 1 0 00000  0 0 0 0 0 1 000 000000 000000 1
  1 1 11111111000000000000000000000000 0 1 000 1 0 00000  0 0 0 0 0 1 000 000000 000000 1
  1 1 11111111000000000000000000000000 1 1 000 1 0 00000  0 0 0 0 0 1 000 000000 000000 1
  1 1 zzzzzzzzzzzzzzzzzzzzzzzzzzzzzzzz 1 1 000 1 0 00000  0 0 0 0 0 1 000 000000 000000 1
  1 1 zzzzzzzzzzzzzzzzzzzzzzzzzzzzzzzz 1 1 000 1 0 00000  0 0 0 0 0 1 000 000000 000000 1
```

Figure 9.18 Extracted test patterns

As we do not intend to bother the reader with an additional simulation language not containing anything basically new, we restrict ourselves to

Figure 9.17 indicating the change of simulation environment. There is a "monitor" observing gate simulation and extracting ATE test patterns.

Figure 9.18 finally shows an extract of the resulting test vectors when simulating the tripling program (Figure 5.15). CP always equals 1, as in every cycle the levels are extracted after the positive clock edge.

After the reset phase lasting 5 cycles with a high impedance data bus, the first instruction is executed by the operating system; the bit pattern at the data bus therefore does not yet constitute the first instruction of the application program. This happens afterwards, beginning with an OR instruction (44080000h). It is valid for three cycles at the data bus, as accesses to main memory simulate two wait cycles. After loading instruction HALT, the data bus shows value FF000000h. Afterwards, the test environment stops the processor, and the data bus becomes high impedance.

In the next section, the transformation of function oriented test patterns is again considered.

9.5 Extraction of Test Data

By simulating assembler programs, we have created in the previous section function oriented test programs for production test by the silicon producer and for our ATE test. This procedure is particularly fruitful in the case of our RISC processor. But even there, additional actions are required to obtain an excellent fault coverage in the sense of abstract fault models. Moreover, the silicon producer prescribes further quality assuring actions.

The second goal of this section is the preparation and adaptation of test data to the special requirements of the ATE tester.

9.5.1 Requirements on Test Patterns and Test Blocks

The silicon producer LSI Logic gives the following requirements for prototype production:

- a test block for tristate test with a test cycle of 2 000 ns corresponding to a test vector frequency of 500 kHz (test block Z);
- a test block for quiescent current with a 2 000 ns test cycle corresponding to 500 kHz (test block Y);
- a block for testing the NAND tree and the process monitor PROCMON (Section 9.3) with 2 000 ns or 500 kHz (test block P);

- a test block for testing RAM cells with 2 000 ns or 500 kHz with given test patterns (test block L);
- at most two functional test blocks with 16 000 vectors each with a test cycle of 50 ns corresponding 20 MHz (test block Y);
- a simulation of test blocks with the LSI simulation system;
- insensitivity of test patterns against signal skew of up to 4 ns due to possible runtime variations of the tester;
- insensitivity of test patterns against extension of cycle time due to varying tester speed during die selection and in final test.

The last four points ensure that all test patterns are really applicable and do not require switching speed and signal synchronization in the test which are not achieved by the tester.

Insensitivity against signal skew and test cycle extension is detected by disturbing the test patterns by a converting program ("dither and scale"). Differences in simulation between disturbed and undisturbed test patterns detect problems, which possibly prevent a faultless but too sensitive circuit from passing a test.

9.5.2 Tristate, Quiescent Current, Process, and Memory Test

In test block Z for tristate drivers, the data and address bus drivers are to be brought to a high impedance state thus checking the essential parts of the bus control unit BCU. The processor executes the following bus operations for the asynchronous and synchronous bus protocol: accesses to instructions and data, delayed and extended access, and a bus separation. We want to test accesses to words, halfwords, and bytes as well as all transitions between 0, 1, and Z for tristate output drivers.

In test block Y for measuring quiescent current, all memory elements have to be initialized completely: RAM, CAM, and registers with and without reset. While the large memories and the reset registers can easily be erased by write accesses, the remaining registers have to be brought to a unique state using instruction sequences. This includes, for instance, the filling of the branch-target cache BTC after a reset with well defined branch instructions.

For precise measurement of quiescent current, an inactive processor state is required, in which all inputs are 1.

In test block P for process parameters, sensitivity of input drivers is determined first by testing in the NAND tree the reaction to maximal voltages for 0 and minimal ones for 1. 0-levels have to be tested directly after a falling signal edge and 1-levels directly after a rising one.

After a reset, the serially connected inputs in the NAND tree are inverted step by step, one change per test vector. Afterwards, they are inverted again in the opposite order.

After the input drivers test, the process monitor is supplied with 8 test vectors. The first two test the selection logic of PROCMON, the others determine transistor speed as the main task of the process monitor. This is accomplished by different delays of signals and pulses.

Test block L for the RAM memory of TOOBSIE is given by the silicon vendor and is quite extensive.

9.5.3 Functional Test

As generally explained in the previous section, functional test blocks A and B have to test all processor components unless this was done by the previous test blocks. We want to achieve a fault coverage as high as possible. The large (and nevertheless small) number of 16 000 test vectors each permit only a rather coarse overview of the various tests in Figure 9.19.

- Test block A
  - Test of content-address memories (CAM)
  - Test of instruction fetch unit (IFU)
    - Test of valid bits of caches in RESET
    - Test of program counter calculator (PCC)
    - Test of branch decision logic (BDL)
    - Test of caches (BTC and MPC)
  - Test of arithmetic logic unit (ALU)
    - Execution of test program "alucheck"
- Test block B
  - Test of instruction decode unit (IDU)
  - Test of forwarding and register unit (FRU)
  - Test of memory access unit (MAU)
    - Execution of test program "ifmcheck"
  - Test of pipeline control unit (PCU)
    - Test of special registers
    - Test of interrupt handling
  - Tests of remaining components (signal change)
  - Tests of scan path and signature scan
  - Tests of remaining components (stuck-at-faults)

Figure 9.19 Structure of functional tests

Except for the large CAM test in the memory test mode and the scan test, the test patterns are based on instruction sequences. These were either programmed manually or extracted in the case of programs alucheck and ifmcheck by tracing appropriate simulation programs. Such test results include branch and store instructions and signature analysis.

For branch instructions it has to be considered that the test result appears at the address bus with a delay of one cycle. Store instructions may output results on data and address bus leading easily to conflicts with a busy memory and memory protection. Therefore, corresponding test outputs were programmed manually at the bit level.

Signature analysis is independent of instructions, the test result can directly be sent to the tester. This saves test vectors in some tests such as program alucheck. The probability of fault detection, however, is lower in this case.

The "tests of remaining components" increase fault coverage and were created after evaluating the previously created test patterns. A limit in the number of test vectors had to be observed.

9.5.4 Evaluation of Test Patterns

We focus on an evaluation of test programs by simulation. As we have not (yet) reached mass production of our processor TOOBSIE, statistical methods do not apply at this point.

A relatively simple evaluation of test patterns is the *toggle test*. One counts the number of circuit nodes reaching values 0 and 1 in simulation, relating this number to the total number of nodes. A toggle rate of 100% thus means that every circuit node has at least once changed state.

With a specially suited program, we computed for the various test blocks the rates in Table 9.20. This table gives more details than a total rate of 100% of all test blocks. For a serious quality evaluation, however, the stuck-at fault coverage is more meaningful.

Test block	A	B	L	P	Y	Z	A+B+L+P+Y+Z
Toggle rate	96.4%	94.5%	34.4%	32.9%	72.0%	46.5%	100%

Table 9.20 Toggle rates of test blocks

The fault coverage with respect to stuck-at faults is computed by a *fault simulation*. A fault simulator sequentially includes all possible stuck-at faults in the circuit and determines, in each case, whether the particular fault is detected by the test program. The simulation effort for this method is quite high. A time-saving and acceptable restriction consists of the inclusion of only *one* such fault at a time.

We have used the fault simulator VERIFAULT of CADENCE. For this purpose, the gate model had to be retranslated into a simulatable VERILOG representation. Before a simulation, the set of possible faults is divided into equivalence classes resulting in equal simulations. From every class, a primary fault is selected as a representative.

An additional important property is the recognition of faults as safe or as potential. A fault is recognized as safe, if a circuit output shows a 0 instead of a 1 or vice versa. A fault is recognized as potential, if the high impedance state Z appears instead of 0 or 1. One may abort simulation after a potential recognition (drop potential) or continue, until a recognition as safe is assured.

Fault simulation of TOOBSIE produced all stuck-at faults and their recognition status as in Table 9.21.

	Total #	Total %	Prime #	Prime %
Untestable	631		631	
Detected	20917	98.9	17632	98.7
Potential	0	0.0	0	0.0
Undetected	224	1.1	219	1.3
Drop_potential	0	0.0	0	0.0
All	21141		17851	

Table 9.21 Results of fault simulation by VERIFAULT

Out of 21 000 possible stuck-at faults of the VERILOG Gate Model, 18 000 are represented as primary faults, of which almost 99% are detectable and only about 1% cannot be detected. We were not satisfied with potentially recognizable faults. Of course, the stuck-at model does not consider all technically possible faults (Section 9.1).

The faults recognized as untestable are due to circuit redundancies and do thus not influence the circuit function.

9.5.5 Preparation of ATE Test Data

The test blocks above were created for production test at the silicon producer. They may also be used for our own ATE. While we did not mention the formats of the production tester, we will now assign formats and templates to our own ATE test vectors. In Section 9.2.2, we explained that a template assigns a format to all signals for one test cycle (signal shape, input or output, etc.; Figures 9.9 and 9.10). For a particular signal, its format may vary with test cycles.

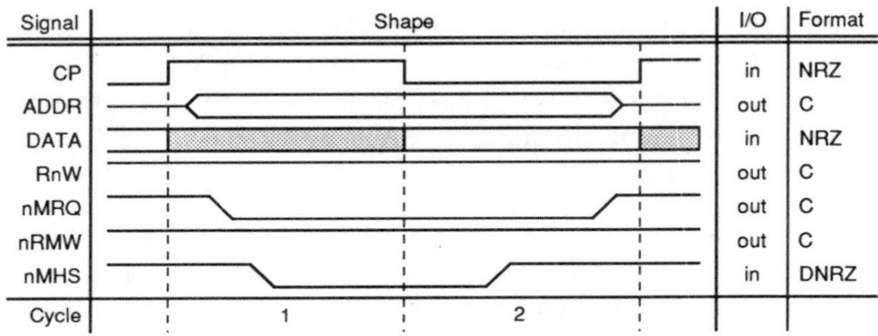

Figure 9.22 Signal formats of asynchronous memory access

At the beginning of a test cycle, the input pins of the chip are normally supplied with input test patterns, then a clock signal is generated, and finally the output pins are compared with output test patterns. Figure 9.22 shows as an example an asynchronous memory access, which also generates a memory handshake signal nMHS. For this operation, by the way, at least two ATE cycles are required. The maximal test speed reduces therefore from 50 to 25 MHz. In a test for speed, a different assignment is necessary, as for TOOBSIE, a clock frequency above 25 MHz is to be expected.

The address bus is an example of a signal requiring more than one format: normally, it is a chip output, during reset, it has to be high impedance.

Groups of signals like buses can be bundled. For every possible format combination of single signals, only one template has to be defined. For simplification, our template names contain the information of Table 9.23. For instance, in the situation of Figure 9.22, template A1 IFO0 R0TM denotes a driving address bus, a data bus as input (that is inactive as output), etc. The data bus has three operation modes: input IFO0, output I0OF, and high impedance I0O0.

Symbol	Application	Value	Explanation	Mode
A	Address bus	0	inactive	MASK
		1	driving	COMPARE
I	Data bus, input	0	inactive	MASK
		F	input	FORCE
O	Data bus, output	0	inactive	MASK
		F	driving	COMPARE
R	RAM test bus	0	inactive	MASK
		1	driving	FORCE
T	Tristate test	0	pull down	FORCE
		1	pull up	FORCE
		M	inactive	MASK

Table 9.23 Naming conventions for templates

Figure 9.24 finally shows ATE test data, which have to be augmented by an initialization header for tester specific settings like test frequency, power supply, etc.

```
* "                                                                P                                    ";
* "                 N                       F N   N N N I N N B    A S S S S S S   R   R  R          N N";
* "                 R    A        D     A K A R R M M I R I H U C  N C C O I I I R T R T  T  P   L L A R";
* "               C S    D        A     C U C M N R H R I R L S N  I A I U S S S T W T A  A  M T A D D T";
* "TEMPLATE       P T    R        T     M M C W W Q S Q D A T P F  C N N T E I O E N S A  B  Z N B B R B";
* "-----------------------------------------------------------------------------------------------------";
* "RESET cycles"
"A0 I0 O0 R0 TM"  1 0 00000000 00000000 0 1 0 1 1 1 1 1 0 1 1 0 0b 0 0 0 0 0 0 0 0 1 0 00 00 0 1 0 0 0 1;
"A0 I0 O0 R0 TM"  0 0 00000000 00000000 0 1 0 1 1 1 1 1 0 1 1 0 0b 0 0 0 0 0 0 0 0 1 0 00 00 0 1 0 0 0 1;
"A0 I0 O0 R0 TM"  1 0 00000000 00000000 0 1 0 1 1 1 1 1 0 1 1 0 0b 0 0 0 0 0 0 0 0 1 0 00 00 0 1 0 0 0 1;
"A0 I0 O0 R0 TM"  0 1 00000000 00000000 0 1 0 1 1 1 1 1 0 1 1 0 0b 0 0 0 0 0 0 0 0 1 0 00 00 0 1 0 0 0 1;
* "first OR instruction"
"A1 IF O0 R0 TM"  1 1 00000000 44080000 2 1 1 1 1 0 0 1 0 1 1 0 0b 0 0 0 0 0 0 1 0 1 0 00 00 0 1 0 0 0 1;
"A0 IF O0 R0 TM"  0 1 00000000 44080000 2 1 1 1 1 1 1 1 0 1 1 0 0b 0 0 0 0 0 0 1 0 1 0 00 00 0 1 0 0 0 1;
"A1 IF O0 R0 TM"  1 1 00000004 0e100008 2 1 1 1 1 0 0 1 0 1 1 0 0b 0 0 0 0 0 0 0 0 1 0 00 00 0 1 0 0 0 1;
"A0 IF O0 R0 TM"  0 1 00000000 0e100008 2 1 1 1 1 1 1 1 0 1 1 0 0b 0 0 0 0 0 0 0 0 1 0 00 00 0 1 0 0 0 1;
"A1 IF O0 R0 TM"  1 1 00000008 49000000 2 1 1 1 1 0 0 1 0 1 1 0 0b 0 0 0 0 0 0 0 0 1 0 00 00 0 1 0 0 0 1;
"A0 IF O0 R0 TM"  0 1 00000000 49000000 2 1 1 1 1 1 1 1 0 1 1 0 0b 0 0 0 0 0 0 0 0 1 0 00 00 0 1 0 0 0 1;
"A1 IF O0 R0 TM"  1 1 0000000c 6a108001 2 1 1 1 1 0 0 1 0 1 1 0 0b 0 0 0 0 0 0 1 0 1 0 00 00 0 1 0 0 0 1;
"A0 IF O0 R0 TM"  0 1 00000000 6a108001 2 1 1 1 1 1 1 1 0 1 1 0 0b 0 0 0 0 0 0 1 0 1 0 00 00 0 1 0 0 0 1;
"A1 IF O0 R0 TM"  1 1 00000020 00000002 2 1 0 1 1 0 0 1 0 1 1 0 0b 0 0 0 0 0 0 0 0 1 0 00 00 0 1 0 0 0 1;
"A0 IF O0 R0 TM"  0 1 00000000 00000002 2 1 0 1 1 1 1 1 0 1 1 0 0b 0 0 0 0 0 0 0 0 1 0 00 00 0 1 0 0 0 1;
"A1 IF O0 R0 TM"  1 1 00000010 fc07ffff 2 1 1 1 1 0 0 1 0 1 1 0 0b 0 0 0 0 0 0 1 0 1 0 00 00 0 1 0 0 0 1;
"A0 IF O0 R0 TM"  0 1 00000000 fc07ffff 2 1 1 1 1 1 1 1 0 1 1 0 0b 0 0 0 0 0 0 1 0 1 0 00 00 0 1 0 0 0 1;
"A1 IF O0 R0 TM"  1 1 00000014 60084003 2 1 1 1 1 0 0 1 0 1 1 0 0b 0 0 0 0 0 0 0 0 1 0 00 00 0 1 0 0 0 1;
"A0 IF O0 R0 TM"  0 1 00000000 60084003 2 1 1 1 1 1 1 1 0 1 1 0 0b 0 0 0 0 0 0 0 0 1 0 00 00 0 1 0 0 0 1;
"A1 IF O0 R0 TM"  1 1 0000000c 6a108001 2 1 1 1 1 0 0 1 0 1 1 0 0b 0 0 0 0 0 0 1 0 1 0 00 00 0 1 0 0 0 1;
"A0 IF O0 R0 TM"  0 1 00000000 6a108001 2 1 1 1 1 1 1 1 0 1 1 0 0b 0 0 0 0 0 0 1 0 1 0 00 00 0 1 0 0 0 1;
"A1 IF O0 R0 TM"  1 1 00000010 fc07ffff 2 1 1 1 1 0 0 1 0 1 1 0 0b 0 0 0 0 0 0 1 0 1 0 00 00 0 1 0 0 0 1;
"A0 IF O0 R0 TM"  0 1 00000000 fc07ffff 2 1 1 1 1 1 1 1 0 1 1 0 0b 0 0 0 0 0 0 1 0 1 0 00 00 0 1 0 0 0 1;
"A1 IF O0 R0 TM"  1 1 0000000c 6a108001 2 1 1 1 1 0 0 1 0 1 1 0 0b 0 0 0 0 0 0 1 0 1 0 00 00 0 1 0 0 0 1;
"A0 IF O0 R0 TM"  0 1 00000000 6a108001 2 1 1 1 1 1 1 1 0 1 1 0 0b 0 0 0 0 0 0 1 0 1 0 00 00 0 1 0 0 0 1;
"A1 IF O0 R0 TM"  1 1 00000018 2e080009 2 1 1 1 1 0 0 1 0 1 1 0 0b 0 0 0 0 0 0 0 0 1 0 00 00 0 1 0 0 0 1;
"A0 IF O0 R0 TM"  0 1 00000000 2e080009 2 1 1 1 1 1 1 1 0 1 1 0 0b 0 0 0 0 0 0 0 0 1 0 00 00 0 1 0 0 0 1;
*"HALT instruction"
"A1 IF O0 R0 TM"  1 1 0000001c ff000000 2 1 1 1 1 0 0 1 0 1 1 0 0b 0 0 0 0 0 0 0 0 1 0 00 00 0 1 0 0 0 1;
"A0 IF O0 R0 TM"  0 1 00000000 ff000000 2 1 1 1 1 1 1 1 0 1 1 0 0b 0 0 0 0 0 0 0 0 1 0 00 00 0 1 0 0 0 1;
"A1 IF O0 R0 TM"  1 1 00000020 00000002 2 1 1 1 1 0 0 1 0 1 1 0 0b 0 0 0 0 0 0 0 0 1 0 00 00 0 1 0 0 0 1;
"A0 IF O0 R0 TM"  0 1 00000000 00000002 2 1 1 1 1 1 1 1 0 1 1 0 0b 0 0 0 0 0 0 0 0 1 0 00 00 0 1 0 0 0 1;
"A1 I0 OF R0 TM"  1 1 00000024 00000006 2 1 0 1 0 0 0 1 0 1 1 0 0b 0 0 0 0 0 0 1 0 1 0 00 00 0 1 0 0 0 1;
"A0 I0 O0 R0 TM"  0 1 00000000 00000000 2 1 0 1 1 1 1 1 0 1 1 0 0b 0 0 0 0 0 0 1 0 1 0 00 00 0 1 0 0 0 1;
"A0 I0 O0 R0 TM"  1 1 00000000 00000000 2 1 1 1 1 1 1 1 0 1 1 0 0b 0 0 0 0 0 0 1 0 1 0 00 00 0 1 0 0 0 1;
```

Figure 9.24 Test data with templates

Figure 9.24 shows ATE test data extracted from the multiplication program (Section 5.3.3). Every line is a test vector with input and output test patterns. For instance, templates beginning with A1 define address bus ADR as chip output to be compared by the ATE with nominal values. Clock signal CP cyclically changes its value, the format being NRZ. The memory address for the instruction to be loaded is given by ADR.

If no branches are executed, it increases by 4. In between, CP changes to 0 and the template to A0xx, because in the second half of the clock, the address is not to be compared by the ATE.

Furthermore, one can see that after an initialization and reset, instruction OR R01 R00 00 with hexadecimal code 44080000h is loaded as a first instruction. The program terminates with a HALT instruction FF000000h.

9.6 ATE Test

For a designer, ATE test and first run on a testboard constitute the highlight of an intensive design effort. For the reader, this section is not quite as exciting.

9.6.1 Set-up of DUT Card

For connecting the chip TOOBSIE with the ATE, a DUT card (device under test, Section 9.2) is required as interface. It is based on a board of the tester producer. On the board, a special test socket is fixed permitting an easy exchange of chip by a suitable contacting mechanism (Figure 9.25).

Figure 9.25 ATE adapter

Next, the power supply pins of the processor are wired and connected with the central power supply of the DUT card. To prevent momentary power breakdown under change of load, all pins should be augmented by suitable capacitors. The remaining processor pins are then wired with an ATE channel by serial protection resistors. In addition, all wires that may have high impedance are connected by a resistor permitting a test of high impedance (tristate test).

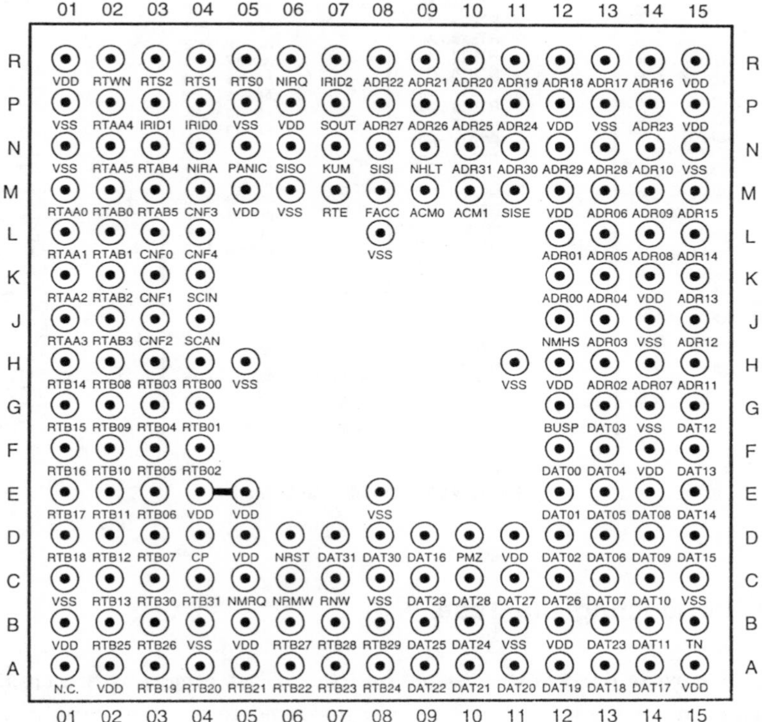

Figure 9.26 Pin diagram

Figure 9.26 shows the pin diagram of TOOBSIE. As compared with the Gate Model, the number of connections has increased significantly, as buses are no longer bundled and as power supply now exists explicitly. Table 9.27 assigns in a *pinout* pin names and their geometric position to the Gate Model ports.

Gate model	Pin-out	Pin	Gate model	Pin-out	Pin	Gate model	Pin-out	Pin	Gate model	Pin-out	Pin
RTSEL	RTS2	R03	NMHS	NMHS	J12	ACCMODE	ACM1	M10	PROCMONZ	PMZ	D10
	RTS1	R04	BUSPRO	BUSP	G12		ACM0	M09	NIRA	NIRA	N04
	RTS0	R05	TN	TN	B15	ADDR_BUS	ADR31	N10	SCANOUT	SOUT	P07
RTWEN	RTWN	R02	RTOUTB	RTB31	C04		ADR30	N11	PANIC	PANIC	N05
RTE	RTE	M07		RTB30	C03		ADR29	N12	KUMODE	KUM	N07
RTADRA	RTAA5	N02		RTB29	B08		ADR28	N13	DATA_BUS	DAT31	D07
	RTAA4	P02		RTB28	B07		ADR27	P08		DAT30	D08
	RTAA3	J01		RTB27	B06		ADR26	P09		DAT29	C09
	RTAA2	K01		RTB26	B03		ADR25	P10		DAT28	C10
	RTAA1	L01		RTB25	B02		ADR24	P11		DAT27	C11
	RTAA0	M01		RTB24	A08		ADR23	P14		DAT26	C12
RTADRB	RTAB5	M03		RTB23	A07		ADR22	R08		DAT25	B09
	RTAB4	N03		RTB22	A06		ADR21	R09		DAT24	B10
	RTAB3	J02		RTB21	A05		ADR20	R10		DAT23	B13
	RTAB2	K02		RTB20	A04		ADR19	R11		DAT22	A09
	RTAB1	L02		RTB19	A03		ADR18	R12		DAT21	A10
	RTAB0	M02		RTB18	D01		ADR17	R13		DAT20	A11
CONFIG	CNF4	L04		RTB17	E01		ADR16	R14		DAT19	A12
	CNF3	M04		RTB16	F01		ADR15	M15		DAT18	A13
	CNF2	J03		RTB15	G01		ADR14	L15		DAT17	A14
	CNF1	K03		RTB14	H01		ADR13	K15		DAT16	D09
	CNF0	L03		RTB13	C02		ADR12	J15		DAT15	D15
SCANIN	SCIN	K04		RTB12	D02		ADR11	H15		DAT14	E15
IRQ_ID	IRID2	R07		RTB11	E02		ADR10	N14		DAT13	F15
	IRID1	P03		RTB10	F02		ADR09	M14		DAT12	G15
	IRID0	P04		RTB09	G02		ADR08	L14		DAT11	B14
NIRQ	NIRQ	R06		RTB08	H02		ADR07	H14		DAT10	C14
SCAN	SCAN	J04		RTB07	D03		ADR06	M13		DAT09	D14
CP	CP	D04		RTB06	E03		ADR05	L13		DAT08	E14
NRESET	NRST	D06		RTB05	F03		ADR04	K13		DAT07	C13
SIGSE	SISE	M11		RTB04	G03		ADR03	J13		DAT06	D13
SIGSI	SISI	N08		RTB03	H03		ADR02	H13		DAT05	E13
NHLT	NHLT	N09		RTB02	F04		ADR01	L12		DAT04	F13
				RTB01	G04		ADR00	K12		DAT03	G13
				RTB00	H04	NMRQ	NMRQ	C05		DAT02	D12
			SIGSO	SISO	N06	RNW	RNW	C07		DAT01	E12
			FACC	FACC	M08	NRMW	NRMW	C06		DAT00	F12

Table 9.27 Pinout of Gate Model

9.6.2 Conducting the Tests

The DUT card is fixed on the tester interface. Test programs are created and converted on a workstation and then transferred to the test equipment. This can be done by a serial interface or by a disk.

The prototypes produced by the silicon vendor can now be tested in the tester. The ATE executes a test program. After a setup phase for initialization of ATE memory, the test vectors are distinguished as input and output vectors. The input vectors supply the chip input pins, the output vectors serve as a reference for output pin evaluation. If the results coincide for every test vector of the test program, the chip has passed the test.

During test program execution, the parameters power supply, chip temperature, and cycle length may vary. For a combination of high chip temperature and high power supply, one has to take care not to overheat the chip.

9.6.3 Test Results

The amount of test results is in no relation to the work done before. The results concern the functioning of a prototype (ok or not) and the maximal delay.

With a surrounding temperature of 20°C, a power voltage of 5 V and a suitable cycle, all test programs with test blocks Z, Y, P, L, A, and B as explained above were executed by all ten prototypes of TOOBSIE. The cycle length of a test block is prescribed by the producer (Section 9.5.1). For statistical purposes, however, it may be varied; of course, the producer no longer guarantees the passing of tests.

All 10 prototypes passed all tests successfully.

It can thus be concluded that the producer correctly implemented our design under consideration of a fault coverage of almost 99% with respect to our test programs. In addition to the production test of the silicon producer, we created another test block T reaching a fault coverage of 100%. For reasons of space, this could not be included in the production test. Also the T-test was passed. In addition, further functional tests with "real" programs on a testboard will be meaningful in the following Sections 9.7 and 9.8.

The following examples indicate two possibilities of statistic analysis with the ATE. The variance of electrical properties and the dependance of circuit speed on temperature is tested.

In Section 9.3, design for testability was explained. This includes a NAND tree with process monitor on the chip, including a test path for electrical parameters. In test block P, signal delay is computed by this test path and is compared with a previously computed value at a certain strobe point. If for a given ATE period, this strobe point is moved step by step, the ATE will detect a difference at a certain point.

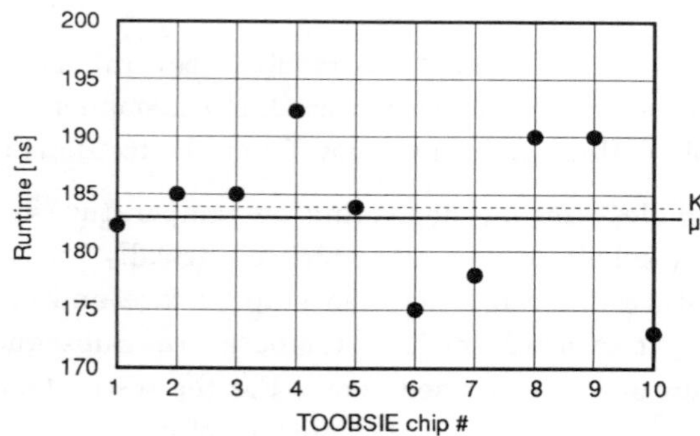

Figure 9.28 Runtimes of prototypes

This procedure is applied to every prototype resulting in Figure 9.28. The runtime ranges between 173 and 192 nanoseconds. The average μ is 183.4 ns, the previously computed value K is 184.6 ns.

This test path is unimportant for the function of TOOBSIE, as it is not a critical path. A critical path depends on the processor configuration and includes the cache RAM cells in the slowest case. Their runtime determines the maximal clock frequency. For a cycle of 36 ns, all prototypes passed extensive functional tests similar to test blocks A and B.

This corresponds to a clock frequency of 27.8 MHz.

The next lower cycle length supported by the ATE is 32 ns corresponding to 31.3 MHz. Only the quite fast prototype #10 (Figure 9.28) passed the test, but only when the chip was cooled down to 10°C. Therefore, the frequency range between 27.8 and 31.3 MHz cannot be analyzed with the given ATE configuration.

Temperature 10 C

o Test failed
x Test passed

Power supply	28ns	32ns	36ns	40ns	42ns	46ns
5,20V	o	x	x	x	x	x
5,15V	o	x	x	x	x	x
5,10V	o	x	x	x	x	x
5,05V	o	x	x	x	x	x
5,00V	o	o	x	x	x	x
4,95V	o	o	x	x	x	x
4,90V	o	o	x	x	x	x
4,85V	o	o	x	x	x	x
4,80V	o	o	x	x	x	x

Cycle length

Figure 9.29 Voltage and cycle length (Schmoo plot)

Figure 9.29 shows a *Schmoo plot* as a result of several ATE runs, in which clock frequency and power supply were varied. For a smaller clock frequency, a lower power supply is thus sufficient, below 32 ns the test fails in every case.

As a second example, runtime depending on temperature is determined in Figure 9.30. Using a Peltier element, which electrically creates a positive or negative temperature difference between chip surface and environment, the prototype is brought to a well-defined temperature. Subsequently, the ATE determines the runtime as described above. For the tested temperature range between 10 and 30°C, a temperature coefficient of 0.9 ns / ^{o}C results.

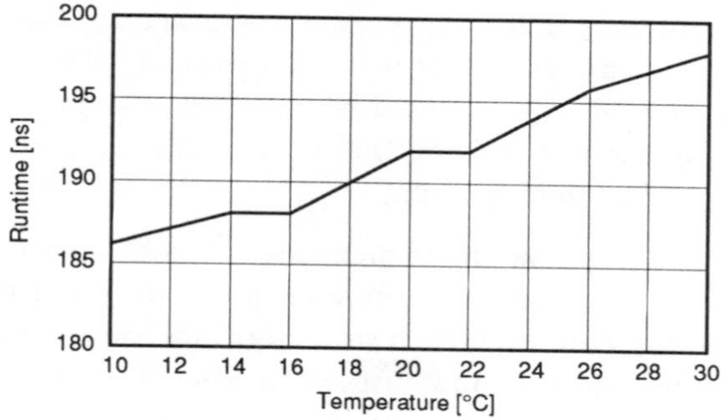

Figure 9.30 Temperature coefficient of runtime

9.7 Testboard

Testing a processor only in an ATE tester is not sufficient, as a high fault coverage only ensures correct production of the Gate Model. Although in our case, the production test contains important parts of a functional test, this covers just a small part of the powerful and complex total function. Aside from all scientific aspects, we are eager to finally have our TOOBSIE *really* running ...

Only under more or less real conditions can real programs be tested in detail. Large benchmarks (standardized test programs) can be performed to obtain various results on real performance. (For the difficult problems of realistic notions of performance, we refer to [Hennessy, Patterson 1990].)

From a testboard we expect good access to the processor to be studied, flexible bus timing, and good extendability. One of the most important requirements is therefore a powerful interface to a host computer, such that programs developed and cross-assembled there can easily and efficiently be written into the test system memory; vice versa, this memory should be readable without participation of the CPU under test. In that case, no loading software has to be developed for the target processor, thus reducing potential sources of error. In this connection, the DMA property is relevant (direct memory access).

During loading, the processor TOOBSIE under test is halted until program and data have been written completely into its memory. After a test program run, it is halted again to return test memory contents to the host for further analysis.

A test of all features of TOOBSIE has to support not only asynchronous bus timing and a 32-bit data bus but also the generation of interrupts. The cache configuration signals should be accessible from outside to determine efficiency.

Such a test system may not only verify the processor using assembler programs, but may also perform other tasks. For example, if we plan to develop an independent computer system based on our CPU, we may implement the basic software using the test system. Due to the DMA property, no complete programs are required at the beginning.

A simple operating system may be implemented step by step using the DMA interface to the host computer for communication with the outside world. Terminal outputs may be deposited in a certain memory section, which the host reads in regular intervals and outputs on a monitor. Equally, keyboard inputs can be put by the host into another memory section, from where they are used by the operating system. Even more complex peripherals such as mass storage and corresponding interfaces can be "emulated" this way. Only after the operating system runs satisfactorily will the cord from test system to the host successively be cut.

This results in another requirement on our test system, namely its extendability. An elegant way to achieve this is a system in which on a base board or *backplane* several cards are plugged in. Even the processor can be included in the system as a plug-in card. This way, the test system may also be used for other processors and thus becomes "universal".

For efficient fault analysis, an optional hardware debugger would be helpful which, for instance, indicates data and address bus state by a 7-segment display or which supports a single-step mode. All signals necessary for such an extension card are present on the backplane.

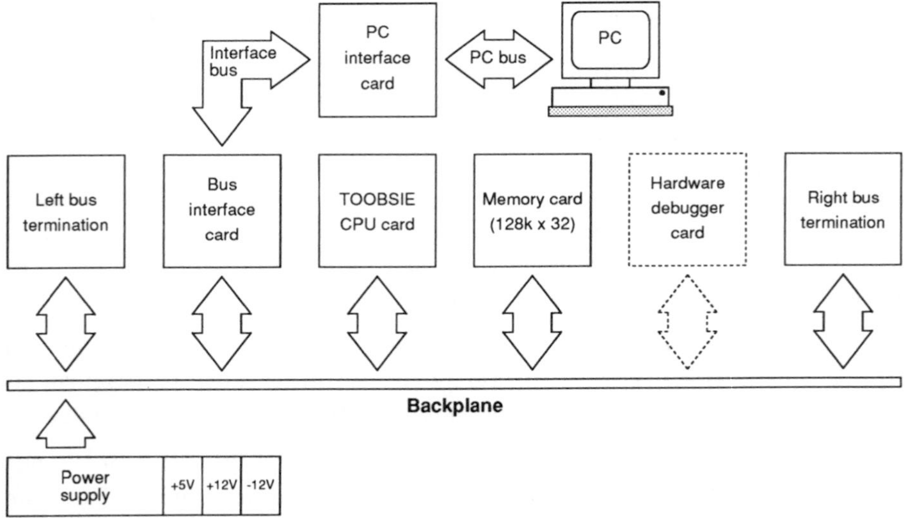

Figure 9.31 The testboard

Figure 9.31 shows the block diagram of a (rather) universal test system. As a backplane, a board with ten 96-pin connectors is used, of which at least five are occupied. Communication with a host computer (in our case an IBM PC-compatible system) is achieved by a bus interface card. Aside from a memory card, there is, of course, a card with test processor TOOBSIE. To avoid signal reflection at the end of the backplane, both ends contain bus termination cards. An optional hardware debugger is indicated by a dotted line. There is a separate power supply delivering 5V for logic and ±12V for a planned RS232 interface card.

The following explanation of the individual components uses the legend in Figure 9.32.

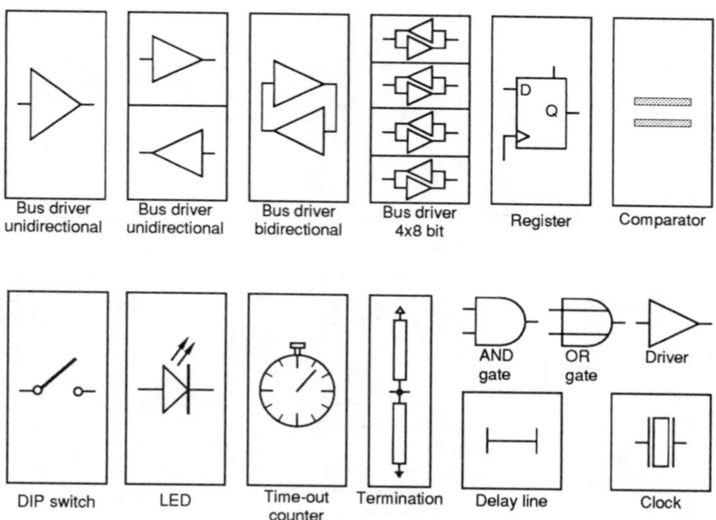

Figure 9.32 Legend of some components

9.7.1 Backplane

The backplane serves as the "backbone" of communication between components. It includes data and address bus as well as control wires for memory access, interrupt and bus arbitration, and a global reset. Moreover, power is distributed. Asynchronous CPU bus timing is also used for the timing of plug-in cards. Thus components of varying speed can be connected independently of a clock.

9.7.2 PC-Interface Card and Bus-Interface Card

For efficient communication of the test system with the host computer, bus and PC interface card are connected by a 60-wire flat cable (*interface bus*), half of the wires being connected to ground for noise suppression. These signals include an 8-bit data bus, a 12-bit address bus, and other control signals.

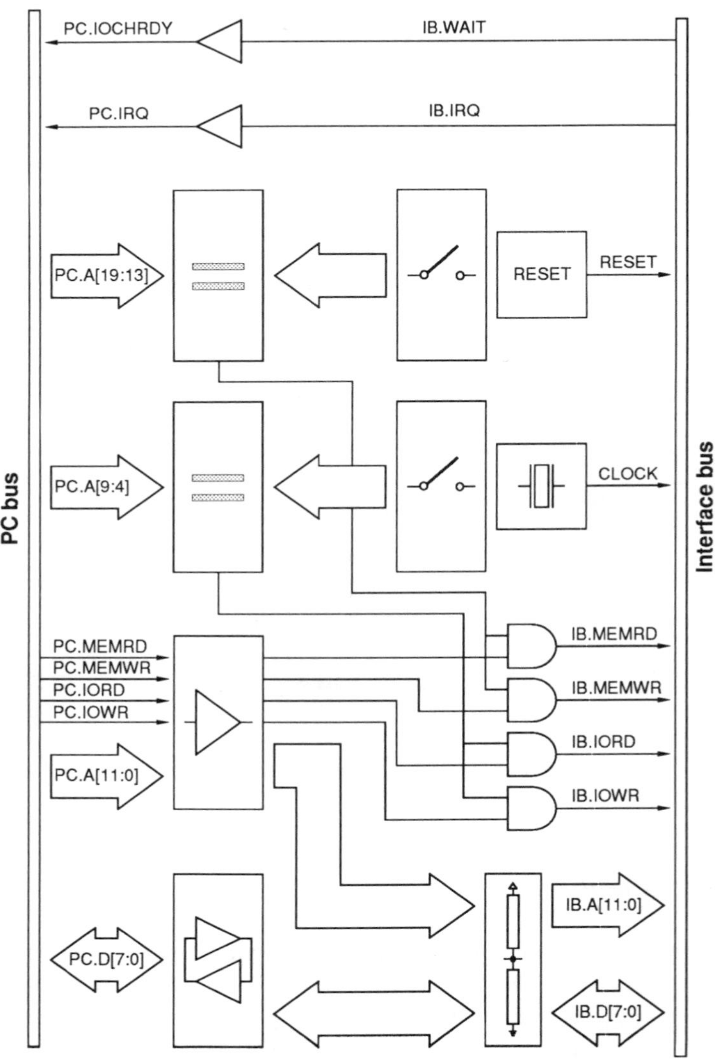

Figure 9.33 PC-interface card

The block diagram of the PC interface card in Figure 9.33 shows two comparators decoding two different memory areas of the PC. First, a 4-kByte page is mapped into the PC program and data memory, by which a 4-kByte memory area of the test system may be accessed (having a 4-GByte address space with 2^{32} addresses). The address of this PC page can be configured by an 8-fold DIP switch. In IBM PC systems, this memory area for extensions is between addresses C0000h and DFFFFh.

Second, 16 addresses of the additional I/O area in the PC are decoded for reading and writing control registers, by which, for instance, the upper address bits of the selected page can be defined. The control lines are separated for both memory areas. Moreover, the data bus PC.D[7:0] and the address bits PC.A[11:0] for the memory page are buffered, in order to reduce the capacitive load of these wires on the PC bus. At the connecting plugs for the interface bus, passive terminations suppress wire reflections.

A reset generator sets the bus interface card to a defined state after power-on (Figure 9.34). The PC system clock is available as CLOCK on the bus interface card for extension purposes. This card can extend a PC read or write access to test memory by IB.WAIT or can request an interrupt in the case of a fault by IB.IRQ.

The address, data, and control signals lead to buffers with Schmitt trigger inputs via terminating resistors for improving voltage level. The data bus IB.D[7:0] is bidirectional from the interface bus to the backplane, such that test memory can be written and read. From the host, only 8-bit accesses can be performed; one of four bus drivers is selected by the two least significant address bits. The twelve PC address wires IB.A[11:0] are connected through both interface cards with address signals A[11:0] of the backplane. The remaining 20 address lines A[31:12] lead through control registers enabling the paging mentioned above.

There is a control unit for the whole bus interface card. As bus interface card and CPU card may initiate bus accesses in the test system, a small bus arbitration logic prevents possible conflicts on the CPU card. Prior to a memory access, the bus interface card requests the bus by nBUSREQ. Only after a bus acknowledge from the CPU card by nBUSACK is memory access initiated. The CPU is halted during this time by the selection logic on the CPU card. As soon as nBUSREQ returns to 1, the CPU may perform the next memory access.

Alternatively, the CPU may be brought to a permanent sleep by a special nHALT signal, which accelerates memory accesses of the host. This way, PC accesses need not be coordinated with CPU accesses. This is particularly useful, if complete program sections are loaded. nHALT is controlled by a special register accessible by the PC.

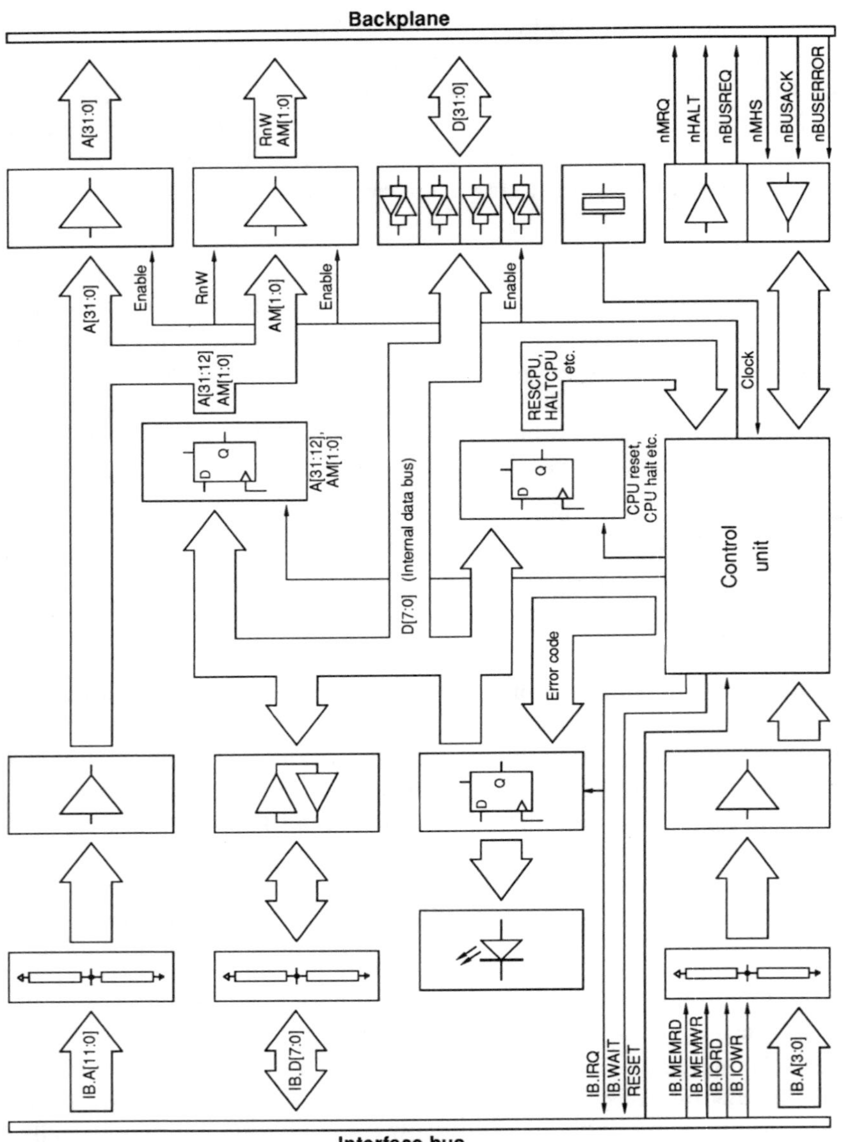

Figure 9.34 Bus interface card

In contrast to PC timing, the bus timing of the test system is asynchronous. After a bus request by nBUSREQ, the memory access is initiated with a falling nMRQ edge. As long as the memory has not generated an enable signal (positive edge of nMHS), the host is halted by the control unit of the bus interface card by IB.WAIT. After a maximal time span of about 2 μs, the control unit clears IB.WAIT (time-out). If for instance, an unselected memory section is accessed, this protection mechanism prevents an endless wait. In the status register, an appropriate fault bit is set, and the exception state is indicated by an LED. Optionally, an interrupt may be requested from the host.

Signal nBUSERROR of the system bus is activated by the selected periphery, if an access could not be completed successfully. Also this exception state is indicated by an LED and is stored in the status register. It is reset by the host.

9.7.3 Memory Card

The memory card of the test system in Figure 9.35 includes maximally 512 kByte of static RAM. The memory is organized as 128 k words of 32 bits. To increase CPU throughput by small access times, commercial cache RAM components are used. These are organized as 32 kByte of 8 bits, and their access time varies between 15 and 35 ns. At most 16 components of this type can be placed in four memory banks.

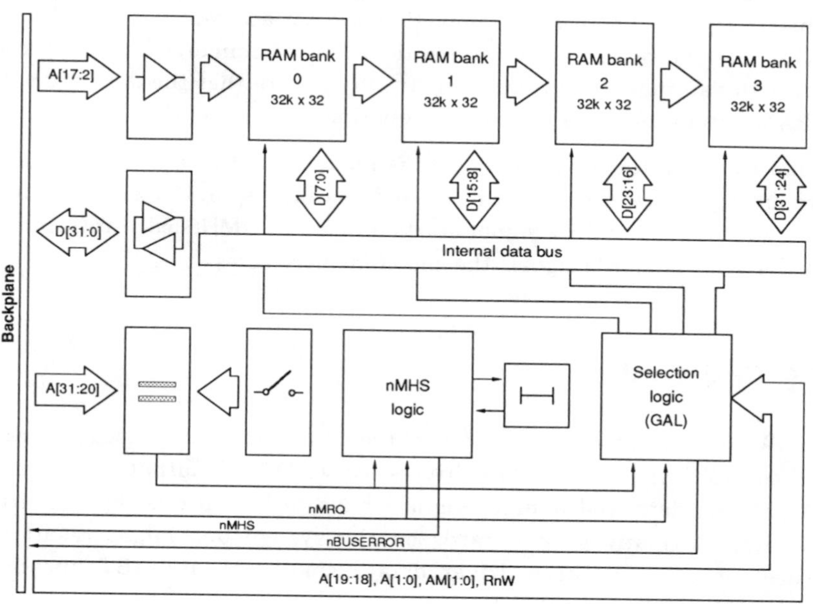

Figure 9.35 Memory card

As with the other cards, data and address bus are buffered by bus drivers. The selection logic of the memory card is quite simple. Addresses A[2:17] are directly connected with addresses RA[0:15] of all RAM components thus selecting a 32-bit word. Addresses A[18:19] select one of the four RAM banks. A[19:31] lead to two 8-bit comparators and are compared with an address preset by DIP switches. If true, a memory access is performed by the card. This allows the inclusion of further cards in the system, of course with a different base address.

Address bits A[0:1], the two access mode signals AM[0:1], and the RnW signal control write and read accesses by a programmable GAL logic component. Depending on the access mode (8, 16, or 32 bits), one, two, or all RAM write lines are activated. For read accesses, only a 32-bit word is put on the bus. (If the CPU performs an 8-bit access, the remaining 24 bits are suppressed by the CPU logic.) If a 16-bit access is performed to an odd address or a 32-bit access to an address not divisible by four, a fault is signaled by nBUSERROR.

The asynchronous bus protocol is more complicated. The CPU initiates a bus access by a memory request nMRQ, which the memory card acknowledges with a falling nMHS edge as a memory handshake. After memory access time, a rising nMHS edge signals the end of access.

There is a difficulty in the design of asynchronous memory cards, namely, how the nMHS logic will detect the completion of RAM access. Only very few RAMs indicate the end of access by an additional pin. Commercial memory components with varying access times usually only ensure that the data are valid at the RAM output after the maximal access time.

The nMHS signal for our memory card is implemented by a delay line delaying an input signal by internal gates. If address bits A[19:31] coincide with the preset address, the nMRQ signal starts a negative nMHS edge returning to 1 after the delayed nMRQ signals the end of memory access.

9.7.4 CPU Card

The CPU card in Figure 9.36 consists of the CPU TOOBSIE, a clock generator, a small control logic, and the bus drivers. As TOOBSIE output pads are weak 4mA drivers, data and address signals have to be buffered by bus drivers; otherwise, too many plug-in cards on the system bus might result in an overload of pads. To keep driver delays small, we use ABT bus drivers (advanced BiCMOS technology).

As peripherals are accessed by an asynchronous interface, the CPU clock is independent and can be adapted to the processor under test. Aside from the CPU, a time-out counter is connected with the clock interrupting accesses to undefined memory sections and indicating this by an LED.

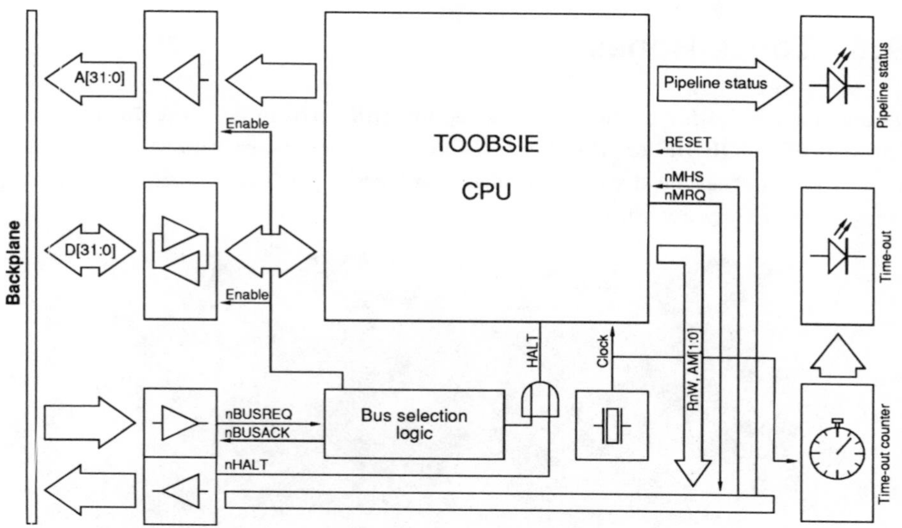

Figure 9.36 The CPU card

Moreover, there is the bus arbitration logic explained above, acknowledging bus requests nBUSREQ from the bus interface card by enable signal nBUSACK and halting the CPU. As there is a special HALT signal for TOOBSIE, the necessary logic is quite simple. For processors without HALT, the CPU has to be halted by the clock during external bus arbitration.

Swap accesses useful for semaphores in multi-tasking operating systems are divided by the CPU card logic into two subsequent memory accesses.

Additional LEDs indicate the pipeline load. This supports illustration of the pipeline concept particularly in single step mode. Also, the cache configuration can be set using a 5-fold DIP switch. This is interesting when evaluating cache strategies by benchmarks.

9.7.5 Evaluation

The bus concept of the TOOBSIE testboard turns out to be meaningful. Later, the system can be extended by additional cards for EPROM, SCSI adapter, and RS-232 asynchronous interface and thus become a more and more independent computer system. However, universality has a price: too many bus drivers of an open system reduce performance. Every read access involves four bus driver delays: address signals from the CPU card to the bus, and from the bus to the memory card, and data signals from memory card to the bus, and from the bus back to the CPU card.

9.8 To Be Honest ...

The attentive reader of the previous section will have noted that no *results* on the test of TOOBSIE on the comfortable testboard were reported. Although design of this testboard was started in parallel to processor design, it was not completed at copy deadline.

Figure 9.37 FPGA based testboard

Instead, a simpler board as in Figure 9.37 was implemented, which was also capable of a processor test with complete non-trivial machine programs.

In the center of this minimal solution, there is aside from CPU TOOBSIE a universally configurable logic component, a field-programmable gate-array (FPGA) XILINX XC3042 with a complexity of up to 4 200 gate equivalents and 73 I/O pins. This FPGA can be reconfigured arbitrarily often, i.e., a single component can subsequently implement different circuits (Section 2.1).

The FPGA is connected with the data and address bus of the CPU. Moreover, four memory components are connected with a total of 128 kByte memory (32k words of 32 bits). By three signals for data input, data output, and clock, the FPGA can be configured after power-on by a PC in such a way that, afterwards on the same wires, the machine program to be executed can be written serially into memory. TOOBSIE is halted during the load procedure with a reset, such that data communication between FPGA and memory is not disturbed.

As soon as the program is loaded completely into memory, the output pins of the FPGA are set high impedance, and the processor is started. After a certain time, it can be halted by another reset, and the memory can be read to the PC.

Also during program execution, the FPGA can be reconfigured in such a way that the state of data and address signals can be observed by the serial PC connection or that the processor is halted when reaching a preset address (break point). Moreover, TOOBSIE can reconfigure the FPGA independently, using it as a peripheral component in "stand-alone mode" (asynchronous interface, keyboard decoder, etc.). As extensions, an LC display and a real time clock are provided. With battery operation, the circuit becomes portable.

As no bus drivers slow down communication between CPU and memory, TOOBSIE can be clocked with 24 MHz in this minimal solution. All test programs were executed correctly even in a 16-hour permanent test.

We finally mention a very special test. A sound generator was controlled by suitable loops playing the *Root Beer Rag*. (Of course, the program spends most of its time in waiting loops.) After turning on the multi-purpose and the branch-target cache, the same melody was played much faster with higher frequency. In this acoustic test output with permanent short loops, the performance-enhancing caches speed up operation optimally.

10 Summary and Prospect

At the end of a book, we should lean back and summarize what we learned (and did not learn), we should mention supplementary material in the expert volume, and we should at least bring up some continuing and related research topics.

It was predicted that in the year 2000, electronics will be the leading industrial sector, and that custom design of integrated circuits will be a key technology. By the exponential increase of chip size and integration density in the last decades, the art of chip design has permanently changed. At the center of modern semi-custom design, there are programming language-like circuit design descriptions by a hardware description language (HDL). They accompany the design from a first abstract, but simulatable behavior model down to the gate level. CAD tools complete the remaining design until production.

A focus of attention was the design of *large* circuits. As a large example and another present-day subject we have selected RISC processors, which have influenced computer architecture to a large extent in the last decade. They are characterized by simple homogeneous instruction sets, which can be implemented by parallel pipelines on the chip.

After a short overview of some technological foundations and VLSI design styles (CMOS, semi- and full-custom design, gate-array, FPGA), we have sketched the design flow: it leads from a first requirement analysis and from an external and internal specification of behavior and coarse structure to the representation by a gate netlist, to placement and routing, and finally to chip production by a silicon vendor. In parallel, there are activities such as consideration of testability and test and planning of a future application in a system. The design is not only refined in the sense of a decomposition hierarchy but is also represented on different abstraction levels.

Hardware description languages, particularly the HDL VERILOG, are thoroughly introduced in Chapter 11 – supported by a VERILOG simulator on the disk – under special consideration of our design. An HDL is a classical higher programming language extended by parallelism, time, and physical data structures. Hierarchically designed HDL models represent a unique documentation and can be simulated. They are the base for a manual or automatic synthesis of a next refined HDL model on a lower abstraction level.

Our large design of a real RISC processor TOOBSIE began with a first selection of processor architecture, and we have put special emphasis on useful on-chip memories (caches). After an external specification of the RISC instruction set, defined by a VERILOG model of an interpreter, and after a more detailed internal specification of data flow, timing, pipeline stages, and caches as well as interrupts, the real modeling began with the design of particular pipeline stages. These execute in a continuous data flow several instructions in parallel, attempting to avoid pipeline hazards. Questions of controller and application in a system environment were not yet treated.

We have selected a Pseudo-Harvard architecture, in which data and instructions use a single memory bus with the danger of a mutual interlock, but where a multi-purpose cache reduces this danger. Moreover, we have used a branch-target cache remembering frequently used or critical branch instructions, thus relieving the pipeline. This cache attempts to speculatively predict the future branch behavior, based on past experiences. Our processor is capable of interrupts and supports a kernel/user mode.

We have striven for a balance between an abstract and well readable Coarse Structure Model and a model well structured with respect to important signals and components permitting an easy gate level synthesis. This synthesis was performed using exemplary parts of the model showing the way to a hierarchic netlist of library components from the silicon vendor, the Gate Model. Synthesis was achieved manually and automatically. Finally, we enjoyed a successful test of the produced processor in an ATE tester and on a first testboard.

We have not yet reached the goal of a complete design and project documentation, but refer to the expert volume. There, instructions are first of all treated in detail, the relevant HDL models are clearly printed, remaining parts of the Coarse Structure Model such as the pipeline controller and the bus controller as well as the branch-target cache and the interrupts are commented, and finally the system environment with first experiments on this model are presented in additional chapters. The complete hierarchic gate model enables the expert to reproduce the processor, possibly after adaptation of the gate library.

Even though we basically manage to give a complete documentation of our design using the expert volume and the enclosed disk, there are wishes remaining. We were often busy with documentation of a difficult solution, but did not mention enough the difficulties avoided or unfavorable alternatives. We have shown how to do something, but often not how not to do it...

For instance, it is in the dynamic nature of large models that they require extensive simulations and produce long simulation results. A book is a rather unfavorable medium and interactive work on a computer is much better. This has the additional learning advantage that the user will find his own simulations and will put own questions to the model. We explicitly recommend this.

We had too little time for simulations with *one* model, let alone time for a thorough vertical verification comparing *several* models and their simulations. This by the way, is for models like our Coarse Structure Model the only realistic method of verification; formal verifications propagated elsewhere are not suited for realistic use due to strongly parallel complexity.

While a large VLSI design example is instructive, sometimes painfully instructive, it is obviously interesting to use it as a starting base for further analysis and research on design methodology. The team members mentioned in the preface have done so, and we will try to give at least a small outlook on the research performed.

Furthermore, we want to mention some more or less up-to-date textbooks on general VLSI design: [Bode 1990, Eschermann 1993, Eveking 1991, Fabricius 1990, Furber 1989, Gajski et al. 1992, Hartenstein 1987, Hennessy, Patterson 1990 and 1994, Kemper, Meyer 1989, Mukherjee 1986, Patterson, Hennessy 1994, Rammig 1989, Rosenstiel, Camposano 1989, Sternheim et al. 1993, Thomas, Moorby 1991, Wojtkowiak 1988, Wolf 1994].

10.1 Efficiency and Complexity

Design decisions on the RISC architecture and the RISC instruction set in Chapter 3 appeared from nowhere to the reader (and even to some of the design team members). In a commercial design with a well-defined application, this requires thorough and early, hence cost-saving analysis. We have partially performed such analysis only later in the project leading to some design iterations.

In particular, extensive simulations and statistical evaluations were performed in [Schäfers 1994] on the instruction level well above the Coarse Structure Model by using abstract pipelines. Different variants of caches, branch instructions and their dynamic behavior were central. Important features and decisions about the instruction set, cache strategies, their sizes, and many other things were deduced or approved afterwards, sometimes even disapproved. It was useful that we focused on a SPARC-like architecture, such that we could start with an analysis of instruction frequencies in SPARC programs and improve those.

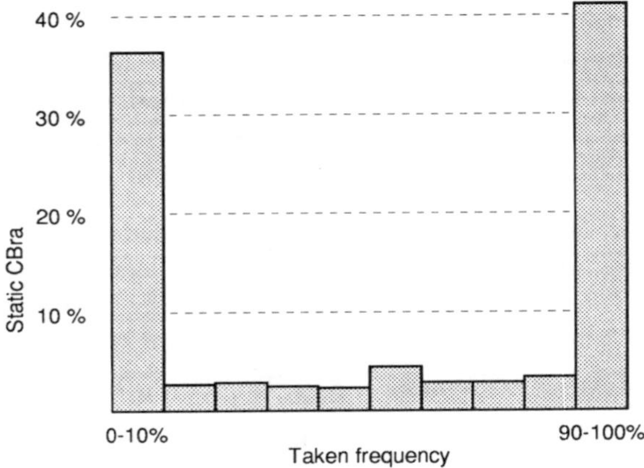

Figure 10.1 Stability of conditional branches

In Section 5.2.2, we have introduced conditional branches of TOOBSIE. Every such BCC instruction (called CBra here) is Taken in a program execution or not. Figure 10.1 summarizes the *stability* of CBra instructions of a program. First for every CBra executed at all, its dynamic taken frequency is counted. Then it is assigned to one of ten frequency classes. Almost 41% of all conditional branches of a program are taken almost always, 36% almost never. This means that about 77% of all conditional branches are quite stable (stability of at least 80%).

Such considerations permit the development of efficient cache strategies. Furthermore, the *run length* of conditional branches is analyzed, i.e., how often the same branch decision Taken or not Taken occurs in a row. This allows the estimation of speculative cache prediction.

The analytical computation of CPI (Cycles Per Instruction) is complicated but interesting: starting from certain single probabilities, the probabilities of caches and finally of the processor are computed. However, many input parameters have to be determined in experiments by a benchmark simulation.

One of the well known tests of computer efficiency is the benchmark Dhrystone based on non-numerical applications (Section 🖫4.2.4). A single execution of a certain loop body of this application is also denoted as one Dhrystone. Figure 10.2 compares TOOBSIE with known processors.

Another focus of the dissertation [Schäfers 1994] is the evaluation of HDL models. From software engineering, quite a few more or less useful software measures or complexity measures are known to determine certain quality features of a program. As hardware description languages include the power

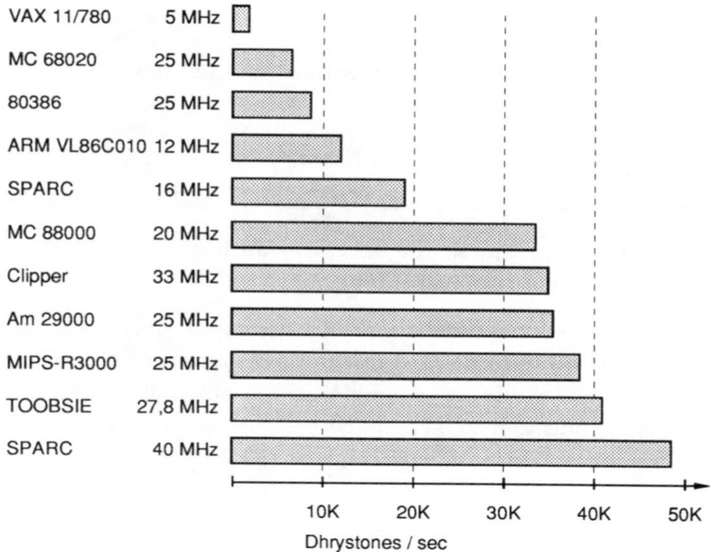

Figure 10.2 Benchmark Dhrystone for some RISC processors

of normal programming languages, one may apply these complexity measures here, too. However, as parallelism is added, there are additional interesting questions such as how to measure readability or design stability of parallel models. This is an inherently difficult area with no simple answers.

Further work in this field is found in [Bray, Flynn 1991, Cragon 1992, Dubey, Flynn 1991, Fenton 1991, Halstead 1977, Hennessy, Patterson 1990 and 1994, Lee, Smith 1984, Mansfeld 1993, Mansfeld, Schäfers 1993, Reitner 1994, Schäfers 1993 and 1994, Schäfers et al. 1993 and 1994, Scholz, Schäfers 1995, Smith 1982, Zuse 1991].

10.2 Specification, Analysis, and Simulation of Large VLSI Designs with Statecharts and Activitycharts

So far, the reader is hopefully convinced of the tremendous advantages, simplifications, and improvements of design stability by using hardware description languages as opposed to the classical "gate jungles". On the other hand, also a Coarse Structure Model was not built in one day, and its understanding requires a high effort in spite of all structures and comments. One may therefore search for CAD tools and methods,

- which operate above HDL modeling,
- which offer better graphic support with state diagrams, flow charts, and similar things,
- which are nevertheless precise and simulatable,
- which offer a connection to normal HDL models, and
- which enable fast design in the specification phase thus supporting, for instance, a search for architectural variants.

Concerning these questions, the concept of *statecharts* and *activitycharts* was researched, as they are implemented in the CAD system STATEMATE. It has so far been used successfully, for example, in the automotive and aeronautics industry, but the application to large VLSI designs has not been much studied. This is the focus of the dissertation [Cochlovius 1994].

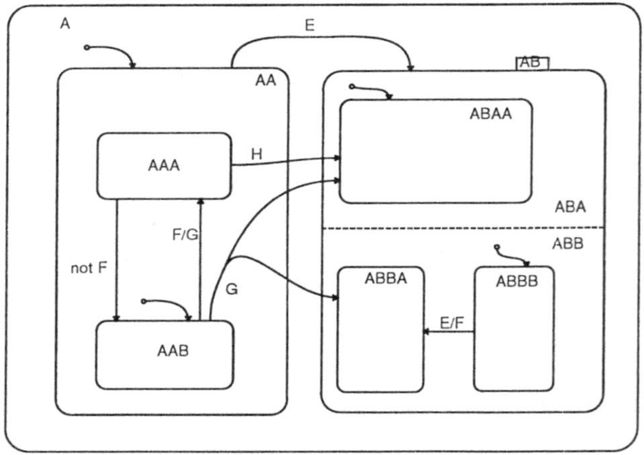

Figure 10.3 A simple statechart

Figure 10.3 shows a simple statechart with transitions. In addition to the well known state transition diagrams, we have the extension by hierarchies of states and in particular parallel substates. For example, the main state or root state A is hierarchically decomposed into AA and AB. This decomposition is meant alternatively, i.e., A is either in substate AA or in AB. In contrast, the latter one is divided into the two parallel substates ABA and ABB, which are simultaneously activated by the activation of AB. Hierarchy is better supported as compared to normal hardware description languages in the sense that with a state, also all of its substates and their predecessors are activated either alternatively or in parallel.

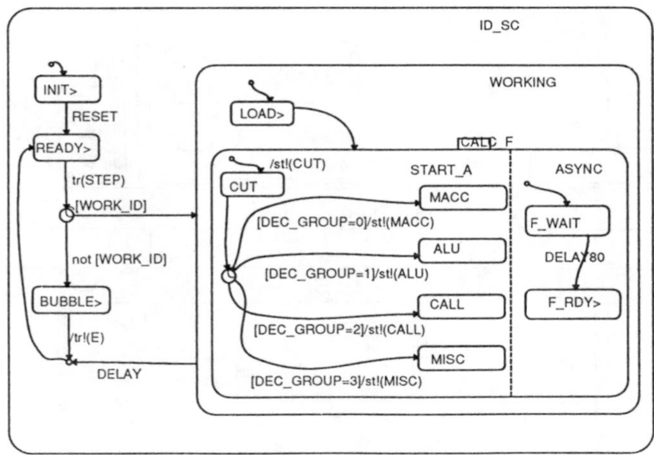

Figure 10.4 Statechart for controlling the instruction decode stage

Figure 10.4 shows a small sub-statechart of the TOOBSIE model. This, by the way, was conducted completely, and the model can execute TOOBSIE programs normally. Aside from statecharts for modeling parallel and structured state or control behavior, there are activitycharts modeling the hierarchic decomposition into functional units. These units are controlled by associated statecharts.

Figure 10.5 shows an interesting graphically and also hierarchically structurable user interface of the processor model that we designed. Like in a cockpit, interesting values, data, activities, and similar things are indicated during simulation and can be controlled at the display by lamps, buttons, switches, etc. This *animation* supports flexible experimentation.

Aside from a direct simulation, STATEMATE includes dynamic test tools which, for instance, discover deadlocks or components that are never or simultaneously used and hence are unsafe. One may ask for the maximal number of empty steps in a pipeline or one may study the absence of races.

The STATEMATE model developed in [Cochlovius 1994, Gummert 1994, Halliger 1994, and Wodtke 1994] of the processor TOOBSIE includes 13 statecharts, 10 activitycharts, and about 1000 lines of C code. In this way, it is better readable than the VERILOG Coarse Structure Model including almost 10 000 lines of code. It may be considered as a specification model containing many important architecture components without being burdened by the details of the Coarse Structure Model. Thus variations of architecture may be tested more easily at the beginning.

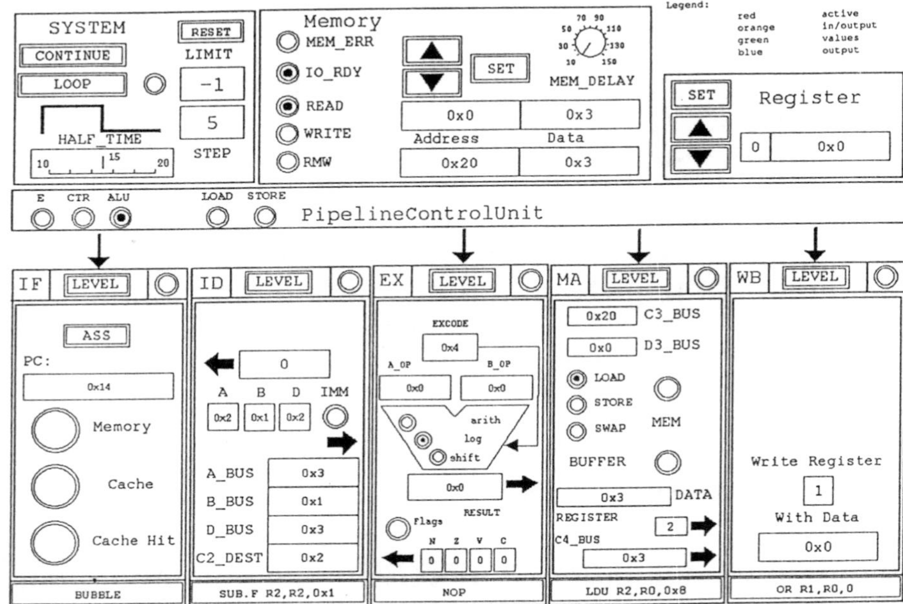

Figure 10.5 Typical user interface

Because of the many powerful modeling features, statechart and activitychart based design requires an extensive learning phase. The corresponding model was developed in part after the Coarse Structure Model. Additional references can be found in [Cochlovius, Golze 1994, Furbach 1993, Harel 1987, Harel et al. 1990, Huizing 1991].

10.3 Fault Models and Test Patterns for HDL Models

Digital chips are tested not only during the design in a simulation, but most of all after production in many different ways, first in a tester, then in a real system. For the production test in an automated tester, test stimuli or test programs are developed (Chapter 9). Typically, such production test patterns are developed exclusively for a gate model. In a fault model, for example, all those faults are considered, where a gate input or output is stuck at a constant value (e.g., stuck-at-0).

The development of such test patterns at the gate level is quite time consuming. VLSI design is moving away from the gate level. In automatic gate synthesis, the designer no longer understands the gate model. Therefore, it appears attractive to develop suitable test patterns at higher HDL levels. For example, in analogy to stuck-at-0, a higher fault model might consist in a stuck-at-then: in an if-else construct, the assumed fault would always take the first branch. The task is to detect such a fault by suitable test patterns. The idea of such higher fault models is not new, but brings with it considerable difficulties.

To explain it in a simplified way, such fault models become more unrealistic, the more abstract and more behavior oriented the HDL model and the more serious the fault is. (It is obviously more difficult to detect a stuck bit of a bus than a bus stuck as a whole.) The test patterns for such faults are less capable of detecting typical real production faults. This is the starting point of the dissertation [Wachsmann 1994]. The applicability of various higher fault models like stuck-at-then is analyzed, first for small models like the simple processor ASIC in Section 11.4 or for the PC logic of TOOBSIE, later for larger models. The resulting test programs are analyzed for usefulness in a production test.

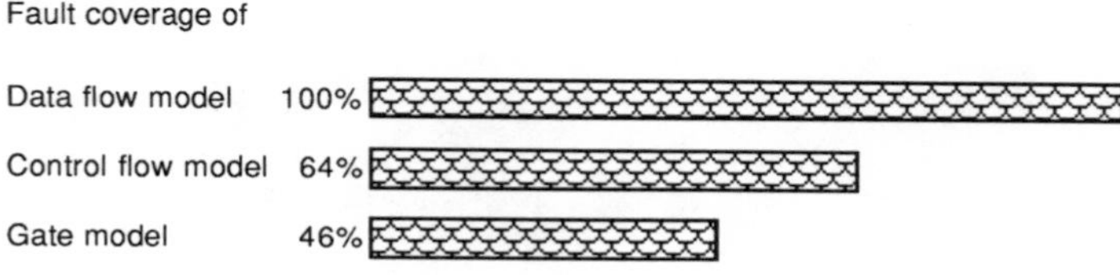

Figure 10.6 Faults of type stuck-at-then or stuck-at-else

In Figure 10.6, for example, three small models that are behaviorally equivalent are considered. For faults of type stuck-at-then and stuck-at-else, we gain a certain test program with a 100% fault coverage in the original data flow model, but with insufficient fault coverage in the remaining two models. This indicates typical difficulties.

It is shown that the usefulness of test patterns on higher design levels depends upon how close to hardware and structured the HDL model is, and it turns out to be helpful to use modeling guidelines that support the development of good test patterns. This can be considered as an abstract extension of the concept of design for testability. Further references are found in [Armstrong 1993, Chakraborty, Ghosh 1988, Chao, Gray 1988, Davidson, Lewandowski 1986, O'Neil et al. 1990, Rao et al. 1993, Rosenthal, Wachsmann 1994, Ward, Armstrong 1990].

Notes:

Notes:

Notes:

HDL Models

for Circuits and Architectures

A Supplementary Introduction
Based on the Hardware Description
Language VERILOG

11 HDL Modeling with VERILOG

This chapter introduces in detail the hardware description language VERILOG. The reader is enabled to create his or her own hardware models and to fully understand the Interpreter Model and the Coarse Structure Model of the RISC processor TOOBSIE. The introduction is conceived as both a course and a reference. A training simulator VeriWell together with the examples of this chapter are included on the disk, so that all programs may be tested on a PC or a SUN. The disk contains instructions for the use of VeriWell.

All relevant VERILOG statements are explained by their syntax, by a text description, by small examples, and by similarities with the language C (Section 11.2). Typical modeling concepts are offered, such as parallelism, time, hierarchy, and pipeline, and are supported by medium sized examples (Section 11.3). Two large examples of a behavior and a structure model of a simple RISC computer are presented (Section 11.4). As very large examples, the TOOBSIE models mentioned before constitute a consistent extension of this introduction.

For a precise representation of the various statements, format EBNF (Extended Backus Naur Form) is used. In Section 11.1, there is a summary of the EBNF technique. For every particular statement, there are some EBNF rules. Section 11.5 summarizes all EBNF rules for reference.

Four large and 42 small tested examples, usually accompanied by a simulation result, support the learning process. VERILOG instructions, variables and similar VERILOG names have print type `courier`.

This introduction is based on [Ackad 1994]. Other textbooks are [Sternheim et al. 1993, Thomas, Moorby 1991].

11.1 Syntax Format EBNF

As for a natural language, a grammar or syntax defines which programs are (syntactically) correct, without explaining the meaning or semantics of the instructions. The Extended Backus-Naur Form EBNF is a way to describe the syntax of a programming language.

One can directly conclude, for example, that an `if` statement in Pascal always consists of an `if` part and a `then` part with an optional `else` part (or that VERILOG has no such `then`). An order with an `else` preceding the `if` is syntactically illegal.

Basic constructs of EBNF are definition, alternative, sequence, and recursion. *Definition* (represented by `::=`) defines an identifier on the left side by a string on the right side. For example,

```
letter_a ::= a
```

describes the letter `a`. If we want to define a small and a capital `A`, the *alternative* | is used:

```
letter_a ::= a | A
```

A digit can be defined in EBNF as

```
digit ::= 0 | 1 | 2 | 3 | 4 | 5 | 6 | 7 | 8 | 9
```

To compose an arbitrary number of arbitrarily many digits, we use *recursion*

```
number ::= <digit> | <digit> <number>
```

Thus a number is a choice between a digit and a digit followed by another number. For `digit`, exactly one digit has to be substituted by the first definition, for `number` a number. The definition of a number is recursive as it refers to itself. An alternate representation of a number is:

```
number ::= <digit> | <number> <number> .
```

Therefore, EBNF descriptions are not unique. Such descriptions officially specify just the syntax, but not the semantics. A definition of a `for` loop in Pascal by EBNF might look as follows:

```
for_loop ::= FOR <variable>:=<number> TO <number> <stepsize> DO
             <statement>;
variable    ::= <variable> <variable> | <digit>  | a | b | c | d | e | f
              | g | h | i | j | k | l | m | n | o | p | q | r | s | t
              | u | v | w | x | y | z | A | B | C | D | E | F | G | H
              | I | J | K | L | M | N | O | P | Q | R | S | T | U | V
              | W | X | Y | Z
stepsize ::=  | STEP <number>
```

A step size is optional. Therefore, `stepsize` is either replaced by the empty word before | or by `STEP <number>`. The definition of `number` and `digit` was explained above. A `statement` is defined elsewhere. By the names `variable`, `number`, and `statement`, a certain meaning is unofficially associated. Clever naming enhances syntax readability. A misleading but also valid representation of a `for` loop would be:

```
for_loop     ::= FOR <number1>:=<for> TO <variable> <statement1> DO <A>;
number1      ::= <number1><number1> | <digit> | a | b | c | d | e | f | g
                 | h | i | j | k | l | m | n | o | p | q | r | s | t | u
                 | v | w | x | y | z | A | B | C | D | E | F | G | H | I
                 | J | K | L | M | N | O | P | Q | R | S | T | U | V | W
                 | X | Y | Z
for          ::= <number>
variable     ::= <number>
statement1   ::= | STEP <for>
A            ::= <statement>
```

Here `number1` stands for a variable, and strings `for` and `variable` are replaced by a number. `Statement1` means the step size, and `A` is a statement still to be defined.

11.2 VERILOG Statements

This section is both for reference and for learning VERILOG. It is classified into structural statements (like `module`), variables (like `integer`), operations (+), program control (`case`), and miscellaneous statements. In addition, each statement or small group of closely related statements is presented as follows.

1. Name and meaning of statement group, numbered by B1, B2, ...;
2. EBNF syntax;
3. verbal description;
4. short example;
5. correspondence to programming language C.

There are the following groups of statements.

B1 `module, endmodule`
B2 `parameter, defparam`
B3 `begin, end`
B4 `task, endtask`
B5 `function, endfunction`
B6 `input, output, inout`
B7 `integer`
B8 `wire`
B9 `reg`
B10 `event`
B11 Constant
B12 Arithmetic `+, -, *, /, %`
B13 Compare `==, !=, ===, !==, <, >, <=, >=`
B14 Logic `!, &&, ||`
B15 Bit-wise logic `~, &, |`
B16 Concatenation `{}`
B17 Repeated concatenation
B18 Shift `<<, >>`
B19 Triggering an event `->`
B20 `assign`
B21 Assignment `=`
B22 Precedence
B23 `always`
B24 `initial`
B25 `at @`
B26 `wait`
B27 Wait `#`
B28 `if, else`
B29 `?, :`
B30 `case, casez`
B31 `while`
B32 `forever`
B33 `for`

B34 fork, join
B35 `define
B36 Comments //, /* ... */
B37 $display, $write
B38 $finish
B39 $stop
B40 $readmemh, $readmemb
B41 $gr_waves
B42 $define_group_waves
B43 $gr_waves_memsize

11.2.1 Structural Statements

B1 module, endmodule

```
VERILOG_program        ::= <module> | <VERILOG_program> <module>
module                 ::= module <name_of_module> <list_of_ports>; <module_item>
                           endmodule
name_of_module         ::= <identifier>
list_of_ports          ::= | ( <port_list> )
port_list              ::= <identifier> | <port_list> , <port_list>
module_item            ::= <parameter_declaration> | <input_declaration>
                           | <output_declaration> | <inout_declaration>
                           | <reg_declaration> | <integer_declaration>
                           | <wire_declaration> | <event_declaration>
                           | <gate_instantiation> | <module_instantiation>
                           | <always_statement> | <initial_statement>
                           | <continuous_assign> | <function> | <task>
                           | <module_item> <module_item>
module_instantiation   ::= <type_of_module>
                           <name_of_instance> ( <module_arguments> );
```

Modules are the basic components of VERILOG. They represent small or large hardware components like AND gates, counters, a CPU, or a complete computer network. A module can be structured hierarchically by submodules that are instances of other modules (cf. Example 11.2 and Section 11.3.3). `Module` and `endmodule` enclose a module. Following `module` and the module name is an optional `list_of_ports` as a connection with other modules. External modules may also access a module variable directly, but this leads to structures hard to verify and should therefore be avoided.

```
module counter;
integer R;

initial
  for (R=1; R <= 10; R = R + 1)
    $display ("R= %d", R);
endmodule
```

Example 11.1 A module

There normally follows a declaration of local variables in the module body. Their type (e.g., `reg`) has to be stated. If the variable is part of the port list, it is input, output, or both.

Example 11.1 outputs numbers 1 to 10 on the screen.

Statement `$display` corresponds to `printf` in C and outputs variables and text in a formated way on the screen. There is no correspondence to a module in C.

```
B2  parameter, defparam
```

```
parameter_declaration    ::= parameter <range> <list_of_assignments>;
range                    ::= | [<expression> : <expression>]
list_of_assignments      ::= <parameter_assignment>
                             | <parameter_assignment> , <list_of_assignments>
parameter_assignment     ::= <lvalue> = <expression>
```

A constant is declared by `parameter`. It cannot be changed by the module, but can be modified in a module instantiation by `defparam`. Thus, several instances of a module may differ in their parameters.

In Example 11.2, two modules of type `counter` are instantiated; `COUNTER1` counts up to 5, `COUNTER2` up to 10. First, a general module `counter` is declared counting up to parameter `max`. This parameter is specified during instantiation.

```
module counter;
parameter Max = 0;

integer R;

initial
  for (R=1; R <= Max; R = R + 1)
    $display ("R= %d", R);
endmodule


module main_module;
defparam COUNTER1.Max   = 5,
         COUNTER2.Max   = 10;

counter COUNTER1 ();
counter COUNTER2 ();
endmodule
```

Example 11.2 Parameters

```
B3  begin, end
```

```
compound_statement     ::= <named_seq_block> | <unnamed_seq_block>
named_seq_block        ::= begin : <name_of_block> <statements> end
name_of_block          ::= <identifier>
statements             ::= <statement> | <statements> <statement>
unnamed_seq_block      ::= begin <statements> end
```

Several statements are grouped by `begin` and `end` as a `compound_statement`. It may be named optionally, in which case the declaration of local variables is possible. Example 11.3 shows a module with four `initial` statements. The first two contain one statement each, the third contains a compound statement, the fourth contains a named compound statement with local variable A_LOCAL.

```
module begin_example;
reg A,
    B;

initial
  A = 1;

initial
  B = 1;

initial begin
  A = 1;
  B = 1;
end

initial begin : block1
  reg A_LOCAL;
  A_LOCAL = 1;
  B = A && A_LOCAL;
end
endmodule
```

Example 11.3 Compound statements

In C, {, } correspond to begin, end.

B4 task, endtask

```
task                 ::= task <name_of_task>; <tf_declaration> <statements>
                         endtask
name_of_task         ::= <identifier>
tf_declaration       ::= <parameter_declaration> | <reg_declaration>
                         | <integer_declaration> | <input_declaration>
reg_declaration      ::= reg <range> <list_of_variables>;
integer_declaration  ::= integer <range> <list_of_variables>;
```

A task contains logically connected program parts. Its limits are the keywords task and endtask. As opposed to a function (B5), a task may contain time controls (delay control #, event control @, and wait, B25–B27).

The module in Example 11.4 consists of two tasks and one initial block, in which first the task add is called with actual parameters 1 and 2. This task has thus two formal parameters. The result of addition is stored in the global variable RESULT. The task display_result has no parameters and outputs the result on a screen.

A task corresponds to a function in C with the restriction that a task may not return a result by its name.

```
module task_example;
reg   [7:0] RESULT;

task add;
input [7:0] A,
            B;
RESULT = A + B;
endtask

task display_result;
$display ("The sum is %d", RESULT);
endtask

initial begin
  add (1, 2);
  display_result;
end
endmodule
```

Example 11.4 A task

B5 function, endfunction

```
function               ::= function <range> <name_of_function>; <tf_declaration>
                           <statements> endfunction
name_of_function       ::= <identifier>
tf_declaration         ::= <parameter_declaration> | <reg_declaration>
                           | <integer_declaration> | <input_declaration>
reg_declaration        ::= reg <range> <list_of_variables>;
integer_declaration    ::= integer <range> <list_of_variables>;
```

A function is enclosed by the keywords `function` and `endfunction`. Like a task, it contains a logically connected piece of program, but a time control is not allowed. Therefore, a function corresponds in combinational logic to compute a result from its arguments without delay. A function returns exactly one value by its name and must have at least one formal parameter.

Function `maximum` in Example 11.5 computes the usual maximum of two values. The `initial` block calls the function several times with test values and outputs the results.

We will often append the simulation result directly to a program, as was done in Example 11.5.

The output begins with some simulator notes (`VERIOLG-XL ...`) and the start module. After the actual simulation output, the number of events simulated, the computation time elapsed, and a final line conclude the output. The initial and final information is not listed in the following, as it is basically the same in all cases.

A function corresponds to a C function with the restriction that it has to return a result by its name.

```
module function_example;

function maximum;
input A,
      B;
if (A > B)
  maximum = A;
else
  maximum = B;
endfunction

initial begin
  $display ("maximum (0,0)=%d", maximum (0,0));
  $display ("maximum (1,0)=%d", maximum (1,0));
  $display ("maximum (0,1)=%d", maximum (0,1));
end
endmodule
```

```
VERILOG-XL 2.0.1   Jun  6, 1995  10:22:48

. . .

Compiling source file "bsp4.v"
Highest level modules:
function_example

maximum (0,0)=0
maximum (1,0)=1
maximum (0,1)=1
11 simulation events
CPU time: 0.5 secs to compile + 0.1 secs to link + 0.0 secs in simulation
End of VERILOG-XL 2.0.1   Jun  6, 1995  10:22:49
```

Example 11.5 Function with simulation output

B6 input, output, inout

```
input_declaration     ::= input <range> <list_of_variables>;
output_declaration    ::= output <range> <list_of_variables>;
inout_declaration     ::= inout <range> <list_of_variables>;
```

A variable is declared as a module input by `input`. An `input` variable can be read but not changed. An `output` variable can only be written by the module, external modules can only read it. `inout` variables are readable and writeable. `input` can also be used for tasks and functions.

Subsequently, the type of inputs and outputs is declared. This may be omitted for a 1-bit wire. Example 11.6 again computes the maximum of two input variables and stores the result in register `RESULT`. `A` and `B` are 1-bit wires by default.

Keyword `inout` is mainly used for modeling bidirectional data buses. For a data exchange in both directions, `input` or `output` would be too restrictive. Example 11.7 implements two modules exchanging data by a bidirectional wire (called DATA in the main module and VALUE in the submodule). Section 11.3.7 treats bidirectional communication in detail.

```
module maximum (A, B, RESULT);
input  A,
       B;
output RESULT;
reg    RESULT;

always @(A or B)
  if (A > B)
    RESULT = A;
  else
    RESULT = B;
endmodule
```

Example 11.6 Module parameters

```
module submodule (VALUE, ENABLE);
inout [7:0] VALUE;
input       ENABLE;

reg   [7:0] BUFFER;
reg   [7:0] MEMORY;
wire  [7:0] VALUE = BUFFER;             // continuous assignment

always @(VALUE or ENABLE)
  if (ENABLE == 1) begin
    BUFFER = 8'bz;
    #2;
    MEMORY = VALUE;
  end
  else
    BUFFER = 255 - MEMORY;
endmodule


module mainmodul;
reg  [7:0] BUFFER;
wire [7:0] DATA = BUFFER;               // continuous assignment
reg        ENABLE;

submodule SUBMODULE (DATA, ENABLE);

initial begin
  BUFFER = 0;
  ENABLE = 1; #10;
  ENABLE = 0; #1;
  BUFFER = 8'bz;
  #10;
  $display ("DATA = %d", DATA);

  BUFFER = 100;
  ENABLE = 1; #10;
  ENABLE = 0; #1;
  BUFFER = 8'bz;
  #10;
  $display ("DATA = %d", DATA);
end
endmodule
```

Example 11.7 Bidirectional connection

```
submodule SUBMODULE (DATA, ENABLE);
```

connects the main module wires with those of the submodule. The main module sends an 8-bit byte to the submodule. The submodule subtracts it from 255 and returns the result on the same wire. As the data wire is used in both directions and by both modules, an additional control wire called `ENABLE` in both modules has to synchronize the write accesses. The submodule reads a value, if the main module has set `ENABLE` to `1`, and stores it in `MEMORY`. If the main module sets `ENABLE` to `0`, the submodule subtracts `MEMORY` from 255 and puts the result on the bidirectional bus.

Note that the party not writing has to set its register `BUFFER` connected with the data wire to value `z`. `z` stands for high impedance (B11), meaning that the party clears the bus for a write access of the other party. Note further that an `inout` variable cannot be a register, but has to be a wire.

Because a `wire` cannot directly be assigned a value, it is permanently connected in the submodule with register `BUFFER` by

```
wire [7:0] VALUE = BUFFER;
```

(continuous assignment, B20). In short, `VALUE` takes with every change of `BUFFER` its contents. If the `BUFFER` of the submodule is `z`, only the `BUFFER` of the main module affects the data wire `DATA = VALUE`. Also in the main module, a register is continuously assigned to the data bus by

```
wire [7:0] DATA = BUFFER;
```

There is no direct equivalent in C, where all variables may be read and written.

11.2.2 Variable Declaration

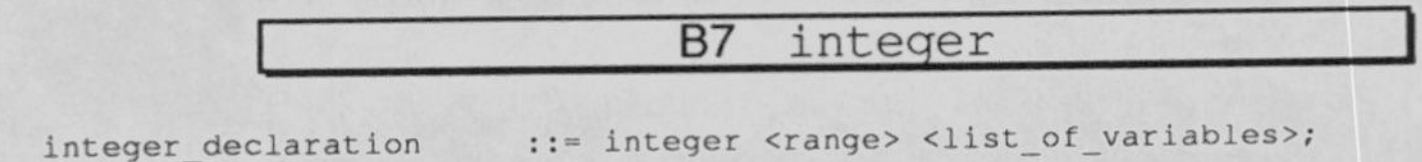

B7 integer

```
integer_declaration      ::= integer <range> <list_of_variables>;
```

One or more integer variables are defined by keyword `integer`. The `range` may be defined in bits, it is the same for all variables of the list.

This corresponds to `int` in C.

B8 wire

```
wire_declaration         ::= wire <range> <list_of_variables>;
                           | wire <range> <list_of_assignments>;
list_of_assignments      ::= <parameter_assignment>
                           | <parameter_assignment> , <list_of_assignments>
parameter_assignment     ::= <lvalue> = <expression>
```

Variables of type `wire` may have per bit values `0`, `1`, `x` (undefined), and `z` (high impedance) (B11). Again the `range` in bits may precede. It is the same for the whole list. A wire is a connecting net between different nodes. A wire is unable to store information. It is impossible to directly assign a value to a wire, but it may receive information by a continuous assignment `assign` or directly during declaration (B20).

```
module submodule1 (CLOCK_SUBMODULE1);
output CLOCK_SUBMODULE1;
reg    CLOCK_SUBMODULE1;

always begin
  CLOCK_SUBMODULE1 = 0;               // reset clock
  #10;                                // wait 10 time steps
  CLOCK_SUBMODULE1 = 1;               // set clock
  #10;                                // wait 10 time steps
end
endmodule


module submodule2 (CLOCK_SUBMODULE2, CLOCK_DIV_2_SUBMODULE2);
input  CLOCK_SUBMODULE2;
output CLOCK_DIV_2_SUBMODULE2;
reg    CLOCK_DIV_2_SUBMODULE2;

always begin
  CLOCK_DIV_2_SUBMODULE2 = 0;         // reset clock
  @(CLOCK_SUBMODULE2);                // wait twice
  @(CLOCK_SUBMODULE2);
  CLOCK_DIV_2_SUBMODULE2 = 1;         // set clock
  @(CLOCK_SUBMODULE2);                // wait twice
  @(CLOCK_SUBMODULE2);
end
endmodule


module mainmodule;
wire CLOCK_MAINMODULE,
     CLOCK_DIV_2_MAINMODULE;

submodule1 SUBMODULE1 (CLOCK_MAINMODULE);
submodule2 SUBMODULE2 (CLOCK_MAINMODULE, CLOCK_DIV_2_MAINMODULE);

always @(CLOCK_DIV_2_MAINMODULE)
  $display ("CLOCK_DIV_2_MAINMODULE changing");

initial begin
  #100;                               // wait 100 time steps
  $finish;                            // and finish simulation
end
endmodule
```

Example 11.8 Wires

When instantiating a submodule in a module, the wires in the parameter list of the submodule are connected with those of the module; this corresponds to a continuous assignment. If a register is continuously assigned to a wire, the value of the wire can be controlled by assigning values to the register.

The mainmodule in Example 11.8 instantiates two modules SUBMODULE1 and SUBMODULE2 of types submodule1 and submodule2. Instance SUBMODULE1 generates pulses of period 20 for the other modules. Because it writes to CLOCK_SUBMODULE1, it has to be a register (B9). By the instantiation

```
submodule1 SUBMODULE1 (CLOCK_MAINMODULE);
```

register CLOCK_SUBMODULE1 of SUBMODULE1 is connected with wire CLOCK_MAINMODULE. This must not be of type reg, as CLOCK_SUBMODULE1 is a register variable. The instantiation

```
submodule2 SUBMODULE2
  (CLOCK_MAINMODULE, CLOCK_DIV_2_MAINMODULE);
```

connects wire CLOCK_SUBMODULE2 with wire CLOCK_MAINMODULE and thus with wire CLOCK_SUBMODULE1. CLOCK_SUBMODULE2 must also be of type wire, as it is implicitly connected to register CLOCK_SUBMODULE1.

Such assignments can produce chains through several modules. Only the ends of a chain may be registers, the remaining members are wires.

As compared to int in C, a wire has additional physical properties.

B9 reg

```
reg_declaration          ::= reg <range> <list_of_variables>;
```

Variables of type reg may assume at every bit position one of the values 0, 1, x (undefined), and z (high impedance) (B11). Preceding the list of variables, a range in bits may be defined. It is the same for all variables of the list. A register variable (in short: register) stores information until a new value is assigned.

The counter in Example 11.9 outputs numbers 1 to 10.

```
module counter;
reg [3:0] R;

initial
  for (R=1; R <= 10; R = R + 1)
    $display ("R= %d", R);
endmodule
```

Example 11.9 Register

As compared to int in C, a register has additional physical properties.

B10 event

```
event_declaration          ::= event <list_of_variables>;
```

A variable of type `event` is an abstract event, whose interpretation remains with the user: it may be interpreted as the arrival of a rising signal edge or an acknowledge of another module. Such events may also be modeled by registers, but less elegantly. Events do not model (permanent) *states*, but their *changes*.

Example 11.10 contains a sender and a receiver. The sender, modeled by an `initial` block, is to send an 8-bit value to the receiver, an `always` block, which the receiver outputs on a screen. Data exchange is accomplished by variable `DATA`. Therefore, type `reg` is selected. The sender reports the existence of a new value to the receiver by an `event` variable `STROBE`. The receiver waits for a new event by

```
always @ STROBE
```

which the sender triggers by

```
-> STROBE;
```

```
module send_receive;
reg [7:0] DATA;
event     STROBE;

// Sender
initial begin
  #10;
  DATA =   0; ->STROBE; #10;      // select DATA
  DATA = 100; ->STROBE; #10;      // trigger STROBE
  DATA = 255; ->STROBE; #10;      // and wait 10 steps
  DATA = 255; ->STROBE; #10;
end

// Receiver
always @ STROBE
  $display ("New value received is: %d", DATA);
endmodule
```

Example 11.10 Event

An alternative model employing a register is shown in Example 11.11.

The receiver waits by

```
always @(posedge STROBE)
```

until `STROBE` changes from `0` to `1`; without `posedge` (B25), *every* change of `STROBE` would be considered.

There is no `event` construct in C.

```
module send_receive_2;
reg [7:0] DATA;
reg       STROBE;

// Sender
initial begin
  #10;
  DATA =   0; STROBE = 1; #5; STROBE = 0; #5;    // select DATA,
  DATA = 100; STROBE = 1; #5; STROBE = 0; #5;    // STROBE pulse,
  DATA = 255; STROBE = 1; #5; STROBE = 0; #5;    // and wait
  DATA = 255; STROBE = 1; #5; STROBE = 0; #5;
end

// Receiver
always @(posedge STROBE)
  $display ("New value received is: %d", DATA);
endmodule
```

Example 11.11 Register instead of event

B11 Constants

```
constant_number      ::= <optional_sign> <width> <base> <number>
optional_sign        ::= | + | -
width                ::= | <decimal_number>
decimal_number       ::= <decimal_digit> | <decimal_digit> <decimal_number>
decimal_digit        ::= 0 | 1 | 2 | 3 | 4 | 5 | 6 | 7 | 8 | 9
base                 ::= | 'b | 'B | 'o | 'O | 'd | 'D | 'h | 'H
number               ::= <digit_of_number> | <digit_of_number> <number>
digit_of_number      ::= <decimal_digit> | <hexadecimal_digit>
                         | x | X | z | Z | ? | _
hexadecimal_digit    ::= a | A | b | B | c | C | d | D | e | E | f | F
```

Constants may have different bases. As the `base`, there are 2 (`'b` or `'B`), 8 (`'o`, `'O`), 10 (`'d`, `'D`), and 16 (`'h`, `'H`), the default being 10. When the `width` is specified, a base has to be mentioned. The `width` precedes the constant `base` as a decimal number.

As a `number`, only numbers of the selected `base` are allowed (e.g., only `0` and `1` for base 2) and `x`, `X`, `z`, `Z`, `?`, and `_`. `z` and `Z` represent "high impedance". `x` and `X` are interpreted as "undefined". Instead of `z` or `Z`, also `?` may be used. An `_` serves for better readability. The semantics of `z` and `x` are now explained in more detail.

In Example 11.12, register `DATA` is assigned some typical constants. The output format is no longer `%d`, but `%b` for a binary number.

By

```
DATA = 1'b1;
```

`DATA` receives value `1`, although the constant has width 1 bit. The remaining bits are filled with `0`. In

```
DATA = 'bz;
```

no width is specified; in this case, it is filled with `z` instead of `0`.

```
module constant_example;
reg  [7:0] DATA;

initial begin
  DATA =           0; $display ("DATA = %b", DATA);  // decimal   0
  DATA =          10; $display ("DATA = %b", DATA);  // decimal  10
  DATA =        'h10; $display ("DATA = %b", DATA);  // decimal  16
  DATA =        'b10; $display ("DATA = %b", DATA);  // decimal   2
  DATA =         255; $display ("DATA = %b", DATA);  // decimal 255
  DATA =        1'b1; $display ("DATA = %b", DATA);
  DATA =  'bxxxxzzzz; $display ("DATA = %b", DATA);
  DATA = 'b1010_1010; $display ("DATA = %b", DATA);
  DATA =        1'bz; $display ("DATA = %b", DATA);
  DATA =         'bz; $display ("DATA = %b", DATA);
end
endmodule
```

```
Highest level modules:
constant_example

DATA = 00000000
DATA = 00001010
DATA = 00010000
DATA = 00000010
DATA = 11111111
DATA = 00000001
DATA = xxxxzzzz
DATA = 10101010
DATA = 0000000z
DATA = zzzzzzzz
```

Example 11.12 Constants

```
module constant_example_2;
reg  [7:0] REG1,
           REG2;
wire [7:0] W = REG1;
assign     W = REG2;

initial begin
                                    $display ("W = %b", W);
  REG1 =  0; REG2 =           0; $display ("W = %b", W);
  REG1 = 10; REG2 =       8'bz; $display ("W = %b", W);
             REG2 = 8'b11111111; $display ("W = %b", W);
             REG2 =       8'bx; $display ("W = %b", W);
             REG2 =       8'bz; $display ("W = %b", W);
end
endmodule
```

```
Highest level modules:
constant_example_2

W = xxxxxxxx
W = 00000000
W = 00001010
W = xxxx1x1x
W = xxxxxxxx
W = 00001010
```

Example 11.13 x and z

Example 11.13 explains the meaning of x and z further. Two registers REG1 and REG2 both drive wire W. This corresponds to the connection of two possibly high impedance drivers with a common output wire. If both drivers are not high impedance, there are conflicts for different output values.

At simulation beginning, REG1 and REG2 are still undefined with x in all bit positions. Their connection also produces x everywhere. If both registers are set to 0, there is no conflict. By

```
REG1 = 10; REG2 = 8'bz;
```

the second driver becomes high impedance, so that the first register drives output W alone. After an assignment

```
REG2 = 8'b11111111;
```

there are conflicts at bit positions with different values. By

```
REG2 = 8'bx;
```

all bits are undefined, which is transferred to the output. Note the important difference between the two cases of all bits of REG2 being z or x. In the first case of z, this bit does *not* influence connected wires; in the second case of x, the variable "drives" the connected wires with an undefined value.

Also in C, constants with bases 2, 8, 10, or 16 may be defined. Values x,z, or ? and a width are not possible.

11.2.3 Operations

B12 Arithmetic +, -, *, /, %

```
expression1           ::= <expression> <four_rules_operator> <expression>
four_rules_operator   ::= + | - | * | / | %
expression2           ::= <sign> <expression>
sign                  ::= + | -
```

+, -, *, and / have the usual meaning. Operator % gives the remainder of a division. + and - may also represent a sign.

These operators have the same meaning in C.

B13 Comparison ==, !=, ===, !==, <, >, <=, >=

```
expression7           ::= <expression> <compare_operator> <expression>
compare_operator      ::= == | != | === | !== | < | > | <= | >=
```

These operators compare expressions. As in C, ==, !=, <, >, <=, and >= mean "equal", "not equal", "less", etc.; === and !== also consider values x and z. While the first operators compare *logically*, operators === and its negation

!== do so *literally*. Example 11.14 explains the difference. We also refer to Chapter 4.

```
module compare;

initial begin
   $display ("1'bx  ==  1'b1  = %b", 1'bx  ==  1'b1);
   $display ("1'bx  === 1'b1  = %b", 1'bx  === 1'b1);
   $display ("1'bx  ==  1'bx  = %b", 1'bx  ==  1'bx);
   $display ("1'bx  === 1'bx  = %b", 1'bx  === 1'bx);
   $display ("1'bz  !=  1'b1  = %b", 1'bz  !=  1'b1);
   $display ("1'bx  <=  1'b1  = %b", 1'bx  <=  1'b1);
   $display ("2'bxx ==  2'b11 = %b", 2'bxx ==  2'b11);
end
endmodule
```

```
Highest level modules:
compare

1'bx  ==  1'b1  = x
1'bx  === 1'b1  = 0
1'bx  ==  1'bx  = x
1'bx  === 1'bx  = 1
1'bz  !=  1'b1  = x
1'bx  <=  1'b1  = x
2'bxx ==  2'b11 = x
```

Example 11.14 Compare operators

"Logical equality" means that both sides contain only `0` or `1` and are equal. The first logic comparison between `1'bx` and `1'b1` is `x`, as the first expression is undefined. The second and "literal comparison" is `0` (false), as `x` is different from `1`.

The comparison of two undefined `x` is logically undefined, but literally equal (result `x` or `1`). Note that in the latter comparison, the result is 1 bit, although the compared expressions are 2 bits.

These operators exist in C with the same semantic except for === and !==.

B14 Logic !, &&, ||

```
expression3              ::= <expression> <binary_logical_operator> <expression>
binary_logical_operator ::= &&  |  ||
expression4              ::= <unary_logical_operator> <expression>
unary_logical_operator  ::= !
```

Logic operators negation (!), OR (||),and AND (&&) have one or two `expressions` as operands. For instance, an `if` condition may require several conditions to be satisfied. As every operand may also contain `x` and `z`, the logic operators have to be defined also for these values. The result of an operation is `x`, if at least one bit position of some operand contains an `x` or `z`. There is an exception if the result is uniquely determined by one of two operands. For example, the value of

```
1'bx && 1'b0
```

is always 0. Table 11.15 defines the AND operator.

&&	0	1	x	z
0	0	0	0	0
1	0	1	x	x
x	0	x	x	x
z	0	x	x	x

Table 11.15 AND operation for x and z

Example 11.16 clarifies operations on the logic level.

```
module logical_operators;

initial begin
  $display ("! 1'b1 = %b", ! 1'b1);
  $display ("! 1'bx = %b", ! 1'bx);
  $display ("! 1'bz = %b", ! 1'bz);
  $display ("1'b1  && 1'b0  = %b", 1'b1  && 1'b0 );
  $display ("1'bx  && 1'b0  = %b", 1'bx  && 1'b0 );
  $display ("1'bx  && 1'b1  = %b", 1'bx  && 1'b1 );
  $display ("1'bx  || 1'b0  = %b", 1'bx  || 1'b0 );
  $display ("1'bx  || 1'b1  = %b", 1'bx  || 1'b1 );
  $display ("2'b00 || 2'bxx = %b", 2'b00 || 2'bxx);
end
endmodule
```

```
Highest level modules:
logical_operators

! 1'b1 = 0
! 1'bx = x
! 1'bz = x
1'b1  && 1'b0  = 0
1'bx  && 1'b0  = 0
1'bx  && 1'b1  = x
1'bx  || 1'b0  = x
1'bx  || 1'b1  = 1
2'b00 || 2'bxx = x
```

Example 11.16 Logic operations

Also the expression

```
1'bx || 1'b1
```

is always 1, as the second operand uniquely determines the result. The last statement of Example 11.16 combines two 2-bit expressions, the result is nevertheless just 1 bit.

These operators exist in C except for x and z.

B15 Bit-wise Logic ~, &, |

```
expression5                ::= <expression> <binary_bitwise_operator> <expression>
binary_bitwise_operator ::= & | |
expression6                ::= <unary_bitwise_operator> <expression>
unary_bitwise_operator   ::= ~
```

In this EBNF of a binary_bitwise_operator, the first | represents an EBNF alternative, whereas the second | is a VERILOG symbol.

Operators negation (~), OR (|), and AND (&) combine expressions bit-wise. The result has the same width as the widest expression. At every bit position, the operands are combined appropriately. As every bit may assume one of the four values 0, 1, x, or z , the definition of bit-wise operators has to be extended. The same rules as with logic operators apply. If at least one of the combined bits has value x or z, the result at this position is x, except for the case that it is determined completely by one of the operands. For instance, this is the case in the operation

```
1'bx & 1'bz & 1'b1 & 1'b0
```

where the result is always 0. Example 11.17 applies operators bit-wise.

```
module bitwise_operators;

initial begin
  $display ("~ 4'bzx10          = %b", ~ 4'bzx10);
  $display ("4'b001x & 4'b0x10 = %b", 4'b001x & 4'b0x10);
  $display ("2'b1x | 2'b00      = %b", 2'b1x | 2'b00);
end
endmodule
```

```
Highest level modules:
bitwise_operators

~ 4'bzx10          = xx01
4'b001x & 4'b0x10 = 0010
2'b1x | 2'b00      = 1x
```

Example 11.17 Bit-wise operations

The first statement $display inverts a 4-bit variable. The second shows an AND operation, the third one an OR operation. Note that the result has several bits.

These operators exist in C, except for x and z.

B16 Concatenation { }

```
concatenation        ::= { <expression_list> }
expression_list      ::= <expression> | <expression> , <expression_list>
```

A `concatenation` appends several `expressions` to form a new one. Two concatenated 3-bit `expressions` are 6 bits. Example 11.18 concatenates three variables of widths 3, 4, and 2.

```
module concatenation;

initial
  $display ("{3'b100, 4'bxxzz, 2'ha} = %b", {3'b100, 4'bxxzz, 2'ha});
endmodule
```

```
Highest level modules:
concatenation

{3'b100, 4'bxxzz, 2'ha} = 100xxzz10
```

Example 11.18 Concatenation

Notice `2'ha` in the third expression. The decimal value `10` would require 4 bits, but only 2 bits are allowed. Thus, only the two least significant bits are used.

Such an operation does not exist in C.

B17 Repeated Concatenation

```
replication          ::= { <expression> { <expression_list> } }
expression_list      ::= <expression> | <expression> , <expression_list>
```

In a `replication`, the `expression` has to be constant.

```
{ 4 { 2'b00, 2'b11} }
```

produces

```
16'b0011001100110011
```

Such an operation does not exist in C.

B18 Shift <<, >>

```
shift                ::= <expression> <shift_operator> <expression>
shift_operator       ::= << | >>
```

Operation << shifts bits in the direction of more significant bit positions, >> in the opposite direction. The right `expression` is the shift distance. If it is negative, it is shifted the opposite way.

Example 11.19 first shifts left by 4 bits, then right by 4 bits, and finally left by -4 bits, hence right.

```
module shift;

initial begin
   $display ("%b", 8'b0000_1111 << 4);
   $display ("%b", 8'b0000_1111 >> 4);
   $display ("%b", 8'b0000_1111 << -4);
end
endmodule
```

```
Highest level modules:
shift

11110000
00000000
00000000
```

Example 11.19 Shift

The same operations exist in C.

B19 Event Triggering ->

```
generate_event_statement::= -> <event_variable>;
event_variable          ::= <identifier>
```

Operation `->` triggers an event (B10). In Example 11.20, an `always` and an `initial` statement are executed simultaneously. The `always` statement is executed always again and waits for a change of `EVENT` by condition

```
@ EVENT
```

In this case, the following `$display` statement is executed, which outputs the present simulation time in `$time`. Events are triggered in the `initial` block. The first one is triggered at time 0, the second and third one at time 10.

However, the `always` condition reacts at time 10 only to one of the two events triggered at time 10. This special case is treated in detail when explaining the time axis (B23, Section 11.3). The fourth event is triggered at time 20; `$finish` completes the simulation.

```
module trigger_event;
event EVENT;

always @ EVENT                          // wait for EVENT
  $display ("EVENT is triggered at time %d", $time);
                                        // $time is the simulation time

initial begin
  ->EVENT; #10;
  ->EVENT;                              // two events for the same
  ->EVENT; #10;                         // simulation time
  ->EVENT; #10;
  $finish;                              // end of simulation
end
endmodule
```

```
Highest level modules:
trigger_event

EVENT is triggered at time                0
EVENT is triggered at time               10
EVENT is triggered at time               20
L16 "bsp18.v": $finish at simulation time 30
```

Example 11.20 Event triggering

There are no events in C.

B20 assign

```
continuous_assign       ::= assign <list_of_assignments>;
list_of_assignments     ::= <parameter_assignment>
                          | <parameter_assignment> , <list_of_assignments>
parameter_assignment    ::= <lvalue> = <expression>
```

In a continuous assignment, denoted by keyword `assign`, the `expression` on the right side of an = is permanently assigned to a wire or a part of it. It is recomputed whenever the right side changes. Aside from `assign`, the continuous assignment can also be stated implicitly in the definition of a wire as in Example 11.21. Here, `REGISTER_VARIABLE` is implicitly assigned to `WIRE1` and explicitly to `WIRE2`. Both `always` blocks monitor `WIRE1` and `WIRE2` and output the result with every change of simulation time. The changes are produced by the `initial` block.

Note that `REGISTER_VARIABLE` changes twice at time 20, which, however, does not lead to a change of `WIRE1` or `WIRE2`, because the resulting state of `REGISTER_VARIABLE` has the same value as before. This specialty is treated in the context of time axis (B23, Section 11.3).

A similar statement does not exist in C.

```
module assign_test;
reg    REGISTER_VARIABLE;
wire   WIRE1 = REGISTER_VARIABLE;   // implicit continuous assignment
wire   WIRE2;
assign WIRE2 = REGISTER_VARIABLE;   // explicit continuous assignment

always @(WIRE1)
  $display ("time = %d: WIRE1 = %d", $time, WIRE1);

always @(WIRE2)
  $display ("time = %d: WIRE2 = %d", $time, WIRE2);

initial begin
  REGISTER_VARIABLE = 0; #10;
  REGISTER_VARIABLE = 1; #10;
  REGISTER_VARIABLE = 0;
  REGISTER_VARIABLE = 1; #10;
  $finish;
end
endmodule
```

```
Highest level modules:
assign_test

time =                    0: WIRE1 = 0
time =                    0: WIRE2 = 0
time =                   10: WIRE1 = 1
time =                   10: WIRE2 = 1
time =                   20: WIRE1 = 1
L21 "bsp19.v": $finish at simulation time 30
```

Example 11.21 Continuous assignment

B21 Assignment =

```
assignment        ::= <lvalue> = <control> <expression>;
control           ::= | <delay_control_construct> | <event_control_construct>
lvalue            ::= <variable> <range> | <concatenation>
                    | <variable> [<expression>]
```

The `expression` on the right side is assigned exactly once to a variable or part of it on the left side. The left side has to be of type `reg` or `integer`. If the = is followed by a time control (`delay_control_construct` or `event_control_construct`), the present value of `expression` is copied into a temporary, transparent register. After waiting for the given time or event, the assignment takes place.

An assignment without time control exists in C.

B22 Precedences

The precedence of operators from high to low in Table 11.22 concludes this section on operations.

```
!    ~
*    /    %
+    -
<<   >>
<    <=   >    >=
==   !==  ===  !==
&
|
&&
||
```

Table 11.22 Precedences

11.2.4 Program Control

B23 always

```
always_statement        ::= always <statement>
```

An `always` statement executes the following `statement` again and again. We often refer to it as an `always` block. It is executed simultaneously to all other `always` and `initial` blocks (B24). Thus all such statements operate *in parallel* (Section 11.3.1).

The statements within an `always` block are executed *sequentially without interrupt* until a time control is reached (Section 11.3.2).

The first two `always` blocks in Example 11.23 display messages whenever `COUNTER` changes. The third one changes `COUNTER`. First, it is checked by `if` whether `COUNTER` was not yet initialized (this is the case in the first run). The literal comparison `===` is required instead of the logic `==`. `COUNTER` is increased until simulation terminates at time 10.

`@(COUNTER)` in the first `always` block executes the following `$display` only, if `COUNTER` has changed. One could also write

```
always
begin
  @(COUNTER);
  $display ("COUNTER has changed");
end
```

All three `always` blocks operate in parallel in the sense that at a given simulation point, the order of execution is arbitrary. The statements within an `always` block are executed as mentioned above sequentially without interrupt until a time control is encountered. Therefore, a simulation result like

```
time = 10
COUNTER has changed
COUNTER = 1
```

```
module always_test;
reg [7:0] COUNTER;

always @(COUNTER)
  $display ("COUNTER has changed");

always @(COUNTER) begin
  $write ("time = %d    ", $time);
  $display ("COUNTER = %d", COUNTER);
end

always begin
  if (COUNTER === 8'bx)
    COUNTER = 0;                     // initialization
  else
    COUNTER = COUNTER + 1;
  if (COUNTER == 10)
    $finish;                         // finish simulation after 10 runs
  #10;                               // wait 10 time units
end

endmodule
```

```
Highest level modules:
always_test

time =                    0     COUNTER =   0
COUNTER has changed
COUNTER has changed
time =                   10     COUNTER =   1
time =                   20     COUNTER =   2
COUNTER has changed
COUNTER has changed
time =                   30     COUNTER =   3
time =                   40     COUNTER =   4
COUNTER has changed
COUNTER has changed
time =                   50     COUNTER =   5
time =                   60     COUNTER =   6
COUNTER has changed
COUNTER has changed
time =                   70     COUNTER =   7
time =                   80     COUNTER =   8
COUNTER has changed
COUNTER has changed
time =                   90     COUNTER =   9
L18 "bsp20.v": $finish at simulation time 100
```

Example 11.23 Parallel `always` blocks

is impossible, because in this case, the second `always` block would be interrupted by the first one, although there is no time control between the `$write` and the `$display` statement. If at the end of the third `always` block, the time control

```
#10
```

were missing, the third block would be executed 10 times in sequence without transferring control to one of the other two blocks. Details may be found in Section 11.3.1.

There is no `always` statement in C having only a sequential program flow.

B24 initial

```
initial_statement        ::= initial <statement>
```

An `initial` statement, often referred to as an `initial` block, executes the following `statement` exactly once. It is executed simultaneously with all other `initial` and `always` blocks. Therefore, all such statements operate *in parallel* (Section 11.3.1).

The statements within an `initial` block are executed *sequentially without interrupt*, until a time control is reached (Section 11.3.2).

Example 11.24 shows two parallel `initial` blocks. It is not determined whether the first or the second block is executed first.

```
module initial_test;
initial begin                          // initial block 1
  $display ("i1: a");
  $display ("i1: b");
  #10;
  $display ("i1: c");
end

initial begin                          // initial block 2
  $display ("i2: a");
  $display ("i2: b");
end
endmodule
```

Example 11.24 Parallel `initial` blocks

A possible simulation result is

```
i1: a
i1: b
i2: a
i2: b
i1: c
```

Here, the first block was executed first. `#10;` interrupted this execution, and then the second block was executed. Another possible simulation result would be

```
i2: a
i2: b
i1: a
i1: b
i1: c
```

There is no `initial` statement in C having only a sequential program flow.

B25 at @

```
event_control_construct ::= @ <event_variable> | @ (<event_expression>)
event_variable          ::= <identifier>
event_expression        ::= <expression> | posedge <expression>
                            | negedge <expression>
                            | <event_expression> or <event_expression>
```

An `event_control_construct` waits for an event to occur (without terminating semicolon). It waits either for a new event of an `event_variable` or for a change of an `event_expression`.

A leading `posedge` waits for a rising edge from `0`, `x`, or `z` to `1`. Analogously, `negedge` waits for a falling edge from `1`, `x`, or `z` to `0`. Several such changes may be combined by `or`.

In Example 11.25, the first `always` block waits for a rising edge of `CLOCK`, the second one for a falling edge, and the third for `EVENT1` or `EVENT2`.

```
module events;
event EVENT1,
      EVENT2;
reg   CLOCK;

always @(posedge CLOCK)
  $display ("time: %d: rising  edge", $time);

always @(negedge CLOCK)
  $display ("time: %d: falling edge", $time);

always @(EVENT1 or EVENT2)
  $display ("time: %d: EVENT1 or EVENT2", $time);

initial begin
  CLOCK = 0; #10;
  CLOCK = 1; #10;
  CLOCK = 0; #10;
  ->EVENT1; #10;
  ->EVENT2; #10;
  $finish;
end
endmodule
```

```
Highest level modules:
events

time:                      0: falling edge
time:                     10: rising  edge
time:                     20: falling edge
time:                     30: EVENT1 or EVENT2
time:                     40: EVENT1 or EVENT2
L21 "bsp22.v": $finish at simulation time 50
```

Example 11.25 Event control @

Already at time 0, there is a falling edge of CLOCK, which changes from x to 0. At time 30, EVENT1 is triggered, condition @(EVENT1 or EVENT2) is therefore satisfied.

A similar construction does not exist in C.

B26 wait

```
wait_statement          ::= wait ( <expression> ) <statement_or_null>
```

A wait starts a wait until the expression is true; it is optionally followed by a statement. If the expression is already true when reaching wait, execution is not interrupted at this point.

```
module wait_test;
reg ENABLE;

always begin
  wait (ENABLE);
  $display ("time: %d", $time);
  #1;
end

always @(ENABLE)
  $display ("ENABLE= %d", ENABLE);

initial begin
  ENABLE = 1; #5;
  ENABLE = 0; #5;
  ENABLE = 1; #5;
  $finish;
end
endmodule
```

```
Highest level modules:
wait_test

ENABLE= 1
time:                    0
time:                    1
time:                    2
time:                    3
time:                    4
ENABLE= 0
ENABLE= 1
time:                   10
time:                   11
time:                   12
time:                   13
time:                   14
L17 "bsp23.v": $finish at simulation time 15
```

Example 11.26 wait

The first always block in Example 11.26 outputs the present simulation time, if ENABLE has value 1. Without

```
#1;
```

the loop would become endless: the first `always` would no longer transfer control to the other `initial` and `always` blocks. The second `always` block outputs `ENABLE` when changing. The `initial` block generates the enable signal.

There is no equivalent to `wait` in C.

B27 Delay

```
delay_control_construct ::= # <number> | # <variable> | # ( <expression> )
```

A `delay_control_construct` is given by a `number`, a `variable`, or an `expression`. Execution is continued after the delay. A delay control is not terminated by a semicolon.

The `always` block in Example 11.27 outputs changes of `WIRE`. The `initial` block contains three time controls; the middle one is inside an assignment. In this case, the assignment of `1` to `WIRE` is delayed by 10 units of time, so that `WIRE` changes to `1` at time 20. The difference between statement

```
WIRE = #10 1;
```

and

```
#10;
WIRE = 1;
```

is treated in detail in Section 11.3.2.

```
module time_delay;
reg WIRE;

always @(WIRE)
  $display ("time: %d, WIRE= %d", $time, WIRE);

initial begin
  WIRE = 0;
  #10;
  WIRE = #10 1;
  #10;
end
endmodule
```

```
Highest level modules:
time_delay

time:                     0, WIRE= 0
time:                    20, WIRE= 1
```

Example 11.27 Delay #

This statement corresponds to `sleep (<seconds>)` in C.

B28 if, else

```
if_statement          ::= if ( <conditional_expression> ) <statement_or_null>
                          <else_clause>
statement_or_null     ::= ; | <statement>
else_clause           ::= | else <statement_or_null>
```

```
module if_test;
reg [7:0] WIRE;                       // 8 bit variable

always @(WIRE) begin
  $display ("time: %d, WIRE= %b", $time, WIRE);
  if (WIRE)
    $display ("if");
  else
    $display ("else");
  $display;
end

initial begin
  WIRE = 0;             #10;        // case 1
  WIRE = 1;             #10;        // case 2
  WIRE = 100;           #10;        // case 3
  WIRE = 8'b0000_001x;  #10;        // case 4
  WIRE = 8'b1111_111z;  #10;        // case 5
  WIRE = 8'bxxxx_xxxx;  #10;        // case 6
  WIRE = 8'bzzzz_zzzz;  #10;        // case 7
end
endmodule
```

```
Highest level modules:
if_test

time:                    0, WIRE= 00000000
else

time:                   10, WIRE= 00000001
if

time:                   20, WIRE= 01100100
if

time:                   30, WIRE= 0000001x
if

time:                   40, WIRE= 1111111z
if

time:                   50, WIRE= xxxxxxxx
else

time:                   60, WIRE= zzzzzzzz
else
```

Example 11.28 Alternatives

If the `conditional_expression` of an `if_statement` is true (at least one bit being `1`), the following (possibly empty) statement is executed, otherwise the else_clause. In other words, the if branch is executed, if the OR of all bits of conditional_expression is 1.

In the first case of Example 11.28, the condition contains no 1-bit, therefore, the else branch is executed. In cases two to five, the condition contains at least one bit that is 1. In the last two cases, the condition is undetermined.

The same statement exists in C.

B29 ?, :

```
selection_expression    ::= <expression> ? <expression> : <expression>
```

If the first expression before ? is not equal 0 (i.e., at least one bit of this expression is 1), the left side selection_expression takes the middle expression between ? and :, otherwise the third expression.

In Example 11.29, RESULT takes the value of SOURCE, if ENABLE contains at least one 1, otherwise 8'bx. For practice only, the enable signal is in this case more than one bit.

```
module selection;
reg  [1:0] ENABLE;
reg  [7:0] SOURCE,
           RESULT;

always @(ENABLE or SOURCE) begin
  RESULT = ENABLE ? SOURCE : 8'bxxxx_xxxx;
  $display ("time: %d, RESULT= %b", $time, RESULT);
end

initial begin
  SOURCE = 0;              #10;      // change of 8'bxxxx_xxxx to 0
  ENABLE = 1;              #10;      // change of 2'bxx to 2'b01
  SOURCE = 8'b0000_1010;   #10;
  ENABLE = 2'b0x;          #10;
  ENABLE = 2'b0z;          #10;
  ENABLE = 2'b1x;          #10;
  $finish;
end
endmodule
```

```
Highest level modules:
selection

time:                        0, RESULT= xxxxxxxx
time:                       10, RESULT= 00000000
time:                       20, RESULT= 00001010
time:                       30, RESULT= xxxxxxxx
time:                       40, RESULT= xxxxxxxx
time:                       50, RESULT= 00001010
L18 "bsp26.v": $finish at simulation time 60
```

Example 11.29 Alternative with ?

At time 0, SOURCE changes from 8'bxxxx_xxxx to 8'b0000_0000, the always block is therefore reached. As ENABLE, however, is x at start of simulation, RESULT begins with 8'bxxxx_xxxx. At time 10, ENABLE changes to 2'b01, thus SOURCE is copied to RESULT. ENABLE changing to 2'b0x and 2'b0z results in another execution of the always block; as the OR of all ENABLE bits, however, is x, RESULT becomes 8'bxxxx_xxxx.

This statement exists in C as well.

B30 case, casez

```
case_statement        ::= case ( <expression> ) <case_items> endcase
casez_statement       ::= casez ( <expression> ) <case_items> endcase
case_items            ::= <case_item> | <case_item> <case_items>
case_item             ::= <expression_list> : <statement_or_null>
                        | default: <statement_or_null>
expression_list       ::= <expression> | <expression> , <expression_list>
statement_or_null     ::= ; | <statement>
```

In a case selection with case, the expression in parentheses is compared in order with each of the case_items bit-wise. If it is true, i.e., if both expressions coincide literally at all bit positions (0, 1, x, or z, B13), the corresponding statement is executed. It is continued after the case_statement. If no comparison is true, the default statement is executed, if it exists.

```
module case_and_casez;
reg [1:0] SELECTION;

always @(SELECTION) begin
  $display ("time: %d, SELECTION= %b", $time, SELECTION);
  $display ("case:");
  case (SELECTION)
    2'b00:   $display ("2'b00");
    2'b01:   $display ("2'b01");
    2'b0x:   $display ("2'b0x");
    2'b0z:   $display ("2'b0z");
    default: $display ("undefined");
  endcase
  $display ("casez:");
  casez (SELECTION)
    2'b00:   $display ("2'b00");
    2'b01:   $display ("2'b01");
    2'b0x:   $display ("2'b0x");
    2'b0z:   $display ("2'b0z");
    default: $display ("undefined");
  endcase
  $display;
end

initial begin
  SELECTION = 2'b00; #10;
  SELECTION = 2'b0x; #10;
  SELECTION = 2'b0z; #10;
  SELECTION = 2'b??; #10;
end
endmodule
```

```
Highest level modules:
case_and_casez

time:                 0, SELECTION= 00
case:
2'b00
casez:
2'b00

time:                10, SELECTION= 0x
case:
2'b0x
casez:
2'b0x

time:                20, SELECTION= 0z
case:
2'b0z
casez:
2'b00

time:                30, SELECTION= zz
case:
undefined
casez:
2'b00
```

Example 11.30 Case selection with case and casez

In a casez statement, however, all z in all expressions are interpreted as "don't care", i.e., a comparison with z is always true. For case, this would only be true if the second value is also z.

Example 11.30 shows the difference between case and casez. Both statements output, which case of SELECTION they did recognize. The initial block generates changes of SELECTION. We recall that a ? is equivalent to z.

At times 0 and 10, the results coincide. At time 20, casez first compares SELECTION (being 2'b0z) with 2'b00. The result is positive. At time 30, no value matches case, therefore, the default statement is executed; in casez, already the first case matches.

In C, case exists as well, but not casez.

B31 while

```
while_statement        ::= while ( <conditional_expression> ) <statement>
```

The statement is executed until the conditional_expression contains no 1-bit. If this is the case before the first evaluation, the statement is not executed at all.

Example 11.31 outputs numbers 0 to 10. The comparison

```
COUNTER <= 10
```

is 1'b1, if COUNTER is less or equal 10, otherwise 1'b0.

```
module while_loop;
reg [3:0] COUNTER;

initial begin
  COUNTER = 0;
  while (COUNTER <= 10) begin
    $display ("%d", COUNTER);
    COUNTER = COUNTER + 1;
  end
end
endmodule
```

Example 11.31 Loop with while

The same statement exists in C.

B32 forever

```
forever_statement        ::= forever <statement>
```

A forever corresponds to a while loop without end. Example 11.32 shows an initial forever loop equivalent to an always block. It is impossible to print the output listing.

```
module forever_loop;
initial
  forever
    $display ("endless loop");

always
  $display ("endless loop");
endmodule
```

Example 11.32 Loop with forever

For example, if a reset signal at simulation start is to change briefly from 0 to 1 followed by a continuous clock, the initial and the always block can be integrated as follows.

```
initial
begin
  RESET = 1;
  CLOCK = 0;
  #10;
  RESET = 0;
  forever
  begin
    CLOCK = 1;
    #10;
    CLOCK = 0;
```

```
        #10;
      end
    end
```

There is no counterpart in C.

B33 for

```
for_statement            ::= for ( <assignment>; <conditional_expression>;
                             <statement> ) <statement>
```

First, the `assignment` is executed. If hereafter, the `conditional_expression` contains at least one bit that is `1`, the second `statement` is executed. Then the first `statement` is performed. A new cycle follows evaluating the `conditional_expression`.

Example 11.33 outputs numbers 0 to 10.

```
module for_loop;
reg [3:0] COUNTER;

initial
  for (COUNTER = 0; COUNTER <= 10; COUNTER = COUNTER + 1)
    $display ("%d", COUNTER);
endmodule
```

Example 11.33 Loop with `for`

This statement exists in C, too.

B34 fork, join

```
fork_statement           ::= fork <statements> join
statements               ::= <statement> | <statements> <statement>
```

All `statements` between `fork` and `join` are executed in parallel. The statement after `join` is only executed if all parallel statements have terminated. Parallel execution means an arbitrary order of execution (Section 11.3.1).

Example 11.34 first outputs `start`. Then three parallel statements are started in a `fork-join` block. By chance, the first block is executed first and outputs a starting message. Execution is stopped by the delay

```
#10;
```

and block 2 is started. After the second block terminates, the third one is executed. Finally, block 1 is started again. The last statement of the `initial` block is only executed at time 10, as only then is the `fork-join` block finished.

```
module fork_join;

initial begin
  $display ("time: %d, begin", $time);
  fork
  begin                          // block 1
    $display ("B1 begin");
    #10;
    $display ("B1 end");
  end
  begin                          // block 2
    $display ("B2 begin");
    $display ("B2 end");
  end
  begin                          // block 3
    $display ("B3 begin");
    $display ("B3 end");
  end
  join
  $display ("time: %d, end", $time);
end
endmodule
```

```
Highest level modules:
fork_join

time:                     0, begin
B1 begin
B2 begin
B2 end
B3 begin
B3 end
B1 end
time:                    10, end
```

Example 11.34 Parallel `fork-join`

In the sequential language C, there can be no parallel parentheses.

11.2.5 Miscellaneous Statements

B35 `` `define ``

```
define_statement        ::= `define <string1> <string2>
```

This is a different kind of statement. Like `#define` in C, it is a preprocessor command to replace everywhere in the following program text `` `string1 `` by `string2`. The strings to be replaced are preceded by a `` ` ``.

These replacements help in writing better readable programs. Note that there are no *local* `` `define `` statements valid only within one module. A `` `define `` is always valid until the end of program. If several files are linked, it remains valid to the last file. In a larger project, all `` `define `` statements can thus be centralized in one file.

Example 11.35 calls `hello` six times. Within `modul2`, `TIMES` and `TEXT` are not specified by an additional `` `define ``.

```
module module1;

`define TEXT "hello"
`define TIMES 3

reg [2:0] COUNTER;

initial
  for (COUNTER = 1; COUNTER <= `TIMES; COUNTER = COUNTER + 1)
    $display (`TEXT);
endmodule


module modul2;
reg [2:0] COUNTER;

initial
  for (COUNTER = 1; COUNTER <= `TIMES; COUNTER = COUNTER + 1)
    $display (`TEXT);
endmodule
```

Example 11.35 `` `define ``

B36 Comments //, /* ... */

```
comment                    ::= // | /* <string> */
```

Comments are marked in two ways. Following //, the remainder of a line is a comment. /* and */ enclose an arbitrarily long comment, which, of course, must not contain another */.

In C there are /* and */.

11.2.6 Verilog-XL Statements

B37 $display, $write

```
display_statement      ::= $display; | $display ( <arguments> );
write_statement        ::= $write; | $write ( <arguments> );
arguments              ::= <argument> | <argument>, <arguments>
argument               ::= "<string>" | <expression>
```

`$display` outputs its `arguments` on a screen and begins a new line. The `arguments` consist either of a `string` in quotation marks with optional formating parameters or of an `expression`, which is output according to formating statements. These are summarized in Table 11.36.

`\n`	New line
`\t`	Tabulator
`\\`	Character \
`\"`	Quotation mark
`%%`	Character %
`%h, %H`	Hexadecimal number
`%d, %D`	Decimal number
`%o, %O`	Octal number
`%b, %B`	Binary number
`%f, %F`	Real number
`%c`	Single character
`%s`	Character string
`%t`	Time
`%m`	Present module name

Table11.36 Formating statements

When outputting hexadecimal, octal, or binary numbers, the number of positions corresponds to the size of the expression. Leading nulls are also output. If they are to be suppressed, the format contains an additional `0` (e.g., `%0b` instead of `%b`). The `$write` statement has the same functionality except that no new line is started.

Example 11.37 demonstrates some outputs. The assignment

```
STRINGVARIABLE = "Testtext";
```

divides `Testtext` into 8-bit characters, which are assigned in order.

```
module display_write;
reg [71:0] STRINGVARIABLE;
reg  [7:0] VARIABLE;

initial begin
  $display ("module name: %m");
  STRINGVARIABLE = "test";
  $display ("This is a %s", STRINGVARIABLE);
  VARIABLE = 100;
  $write ("100 decimal: %d, hexadecimal: %H\n ",
    VARIABLE, VARIABLE);
  $display ("octal: %O, binary: %b", VARIABLE, VARIABLE);
  $display ("binary without leading nulls: %0b", VARIABLE);
end
endmodule
```

```
Highest level modules:
display_write

module name: display_write
This is a      test
100 decimal: 100, hexadecimal: 64
 octal: 144, binary: 01100100
binary without leading nulls: 1100100
```

Example 11.37 Output by `$display` and `$write`

`$write` is equivalent to `$display`, if a new line is produced by an `\n` at the end of the string.

This corresponds to `printf` in C.

B38 $finish

```
finish_statement        ::= $finish;
```

`$finish` terminates a VERILOG simulation. It may occur at any place in the program. All active modules and `initial` and `always` blocks are immediately terminated.

An `always` loop without end can be stopped as in Example 11.38 by a `$finish` in a separate `initial` block.

```
module finish;
`define SIMULATIONTIME 4

always begin
  $display ("working");
  #1;
end

initial begin
  #`SIMULATIONTIME;
  $finish;
end
endmodule
```

```
Highest level modules:
finish

working
working
working
working
```

Example 11.38 End of simulation by `$finish`

Without the delay `#1`, the `always` block would at time 0 never give control away.

An equivalent in C is `exit`.

B39 $stop

```
stop_statement          ::= $stop; | $stop ( <expression> );
```

`$stop` interrupts simulation at any place in the program. For debugging purposes, VERILOG statements may be input interactively to read or set variables.

B40 $readmemh, $readmemb

```
readmemb_statement      ::= $readmemb (<filename>, <field_of_variables>);
readmemh_statement      ::= $readmemh (<filename>, <field_of_variables>);
filename                ::= "<string>"
field_of_variables      ::= <identifier>
```

`$readmemb` and `$readmemh` read a file `filename` into a variable array called `field_of_variables`. This helps filling a large array with values of a file. The file must only contain spaces, new lines, tabs, comments, and binary or hexadecimal numbers.

Example 11.39 loads a memory.

```
module memory (S_ADDRESS, S_DATA);
input   [3:0] S_ADDRESS;                    // address
output  [7:0] S_DATA;                       // output
reg     [7:0] MEMORY [15:0];                // 16 8-bit words

assign        S_DATA = MEMORY [S_ADDRESS]; // continuous assignment

initial
  $readmemb ("memory_initial", MEMORY);     // initialize memory
endmodule
```

Example 11.39 Reading an array

An address at `S_ADDRESS` results in a data byte at `S_DATA`. At the beginning, array `MEMORY` is loaded with the contents of a file `memory_data`. This might have the structure of Example 11.40.

```
// initial memory data
0000_0000 0000_0001 0000_0010 0000_0011
0000_0100 0000_0101 0000_0110 0000_0111
0000_1000 0000_1001 0000_1010 0000_1011
0000_1100 0000_1101 0000_1110 0000_1111
```

Example 11.40 Sample data

The first binary number is assigned to the array element with the lowest index, and so on. In the example, the memory is filled with values 0 to 15.

This statement corresponds in C to

```
fscanf (<stream>, <format>, <list_of_variables>)
```

B41 $gr_waves

```
gr_waves_statement      ::= $gr_waves ( <arguments2> );
arguments2              ::= <variable2> | <arguments2>, <arguments2>
variable2               ::= <string_with_formatting_parameters>, <variable2>
```

`$gr_waves` is a graphic output. As an alternative, a state time diagram can be produced. It can be defined which variables are shown according to the formatting.

```
$gr_waves("notRESET", nRESET);
```

outputs `nReset` with name `notReset` graphically. In the case of more than one bit, the base may be defined; for example,

```
$gr_waves ("notRESET", nRESET, "DATA %h", DATA_BUS);
```

outputs `nReset` normally and `DATA_BUS` as a hexadecimal number.

B42 $define_group_waves

```
define_group_waves_state::= $define_group_waves
                            ( <number_of_group>, <name_of_group>, <arguments3> );
number_of_group         ::= <number>
name_of_group           ::= <string>
arguments3              ::= <variable3> | <arguments3>, <arguments3>
variable3               ::= <string_with_formatting_parameters>
```

This allows the graphic output of variables in a concentrated way.

B43 $gr_waves_memsize

```
gr_waves_memsize_stateme::= $gr_waves_memsize ( <size> );
size                    ::= <number>
```

The internal memory `size` can be defined, in which the variable states are stored during simulation.

11.3 Basic Modeling Concepts

Aside from the previous section on VERILOG statements, this part is particularly important.

11.3.1 Parallelism and Event Control of the Simulator

"Normal" programming languages like C execute statements in order. A program counter `PC` points to the present statement. After execution of this statement, `PC` is increased by 1 or adapted in the case of branches, loops, and similar things. In any case, there is only *one* flow of control.

All components of a real circuit operate in parallel, which should therefore be somehow considered in a circuit simulation. For example, a clock edge may trigger actions at many places simultaneously, or there may be `always` blocks operating in parallel.

In the previous section, we got to know the following alternatives to model parallelism in VERILOG.

1. (Instances of) modules (B1),
2. `initial` and `always` blocks (B23, B24),
3. continuous assignments (B20),
4. `fork-join` (B34), and
5. mixed combinations of 1 to 4.

We first consider simulation by event control somewhat more abstractly. A global variable contains the simulation time. At any point in time, one or more events may be scheduled for parallel execution. An event scheduler of a VERILOG simulator replaces the program counter. Figure 11.41 shows the simulation time axis with several events scheduled at different points in time.

The simulator executes all events scheduled for present simulation time t_1 and removes them from the present list of events (events A_1 and B_1). This is not accomplished by truly parallel execution, but rather by sequential execution in an arbitrary order. When there are no further events at present simulation time t_1, this time is increased to a time t_2 of a next event scheduled. The execution of events will often produce new events for the future or even for the present time. For instance, the execution of event B_1 might produce an event D_3 for t_3, event A_3 might produce an event E_3 at the same time t_3, etc.

The order of event execution at a given simulation time is undetermined in the general case.

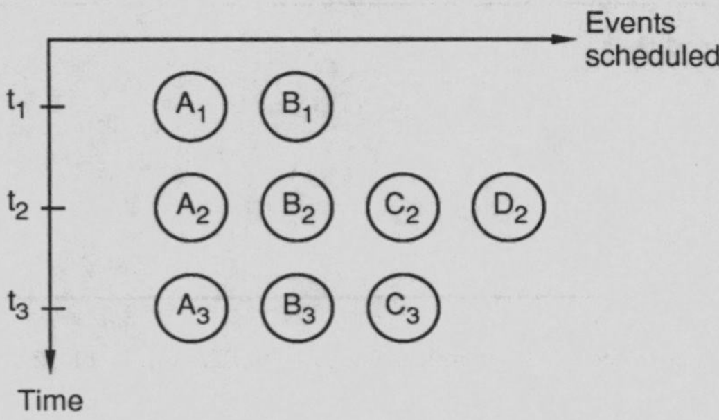

Figure 11.41 Time and parallelism

One may therefore not rely upon a special order. Also, this order may differ between simulators: VERILOG-XL, for example, has a different order than VeriWell, but neither of the two violates the rules.

It is guaranteed, however, that subsequent code *without* time control statements is executed as a single event without interrupt. Example 11.42 illustrates this point. Moreover, it is ensured that execution order does not vary between two equal simulation runs.

```
module event_control;

reg[4:0] N;

initial begin
  $display ("AAA");
  $display ("BBB");
end

initial
  for (N=0; N<=3; N=N+1)
    $display (N);

endmodule
```

Example 11.42 Parallelism and order of execution

Execution of module `event_control` produces the results in Figure 11.43.

Both `initial` blocks are scheduled for the same simulation time 0. A second simulator might therefore output

```
  0
  1
  2
  3
AAA
BBB
```

```
Highest level modules:
event_control

AAA
BBB
 0
 1
 2
 3
```

Figure 11.43 Simulation result of Example 11.42

However, the result

```
AAA
 0
 1
BBB
 2
 3
```

may appear to be meaningful, but it is impossible here, as both `initial` blocks do not contain time controls.

Once again: the order of event execution at a given simulation time is undetermined in the general case.

Unfortunately, the tree of possible simulation states of the whole system branches with degree n at every time, where n events are to be executed. In the worst case, the simulation tree of a system may therefore become extremely large. A simulator, however, can select in this tree *only a single* path.

This is the big handicap of parallel modeling. *One* correct simulation result does often not prove too much. The simulation of the complete tree, however, is quite impossible for reasons of complexity.

Theoreticians can prove properties for a complete simulation tree like liveness, safety, or the Church-Rosser property. This proof, however, is often too hard to compute and does not answer the really interesting questions in many cases.

As a main evil of sequential programming, the `go to` was once banned. Unfortunately, the parallel control structures mentioned above correspond to the use of many `go to` simultaneously. As humans have problems in understanding parallel events, we recommend a high degree of attention and care.

Whenever parallel events do not operate completely independently, but communicate by signals and common data, one should apply a conservative strategy. This can be done synchronously by scheduling events for *different* points in time (cf. `#1`); this, however, requires an overview of future simulation time. Or one can enforce order by a handshake mechanism using events or synchronization registers.

Simulation ends

- explicitly by a `$finish` or `$stop` statement (B38, B39) or
- as soon as there are no further events.

11.3.2 Time Control

In VERILOG, there are three kinds of so-called time control:

- delay control `#`,
- event control `@`, and
- statement `wait`.

All three time controls may interrupt the sequential and connected execution of statements within an `initial` or `always` block. For delay and event control, this is always the case, i.e., the interrupted execution of statements is continued at a future (or the same) time. The `wait` statement interrupts execution only if the condition is not already satisfied. In the block

```
$display ("start of block");
RESULT = IN1 + IN2;
#1;
$display ("end of block");
```

the first two statements are always executed directly without interrupt, i.e., definitely no other statement of another `always` or `initial` block or any other parallel process is executed in between. Just as one would expect that the sum of `IN1` and `IN2` and the assignment to `RESULT` are executed without interrupt and as a whole, also subcalculations of several statements without time control are executed as a whole.

In contrast, delay control

```
#1;
```

interrupts block execution at present time t_1, and an event is generated for $t_2=t_1+1$, namely, that the statements following the time control are executed. Other parallel events scheduled for t_1 can now be executed. Otherwise, t_1 is increased.

Given a block

```
$display ("start of block");
RESULT = IN1 + IN2;
@ EVENT;
$display ("end of block");
```

execution is stopped when reaching the event control

```
@ EVENT;
```

An event is generated consisting of the test of EVENT at the end of the present simulation time t_1. Then other parallel events at t_1 are executed. When testing event at t_1, there are two possibilites: either EVENT has occurred, in which case execution continues at t_1 after EVENT (possibly after executing other t_1-events); or a new test of EVENT is scheduled for the next $t_2 > t_1$. This behavior is illustrated by Example 11.44.

```
module test_events;
event EVENT;

initial begin                          // begin at time 0
  $display ("begin at %d", $time);
  @ EVENT;
  $display ("EVENT at %d", $time);
end

initial begin                          // begin at time 0
  #1;
  ->EVENT;
end
endmodule
```

Example 11.44 Time control and event

Both initial blocks start at time 0, of which the simulator selects one block as the first. One may not rely upon the first being selected. But if, for example, the first initial block is started first, it outputs the text and the simulation time 0. Then

```
@ EVENT;
```

interrupts execution, and the second initial block is started, which first shifts further execution by

```
#1;
```

to time 1, but *before* the test of event in the first initial block. Then event is triggered. In the first block, EVENT is therefore tested successfully at t=1, and the second $display statement is executed. The simulation output in Figure 11.45 is unambiguous.

```
Highest level modules:
test_events

begin at                    0
EVENT at                    1
```

Figure 11.45 Simulation output of Example 11.44

The delay `#1` in the second block is important. Without it, there would be an undesired nondeterminism in the simulation output depending on which `initial` block the programmer or simulator executes first! If the first block is executed without `#1`, the output is

```
begin at                    0
```

otherwise,

```
begin at                    0
EVENT at                    0
```

Delay and event control may also be used within assignments, for example,

```
OUTPUT = #10 INPUT;
```

The delay (without terminating `;`) is located between = and `INPUT`. The value of `INPUT` valid at t is buffered temporarily and invisibly to the designer, and is assigned to `OUTPUT` only at t+10. Equivalent would be

```
begin : block
  reg TEMP;
  TEMP = INPUT;
  #10;
  OUTPUT = TEMP;
end
```

If `INPUT` changes after t, this does not influence `OUTPUT` immediately. The statement before is to be distinguished from

```
#10 OUTPUT = INPUT;
```

and

```
OUTPUT = INPUT; #10;
```

In the first case, 10 units of time pass until `OUTPUT` receives the value of `INPUT` at t=10. In the second case, the assignment occurs immediately, and then there is a wait of 10 units of time.

Analogously, an event control may occur within an assignment:

```
OUTPUT = @EVENT INPUT;
```

This is equivalent to

```
begin : block
  reg TEMP;
  TEMP = INPUT;
  @ EVENT;
  OUTPUT = TEMP;
end
```

Example 11.46 demonstrates a meaningful application of time delay. A mini-pipeline is to be simulated consisting of two subsequent memory elements. Data at the first memory `INPUT` are delayed in the pipeline by two clock cycles. The first memory output MIDDLE coincides with the second memory input. Both memory inputs take values with a rising edge of CP and set the output again. This happens in the first two always blocks.

The proper functioning of this example depends on the time delay #1 explained below. The third always block displays the two inputs and outputs when changing. The fourth block generates a clock with period 20. The initial block generates test values by assigning new values to INPUT with the falling edge at time 0, 20, and 40. After a rising edge, these values reach MIDDLE, and after another positive edge, OUTPUT.

```
module flipflop_chain;
`define WIDTH 8

reg                CP;
reg   [`WIDTH-1:0] INPUT,
                   MIDDLE,
                   OUTPUT;

always @(posedge CP)
  MIDDLE = #1 INPUT;

always @(posedge CP)
  OUTPUT = #1 MIDDLE;

always @(INPUT or MIDDLE or OUTPUT)
  $display ("time: %d, INPUT= %h MIDDLE= %h, OUTPUT= %h",
    $time, INPUT, MIDDLE, OUTPUT);

always begin
  CP = 0; #10;
  CP = 1; #10;
end

initial begin
  INPUT = 0;      #20;
  INPUT = 255;    #20;
  INPUT = 8'haa; #20;
  $finish;
end
endmodule
```

```
Highest level modules:
flipflop_chain

time:                    0, INPUT= 00 MIDDLE= xx, OUTPUT= xx
time:                   11, INPUT= 00 MIDDLE= 00, OUTPUT= xx
time:                   20, INPUT= ff MIDDLE= 00, OUTPUT= xx
time:                   31, INPUT= ff MIDDLE= ff, OUTPUT= 00
time:                   40, INPUT= aa MIDDLE= ff, OUTPUT= 00
time:                   51, INPUT= aa MIDDLE= aa, OUTPUT= ff
L33 "bsp38.v": $finish at simulation time 60
```

Example 11.46 Flip-flop chain

Without delay #1, the value of INPUT might be transferred with a positive edge to MIDDLE and at the same time to OUTPUT – it would "rush" through. With the delay, the INPUT value is first kept in an invisible auxiliary register until the old value of MIDDLE was saved by the same token. (One could do without the second delay, but then the second pipeline stage could not be extended further.)

Instead of recognizing the #1 as quite important, the large TOOBSIE models use a #'DELTA that is small compared to the clock period ('DELTA is usually also 1).

11.3.3 Hierarchies of Modules and Instances

As everywhere in computer science and engineering, complex systems require a hierarchic structure: decomposition hierarchy, stepwise refinement, top-down, bottom-up, and yoyo design are some typical notions in this context (Section 2.2). VERILOG supports these ideas by the concept of module: a module can be divided into different or equal submodules; a module processor into ALU, registers, etc., the ALU into adders and multipliers, and a 4-bit adder into four 1-bit adders. *All modules operate in parallel* in the sense explained. Example 11.47 shows a 4-bit adder.

```
module four_bit_adder (A4, B4, SUM5, NULL_FLAG);
input          A4,
               B4;
output         SUM5,
               NULL_FLAG;

wire     [3:0] A4,
               B4;
wire     [4:0] SUM5;
wire     [2:0] CARRY;

one_bit_adder Bit0 (A4[0], B4[0],     1'b0, SUM5[0], CARRY[0]);
one_bit_adder Bit1 (A4[1], B4[1], CARRY[0], SUM5[1], CARRY[1]);
one_bit_adder Bit2 (A4[2], B4[2], CARRY[1], SUM5[2], CARRY[2]);
one_bit_adder Bit3 (A4[3], B4[3], CARRY[2], SUM5[3], SUM5 [4]);

nor Nor_for_zeroflag
  (NULL_FLAG, SUM5[0], SUM5[1], SUM5[2], SUM5[3], SUM5[4]);
endmodule
```

Example 11.47 Structure model of a 4-bit adder

By

```
one_bit_adder Bit0 (A4[0], B4[0], 1'b0, SUM5[0], CARRY[0]);
...
```

four instances of module type one_bit_adder are generated with individual instance names bit0 ,... and are wired mutually and with the surrounding module four_bit_adder. One also needs the declaration of module type one_bit_adder in Example 11.48.

```
module one_bit_adder (A, B, CARRY_IN, SUM, CARRY_OUT);
input         A,
              B,
              CARRY_IN;
output        SUM,
              CARRY_OUT;
reg           SUM,
              CARRY_OUT;

always @(A or B or CARRY_IN)
  {CARRY_OUT, SUM} = A + B + CARRY_IN;
endmodule
```

Example 11.48 Behavior model of a 1-bit adder

The combination of the two modules in Examples 11.47 and 11.48 is a structure model of a 4-bit full adder. This program contains only a `four_bit_adder` with four `one_bit_adder` instances, it does not contain outside the `four_bit_adder` an additional `one_bit_adder` instance. The declaration of `one_bit_adder` (its type) and the definition (its type and instantiation) have the same syntax, namely the `module` statement.

How can VERILOG detect whether it is only a type declaration as with the `one_bit_adder` or also an instantiation as with the `four_bit_adder`? The answer is that every module not instantiated by some other module also implicitly generates an instance.

By instantiating modules, a hierarchy "contained-in" structure arises, which may include several nested modules.

11.3.4 Behavior and Structure Models

A behavioral description as in the `one_bit_adder` of the previous section uses "classical" constructs like sequences of statements, loops, and cases. A structural description as in the `four_bit_adder` delegates work to a structure of submodules. (According to Section 11.3.6, also the decomposition in groups of `always` and `initial` blocks has a strong structural character.)

Moreover, there may be arbitrary mixes of behavior and structure (mixed-mode). Section 2.2 discusses the difference between behavior – *what* a circuit does – and structure – *how* it is implemented. In a behavior description of an adder, for example, a future implementation by structures remains open, be it by a carry-look-ahead adder or by a Manchester carry chain. A structural model usually reflects the future hardware to some extent.

Example 11.49 shows a possible behavior model of the `four_bit_adder` of the previous section.

```
module four_bit_adder (A4, B4, SUM5, NULL_FLAG);
input          A4,
               B4;
output         SUM5,
               NULL_FLAG;

wire    [3:0]  A4,
               B4;
reg            NULL_FLAG;
reg     [4:0]  SUM5;

always @(A4 or B4) begin
  SUM5 = A4 + B4;
  NULL_FLAG = SUM5 == 0;
end
endmodule
```

Example 11.49 Behavior model of the 4-bit adder

11.3.5 Arrays of Variables

Variables may contain one or more bits. In addition, there are one-dimensional arrays of variables. This was used before in a memory implementation of 16 memory locations. An array of 1000 1-bit variables of type `reg` is defined by

```
reg FIELD [1:1000];
```

or

```
reg FIELD [1000:1];
```

Other index ranges are allowed. Variable 500 of this array is accessed by

```
RESULT = FIELD [500];
```

The syntax is the same as for the selection of bit 500 of a normal variable. An array of 1000 16-bit registers is defined by

```
reg [16:1] FIELD [1:1000];
```

To assign bit 8 of variable 500 to `RESULT`, an auxiliary 16-bit register `TEMP` has to be defined:

```
TEMP = FIELD [500];
RESULT = TEMP [8];
```

11.3.6 Modules and Groups

Logically connected parts or future hardware components should be collected in modules. Modules can be reused at different places. In a complex program like the Coarse Structure Model of the processor TOOBSIE, there are often relatively small logically connected blocks with a large interface of relatively many variables. From the viewpoint of methodology, collecting them into a module would make sense, but it would inflate the program and decrease readability considerably, as the interface variables have to be listed three times in the module head:

- in the parameter list,
- in the declaration (`input`, `output`, or `inout`),
- in the type declaration (`reg`, `wire`, ...).

In such cases it is convenient to work with *groups* instead of modules. A group, which is not a notion of VERILOG, collects on the comment level one or several `always` blocks and gives them a name.

11.3.7 Bidirectional Communication

By bidirectional connections, two or more modules may communicate on a common data bus in both directions. This construction as a model for real bidirectional tristate buses is not easy to understand; this section, however, is of basic importance.

Example 11.51 (Figure 11.50) contains two instances `M1` and `M2` of a submodule of type `m`. On the comment level, we distinguish the two instances by a preceding instance name, thus `M1.DATA` is the formal parameter `DATA` of instance `M1` .

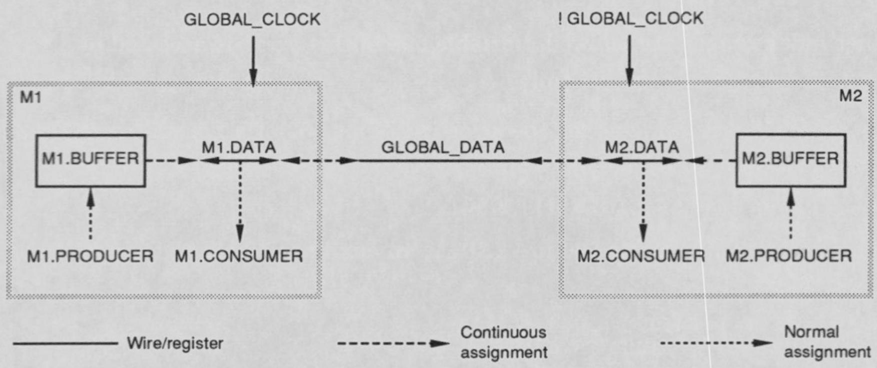

Figure 11.50 Bidirectional producer-consumers

The interface of each instance consists of an input `CLOCK` and a bidirectional port `DATA` (line 2). Both clock inputs are stimulated by an external `GLOBAL_CLOCK`, and being a little tricky, `M2` is controlled by the inverted counter-phase clock. The two data ports are connected by the external wire `GLOBAL_DATA` (lines 38 to 39).

```
module m (CLOCK, DATA);                                              //00
input        CLOCK;                  // local clock                  //01
inout  [7:0] DATA;                   // bidirectional data port      //02
                                                                     //03
reg    [7:0] BUFFER;                 // output driver                //04
wire   [7:0] DATA = BUFFER;          // continuous assignment        //05
reg    [7:0] COUNTER;                // counter                      //06
                                                                     //07
parameter    Start = 0;                                              //08
                                                                     //09
initial                                                              //10
  COUNTER = Start;                   // initialization by parameter  //11
                                                                     //12
always @(posedge CLOCK) begin                                        //13
  BUFFER = COUNTER;                  // PRODUCER (write)             //14
  COUNTER = COUNTER + 1;                                             //15
end                                                                  //16
                                                                     //17
always @(negedge CLOCK)                                              //18
  BUFFER = 8'bz;                     // PRODUCER (drive high impedance) //19
                                                                     //20
always @(CLOCK or DATA)                                              //21
  if (Start == 0)                                                    //22
    $display ("%3.0f      %d              %d", $time, CLOCK, DATA);  //23
  else                                                               //24
    $display ("%3.0f                 %d          %d",                //25
      $time, CLOCK, DATA);           // CONSUMER (read and display)  //26
endmodule // m                                                       //27
                                                                     //28
                                                                     //29
                                                                     //30
module mainmodule;                                                   //31
wire [7:0] GLOBAL_DATA;              // wire between instances       //32
reg        GLOBAL_CLOCK;             // global clock                 //33
                                                                     //34
defparam M1.Start =   0;             // initialize counter of instances //35
defparam M2.Start = 100;             // individually                 //36
                                                                     //37
m M1 ( GLOBAL_CLOCK, GLOBAL_DATA);   // instance M1                  //38
m M2 (!GLOBAL_CLOCK, GLOBAL_DATA);   // instance M2 with clock inverted //39
                                                                     //40
initial begin                        // global clock                 //41
  $display ("time   M1.CLOCK  M2.CLOCK  M1.DATA  M2.DATA");          //42
  #10;                                                               //43
  GLOBAL_CLOCK = 1; #10; GLOBAL_CLOCK = 0; #10;                      //44
  GLOBAL_CLOCK = 1; #10; GLOBAL_CLOCK = 0; #10;                      //45
  GLOBAL_CLOCK = 1; #10; GLOBAL_CLOCK = 0; #10;                      //46
end                                                                  //47
endmodule // mainmodule                                              //48
```

Example 11.51 Producer-consumer communication

Inside an instance, the data connection is used in both directions, that is, one may write from inside to outside and read from outside to inside. First, a permanent connection as a continuous assignment is created in line 5 from register `BUFFER` to wire `DATA`; hence all values of `BUFFER` and its changes are transferred on bus `M1.DATA` or `M2.DATA` and through the permanent connections of the instance ports also to the external wire `GLOBAL_DATA` and thus to `M2.DATA` or `M1.DATA`, respectively. The whole net

```
M1.DATA - GLOBAL_DATA - M2.DATA
```

is driven by *both* sources `M1.BUFFER` and `M2.BUFFER`. If these have different 0-1 values, the data bus is in the undefined state `x`. Instead, line 19 takes care that during the second local clock phase, `BUFFER` is set high impedance and will thus do no harm to the data wire; as the local `M1.CLOCK` and `M2.CLOCK` operate at opposite phases, no accident may occur.

In each of the two submodules, there is a CONSUMER taking from line 21 values of bus DATA whenever it changes. In this case, the CONSUMER is a $display statement, but it might just as well be a connected data processing. With every rising local clock edge, a PRODUCER, in this case the COUNTER in line 14, sends a value to BUFFER and thus to the long distance wire. By the appropriate clock this occurs only when the BUFFER is not high impedance; writing a z into the BUFFER is another function of the PRODUCER.

Both submodules M1 and M2 of module type m are personalized on the one hand by their instance names, on the other hand by their different starting values 0 and 100 of COUNTER in lines 35 and 36.

Thus both instances play ping-pong by alternatingly sending the starting value counted up to the long distance wire. This message is understood by the partner module and is output by $display.

```
Highest level modules:
mainmodule

time   M1.CLOCK  M2.CLOCK  M1.DATA  M2.DATA
 10                  0                  x
 10        1                   x
 10                  0                  0
 10        1                   0
 20                  1                  0
 20        0                   0
 20        0                 100
 20                  1                100
 30                  0                100
 30        1                 100
 30                  0                  1
 30        1                   1
 40                  1                  1
 40        0                   1
 40        0                 101
 40                  1                101
 50                  0                101
 50        1                 101
 50                  0                  2
 50        1                   2
 60                  1                  2
 60        0                   2
 60        0                 102
 60                  1                102
209 simulation events
```

Figure 11.52 Simulation result of Example 11.51

The simulation result in Figure 11.52 shows that the data bus permanently contains values different from x and z. Moreover, one can see that both submodules output both counter values alternately. This example is one possible solution of the *producer-consumer problem*.

11.3.8 Some Practical Guidelines

In this section, we sketch a VERILOG style and conventions for a unique outlook, as they were applied to the large TOOBSIE models (mostly).

- Identifiers for `` `define `` are written with capital letters only.
- Identifiers of registers, wires, etc. are also completely written with capitals; `` `define `` identifiers can be distinguished by the leading hyphen.
- Identifiers for modules, tasks, functions, and parameters begin with a capital letter, but are written otherwise with small letters. To distinguish the declaration and the instance of a module, the instance name starts with a capital letter whereas the definition consists of small letters only.
- There are no tabulators; listings are indented by two spaces per level.
- Line length is at most 80 characters.
- No time is consumed in tasks.

11.4 Examples

By four increasingly complex examples, we study the difference between behavior and structure and the pipeline concept.

11.4.1 A Simple Pipeline

The first example consists of a pipeline of four stages with a master-slave flip-flop each. Between the stages, there is combinational logic, i.e., a function without memory, which is computed when data move in the pipeline from left to right. A master-slave flip-flop consists of a master and a slave register as in Figure 11.53.

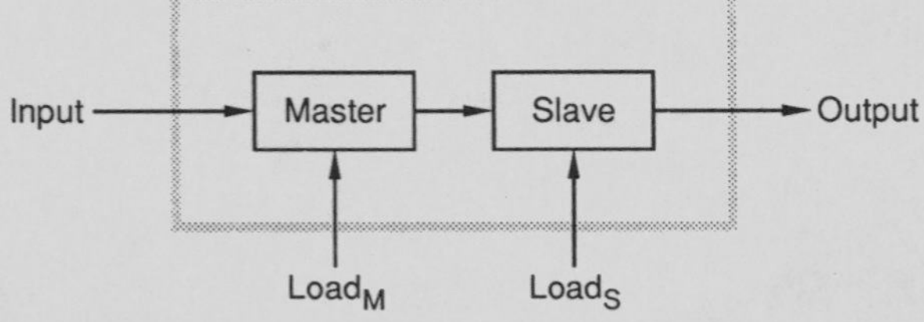

Figure 11.53 Master-slave flip-flop

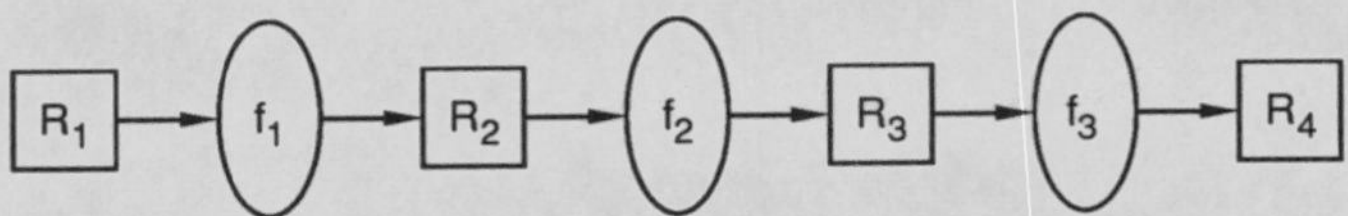

Figure 11.54 Pipeline of flip-flops and combinational logic

All four master registers are loaded with the positive edge of clock CP, the slave registers with the negative edge. The output changes only when loading the slave, not when loading the master. Three combinational logics f1...f3 are located between the four flip-flops as in Figure 11.54. The input data reach the first master M1 and after a transition delay, the slave S4 at the right end. The function of the pipeline is

```
S4 = ((M1 * 2) + 5)^2
```

R1...R4 are the master-slave flip-flops with element i consisting of a master Mi and a slave Si .

Lines 21...25 of Example 11.55 constitute the pipeline heart. Starting from the previous slave, a new function is computed with the positive edge of CP and is buffered in the next master. With the negative edge it is transferred to the slave. Due to the alternating edges, there is no danger that data rush through the whole pipeline at once.

The combinational logics are defined in lines 27...43 as functions. The clock is generated in lines 45...49. CP is High steps valid and Low steps 0.

After outputting a simulation headline, lines 59...67 produce test stimuli synchronously with every rising CP edge. The for loop at the end clears the pipeline.

```
//-----------------------------------------------------------------           //00
//                                                                            //01
// Model of one-phase pipeline                                                //02
//                                                                            //03
//-----------------------------------------------------------------           //04
                                                                              //05
module pipeline;                                                              //06
                                                                              //07
parameter        High  = 10,            // clock high                         //08
                 Low   =  5;            // clock low                          //09
                                                                              //10
reg              CP;                    // clock                              //11
                                                                              //12
reg      [31:0]  M1, S1,                // master 1, slave 1                  //13
                 M2, S2,                // master 2, slave 2                  //14
                 M3, S3,                // master 3, slave 3                  //15
                 M4, S4;                // master 4, slave 4                  //16
                                                                              //17
integer          i;                     // scratch                            //18
                                                                              //19
                                                                              //20
// Control pipeline and apply functions                                       //21
                                        always @(negedge CP) S1 = M1;         //22
always @(posedge CP) M2 = f1(S1);       always @(negedge CP) S2 = M2;         //23
always @(posedge CP) M3 = f2(S2);       always @(negedge CP) S3 = M3;         //24
always @(posedge CP) M4 = f3(S3);       always @(negedge CP) S4 = M4;         //25
                                                                              //26
```

```
// Logic between S1 and M2
function [31:0] f1;
input  [31:0] IN;
  f1 = 2 * IN;
endfunction

// Logic between S2 and M3
function [31:0] f2;
input   [31:0] IN;
  f2 = IN + 5;
endfunction

// Logic between S3 and M4
function [31:0] f3;
input  [31:0] IN;
  f3 = IN * IN;
endfunction

// One-phase clock
always begin
  CP = 1; #High;                      // clock high
  CP = 0; #Low;                       // clock low
end

// Monitor of CP and all registers
always @(CP or M1 or S1 or M2 or S2 or M3 or S3 or M4 or S4)
begin
  $write ("%5.0f  %5.0f  %3.0f  %3.0f  %3.0f  %3.0f  %3.0f  ",
  $time, CP, M1, S1, M2, S2, M3);
  $display ("%3.0f  %3.0f  %3.0f", S3, M4, S4);
end

// Output, test patterns
initial begin
  $write (" Time      CP   M1   S1   M2 ");
  $display  ("  S2   M3   S3   M4   S4 ");

  @(posedge CP) M1 = 1;               // set M1
  @(posedge CP) M1 = 2;               // set M1
  @(posedge CP) M1 = 3;               // set M1
  @(posedge CP) M1 = 4;               // set M1

  for(i=1;i<=5;i=i+1)                 // clear pipeline
    @(negedge CP);
  $finish;
end

endmodule // pipeline
```

```
Highest level modules:
pipeline

 Time     CP   M1   S1   M2   S2   M3   S3   M4   S4
   10      0    0    0    0    0    0    0    0    0
   15      1    0    0    0    0    0    0    0    0
   15      1    1    0    0    0    0    0    0    0
   25      0    1    0    0    0    0    0    0    0
   25      0    1    1    0    0    0    0    0    0
   30      1    1    1    0    0    0    0    0    0
   30      1    2    1    2    0    0    0    0    0
   40      0    2    1    2    0    0    0    0    0
   40      0    2    2    2    2    0    0    0    0
   45      1    2    2    2    2    0    0    0    0
   45      1    3    2    4    2    7    0    0    0
   55      0    3    2    4    2    7    0    0    0
   55      0    3    3    4    4    7    7    0    0
   60      1    3    3    4    4    7    7    0    0
   60      1    4    3    6    4    9    7   49    0
   70      0    4    3    6    4    9    7   49    0
   70      0    4    4    6    6    9    9   49   49
   75      1    4    4    6    6    9    9   49   49
   75      1    4    4    8    6   11    9   81   49
   85      0    4    4    8    6   11    9   81   49
   85      0    4    4    8    8   11   11   81   81
   90      1    4    4    8    8   11   11   81   81
   90      1    4    4    8    8   13   11  121   81
  100      0    4    4    8    8   13   11  121   81
  100      0    4    4    8    8   13   13  121  121
  105      1    4    4    8    8   13   13  121  121
  105      1    4    4    8    8   13   13  169  121
  115      0    4    4    8    8   13   13  169  121
  115      0    4    4    8    8   13   13  169  169
  120      1    4    4    8    8   13   13  169  169
  130      0    4    4    8    8   13   13  169  169
L72 "bsp101.v": $finish at simulation time 130
488 simulation events
```

Example 11.55 VERILOG model of the pipeline

CP and all registers are monitored in lines 51...57; with every change, simulation time and all states are output.

The slaves take data with the falling CP edge. Alternatively, the slaves could take data also with the positive edge after an additional delay. The pipeline control in lines 22...25 would then look as follows, the slaves loading the master values two time units after the positive CP edge:

```
always @(posedge CP) begin
  #2;
  S1 = M1;
end

always @(posedge CP) begin
  M2 = f1(S1);
  #2;
  S2 = M2;
end
```

etc. The pipeline control could further be simplified as

```
always @(posedge CP) S1 = #2 M1;
always @(posedge CP) S2 = #2 f1(S1);
```

etc.

11.4.2 A Complex Pipeline

The example consists of a pipeline with three stages, input FIFO, ALU, and output FIFO.

The pipeline reads data coming irregularly from a source. The input FIFO levels the variations when reading new source data and transferring them to the ALU, if it is not busy. The ALU operates on the data and transfers them to the output FIFO, which offers them to a data sink.

The pipeline is synchronized by a global one-phase clock CP. The two FIFOs are identical constructions. The ALU knows addition, subtraction, multiplication, and division with two operands from the input FIFO. As in reality, multiplication and division are assumed to take longer (in the example 10 clocks) than addition and subtraction (5 clocks). As the ALU does not produce new results with every CP, the output FIFO has to take this into account. On the one hand, the ALU must not send values to a full output FIFO, which therefore must be reported (SPACELEFT_OUT or SPACELEFT_IN). Because of these back-reports, it is no longer a pure pipeline.

11.4.2.1 Interfaces

There are interfaces

- at the input of the input FIFO,
- between input FIFO and ALU,
- between ALU and output FIFO, and
- at the output of the output FIFO.

Figure 11.56 shows the equally constructed inputs and outputs of FIFO and ALU.

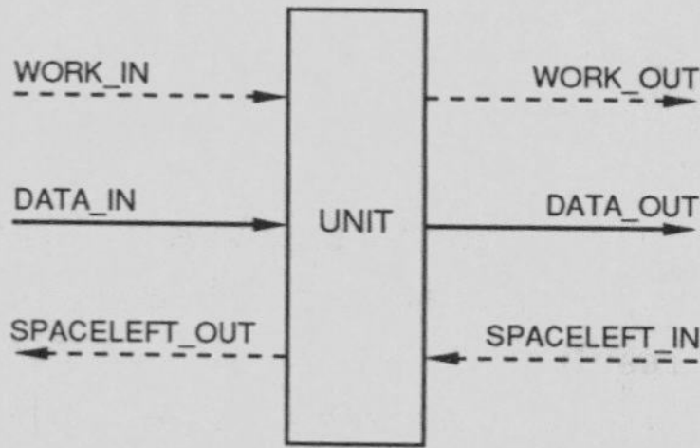

Figure 11.56 Interface structure

Execution takes place from left to right. Reset and clock are not drawn. By `SPACELEFT_OUT`, ALU and FIFO signal to be ready for reading to their predecessor stage. Then the predecessor may write by setting `WORK_IN` and writing its data to `DATA_IN`. The unit reads during `CP`. With a negative `CP` edge, `WORK_IN` is reset. `SPACELEFT_OUT` only changes when `CP` is 0.

Analogously, the unit writes to the following stage only if this one has indicated by `SPACELEFT_IN` that it is ready to read.

11.4.2.2 FIFOs

The two FIFOs only differ by the `WIDTH` of the data words stored. This is adapted by a `parameter` statement during FIFO instantiation (B2). Parameter `WIDTH_LD_2` denotes the FIFO address width, therefore, `2^WIDTH_LD_2-1` FIFO locations may be written and stored in array `MEMORY`. `HEAD` points to the next writable data in `MEMORY`, `TAIL` to the next word to be read. These three variables constitute a data structure "ring buffer".

Only 2^WIDTH_LD_2-1 rather than 2^WIDTH_LD_2 can be stored for the following technical reason. If the FIFO is empty, i.e., HEAD and TAIL point to the same data word, HEAD may assume WIDTH_LD_2 different positions. One of them is HEAD=TAIL. The remaining WIDTH_LD_2-1 locations may be used.

The FIFO reads data from DATA_IN, when CP and WORK_IN are valid. Then the HEAD address is increased; this intention is first stored by setting READ and then incrementing HEAD with the next falling CP edge. HEAD must not be increased during CP, as a change of DATA_IN in the same CP cycle would again increase HEAD illegally.

In the same way, it is written. If the FIFO is not empty (HEAD!=TAIL) and if the next unit is not busy (SPACELEFT), data are written; this fact is remembered by setting WRITE. With the next falling CP edge, TAIL is increased.

11.4.2.3 ALU

The ALU has basically the same interface. DATA_IN consists of OPERAND1, OPERAND2, and OPERATION; the last one controls computation, when WORK_IN is active, and buffers the result in TEMPMEMORY. CYCLES is 5 or 10 cycles depending on the operation and is decreased by 1 per cycle, when NEW_RESULT is active.

Furthermore, the previous pipeline stage must not deliver new data, while the ALU is computing (CYCLES being counted down). Therefore, SPACELEFT_OUT is set to 0, also, when SPACELEFT_IN changes from 1 to 0. In this case, another active SPACELEFT_IN is awaited. As SPACELEFT_OUT only changes for CP==0, this is awaited.

With the falling CP edge, WORK_OUT is reset. CYCLES is decremented, when NEW_RESULT is active. When CYCLES has reached 0, NEW_RESULT is cleared, and the result is transferred with the next positive CP edge.

11.4.2.4 Test Module

The test environment implemented in module test offers a data source and sink and generates CP and RESET. It instantiates three pipeline stages. It defines the width of the FIFO data words by defparam. The input FIFO is like the data bus DATA_FIFO1_ALU to the ALU 20 bits (8 for the operands and 4 for the operation). The ALU result and the data bus to the output FIFO are like the output FIFO itself only 8 bits. Figure 11.57 defines wire names in the pipeline stages.

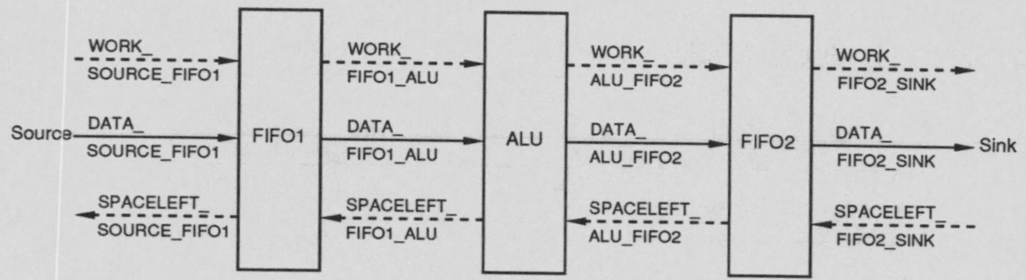

Figure 11.57 The complete pipeline

`DATA_FIFO1_ALU` is structured as follows:

```
DATA_FIFO1_ALU [19:16]   opcode
DATA_FIFO1_ALU [15: 8]   first operand
DATA_FIFO1_ALU [ 7: 0]   second operand.
```

In the model (Example 11.58), the first `initial` block initializes `CP` and implements the global clock by a `forever` loop. Task `Fifo1_write` is the data source and writes during `CP` and with `SPACELEFT_SOURCE_FIFO1` one piece of data to the input FIFO.

The first `always` block is the data sink and reads incoming data from FIFO2 with the positive clock edge from `WORK_FIFO2_SINK` and indicates this. The next `initial` block defines the wires to be represented graphically and then initializes source and sink and generates a reset signal for the pipeline stages.

`SPACELEFT_FIFO2_SINK` is initialized with 0, i.e., the sink cannot take data. Therefore, the pipeline is first filled. As the pipeline in both FIFOs can store six values in total, the input FIFO accepts six values generated by the next `initial` block. Then the pipeline is full. At time 5005, `SPACELEFT_FIFO2_SINK` is set, hence the sink accepts data. Obviously, the output FIFO sends data faster than they are coming from the ALU, it thus becomes empty. Afterwards, data are transferred with a clock delay from ALU to sink, so that the output FIFO is no longer needed.

The last `initial` block generates the test patterns. After waiting for the reset phase, the computation order `0+0` is written into the input FIFO, then `20+10`, etc. In a `for` loop, computation orders of type `I+10 (0≤I<10)` are written. Finally, after waiting 10 000 time units, the pipeline is empty.

11.4.2.5 VERILOG Model

```
//-------------------------------------------------------------------
//
// Asynchronous ALU pipeline
//
//-------------------------------------------------------------------

//-------------------------------------------------------------------
//
// Module FIFO
//
// Pipeline
//
//-------------------------------------------------------------------

module fifo (CP, RESET, WORK_IN, DATA_IN, SPACELEFT_OUT,
             WORK_OUT, DATA_OUT, SPACELEFT_IN);

parameter        WIDTH_LD_2 = 0;     // FIFO locations - 1
parameter        DATA_WIDTH = 0;     // width of data


`define          WIDTH (1 << WIDTH_LD_2)

input            CP,                 // clock
                 RESET,              // reset
                 WORK_IN,            // predecessor writing
                 DATA_IN,            // data from predecessor
                 SPACELEFT_IN;       // successor ready to read

output           WORK_OUT,           // FIFO writing to successor
                 DATA_OUT,           // data to successor
                 SPACELEFT_OUT;      // FIFO ready to read

wire [DATA_WIDTH-1:0]
                 DATA_IN;            // data from predecessor

reg              WORK_OUT,           // message to successor
                 SPACELEFT_OUT;      // FIFO ready to read
reg  [DATA_WIDTH-1:0]
                 DATA_OUT;           // data to successor

// Internal variables
reg              READ,               // did read
                 WRITE;              // did write
reg  [WIDTH_LD_2 -1:0]
                 HEAD,               // pointer to begin of data
                 TAIL;               // pointer to end of data
reg  [DATA_WIDTH-1:0]
                 MEMORY[0:`WIDTH-1]; // memory

//
// Space left in FIFO
//
task Set_spaceleft;
if ((HEAD + 1) % `WIDTH != TAIL)    // ring buffer
  SPACELEFT_OUT = 1;
else
  SPACELEFT_OUT = 0;
endtask // Set_spaceleft

//
// Initialize FIFO
//
always @(posedge RESET) begin
  HEAD = 0;
  TAIL = 0;
  SPACELEFT_OUT = 1;
  WORK_OUT = 0;
  READ = 0;
  WRITE = 0;
end

//
// Read
//
always @(CP or DATA_IN or WORK_IN)
  if (CP == 1 && WORK_IN == 1) begin
    MEMORY [HEAD] = DATA_IN;
    READ = 1;                          // did read
  end

//
// Write
//
```

```
always @(CP)
  if (CP == 1 && HEAD != TAIL && SPACELEFT_IN == 1)
  begin
    DATA_OUT = MEMORY [TAIL];       // data to successor
    WORK_OUT = 1;                   // message to successor
    WRITE = 1;                      // did write
  end

//
// Increase HEAD, TAIL, update SPACELEFT_OUT and WORK_OUT
//
always @(negedge CP) begin
    if (READ == 1) begin
      HEAD = (HEAD + 1) % `WIDTH;  // increase HEAD
      READ = 0;
    end
    if (WRITE == 1) begin
      TAIL = (TAIL + 1) % `WIDTH;  // increase TAIL
      WRITE = 0;
    end
    Set_spaceleft;                  // set SPACELEFT_OUT
    WORK_OUT = 0;
  end
endmodule // fifo


//---------------------------------------------------------------------
//
// Module ALU
//
//---------------------------------------------------------------------

module alu (CP, RESET, WORK_IN, OPERAND1, OPERAND2, OPERATION,
            SPACELEFT_OUT, RESULT, WORK_OUT, SPACELEFT_IN);

input               CP,                 // clock
                    RESET,              // reset
                    OPERAND1,           // ALU operands
                    OPERAND2,
                    OPERATION,          // ALU opcode
                    WORK_IN,            // predecessor writing
                    SPACELEFT_IN;       // successor ready to read

output              WORK_OUT,           // message to successor
                    SPACELEFT_OUT,      // ALU ready to read
                    RESULT;             // ALU result

wire        [3:0]   OPERATION;          // ALU opcode
wire        [7:0]   OPERAND1,           // ALU operands
                    OPERAND2;

reg         [7:0]   RESULT,             // ALU result
                    TEMPMEMORY;         // result ALU (buffer)
reg                 WORK_OUT,           // message to successor
                    NEW_RESULT,         // ALU computing
                    SPACELEFT_OUT;      // ALU ready to read

integer             CYCLES;             // remaining computing time


`define             ADD 0
`define             SUB 1
`define             MUL 2
`define             DIV 3

//
// Initialization
//
always @(posedge RESET) begin
  WORK_OUT = 0;
  NEW_RESULT = 0;
  SPACELEFT_OUT = 1;
end

//
// Execute operation
//
always @(CP or WORK_IN or OPERAND1 or OPERAND2 or OPERATION)
  if (CP == 1 && WORK_IN == 1) begin
    case (OPERATION)
      `ADD: TEMPMEMORY = OPERAND1 + OPERAND2;
      `SUB: TEMPMEMORY = OPERAND1 - OPERAND2;
      `MUL: TEMPMEMORY = OPERAND1 * OPERAND2;
      `DIV: TEMPMEMORY = OPERAND1 / OPERAND2;
    endcase
    if (OPERATION > 1)
      CYCLES = 10;                      // multiplication and division
    else
      CYCLES = 5;                       // addition and subtraction
    NEW_RESULT = 1;                     // ALU computing
    SPACELEFT_OUT = 0;                  // no new inputs
  end
```

```
//
// Report successor status to
// predecessor
//
always @(negedge SPACELEFT_IN) begin
  SPACELEFT_OUT = 0;
  @(posedge SPACELEFT_IN);          // successor ready
  wait (CP == 0);                   // wait
  SPACELEFT_OUT = 1;
end

//
// Count down CYCLES;
// result to output;
// synchronization
//
always @(negedge CP) begin
  WORK_OUT = 0;                     // disable successor
  if (NEW_RESULT) begin             // ALU computing
    CYCLES = CYCLES - 1;            // emulate computation time
    if (CYCLES == 0) begin
      NEW_RESULT = 0;               // ALU not computing
      @(posedge CP);                // wait
      RESULT = TEMPMEMORY;
      WORK_OUT = 1;                 // enable successor
      SPACELEFT_OUT = 1;            // ALU ready to read
    end
  end
end
endmodule // alu


//----------------------------------------------------------------------
//
// Test module
//
// System environment of pipeline
//
//----------------------------------------------------------------------

module test;

// Data widths
`define         DATA_WIDTH_OPERAND 8
`define         DATA_WIDTH_OPCODE  4
`define    DATA_WIDTH_TOTAL (2*`DATA_WIDTH_OPERAND+`DATA_WIDTH_OPCODE)

// Size of FIFO
defparam        FIFO1.DATA_WIDTH = `DATA_WIDTH_TOTAL;
defparam        FIFO1.WIDTH_LD_2 = 2;
defparam        FIFO2.DATA_WIDTH = `DATA_WIDTH_OPERAND;
defparam        FIFO2.WIDTH_LD_2 = 2;

// Connections between pipeline stages
reg             WORK_SOURCE_FIFO1;       // enable FIFO1
wire            WORK_FIFO1_ALU,          // enable ALU
                WORK_ALU_FIFO2,          // enable FIFO2
                WORK_FIFO2_SINK;         // enable sink

reg  [`DATA_WIDTH_TOTAL -1:0]
                DATA_SOURCE_FIFO1;       // data FIFO1
wire [`DATA_WIDTH_TOTAL -1:0]
                DATA_FIFO1_ALU;          // data ALU
wire [`DATA_WIDTH_OPERAND -1:0]
                DATA_ALU_FIFO2,          // data FIFO2
                DATA_FIFO2_SINK;         // data sink

wire            SPACELEFT_SOURCE_FIFO1, // space in FIFO1
                SPACELEFT_FIFO1_ALU,    // space in ALU
                SPACELEFT_ALU_FIFO2;    // space in FIFO2
reg             SPACELEFT_FIFO2_SINK;   // space in sink

// Miscellaneous
reg             RESET,                  // reset
                CP;                     // global clock
reg [`DATA_WIDTH_OPERAND -1:0]
                I;                      // test pattern

//
// Instances
//

// First FIFO
fifo FIFO1      (CP, RESET, WORK_SOURCE_FIFO1, DATA_SOURCE_FIFO1,
                SPACELEFT_SOURCE_FIFO1,
                WORK_FIFO1_ALU, DATA_FIFO1_ALU, SPACELEFT_FIFO1_ALU);

// ALU
alu ALU         (CP, RESET, WORK_FIFO1_ALU, DATA_FIFO1_ALU [15:8],
                DATA_FIFO1_ALU [7:0], DATA_FIFO1_ALU [19:16],
                SPACELEFT_FIFO1_ALU,
```

```
                 DATA_ALU_FIFO2, WORK_ALU_FIFO2, SPACELEFT_ALU_FIFO2);

// Second FIFO
fifo FIFO2       (CP, RESET, WORK_ALU_FIFO2, DATA_ALU_FIFO2,
                 SPACELEFT_ALU_FIFO2, WORK_FIFO2_SINK,
                 DATA_FIFO2_SINK, SPACELEFT_FIFO2_SINK);

//
// Global clock
//
initial begin
  CP = 0;
  forever begin
    #100;
    CP = ~ CP;
  end
end

//
// Fifo1_write writing to FIFO, if space
//
task Fifo1_write;

input [`DATA_WIDTH_TOTAL -1:0]
                 DATA;              // data

reg              DONE;              // writing done

begin
  DONE = 0;                         // initialize
  while (! DONE) begin              // writing in progress
    @(posedge CP);                  // wait
    if (SPACELEFT_SOURCE_FIFO1==1)  // FIFO1 ready to read
    begin
      DATA_SOURCE_FIFO1 = DATA;
      WORK_SOURCE_FIFO1 = 1;        // enable
      @(negedge CP);
      WORK_SOURCE_FIFO1 = 0;
      DONE = 1;
    end
  end
end
endtask // Fifo1_write

//
// Monitor interfaces
//
always @(DATA_SOURCE_FIFO1 or DATA_FIFO1_ALU or DATA_ALU_FIFO2 or
  DATA_FIFO2_SINK)
  $display ("%5.0f      %h            %h          %h\t\t    %h",
    $time, DATA_SOURCE_FIFO1, DATA_FIFO1_ALU, DATA_ALU_FIFO2,
    DATA_FIFO2_SINK);

//
// Initialization
//
initial begin
  $display (" time  SOURCE_FIFO1       FIFO1_ALU    ALU_FIFO2%s",
     "       FIFO2_SINK");
  $gr_waves      ("CP", CP, "RESET", RESET,
                 "1_WORK", WORK_SOURCE_FIFO1, "1_DATA",
                 DATA_SOURCE_FIFO1, "1_SPAC", SPACELEFT_SOURCE_FIFO1,
                 "A_WORK", WORK_FIFO1_ALU, "A_DATA", DATA_FIFO1_ALU,
                 "A_SPAC", SPACELEFT_FIFO1_ALU,
                 "2_WORK", WORK_ALU_FIFO2, "2_DATA", DATA_ALU_FIFO2,
                 "2_SPAC", SPACELEFT_ALU_FIFO2,
                 "S_WORK", WORK_FIFO2_SINK, "S_DATA", DATA_FIFO2_SINK,
                 "S_SPAC", SPACELEFT_FIFO2_SINK);
  WORK_SOURCE_FIFO1 = 0;
  SPACELEFT_FIFO2_SINK = 0;
  RESET = 1;
  #5;                               // reset 5 time units
  RESET = 0;
  #5000;                            // wait 5000 time units,
  SPACELEFT_FIFO2_SINK = 1;         // enable FIFO2,
                                    // fill pipeline
end

//
// Generate test patterns
//
initial begin
  @(negedge RESET);                     // end of reset
  Fifo1_write ({4'd0, 8'd00, 8'd00}); //  0 +  0
  Fifo1_write ({4'd0, 8'd20, 8'd10}); // 20 + 10
  Fifo1_write ({4'd1, 8'd20, 8'd10}); // 20 - 10
  Fifo1_write ({4'd2, 8'd20, 8'd10}); // 20 * 10
  Fifo1_write ({4'd3, 8'd20, 8'd10}); // 20 / 10

  for (I=0; I<10; I = I+1) begin      // add 0..9 to 10
    #1;
    Fifo1_write ({4'd0, I, 8'd10});
```

```
    end                                                        //360
    #10000;                        // clear pipeline           //361
    $finish;                                                   //362
  end                                                          //363
  endmodule // test                                            //364
```

Example 11.58 VERILOG model of ALU pipeline

```
Highest level modules:
test

 time  SOURCE_FIFO1     FIFO1_ALU   ALU_FIFO2      FIFO2_SINK
  100      00000          xxxxx        xx              xx
  300      0140a          xxxxx        xx              xx
  300      0140a          00000        xx              xx
  500      1140a          00000        xx              xx
  700      2140a          00000        xx              xx
 1300      2140a          00000        00              xx
 1500      2140a          0140a        00              xx
 1700      3140a          0140a        00              xx
 2500      3140a          0140a        1e              xx
 2700      3140a          1140a        1e              xx
 2900      0000a          1140a        1e              xx
 3700      0000a          1140a        0a              xx
 5100      0000a          1140a        0a              00
 5300      0000a          2140a        0a              1e
 5500      0010a          2140a        0a              1e
 5500      0010a          2140a        0a              0a
 7300      0010a          2140a        c8              0a
 7500      0010a          3140a        c8              c8
 7700      0020a          3140a        c8              c8
 9500      0020a          3140a        02              c8
 9700      0020a          0000a        02              02
 9900      0030a          0000a        02              02
10700      0030a          0000a        0a              02
10900      0030a          0010a        0a              0a
11100      0040a          0010a        0a              0a
11900      0040a          0010a        0b              0a
12100      0040a          0020a        0b              0b
12300      0050a          0020a        0b              0b
13100      0050a          0020a        0c              0b
13300      0050a          0030a        0c              0c
13500      0060a          0030a        0c              0c
14300      0060a          0030a        0d              0c
14500      0060a          0040a        0d              0d
14700      0070a          0040a        0d              0d
15500      0070a          0040a        0e              0d
15700      0070a          0050a        0e              0e
15900      0080a          0050a        0e              0e
16700      0080a          0050a        0f              0e
16900      0080a          0060a        0f              0f
17100      0090a          0060a        0f              0f
17900      0090a          0060a        10              0f
18100      0090a          0070a        10              10
19100      0090a          0070a        11              10
19300      0090a          0080a        11              11
20300      0090a          0080a        12              11
20500      0090a          0090a        12              12
21500      0090a          0090a        13              12
21700      0090a          0090a        13              13
L362 "bsp102.v": $finish at simulation time 27200
11692 simulation events
```

Figure 11.59 Simulation output of Example 11.58

11.4.2.6 Simulation Output

For example, the source in Figure 11.59 generates at time 1700 input `3140a` consisting of opcode `3` for division, dividend `14` (20 decimal) and divisor `0a` (10 decimal). Due to the sink being artificially disabled, the order reaches the ALU only at time 7500. The result `02` reaches the output FIFO at time 9500.

The graphic model output by `$gr_waves` (line 327) is not shown here, as it looks similar to Figure 4.62.

11.4.3 Behavior Model of Processor ASIC

This example implementing a 32-bit processor with a very limited number of instructions is called ASIC (a simple instruction computer). It is a derivative of the SISC computer of [Sternheim et al. 1993], which we have modified and simplified.

We first define a behavior model. The processor has no registers, but reads and writes operands directly from and to memory. Thus instructions can easily be implemented in this exercise.

11.4.3.1 Instructions

The processor has the instructions of Table 11.60, which uses the names and instruction formats of Figure 11.61.

Opcode	Name	Explanation	
NOP	No operation		
HLT	Halt		
BRA	Branch	if flag of type CCODE is set, branch to BB	
STR	Store	if IMMED, else	MEM[BB] ← AA , MEM[BB] ← MEM[AA]
CPL	Complement	if IMMED, else	MEM[BB] ← ~AA , MEM[BB] ← ~MEM[AA]
ADD	Add		MEM[BB] ← MEM[BB] + AA
MUL	Multiply		MEM[BB] ← MEM[BB] * AA
SHF	Shift	if SHLEFT, else	shift MEM[BB] left by SHDIST , shift right

Table 11.60 Opcodes for the ASIC processor

Flags ALWAYS, CARRY, EVEN, PARITY, ZERO, and NEG with the obvious meaning are set by ALU instructions ADD, MUL, CPL, and SHF.

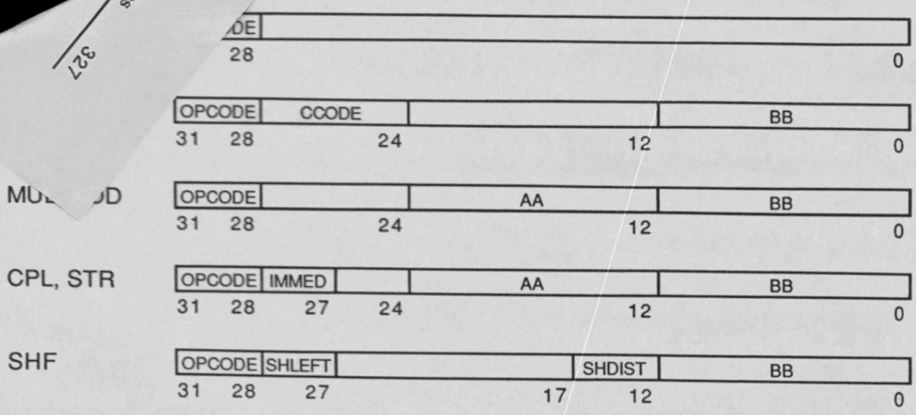

Figure 11.61 Instruction formats

11.4.3.2 VERILOG Model

The source code of Example 11.62 consists of modules `system` and `application`. The first one implements processor and memory and generates a reset by setting the program counter to 0. Module `application` loads a program into memory and monitors execution. It is clearly separated from the hardware model.

In `system`, variable declaration begins with main memory `MEM` as an array of 2^{12} memory locations of 32 bits. Hence the program counter `PC` is 12 bits. The `` `define `` statements in lines 33...43 abbreviate the instruction fields of Figure 11.61.

Lines 46...53 define instruction opcodes, followed by the definition of branch condition code, which will determine the position in the status register. Task `setcondcode` computes the new flags depending on the result of an operation.

The `always` block from lines 89...136 always executes one instruction of the application program. First, an instruction is fetched from `MEM`, and `PC` is increased. Then, the instruction is decoded by a `case` statement. The selection

```
if (`IMMED)
  MEM[`BB] = `AA;
else
  MEM[`BB] = MEM[`AA];
```

distinguishes the two address modes.

In module `application`, the `initial` block initializes main memory by loading a file `asic.prog` with a machine program to be executed. Furthermore, a simulation headline is displayed. The `always` block monitors the variables of interest in this particular application.

```
//---------------------------------------------------------------------
//
// Behavior model of the ASIC processor
//
//---------------------------------------------------------------------

//---------------------------------------------------------------------
//
// Module system
//
// Processor and memory
//
//---------------------------------------------------------------------

module system;

// Declaration of parameters
parameter       Step = 10,          // execution time of one instruction
                Width = 32,         // data bus width
                Addrsize = 12,      // address bus width
                Memsize = 1<<Addrsize,
                                    // memory size
                Sbits = 6;          // number of status bits

reg [Width-1:0] MEM[0:Memsize-1],  // memory
                IR;                 // instruction register

reg [Sbits-1:0] SR;                 // status register

reg [Addrsize-1:0]
                PC;                 // program counter

// Definition of instruction fields
`define OPCODE  IR[31:28]           // opcode
`define AA      IR[23:12]           // operand AA
`define BB      IR[11:0]            // operand BB
`define IMMED   IR[27]              // operand type
                                    //   1: immediate
                                    //   0: memory
`define CCODE   IR[27:24]           // branch condition
`define SHLEFT  IR[27]              // shift direction
                                    //   1: left
                                    //   0: right
`define SHDIST  IR[16:12]           // shift distance

// Instruction code
`define HLT     4'b0000             // halt
`define BRA     4'b0001             // branch
`define NOP     4'b0010             // no operation
`define STR     4'b0011             // store
`define SHF     4'b0100             // shift
`define CPL     4'b0101             // complement
`define ADD     4'b0110             // add
`define MUL     4'b0111             // multiply

// Condition code and status bit position
`define ALWAYS  0
`define CARRY   1
`define EVEN    2
`define PARITY  3
`define ZERO    4
`define NEG     5


//
// New flags
//
task setcondcode;
input [Width:0] RES;
begin
  SR[`ALWAYS] = 1;
  SR[`CARRY]  = RES[Width];
  SR[`EVEN]   = ~RES[0];
  SR[`PARITY] = ^RES;
  SR[`ZERO]   = ~(|RES);
  SR[`NEG]    = RES[Width-1];
end
endtask // setcondcode


//
// Reset
//
initial
  PC = 0;                           // start program


//
// Main cycle: one instruction
//
```

```
   n
                                      // execution time of one instruction
   PC];                               // fetch instruction
    1;                                // increment program counter

   CODE)                              // execute instruction


    `BRA: if (SR[`CCODE])             // branch
              PC = `BB;

    `STR: if (`IMMED)                 // store into memory
            MEM[`BB] = `AA;           // immediate
          else
            MEM[`BB] = MEM[`AA];      // memory

    `ADD: begin                       // add
            MEM[`BB] = `AA + MEM[`BB];
            setcondcode(MEM[`BB]);
          end

    `MUL: begin                       // multiply
            MEM[`BB] = `AA * MEM[`BB];
            setcondcode(MEM[`BB]);
          end

    `CPL: begin                       // complement
            if (`IMMED)
              MEM[`BB] = ~`AA;        // immediate
            else
              MEM[`BB] = ~MEM[`AA];// memory
            setcondcode(MEM[`BB]);
          end

    `SHF: begin                       // shift
            if (`SHLEFT)
              MEM[`BB] = MEM[`BB] << `SHDIST;
            else
              MEM[`BB] = MEM[`BB] >> `SHDIST;
            setcondcode(MEM[`BB]);
          end

    `HLT: $finish;                    // halt

   default: $display("Error: wrong opcode in instruction.");
  endcase
end

endmodule // system


//------------------------------------------------------------------
//
// Module application
//
// Depends on the application program
//
//------------------------------------------------------------------

module application;

reg      [31:0] MNEMONIC;             // opcode name

//
// Load program into memory
//
initial
begin
  $readmemb("asic.prog", system.MEM);
  $display("                   Time    PC  Mnemonic    Result\n");
end


//
// Monitor
//
always @(system.PC or system.IR[31:28] or system.MEM[10])
begin
  case (system.IR[31:28])             // opcode name
    `HLT:    MNEMONIC = "HLT";
    `BRA:    MNEMONIC = "BRA";
    `NOP:    MNEMONIC = "NOP";
    `STR:    MNEMONIC = "STR";
    `SHF:    MNEMONIC = "SHF";
    `CPL:    MNEMONIC = "CPL";
    `ADD:    MNEMONIC = "ADD";
    `MUL:    MNEMONIC = "MUL";
   default: MNEMONIC = "???";
  endcase
  $display ("%d %d   %s       %h", $time, system.PC, MNEMONIC,
```

```
        system.MEM[10]);                                         //180
end                                                              //181
                                                                 //182
endmodule // application                                         //183
```

Example 11.62 Behavior model of processor ASIC

11.4.3.3 Simulation Output

```
0011_1000_0000_0000_0000_0000_0000_1010 // 3800000a 0          STR output, #0
0110_1000_0000_0000_0000_0000_0000_1001 // 68000009 1 loop:    ADD input, #0
0001_0100_0000_0000_0000_0000_0000_1000 // 14000008 2          BRA end, ZERO
0110_1000_0000_0000_0011_0000_0000_1010 // 6800300a 3          ADD output, #3
0101_0000_0000_0000_1001_0000_0000_1001 // 50009009 4          CPL input
0110_1000_0000_0000_0001_0000_0000_1001 // 68001009 5          ADD input, #1
0101_0000_0000_0000_1001_0000_0000_1001 // 50009009 6          CPL input
0001_0000_0000_0000_0000_0000_0000_0001 // 10000001 7          BRA loop, ALW
0000_1111_1111_1111_1111_1111_1111_1111 // 0fffffff 8 end:     HLT
0000_0000_0000_0000_0000_0000_0000_0010 // 00000002 9 input:   DATA 00000002
0000_0000_0000_0000_0000_0000_0000_0100 // 00000004 a output:  DATA 00000004
```

Example 11.63 Application program for ASIC

The application program of Example 11.63 multiplies value `input` stored at memory location 9 by 3. The result will be in `output` (address `a`, hexadecimal). With each loop iteration, `input` is decremented by 1 and `output` is incremented by 3. Since ASIC does not have a subtract instruction, this is done by complementing, adding 1, and complementing again. Figure 11.64 shows the simulation output.

```
Highest level modules:
system
application

              Time     PC   Mnemonic      Result

                10     1      STR        00000000
                20     2      ADD        00000000
                30     3      BRA        00000000
                40     4      ADD        00000003
                50     5      CPL        00000003
                60     6      ADD        00000003
                70     7      CPL        00000003
                80     1      BRA        00000003
                90     2      ADD        00000003
               100     3      BRA        00000003
               110     4      ADD        00000006
               120     5      CPL        00000006
               130     6      ADD        00000006
               140     7      CPL        00000006
               150     1      BRA        00000006
               160     2      ADD        00000006
               170     8      BRA        00000006
L133 "asic.v": $finish at simulation time 180
344 simulation events
```

Figure 11.64 Simulation output of Examples 11.62 and 11.63

11.4.4 Structure Model of Processor ASIC

The structure model has the same behavior as the behavior model. We are now interested in a partitioning into hardware oriented components (Figure 11.65):

- a `Memory` holds an application program, data, and operands;
- an ALU performs arithmetic-logic operations;
- there are an instruction register `Ir`, a program counter `Pc`, and a processor status register `Sr` for the flags;
- a controller coordinates all components.

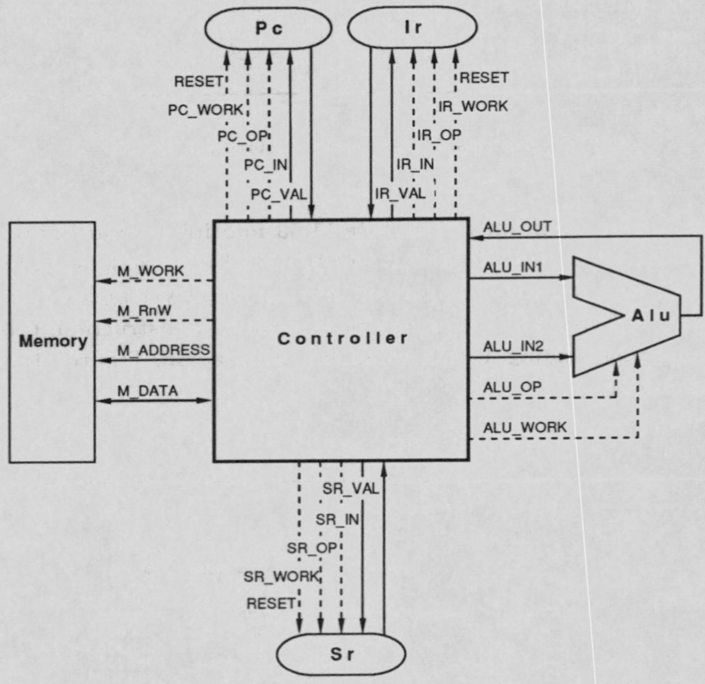

Figure 11.65 Structure of ASIC

11.4.4.1 Module `memory`

In this part of the ASIC structure model, which is listed in Example 11.66, the main memory with the application program and its data is implemented. It communicates with its environment by four signals:

`M_WORK` enables the module for read and write accesses;

M_RnW differentiates between read and write;

M_ADDRESS contains the read and write address;

M_DATA supports data exchange in both directions.

Write data are buffered and transferred to memory after Write_access time units (lines 243, 244). In a read access, data are valid only after Read_access units of time (lines 238, 239).

After reading, DATA contains the information just read. By an assign statement in line 230, DATA is continuously connected with wire M_DATA in order to send the read data outside. In a write access, the write data come from outside also using wire M_DATA and are stored in RAM_DATA (line 243).

To avoid the situation where these data from outside and the value in register DATA are in conflict, producing the undefined value x, DATA is set high impedance when switching from reading to writing (line 240). This, however, does not influence M_DATA immediately, as statements in an always block are executed without interruption, unless a time control occurs. By inserting

```
#1;
```

in line 242, the continuous assignment M_DATA=DATA in line 230 is executed first, thus "disconnecting" DATA (cf. Section 11.3.7).

11.4.4.2 Module regcntr

This module has a double function. As a register, it may be reset, erased, loaded, or simply hold its information; as a counter, it may be incremented. Register width is a parameter. In the model, it is 0 at the beginning, as it is only personalized during instantiation. The interface contains five elements:

WORK enables the module;

RESET initializes the register at any time;

OP selects one of the operations erase, hold, load, or increment;

IN contains a new value;

VAL contains the present register value.

11.4.4.3 Module alu

Addition, multiplication, shift, and complement are offered as arithmetic-logic operations. The module has the following interface:

ALU_WORK enables the ALU;

ALU_OP determines the operation to be executed;

ALU_IN1, 2 are the operands;

ALU_OUT contains the operation result.

The complement is taken from ALU_IN1. In case of a shift, ALU_IN2 is shifted by ALU_IN1[30:0] positions in direction ALU_IN1[31]. Note that we no longer use symbolic names like SHDIST in line 38, as we assume the ALU interface to be a fixed piece of hardware.

11.4.4.4 Module controller

In this module, enable, control, and data signals are handled. Phases fetch, execute, and write-result are triggered in the always block starting at line 581. A reset disables all phases, and there is a wait of one phase.

The fetch phase begins at line 445. The entry condition is

```
@(FETCH or M_DATA or PC_VAL)
```

as M_DATA or PC_VAL may change at the same simulation time, but after FETCH. The opcode is fetched from the memory location given by the program counter. It is therefore set to "hold" its value and activated by PC_WORK.

Furthermore, main memory is activated to read, and the driving register M_DATA_REG is set to tristate, to avoid a collision with memory data (cf. Section 11.3.7).

To fetch an instruction, instruction register Ir is set to "load". The value coming from memory need not be stable at the beginning of the fetch phase, as the memory has a certain access time Read_access. If M_DATA changes after the access, the always loop is run again.

The execute phase begins in line 466. The instruction register is set to "hold" the present value. The opcode of Ir is decoded (`OPCODE being defined as a part of IR_VAL). If a branch is taken, the ALU is turned off, and the Pc is loaded with the destination address; otherwise, Pc is incremented. In case of HLT, the ALU is turned off, the Pc is incremented, and simulation terminates at line 565.

For a store instruction STR, two address modes have to be distinguished by taking `AA either as an immediate or as a memory address to be loaded from. In the first case, `AA as part of IR_VAL is copied to STR_RESULT, which is written back to memory in the write-result phase. In the second case, the operand has to be loaded from memory. Therefore, memory is enabled and the address `AA is used. Also in this case, the operand will be ready only after an access time, so that the assignment

```
STR_RESULT = M_DATA;
```

at the beginning of the execute phase does not produce the final value. By the event control at the beginning of the `always` block, however, a change of `M_DATA` is awaited.

For the remaining operations, the ALU is turned on by `default` (line 515). The ALU operation is specified by `ALU_OP`. `CPL` is the only ALU operation with two addressing modes: `` `AA `` can be used directly or as an address (lines 521...527). Finally, `Pc` is incremented.

When executing `SHF`, `CPL`, `ADD`, or `MUL`, the flags must be updated (line 537). Therefore, the processor status register is set to "load", and the flags are computed.

The write-result phase begins at line 559. First, `Pc` and `Sr` are turned off. Then simulation terminates in case of a `HLT`. If an ALU result is to be written back to memory (`ADD`, `MUL`, `SHF`, or `CPL`), memory is enabled and set to write, and `ALU_OUT` is used. In case of an `STR`, `STR_RESULT` is written.

11.4.4.5 Module `system`

This module instantiates and connects the submodules. The `initial` block generates a reset. After waiting `Simtime`, the simulation is finished.

11.4.4.6 Module `application`

As in the behavior model of ASIC, the application program is not part of the processor, but is separated in its own module (line 613). The `initial` block loads the program `asic.prog` into memory. Then it displays a headline of simulation output. The `always` block monitors `PC_VAL`, `` `OPCODE ``, and `RAM_DATA[10]`, in which the result is stored after simulation.

11.4.4.7 VERILOG Model

```
//-------------------------------------------------------------------        //000
//                                                                           //001
// Structure model of the ASIC processor                                     //002
//                                                                           //003
//-------------------------------------------------------------------        //004
                                                                             //005
//-------------------------------------------------------------------        //006
//                                                                           //007
// Module system                                                             //008
//                                                                           //009
// Processor and memory                                                      //010
//                                                                           //011
//-------------------------------------------------------------------        //012
                                                                             //013
module system;                                                               //014
                                                                             //015
parameter     Width    = 32,        // data bus width                        //016
```

```
                Addrsize = 12,          // address bus width
                Simtime  = 5000;        // simulation time

defparam        Controller.Phase = 10,// execution time for one phase
                Memory.Words
                  = 1<<Addrsize,        // memory size
                Sr.Width = 6,           // number of status bits
                Pc.Width = Addrsize,    // program counter width
                Ir.Width = Width;       // instruction register width

// Definition of instruction fields
`define         OPCODE   IR_VAL[31:28]  // opcode
`define         AA       IR_VAL[23:12]  // operand AA
`define         BB       IR_VAL[11:0]   // operand BB
`define         IMMED    IR_VAL[27]     // operand type
                                        //   1: immediate
                                        //   0: memory
`define         CCODE    IR_VAL[27:24]  // branch condition
`define         SHLEFT   IR_VAL[27]     // shift direction
                                        //   1: left
                                        //   0: right
`define         SHDIST   IR_VAL[16:12]  // shift distance

// Instruction code
`define         HLT         4'h0        // halt
`define         BRA         4'h1        // conditional branch
`define         NOP         4'h2        // no operation
`define         STR         4'h3        // store
`define         SHF         4'h4        // shift
`define         CPL         4'h5        // complement
`define         ADD         4'h6        // add
`define         MUL         4'h7        // multiply

// Condition code and status bit position
`define         ALWAYS      0
`define         CARRY       1
`define         EVEN        2
`define         PARITY      3
`define         ZERO        4
`define         NEG         5

// Instruction code for register-counter
`define         ERASE       2'h0
`define         HOLD        2'h1
`define         LOAD        2'h2
`define         INCREMENT   2'h3

// Reset delays
`define         RESET_LOW_DELAY  1      // time before reset
`define         RESET_HIGH_DELAY 1      // reset time


//
// Connections between modules
// (Comments see below)
//

wire            M_RnW,
                M_WORK,
                IR_WORK,
                PC_WORK,
                SR_WORK,
                ALU_WORK;

wire    [1:0]   IR_OP,
                PC_OP,
                SR_OP;

wire    [3:0]   ALU_OP;

wire    [5:0]   SR_VAL,
                SR_IN;

wire [Addrsize-1:0]
                PC_VAL,
                PC_IN,
                M_ADDRESS;

wire [Width-1:0]
                M_DATA,
                IR_VAL,
                IR_IN,
                ALU_IN1,
                ALU_IN2;

wire [Width:0]
                ALU_OUT;

//
// Registers for reset and halt
//
```

```
reg            RESET,
               HLT;

//
// Instances
//

// Memory
memory Memory (
               M_WORK,                 // enable
               M_RnW,                  // read/not write
               M_ADDRESS,              // address
               M_DATA);                // input/output

// Program counter
regcntr Pc    (PC_WORK,                // enable PC
               RESET,                  // reset  PC
               PC_OP,                  // opcode PC
               PC_IN,                  // input  PC
               PC_VAL);                // value  PC

// Instruction code register
regcntr Ir    (IR_WORK,                // enable IR
               RESET,                  // reset  IR
               IR_OP,                  // opcode IR
               IR_IN,                  // input  IR
               IR_VAL);                // value  IR

// Status register
regcntr Sr    (SR_WORK,                // enable SR
               RESET,                  // reset  SR
               SR_OP,                  // opcode SR
               SR_IN,                  // input  SR
               SR_VAL);                // value  SR

// ALU
alu Alu       (ALU_WORK,               // enable   ALU
               ALU_OP,                 // opcode   ALU
               ALU_IN1,                // operands ALU
               ALU_IN2,
               ALU_OUT);               // result   ALU

// Controller
controller Controller (
               RESET,                  // reset controller
               HLT,                    // halt  controller

               M_WORK,                 // enable           memory
               M_RnW,                  // read/not write memory
               M_ADDRESS,              // address          memory
               M_DATA,                 // input/output     memory

               PC_WORK,                // enable PC
               PC_OP,                  // opcode PC
               PC_VAL,                 // value  PC
               PC_IN,                  // input  PC

               IR_WORK,                // enable IR
               IR_OP,                  // opcode IR
               IR_VAL,                 // value  IR
               IR_IN,                  // input  IR

               SR_WORK,                // enable SR
               SR_OP,                  // opcode SR
               SR_VAL,                 // value  SR
               SR_IN,                  // input  SR

               ALU_WORK,               // enable   ALU
               ALU_OP,                 // opcode   ALU
               ALU_OUT,                // result   ALU
               ALU_IN1,                // operands ALU
               ALU_IN2);


//
// Apply reset and finish simulation
//

initial
begin
  RESET = 0;
  HLT   = 0;
  #`RESET_LOW_DELAY
  RESET = 1;                           // apply reset
  #`RESET_HIGH_DELAY
  RESET = 0;                           // disable reset
  #Simtime
  $finish;
end

endmodule // system
```

```
//------------------------------------------------------------------
//
// Module memory
//
// Main memory
//
//------------------------------------------------------------------

module memory (
               M_WORK,                  // enable
               M_RnW,                   // read/not write
               M_ADDRESS,               // address
               M_DATA);                 // input/output

parameter      Words = 0,               // memory size
               Write_access = 3,        // write delay
               Read_access  = 1;        // read delay

input          M_WORK,                  // enable
               M_RnW;                   // read/not write
input   [11:0] M_ADDRESS;               // address
inout   [31:0] M_DATA;                  // input/output

reg     [31:0] DATA,                    // output register
               RAM_DATA [0:Words-1];
                                        // memory

assign         M_DATA = DATA;           // continuous assignment

//
// Read or write
//
always @(M_WORK or M_ADDRESS or M_RnW or M_DATA)
  if (M_WORK)
    if (M_RnW)                          // read
      DATA = #Read_access
        RAM_DATA[M_ADDRESS];
    else begin                          // write
      DATA = 32'bz;                     // disable output register
      #1;                               // wait until this becomes effective
      RAM_DATA[M_ADDRESS] =
        #Write_access M_DATA;
    end

endmodule // memory

//------------------------------------------------------------------
//
// Module regcntr
//
// Combination of register and counter
//
//------------------------------------------------------------------

module regcntr (
               WORK,                    // enable regcntr
               RESET,                   // reset  regcntr
               OP,                      // opcode regcntr
               IN,                      // input  regcntr
               VAL);                    // value  regcntr

parameter      Width = 0;

input          WORK,                    // enable regcntr
               RESET;                   // reset  regcntr
input   [1:0]  OP;                      // opcode regcntr
input [Width-1:0]
               IN;                      // input  regcntr

output [Width-1:0]
               VAL;                     // value  regcntr

reg [Width-1:0]
               VAL;

//
// Reset
//
always @(posedge RESET)
  VAL = 0;

//
// Execute operation
//
always @(WORK or OP or RESET or IN)
  if (!RESET && WORK)
    case (OP)
      `ERASE:     VAL = 0;
      `HOLD:      ;
```

```
      `LOAD:      VAL = IN;
      `INCREMENT: VAL = VAL + 1;
      default:    $display
                    ("Illegal command for Register (%m, OP=$%h).", OP);
    endcase

endmodule // regcntr


//-------------------------------------------------------------------
//
// Module ALU
//
// Add, multiply, shift, complement
//
//-------------------------------------------------------------------

module alu   (ALU_WORK,               // enable   ALU
              ALU_OP,                 // opcode   ALU
              ALU_IN1,                // operands ALU
              ALU_IN2,
              ALU_OUT);               // result   ALU

input         ALU_WORK;               // enable   ALU
input   [3:0] ALU_OP;                 // opcode   ALU
input  [31:0] ALU_IN1,                // operands ALU
              ALU_IN2;

output [32:0] ALU_OUT;                // result   ALU

reg    [32:0] ALU_OUT;                // result   ALU

//
// Execute operation
//
always @(ALU_WORK or ALU_OP or ALU_IN1 or ALU_IN2)
  if (ALU_WORK)
    case (ALU_OP)
      `ADD:    ALU_OUT = ALU_IN1 + ALU_IN2;
      `MUL:    ALU_OUT = ALU_IN1 * ALU_IN2;
      `SHF:    if (ALU_IN1[31])      // shift left
                 ALU_OUT = ALU_IN2 << ALU_IN1[30:0];
               else
                 ALU_OUT = ALU_IN2 >> ALU_IN1[30:0];
      `CPL:    ALU_OUT = ~ALU_IN1;  // complement
      default: $display("Illegal instruction (=$%h) for ALU.", ALU_OP);
    endcase

endmodule // alu


//-------------------------------------------------------------------
//
// Module controller
//
// Controller for all components
//
//-------------------------------------------------------------------

module controller (
              RESET,                  // reset
              HLT,                    // halt

              M_WORK,                 // enable         memory
              M_RnW,                  // read/not write memory
              M_ADDRESS,              // address        memory
              M_DATA,                 // input/output   memory

              PC_WORK,                // enable PC
              PC_OP,                  // opcode PC
              PC_VAL,                 // value  PC
              PC_IN,                  // input  PC

              IR_WORK,                // enable IR
              IR_OP,                  // opcode IR
              IR_VAL,                 // value  IR
              IR_IN,                  // input  IR

              SR_WORK,                // enable SR
              SR_OP,                  // opcode SR
              SR_VAL,                 // value  SR
              SR_IN,                  // input  SR

              ALU_WORK,               // enable   ALU
              ALU_OP,                 // opcode   ALU
              ALU_OUT,                // result   ALU
              ALU_IN1,                // operands ALU
              ALU_IN2);

parameter     Phase = 0;              // execution time for one phase

input         RESET,                  // reset
```

```
                HLT;                      // halt

output          M_WORK,                   // enable          memory
                M_RnW;                    // read/not write memory
output [11:0]   M_ADDRESS;                // address         memory
inout  [31:0]   M_DATA;                   // input/output    memory

output          PC_WORK;                  // enable PC
output  [1:0]   PC_OP;                    // opcode PC
input  [11:0]   PC_VAL;                   // value  PC
output [11:0]   PC_IN;                    // input  PC

output          IR_WORK;                  // enable IR
output  [1:0]   IR_OP;                    // opcode IR
input  [31:0]   IR_VAL;                   // value  IR
output [31:0]   IR_IN;                    // input  IR

output          SR_WORK;                  // enable SR
output  [1:0]   SR_OP;                    // opcode SR
input   [5:0]   SR_VAL;                   // value  SR
output  [5:0]   SR_IN;                    // input  SR

output          ALU_WORK;                 // enable   ALU
output  [3:0]   ALU_OP;                   // opcode   ALU
input  [32:0]   ALU_OUT;                  // result   ALU
output [31:0]   ALU_IN1,                  // operands ALU
                ALU_IN2;


reg             M_WORK,
                M_RnW,
                ALU_WORK,
                IR_WORK,
                PC_WORK,
                SR_WORK;
reg     [1:0]   IR_OP,
                PC_OP,
                SR_OP;
reg     [3:0]   ALU_OP;
reg     [5:0]   SR_IN;
reg    [11:0]   M_ADDRESS,
                PC_IN;

reg    [31:0]   ALU_IN1,
                ALU_IN2,
                IR_IN;

// Local registers and wires
reg             FETCH,                    // activation of phases
                EXECUTE,
                WRITE_RESULT;
reg    [31:0]   M_DATA_REG;               // output register
reg    [31:0]   STR_RESULT;               // result of STR

wire   [31:0]   M_DATA = M_DATA_REG;      // continuous assignment


//
// Fetch phase
//
always @(FETCH or M_DATA or PC_VAL)
if (FETCH) begin
  PC_OP = `HOLD;                          // PC: save value
  PC_WORK = 1;                            // enable PC

  M_RnW = 1;                              // memory: read
  M_WORK = 1;                             // enable memory
  M_DATA_REG = 32'hz;                     // disable output register
  M_ADDRESS = PC_VAL;                     // set address for memory access

  IR_OP = `LOAD;                          // IR: load value
  IR_WORK = 1;                            // enable IR
  IR_IN = M_DATA;                         // data from memory to IR

  SR_WORK = 0;                            // disable SR
end


//
// Execute phase
//
always @(EXECUTE or M_DATA or ALU_OUT or IR_VAL)
if (EXECUTE) begin
  IR_OP = `HOLD;                          // IR: hold value
  IR_WORK = 1;                            // enable IR

  PC_WORK = 1;                            // enable PC

  case (`OPCODE)                          // execute opcode
    `BRA: begin
          SR_WORK = 1;                    // enable SR
          #1;
```

```
            if (SR_VAL[`CCODE])      // branch condition
            begin
              ALU_WORK = 0;          // disable ALU
              PC_OP = `LOAD;         // PC: load value
              PC_IN = `BB;           // set target address
            end
            else
              PC_OP = `INCREMENT;    // increment PC
          end

    `HLT: begin
            ALU_WORK = 0;            // disable ALU
            PC_OP = `INCREMENT;      // increment PC
          end

    `STR: begin
            PC_OP = `INCREMENT;      // increment PC
            ALU_WORK = 0;            // disable ALU
            if (`IMMED)
            begin                    // immediate value
              M_WORK = 0;            // disable memory
              STR_RESULT = `AA;      // save for write_result phase
            end
            else
            begin                    // memory value
              M_RnW = 1;             // memory: read
              M_WORK = 1;            // enable memory
              M_ADDRESS = `AA;       // set memory address
              M_DATA_REG = 32'bz;    // disable output register
              STR_RESULT = M_DATA;   // save for write_result phase
            end
          end

    `NOP: begin
            ALU_WORK = 0;            // disable ALU
            PC_OP = `INCREMENT;      // increment PC
          end

    default:                         // ALU instructions ADD, MUL, CPL, SHF
         begin
           M_WORK = 1;               // enable memory
           M_DATA_REG = 32'bz;       // disable output register
           ALU_WORK = 1;             // enable ALU
           ALU_OP = `OPCODE;         // set ALU opcode
           if (`IMMED == 0 && `OPCODE == `CPL)
             ALU_IN1 = M_DATA;
           else
             if (`OPCODE == `SHF)    // shift format of ALU
               ALU_IN1 = {`SHLEFT, 26'b0, `SHDIST};
             else
               ALU_IN1 = `AA;
           if (`OPCODE == `CPL)
             M_ADDRESS = `AA;
           else
             M_ADDRESS = `BB;
           ALU_IN2 = M_DATA;         // operand 2
           PC_OP = `INCREMENT;       // increment PC
         end
  endcase

                                     // calculate flags
  if (`OPCODE == `SHF ||
      `OPCODE == `CPL ||
      `OPCODE == `ADD ||
      `OPCODE == `MUL)
  begin
    SR_WORK = 1;                     // enable SR
    SR_OP = `LOAD;                   // SR: load value

    SR_IN[`ALWAYS] = 1;              // calculate flags, send to SR
    SR_IN[`CARRY]  = ALU_OUT[32];
    SR_IN[`EVEN]   = ~(ALU_OUT[0]);
    SR_IN[`PARITY] = ^(ALU_OUT[31:0]);
    SR_IN[`ZERO]   = ~(|ALU_OUT[31:0]);
    SR_IN[`NEG]    = ALU_OUT[31];
  end
end


//
// Write_result phase
//
always @(WRITE_RESULT or ALU_OUT or STR_RESULT)
if (WRITE_RESULT) begin
  PC_WORK = 0;                       // disable PC
  SR_WORK = 0;                       // disable SR

  case (`OPCODE)
    `HLT: $finish;                   // halt
    `SHF, `CPL, `ADD, `MUL, `STR:
    begin
      M_RnW = 0;                     // write to memory
```

```
      M_WORK = 1;                       // enable memory
      M_ADDRESS = `BB;                  // set address
      if (`OPCODE == `STR)
        M_DATA_REG = STR_RESULT;        // STR data to memory
      else
        M_DATA_REG = ALU_OUT;           // ALU output to memory
    end
  endcase
end


// Control of three phases
always begin
  if (!RESET) begin                     // fetch
    WRITE_RESULT = 0;
    FETCH = 1;
    #Phase;
  end

  if (!RESET) begin                     // execute
    FETCH = 0;
    EXECUTE = 1;
    #Phase;
  end

  if (!RESET) begin                     // write_result
    EXECUTE = 0;
    WRITE_RESULT = 1;
    #Phase;
  end

  if (RESET !== 0) begin                // if reset, break all phases
    FETCH = 0;
    EXECUTE = 0;
    WRITE_RESULT = 0;
    #Phase;
  end
end

endmodule // controller


//----------------------------------------------------------------------
//
// Module application
//
// Depends on the application program
//
//----------------------------------------------------------------------

module application;

reg    [31:0] MNEMONIC;                // opcode name


//
// Load program into memory
//
initial
begin
  $readmemb("asic.prog", system.Memory.RAM_DATA);
  $display("                 Time    PC  Mnemonic    Result\n");
end


//
// Monitor
//
always @(system.Controller.PC_VAL or system.Controller.IR_VAL[31:28] or
  system.Memory.RAM_DATA[10])
begin
  case (system.Controller.IR_VAL[31:28])  // opcode name
    `HLT:    MNEMONIC = "HLT";
    `BRA:    MNEMONIC = "BRA";
    `NOP:    MNEMONIC = "NOP";
    `STR:    MNEMONIC = "STR";
    `SHF:    MNEMONIC = "SHF";
    `CPL:    MNEMONIC = "CPL";
    `ADD:    MNEMONIC = "ADD";
    `MUL:    MNEMONIC = "MUL";
    default: MNEMONIC = "???";
  endcase
  $display ("%d %d   %s       %h", $time, system.Controller.PC_VAL,
    MNEMONIC, system.Memory.RAM_DATA[10]);
end

endmodule // application
```

Example 11.66 Structure model of ASIC

11.4.4.8 Simulation Output

The application program is the same as with the behavior model and produces in Figure 11.67 a corresponding (but more detailed) simulation output.

```
Highest level modules:
system
application

                Time    PC  Mnemonic    Result

                   1    0     HLT      00000004
                  10    0     ???      00000004
                  11    0     STR      00000004
                  20    1     STR      00000004
                  34    1     STR      00000000
                  40    1     ???      00000000
                  41    1     ADD      00000000
                  50    2     ADD      00000000
                  70    2     ???      00000000
                  71    2     BRA      00000000
                  81    3     BRA      00000000
                 101    3     ADD      00000000
                 110    4     ADD      00000000
                 124    4     ADD      00000003
                 130    4     ???      00000003
                 131    4     CPL      00000003
                 140    5     CPL      00000003
                 160    5     ???      00000003
                 161    5     ADD      00000003
                 170    6     ADD      00000003
                 190    6     ???      00000003
                 191    6     CPL      00000003
                 200    7     CPL      00000003
                 220    7     ???      00000003
                 221    7     BRA      00000003
                 231    1     BRA      00000003
                 251    1     ADD      00000003
                 260    2     ADD      00000003
                 280    2     ???      00000003
                 281    2     BRA      00000003
                 291    3     BRA      00000003
                 311    3     ADD      00000003
                 320    4     ADD      00000003
                 334    4     ADD      00000006
                 340    4     ???      00000006
                 341    4     CPL      00000006
                 350    5     CPL      00000006
                 370    5     ???      00000006
                 371    5     ADD      00000006
                 380    6     ADD      00000006
                 400    6     ???      00000006
                 401    6     CPL      00000006
                 410    7     CPL      00000006
                 430    7     ???      00000006
                 431    7     BRA      00000006
                 441    1     BRA      00000006
                 461    1     ADD      00000006
                 470    2     ADD      00000006
                 490    2     ???      00000006
                 491    2     BRA      00000006
                 501    8     BRA      00000006
                 521    8     HLT      00000006
                 530    9     HLT      00000006
L566 "asic2.v": $finish at simulation time 540
```

Figure 11.67 Simulation output of Example 11.66

11.5 EBNF Syntax of Statements

The EBNF syntax of statements is listed here (cf. Sections 11.1 and 11.2). The following lines are in alphabetical order. A complete VERILOG program is represented by `VERILOG_program`.

```
always_statement         ::= always <statement>
argument                 ::= "<string>" | <expression>
arguments                ::= <argument> | <argument>, <arguments>
arguments2               ::= <variable2> | <arguments2>, <arguments2>
arguments3               ::= <variable3> | <arguments3>, <arguments3>
arguments_or_null        ::= | <arguments>
assignment               ::= <lvalue> = <control> <expression>;
base                     ::= | 'b | 'B | 'o | 'O | 'd | 'D | 'h | 'H
binary_bitwise_operator  ::= & | |
binary_logical_operator  ::= && | ||
casez_statement          ::= casez ( <expression> ) <case_items> endcase
case_item                ::= <expression_list> : <statement_or_null>
                             | default: <statement_or_null>
case_items               ::= <case_item> | <case_item> <case_items>
case_statement           ::= case ( <expression> ) <case_items> endcase
character_or_underscore  ::= a | b | c | d | e | f | g | h | i | j | k | l | m | n
                             | o | p | q | r | s | t | u | v | w | x | y | z | A | B
                             | C | D | E | F | G | H | I | J | K | L | M | N | O | P
                             | Q | R | S | T | U | V | W | X | Y | Z | _
comment                  ::= // | /* <string> */
compare_operator         ::= == | != | === | !== | < | > | <= | >=
compound_statement       ::= <named_seq_block> | <unnamed_seq_block>
concatenation            ::= { <expression_list> }
conditional_expression   ::= <expression>
constant_number          ::= <optional_sign> <width> <base> <number>
continuous_assign        ::= assign <list_of_assignments>;
control                  ::= | <delay_control_construct> | <event_control_construct>
decimal_digit            ::= 0 | 1 | 2 | 3 | 4 | 5 | 6 | 7 | 8 | 9
decimal_number           ::= <decimal_digit> | <decimal_digit> <decimal_number>
define_group_waves_state::= $define_group_waves
                             ( <number_of_group>, <name_of_group>, <arguments3> );
define_statement         ::= `define <string1> <string2>
delay_control_construct  ::= # <number> | # <variable> | # ( <expression> )
digit_of_number          ::= <decimal_digit> | <hexadecimal_digit>
                             | x | X | z | Z | ? | _
display_statement        ::= $display; | $display ( <arguments> );
else_clause              ::= | else <statement_or_null>
event_control_construct  ::= @ <event_variable> | @ (<event_expression>)
event_declaration        ::= event <list_of_variables>;
event_expression         ::= <expression> | posedge <expression>
                             | negedge <expression>
                             | <event_expression> or <event_expression>
event_variable           ::= <identifier>
expression               ::= <expression1> | <expression2> | <expression3>
                             | <expression4> | <expression5> | <expression6>
                             | <expression7> | <selection_expression>
                             | <constant_number> | <concatenation> | <replication>
                             | <function_call> | <shift> | <variable>
                             | <variable> <range>
                             | <variable> [<expression>]
expression1              ::= <expression> <four_rules_operator> <expression>
expression2              ::= <sign> <expression>
expression3              ::= <expression> <binary_logical_operator> <expression>
expression4              ::= <unary_logical_operator> <expression>
expression5              ::= <expression> <binary_bitwise_operator> <expression>
expression6              ::= <unary_bitwise_operator> <expression>
expression7              ::= <expression> <compare_operator> <expression>
expression_list          ::= <expression> | <expression> , <expression_list>
field_of_variables       ::= <identifier>
filename                 ::= "<string>"
finish_statement         ::= $finish;
forever_statement        ::= forever <statement>
fork_statement           ::= fork <statements> join
for_statement            ::= for ( <assignment>; <conditional_expression>;
                             <statement> ) <statement>
four_rules_operator      ::= + | - | * | / | %
function                 ::= function <range> <name_of_function>; <tf_declaration>
                             <statements> endfunction
function_call            ::= <identifier> ( <arguments_or_null> );
gate_instantiation       ::= <type_of_gate> <name_of_instance> ( <arguments> );
generate_event_statement::= -> <event_variable>;
gr_waves_memsize_stateme::= $gr_waves_memsize ( <size> );
gr_waves_statement       ::= $gr_waves ( <arguments2> );
hexadecimal_digit        ::= a | A | b | B | c | C | d | D | e | E | f | F
```

```
identifier                ::= <character_or_underscore> <rest>
if_statement              ::= if ( <conditional_expression> ) <statement_or_null>
                              <else_clause>
initial_statement         ::= initial <statement>
inout_declaration         ::= inout <range> <list_of_variables>;
input_declaration         ::= input <range> <list_of_variables>;
integer_declaration       ::= integer <range> <list_of_variables>;
list_of_assignments       ::= <parameter_assignment>
                              | <parameter_assignment> , <list_of_assignments>
list_of_ports             ::= | ( <port_list> )
list_of_variables         ::= <variable> | <variable>, <list_of_variables>
lvalue                    ::= <variable> <range> | <concatenation>
                              | <variable> [<expression>]
module                    ::= module <name_of_module> <list_of_ports>; <module_item>
                              endmodule
module_arguments          ::= <variable> | <module_arguments>, <module_arguments>
module_instantiation      ::= <type_of_module>
                              <name_of_instance> ( <module_arguments> );
module_item               ::= <parameter_declaration> | <input_declaration>
                              | <output_declaration> | <inout_declaration>
                              | <reg_declaration> | <integer_declaration>
                              | <wire_declaration> | <event_declaration>
                              | <gate_instantiation> | <module_instantiation>
                              | <always_statement> | <initial_statement>
                              | <continuous_assign> | <function> | <task>
                              | <module_item> <module_item>
named_seq_block           ::= begin : <name_of_block> <statements> end
name_of_block             ::= <identifier>
name_of_function          ::= <identifier>
name_of_group             ::= <string>
name_of_instance          ::= <identifier>
name_of_module            ::= <identifier>
name_of_task              ::= <identifier>
number                    ::= <digit_of_number> | <digit_of_number> <number>
number_of_group           ::= <number>
optional_sign             ::= | + | -
output_declaration        ::= output <range> <list_of_variables>;
parameter_assignment      ::= <lvalue> = <expression>
parameter_declaration     ::= parameter <range> <list_of_assignments>;
port_list                 ::= <identifier> | <port_list> , <port_list>
range                     ::= | [<expression> : <expression>]
readmemb_statement        ::= $readmemb (<filename>, <field_of_variables>);
readmemh_statement        ::= $readmemh (<filename>, <field_of_variables>);
reg_declaration           ::= reg <range> <list_of_variables>;
replication               ::= { <expression> { <expression_list> } }
rest                      ::= <character_or_underscore> | <decimal_digit>
                              | <rest> <rest>
selection_expression      ::= <expression> ? <expression> : <expression>
shift                     ::= <expression> <shift_operator> <expression>
shift_operator            ::= << | >>
sign                      ::= + | -
size                      ::= <number>
statement                 ::= <generate_event_statement>
                              | <event_control_construct> <statement_or_null>
                              | <compound_statement> | <case_statement>
                              | <casez_statement> | <define_group_waves_state>
                              | <display_statement> | <finish_statement>
                              | <for_statement> | <forever_statement>
                              | <fork_statement>
                              | <gr_waves_statement> | <gr_waves_memsize_stateme>
                              | <if_statement> | <readmemb_statement>
                              | <readmemh_statement> | | <stop_statement>
                              | <wait_statement> | <while_statement>
                              | <write_statement> | <delay_control_construct> ;
                              | <assignment> ; | <task_invocation>
statements                ::= <statement> | <statements> <statement>
statement_or_null         ::= ; | <statement>
stop_statement            ::= $stop; | $stop ( <expression> );
task                      ::= task <name_of_task>; <tf_declaration> <statements>
                              endtask
task_invocation           ::= <identifier>; | <identifier> ( <arguments> );
tf_declaration            ::= <parameter_declaration> | <reg_declaration>
                              | <integer_declaration> | <input_declaration>
delay_control_construct   ::= # <number> | # <variable> | # ( <expression> )
```

```
type_of_gate               ::= <identifier>
type_of_module             ::= <identifier>
unary_bitwise_operator     ::= ~
unary_logical_operator     ::= !
unnamed_seq_block          ::= begin <statements> end
variable                   ::= <identifier>
variable2                  ::= <string_with_formatting_parameters>, <variable2>
variable3                  ::= <string_with_formatting_parameters>
VERILOG_program            ::= <module> | <VERILOG_program> <module>
wait_statement             ::= wait ( <expression> ) <statement_or_null>
while_statement            ::= while ( <conditional_expression> ) <statement>
width                      ::= | <decimal_number>
wire_declaration           ::= wire <range> <list_of_variables>;
                             | wire <range> <list_of_assignments>;
write_statement            ::= $write; | $write ( <arguments> );
```

Bibliography

Ackad, C. (1994) VLSI-Entwurf eines großen realen RISC-Prozessors: kritische Analyse und Korrektur der Projektdokumentation und gründliche Einführung in die verwendete Hardware-Beschreibungssprache VERILOG, Diplomarbeit, Abteilung E.I.S., Technische Universität Braunschweig.

Advanced Micro Devices (1988) AM29000 – 32-bit streamlined instruction processor, Users Manual.

Armstrong, J.R. (1993) Hierarchical test generation: where we are, and where we should be going, Proc. European Design Automation Conference, Hamburg, pp. 434–439.

Blinzer, P. (1994) Der Produktionsendtest des RISC-Prozessors TOOBSIE2, Diplomarbeit, Abteilung E.I.S., Technische Universität Braunschweig.

Bode, A. (1990) RISC-Architekturen, Wissenschaftsverlag, Mannheim.

Bray, B.K., Flynn, M.J. (1991) Strategies for branch target buffers, Proc. 24th Annual International Symposium on Microarchitecture, Albuquerque, NM, pp. 42–50.

Chakraborty, T., Ghosh, S. (1988) On behavior fault modelling for combinational digital designs, Proc. International Test Conference, Washington, DC, pp. 593–600.

Chao, C.H., Gray, F.G. (1988) Micro-operation perturbations in chip level fault modeling, Proc. 25th Design Automation Conference, Anaheim, CA, pp. 579–582.

Cochlovius, E. (1994) Spezifikation, Analyse und Simulation großer VLSI-Entwürfe mit Statecharts und Activitycharts, Dissertation, Abteilung E.I.S., Technische Universität Braunschweig.

Cochlovius, E., Golze, U., Schäfers, M., Wachsmann, K.-P. (1993) Experiences with an HDL-based design method for complex architectures, Proc. 6th IEEE International ASIC Conference, Rochester, NY, pp. 297–300.

Cochlovius, E., Golze, U. (1994) Analyzing STATEMATE-models of large pipeline architectures, Proc. Second Asia Pacific Conference on Hardware Description Languages APCHDL '94, Toyohashi.

Courtois, B. (1993) CAD and testing of ICs and systems: where are we going?, TIMA Techniques of Informatics and Microelectronics for Computer Architecture, INPG, Grenoble.

Cragon, H.G. (1992) Branch taxonomy and performance models, IEEE Computer Society Press, Los Alamitos, CA.

Davidson, S., Lewandowski, J. (1986) ESIM/AFS – a concurrent architectural level fault simulator, Proc. International Test Conference, Washington, DC, pp. 375–377.

Dubey, P.K., Flynn, M.J. (1991) Branch strategies: modelling and optimization, IEEE Transactions on Computers, 14, pp. 1159–1167.

Ein Markt im Umbruch, Elektronik, 21, pp. 20–22 (1991).

Eschermann, B. (1993) Funktionaler Entwurf digitaler Schaltungen, Springer, Berlin.

Eveking, H. (1991) Verifikation digitaler Systeme, Teubner, Stuttgart.

Fabricius, E.D. (1990) Introduction to VLSI design, McGraw-Hill, New York, NY.

Fenton, N.E. (1991) Software metrics – a rigorous approach, Chapman & Hall, London.

Furbach, U. (1993) Formal specification methods for reactive systems, Journal of Systems and Software, 21, pp. 129–139.

Furber, S.B. (1989) VLSI RISC architecture and organization, Marcel Dekker, New York.

Gajski, D., Dutt, N., Wu, A., Lim, S. (1992) High-level synthesis, Kluwer, Boston, MA.

Gummert, M. (1994) Die Modellierung des TOOBSIE-Prozessors als Beispiel eines großen STATEMATE-Modells – Teil I: Dokumentation, Entwurfsentscheidungen und Alternativen, Studienarbeit, Abteilung E.I.S., Technische Universität Braunschweig.

Halliger, M. (1994) Die Modellierung des TOOBSIE-Prozessors als Beispiel eines großen STATEMATE-Modells – Teil II: Simulation, Analyse und Architektur-Experimente, Studienarbeit, Abteilung E.I.S., Technische Universität Braunschweig.

Halstead, M.H. (1977) Elements of software science, North-Holland, Amsterdam.

Harel, D. (1987) Statecharts – a visual formalism for complex systems, Science of Computer Programming, 8, pp. 231–274.

Harel, D., Lachover, H., Naamad, A., Pnueli, A., Politi, M., Sherman, R., Shtull-Trauring, A., Trakhtenbrot, M. (1990) Statemate – a working environment for the development of complex reactive systems, IEEE Transactions on Software Engineering, 10, pp. 403–414.

Hartenstein, R.W. (1987) Hardware description languages, Elsevier Science, Amsterdam.

Hennessy, J.L., Patterson, D.A. (1990) Computer architecture – a quantitative approach, Morgan Kaufmann, Palo Alto, CA.

Hennessy, J.L., Patterson, D.A. (1994) Rechnerarchitektur, Vieweg.

Hill, M., Eggers, S., et al. (1986) Design decisions in SPUR, IEEE Computer, 11, pp. 8–22.

Huck, J.C., Flynn, M.J. (1989) Analyzing computer architectures, IEEE Society Press, Washington, DC.

Huizing, C. (1991) Semantics of reactive systems – comparison and full abstraction, Institut für Mathematik und Informatik, Technische Universität Eindhoven.

Jove, T., Cortadella, J. (1989) Reduced instruction buffer for RISC architectures, Proc. 15th Euromicro Conference, Köln, pp. 87–94.

Kane, G. (1987) MIPS R2000 RISC architecture, Prentice-Hall, Englewood Cliffs, NJ.

Katevenis, M.G. (1985) Reduced instruction set computer architectures for VLSI, MIT Press, Cambridge, MA.

Kemper, A., Meyer, M. (1989) Entwurf von Semicustom-Schaltungen, Springer, Berlin.

Lee, J.K.F., Smith, A.J. (1984) Branch prediction strategies and branch target buffer design, IEEE Computer, 17, pp. 6–12.

LSI Logic Corporation (1989) Logic design manual for ASICs.

Mansfeld, M. (1993) Über Eigenschaften von Kontroll-Transfer-Instruktionen in Prozessoren und Optimierungstechniken unter besonderer Berücksichtigung von Branch-Target-Caches und Instruktions-Schedulern, Diplomarbeit, Abteilung E.I.S., Technische Universität Braunschweig.

Mansfeld, M., Schäfers, M. (1993) Branch-Target-Caches für RISC-Prozessoren, 6. E.I.S.-Workshop, Tübingen, pp. 67–76.

Mead, C., Conway, L. (1980) Introduction to VLSI systems, Addison-Wesley, Reading, MA.

Mierse, G. (1994) Ein konfigurierbarer Assembler für RISC-Prozessoren, Studienarbeit, Abteilung E.I.S., Technische Universität Braunschweig.

Mukherjee, A. (1986) Introduction to nMOS and CMOS VLSI systems design, Prentice-Hall, Englewood Cliffs, NJ.

O'Neil, M.D., Jani, D.D., Cho, C.H., Armstrong, J.R. (1990) BTG: a behavioral test generator, Proc. 9th International Symposium on Computer Hardware Description Languages and their Applications, Washington, DC, pp. 347–360.

Patterson, D.A., Hennessy, J.L. (1994) Computer organization and design: the hardware software interface, Morgan Kaufmann, San Mateo, CA.

Quammen, D.J., Miller, D.R., Tabak, D. (1989) Register window management for a real-time multi-tasking RISC, Proc. 22nd Hawaian International Conference on System Science HICSS, pp. 230–237.

Rammig, F.J. (1989) Systematischer Entwurf digitaler Systeme, Teubner, Stuttgart.

Rao, S.R., Pan, B.-Y., Armstrong, J.R. (1993) Hierarchical test generation for VHDL behavioral models, Proc. European Conference on Design Automation, Paris, pp. 175–179.

Reitner, J. (1994) Komplexitätsmaße für VERILOG-Programme und deren praktische Anwendung, Diplomarbeit, Abteilung E.I.S., Technische Universität Braunschweig.

Rosenstiel, W., Camposano, R. (1989) Rechnergestützter Entwurf hochintegrierter MOS-Schaltungen, Springer, Berlin.

Rosenthal, T., Wachsmann, K.-P. (1994) Fault simulation of Verilog models above the gate level, Proc. 5th EUROCHIP Workshop, Dresden, pp. 146–151.

Schäfers, M. (1993) Branch optimization of the TOOBSIE2 RISC-processor and classification, Proc. 19th Euromicro Conference, Barcelona, pp. 141–147.

Schäfers, M. (1994) Effizienter Entwurf großer RISC-Rechner, Dissertation, Abteilung E.I.S., Technische Universität Braunschweig.

Schäfers, M., Golze, U., Cochlovius E. (1993) VERILOG HDL models of a large RISC processor, Proc. 4th EUROCHIP Workshop, Toledo, pp. 242–246.

Schäfers, M., Blinzer, P., Reitner, J. (1994) Complexity measures for Verilog-HDL models, Proc. 5th EUROCHIP Workshop, Dresden pp. 38–43.

Scholz, T., Schäfers, M. (1995) An improved dynamic register array concept for high-performance RISC processors, Proc. 28th Hawaian International Conference on System Sciences HICSS.

Smith, A.J. (1982) Cache memories, ACM Computing Surveys, 14, pp. 473–530.

Sternheim, E., Singh, R., Trivedi, Y. (1993) Digital design and synthesis with VERILOG® HDL, Automata Publishing Company, Cupertino, CA.

Stuckenberg, H. (1992) Entwurf und Implementierung eines Testboards für den RISC-Prozessor, Studienarbeit, Abteilung E.I.S., Technische Universität Braunschweig.

Telkamp, G. (1995) Entwurf und Implementierung eines Testboards für den RISC-Prozessor, Diplomarbeit, Abteilung E.I.S., Technische Universität Braunschweig.

Thomas, D.E., Moorby, P. (1991) The Verilog hardware description language, Kluwer, Boston, MA.

Wachsmann, K.-P. (1994) Fehlermodelle für höhere Hardware-Beschreibungen beim Entwurf großer VLSI-Chips, Dissertation, Abteilung E.I.S., Technische Universität Braunschweig.

Ward, P.C., Armstrong, J.R. (1990) Behavioural fault simulation in VHDL, Proc. 27th Design Automation Conference, Orlando, FL, pp. 587–593.

Wodtke, D. (1994) Das dynamische Test-Tool in Statemate – Anwendung, Beispiele und Bewertung, Diplomarbeit, Abteilung E.I.S., Technische Universität Braunschweig.

Wojtkowiak, H. (1988) Test und Testbarkeit digitaler Schaltungen, Teubner, Stuttgart.

Wolf, W. (1994) Modern VLSI Design, Prentice-Hall, Englewood Cliffs, NJ.

Zuse, H. (1991) Software complexity – measures and methods, de Gruyter, New York, NY.

Index

We distinguish the following index sections: general, names and abbreviations, VERILOG terms, instructions of processor TOOBSIE, and components of the Coarse Structure Model. Sometimes, a term fits in more than one section, but is listed only once.

Numbers beginning with H point to the expert volume (see p. 359). Numbers beginning with B refer to the VERILOG statement groups in Section 11.2.

For the components of the Gate Model including the cells of the silicon vendor, there are separate tables and summaries in Chapters 8 and H5 (Section 8.1, Section H5.1: Figure H5.1, Tables H5.2 and H5.3, Sections H5.2 to H5.4, Section H5.5: Tables H5.5 and H5.6).

General Terms

Absolute address 53
abstraction hierarchy 15
action of a pipeline stage 79
activitychart 252
adder 167
arithmetic logic unit 30,76,116,147,H121
assembler 48,H3
asynchronous bus protocol 197,242
asynchronous interface 80
asynchronous memory access 228
ATE test 230
automated test equipment 20,*209*

Backplane 236,237
behavior 14
behavior specification H3
benchmark Dhrystone 250
branch 53,55
branch decoding 115
branch-target cache
33,99,*100*,115,128,245,H55
bridging fault model 206
buffer 165
bus acknowledge 239
bus arbitration logic 239,243
bus control unit 116,H53,H149
bus interface card 237,238
bus protocol 80,116,152
bus request 239
bus termination card 237

Cache 6,76,98
cache mode 108
cache strategy 98
CAD tool 15
cell (of a library) H205
CISC computer 25
clock (see also CP) 79
clock frequency 71
clock pulse 79
clocking scheme 79
Coarse Structure Model 19,*113*,H39
compare (test channel) 212
conditional 55
conditional branch 53
consistent test strategy 69,221
control transfer 53,55
CPU card 242
cycle 79
cycles per instruction (see also CPI) 71,250

Data cache 98
data dependency 27,H37,H75
data flow 74
decode logic 90
decomposition hierarchy 15

delay instruction 31,*53*,*77*,H55
delay line 242
delay slot 31,*53*,62,*77*,H55
delayed branch 27,31,*77*
delayed load 27,*77*
delayed software interrupt 78
design fault 206
design for testability 214, 255
design style 9
device under test 209
Dhrystone (benchmark) 250
direct memory access 235
dither and scale 224
double-byte 52
DUT card 211, 230

Empty pipeline step 77
EX stage 76
exception 58,H43,H63
execute stage 31,76,92
external specification 19,47

Fault coverage 21, 206
fault model 206
fault simulation 226
fault simulator 226
field-programmable gate-array 12, 245
flag 76
flip-flop 165
force (test channel) 212
format generator 212
forwarding 27,*78*,154
forwarding and register unit 116,154,H129
forwarding logic 88,116
forwarding mechanism 31
full-custom 3,10
function oriented test 220
functional test 220
functional test block 225

Gate Model 20,163,H203
Gate Model hierarchy H204
gate 164
gate equivalent 12
gate level 15
gate-array 11
general pipeline stage 84
general-purpose register 29,49,116,154
group *117*,H39

Handshake protocol 80
handshake signal H53
hardware debugger 236
hardware description language
3,16,39,247,261
hardware interrupt 58,H43,H63
heuristic branch decision 103
higher fault model 255
history bit 102,H55
hit rate 98

ID stage 76
IF stage 76
immediate 55
instruction 55
instruction cache 98
instruction decode stage 30,76,88
instruction decode unit 115,139,H116
instruction decoding 140
instruction fetch stage 30,76,87
instruction fetch unit 115,*123*,H91
instruction format 50
instruction register 28,76
instruction set 49,H3
integration density 2
internal specification 19,*73*
Interpreter Model 19,59,H21
interrupt 33,57,*110*,H44,H63
interrupt identification H44
interrupt routine 110

Kernel/user mode 33

Latch 166
late signal 84
layout 3,10
library of the silicon vendor 164
load/store 26
locality principle 98
logic level 15
logic simulation 199
logic synthesis 181

MA stage 76
main memory 98
mask (test channel) 212
master-slave flip-flop 315
megafunction 164
memory access stage 31,76,94
memory access unit 116,152,H126
memory card 237, 241
memory handshake 228, 242
memory interface 76,80
memory request 242
module H205
MOS transistor 9
multi-purpose cache 32,99,115,129, 245
multi-windows 32

NAND tree 214, 218, 223
nomenclature of buses 85

One-phase clock 79
overlay register 111

Parallelism 302
parametric measurement unit 212
parametric test 214
PC logic 30,88,115
PC-interface card 238
performance 70
pin diagram 231

pinout 22,232
pipeline 76,315
pipeline control unit 116,H39,H135
pipeline hazard 27
pipeline stage 84
pipeline step 80
pipelining 26
placement and routing 3,21
post-layout simulation 21,199
primary fault 227
process monitor 167,214,218,223
processor status register 76
production fault 206
production test 20
program counter 76,115
Pseudo-Harvard architecture 32
pseudo-random generation 217

Quad-byte 52
quantitative specification 70
quiescent current test 223

Read protocol 82
reduced instruction buffer 32,99
register file 29,76,109,116,154
register transfer level 15
relative address with offset 52
relative addressing with index register 52
rerun 58,111,H68
RIB-mode 32,99
RISC processor 4,25
root beer rag 245
run length 250
runtime of prototype 233

Scanpath 169,214,*216*
schematics 3,169,H203,H232
Schmoo plot 214,234
sea-of-gates 11
semi-custom 3,10
shifter 167
signature analysis 214,216
signature analysis register 69
simulation H74
simulator 16
software interrupt 58,H43,H63
software measure 250
specification 14
stability of conditional branch 250
stability principle 103
standard cell circuit 10
standard circuit 9
statechart 252
STATEMATE 252
step 80
stored-response principal 209
stored-response tester 211
structure oriented test 209
stuck-at 254
stuck-at fault 227
stuck-at fault model 206
stuck-at-then 255
superscalar 33
swap access 243
synchronous bus protocol H53
synthesis 163
system enviroment 21,48,H154,H69

TAG field 100,106
template 213,228
test block 223
test channel 211
test circuit 214
test cycle 209
test program 210
test vector 210
testability 214
testboard 21,49,235,244
timing 79
timing simulation 199,202
toggle test 226
trace H37,H76
transparent 57,111
tristate test 223

Unconditional branch 55

Vector base register 111
VERILOG 39
von-Neumann computer 25

Walking one test 208
WB stage 76
write protocol 82
write-back stage 31,76,95,116

Names and Abbreviations

A_BUS 75,86,89,92,147,154
ACC_MODE 80,118,H54
ADDR 76,80
ADDR_A 89,109,139,141,154
ADDR_B 89,109,139,141,154
ADDR_BUS 118,H54
ADDR_C 139,154
ADDR_D 89,109,139,141,154
ADDR_OUT 87,94
ADDR_SREG 139
Address30 50
ALU 28,76,116
ALU_CARRY 147,H40
ALU_OPCODE 89,92,139,141,147
ANNUL 134
AR 94,96
ASIC 1
ATE 20,*209*,227
B_BUS 75,86,89,92,147,154,H40
BCC 53,55,107,250
BCU 116
BCU_ACC_DIR H40,H54
BCU_ACC_MODE H40,H54
BCU_READY H40,H54
BDL_TAKEN 132
BIG_MODE 108
BRANCH 129,130,134
BREAK_MEM_ACC 124,H54
BTC 75,99,104
BTC_ACTIVE 107
BTC_BCC H73
BTC_CALL H73
BTC_CHECK 105
BTC_CORRECT 129,134
BTC_DATA 87,107
BTC_DELAYSLOT 129

BTC_DIS_ALU 129,134
BTC_DIS_IDU 129,134
BTC_HIT 87,105,129,134
BTC_MODE 107
BTC_PC 87,107,129
BTC_TAKEN 107,129
BTC_TYPE 129
BTC_USE_LAST 129
BTCDUMP H72
BUS_FREE 87
BUS_PRO 118,H54
C 51,55
C2_DEST 86,89,92
C3_BUS
86,92,94,147,152,154
C3_DEST 86,92,94
C4_BUS 86,94,95,152,154
C4_DEST 86,94,95
C5_BUS 86,95,109
C5_DEST 86,95,109
C_BUS 75
CACHE_MODE 124
CACHE_PC 87,101,107
CALL 107
CALL_NOW 124,H40
CC 50,51
CCLR 101,107,124,129,
130,139,141,145
CCODE 132
CISC 25
CMOS 9
CONFIG 118,129,130
CP 80,118,124,129,130,
133,135,137,138,139,
147,152,154,H40,H54
CPC 133
CPI 4,26,71,250
CTR 28,89
D2_BUS 86,89,92
D3_BUS 86,92,94
D_BUS 75,152
DATA 76,80
DATA_A 89,109
DATA_B 89,109
DATA_BUS 118,H54
DATA_D 89,109
DATA_IN 87,94,101,107
DATA_OUT 94
DEST 50,51
DIS_ALU 124,134,H40
DIS_IDU 124,134,H40
DIST 133
DMA 235
DNRZ 213
DO_FETCH H54
DO_HALT
139,141,145,H40
DO_IF 129,130
DO_RETI
139,141,145,H40
DR 94,96
DS_IN_IFU H40
DS_NOW 124
DUMP H72
DUT 209,211,230
EBNF 262
EMERG_FETCH
124,135,H40
EN_MEM_BRK H73
EX 76
Exc 59
EXCADR 51,H50
EXCEPT 124
EXCEPT_CTR 139
EXCEPT_ID
139,141,144,H40
EXCEPT_RQ 139,141,H40
EXCRPC 51,H50
EXCSR 51,H50
EXTRACE H72
.F-option 89
FD_FLAGS H40
FETCH_MODE 101
FLAG 90
FLAGS 89,92,132
FLAGS_FD 124,129
FLAGS_FROM_ALU
147,H40
FLAGS_IF 124,129
FPGA 12,245
FRU 116
HDL 3,16
HIBITS 103
HIT 101,107,137
Hwi 59
HWIADR 51,H50
HWIRPC 51,H50
HWISR 51,H50
I_BUS 86,87,89,124,139
IC_MODE 108,H73
ID 76
ID_ANNUL 129,135
ID_BRANCH 135
ID_CCODE 129,135
ID_CPC 135
ID_CTR 135
ID_DIST 135
ID_INSTR 135
ID_KUMODE 139,H40
ID_LAST_BRANCH 135
ID_LAST_CTR 135
ID_TYPE 135
IDU 115
IF 76
IF_FLAGS H40
IF_KUMODE H40
IFU 115
IFU_ADDR_BUS
124,H40,H54
IFU_CORRECT 124,H40
IFU_DATA_BUS 124,H54
IFU_FETCH_RQ 124
IGNORE_HIT 129
Imm n 50
IMMEDIATE 139,141,154
Immediate n 50
INSTR 130,135
INT_STATE 154,H40
IO_READY 80,84
IR 75,90
IRQ_ID 118,H40
JPC 87,129,133
KERNEL_MODE 56
KERNEL_RAM_SIZE H72
KILL_IDU 139,H40
KU_MODE 101,107,118,
124,129,130
LAST_CORRECTION 130
LAST_HIT 130
LAST_KU_MODE 129,130
LAST_LDST 130
LAST_NO_ACC 130
LAST_PC_BUS 138
LAST_USE_PCU_PC 138
LD/ST 28
LDST_ACC_NOW 124,H40
LPC 51,129,130,133,H50
LPC_2 133
MA 76
MA_OPCODE 89,94
MAU 116
MAU_ACC_MODE 141
MAU_ACC_MODE2
139,H40
MAU_ACC_MODE3 H40
MAU_ACC_MODE_3 152
MAU_ADDR_BUS
152,H40,H54
MAU_OPCODE 144
MAU_OPCODE2
139,141,H40
MAU_OPCODE3 H40
MAU_OPCODE_3 152
MAU_READ_DATA
152,H54
MAU_WRITE_DATA
152,H54
MAX_CYCLES H72
MDUMPHI H72
MDUMPLO H72
MEM[n] 51
MEM_ACC 101
MEMDUMP H72
MHS_TIME H72
MIPS 71
MOS 9
MPC 75,99
MPC_ACTIVE 101
MPC_DATA 87,101
MPC_HIT 87,130,134
MPC_INSTR 130
MPC_MODE 101
MPCDUMP H72
N 51,55
NEW_FLAGS 107,124,
129,139,141,143,H40
NEW_PC 133
nHLT 118,H54
nIRA 118,H40
nIRQ 118,H40
nMHS 80,118,228,H54
nMRQ 80,118,H54
NO_ACC 129,134
NO_FETCH 137
NPC H40
NPC_BUS 124
nRESET
118,124,129,130,135,
137,138,139,H40,H54
nRMW 118,H54
NRZ 212
Offset n 50
OPCODE 129
Opcode 50
OS_FORMAT H72
OS_ROM H72
PAGEFAULTS H72
PC
51,75,129,130,133,H50
PC_1 133
PC_2 133
PC_BUS 124,138,H40
PCU 116
PMU 212
PRG_FORMAT H72
PROCMON 214,218,223
PROGRAM H72
PROTOCOL H72
QUAD_CYCLE H72
RA 50,51
RAMTIME H72
RB 50,51
RC 50,51
REG 51,76,109
REG_RnW 109
REGDUMP H72
REGS H72
RESET 101,107
RESET_TIME H72
RIB_MODE 32,99,108,H73
RISC 4,25
RMW 80
RnW 80,118,H54
ROM_SIZE H72
ROMTIME H72
RPC 51,H50
RTADRA 215
RTADRB 215
RTE 215
RTL 15
RTO 213
RTSEL 215
RTWEN 215
RTZ 213
SA 50,51
SC 50,51
Schmoo 214,234
SEL 87
SERIAL_MODE 137,H73
SHIFT 133,135,138
SMALL_MODE 108
Special 28
SR 51,H50
SRCA 50,51
SRCB 50,51
SREG 51
SREG_ACC_DIR
139,141,143,H40
SREG_ADDR 89,H40
SREG_DATA 89,154,H40
STATEMATE 252
STATISTICS H72
STEP 87,89,92,94,95,139,
154,H40,H72
STORE_DATA 154
Swi 59
SWI_ID 139,141,H40
SWI_RQ 139,141,143,H40
SWIRPC 51,H50
SWISR 51,H50
SYS_KUMODE H40
TAG 100,106
TAKEN 107,129,134
TOOBSIE 7
TOOBSIE1 27
TOOTSIE 7
TRACE H72
TYPE 129,133
USE_IMMEDIATE
139,141,154
USE_PCU_PC
124,138,H40
USE_SREG_DATA
139,141,154
USER_MODE 56
USER_RAM_SIZE H72
V 51,55
VALID 100
VBR 51,H50
VERILOG 39
VeriWell viii,7,39,261,303
VLSI 2

WAITSTATE H72
WAVES H72
WB 76
WORK 84
WORK_EX 92,147,154,H40
WORK_FD 124,135,H40
WORK_ID 89,139,H40
WORK_IF 87,124,129, 130,135,137,138,H40
WORK_MA 94,152, 154,H40
WORK_WB 95,154,H40
Z 51,55

VERILOG Terms

(wait, delay control) B21,283,B27,289,305
-> (trigger event) B19,281
? (selection) B29,291
@ (at, event control) 41,B21,283, B25,287,305
always 40,B23,284
always block B23,284
arithmetic +, -, *, /, % B12,276
array of variables 311
assign B8,271,B20,282
assignment = B21,283
at @ 41,B21,283, B25,287,305
begin B3,265
behavior 310
bidirectional connection 312
bidirectional data bus B6,268
case 43, 45,B30,292
case selection B30,292
casez 45,B30,292
comments //, /* ... */ B36,297
comparison ==, !=, ===, !==, <, >, <=, >= B13,276
compound_statement B3,265
concatenation { } B16,280
conflict B11,276
constant B11,274
continuous assignment B8,271,B20,282
define (`define) 43,B35,296
define_group_waves ($def.) B42,301
defparam B2,265
delay control # B21,283,B27,289,305
display ($display) 39,B37,297
EBNF syntax 343
else B28,290
end B3,265
endfunction B5,267
endmodule B1,264
endtask B4,266
event B10,273
event control @ 41,B21,283, B25,287,305
event control of the simulator 302
event triggering -> B19,281
falling edge B25,287
finish ($finish) B38,299
flip-flop chain 308
for B33,295
forever B32,294
fork, join B34,295
formating B37,297
function B5,267
gr_waves ($gr_waves) B41,301
gr_waves_memsize ($gr.) B43,301
group 311
hierarchy 309
high impedance (z) B11,274
if B28,290
initial 39,B24,286
initial block B24,286
inout B6,268
input B6,268
instance B1,264
integer B7,270
join B34,295
literal comparison B13,277
logical equality B13,277
mixed-mode 310
module 39,B1,264
negedge B25,287
operators (bit-wise) ~, &, | B15,279
operators (logical) !, &&, || B14,277
output B6,268
parallelism 302
parameter B2,265
parameter list 40
pipeline 315
posedge B25,287
precedences B22,283
producer-consumer 312
program control 284
readmemb ($readmemb) B40,300
readmemh ($readmemh) B40,300
reg B9,272
register 40,B9,272
repeated concatenation B17,280
rising edge B25,287
selection B29,291
shift <<, >> B18,280
simulation time axis 302
simulator 302
stop ($stop) B39,299
structure 310
submodule 44,B1,264
task B4,266
time control 41,305,B21,283
undefined (x) B11,274
variable declaration 270
VERILOG 261
VERILOG statements 263
VeriWell viii,7,39,261,303
wait 41,B26,288,305
while B31,293
wire 40,B8,270, 271
write ($write) B37,297
x (undefined) B11,274
z (high impedance) B11,274

Instructions of Processor TOOBSIE

.A-option 54,77
ADD 56,H4
ADDC 56,H4
ALU instruction 55,89
AND 56,H4
ANNUL option 53,77
Arithmetic shift right 56
ASR 56,H5
BCC 54,H5
BCS 54,H6
BEQ 54,H6
BF 54,H6
BGE 54,H7
BGT 54,H7
BHI 54,H7
BLE 54,H8
BLS 54,H8
BLT 54,H8
BMI 54,H9
BNE 54,H9
BPL 54,H9
Branch 54
BT 54,H10
BVC 54,H10
BVS 54,H10
CALL 54,H11
CLC 57,H11
Clear 57
Clear cache 57
CLR 57,H11
CTR instruction 53,55,91
Exclusive or 56
.F-option 56
HALT 54,H11
instruction format 50
instruction set 49,H3
Inversion bitwise 57
JMP 54,57,H12
Jump 54,57
LD/ST instruction 52,89
LDH 56,H12
LDS 52,H12
LDU 52,H13
Load high 56
Load register from special
register 57
Load signed 53
Load unsigned 53
Logical shift 56
LRFS 57,H14
LSL 56,H14
LSR 56,H15
NEG 57,H15
Negate 57
No operation 57
NOP 57,H16
NOT 57,H16
OR 56,H16
RET 54,57,H17
RETI 54,H17
Return 54
Return from interrupt 54
Return from subroutine 57
ROT 56,H17
Rotate 56
Software interrupt 54
Special instruction 56,91
SRIS 55,57,H17
ST 52,H18
Store 53
Store register into special
register 57
SUB 56,H19
SUBC 56,H19
Subtract 56
Swap 53,82
SWI 54,H20
SWP 52,H20
synthetic instruction 53,57
XOR 56,H20

Components of the Coarse Structure Model

ARITHMETIC 151
arithmetic logic unit 30,76,116,147,H121
BCU logic H46
branch cache BCACHE H59
branch correction logic BCL H62
branch decision logic BDL 132
branch-target cache
33,99,*100*,115,128,245,H55
bus control unit 116,H53,H149
bus monitor CHECKBUS H74,H197
CALL write multiplexer H58
call detection logic CDL H60
Coarse Structure Model 19,*113*,H39
control file TEST H72,H168
control MCTRL H201
data and address pipeline 161
decode group DG1 etc. 141
DIS_IDU multiplexer H58
external PC logic EPL 138
forwarding comparator CMP 157
forwarding selection logic FSL 159
graphic output GRAPHWAVES H74,H189
history decision logic HIL H61
history update logic HUL H62
I_BUS multiplexer 126
instruction cache ICACHE 131
instruction decode logic IDL 135
instruction decode unit 115,139,H116
instruction fetch unit 115,*123*,H91
instruction write logic IWL 130
interrupt logic H43
LOGIC 152
memory access unit 116,152,H126
memory and register DUMP H73,H183
multi-purpose cache 32,99,115,129,245
NPC_BUS multiplexer 128
PC multiplexer H57
PC_BUS logic H45
pipeline control logic PCL H61
pipeline control unit 116,H39,H135
pipeline disable logic PDL 134
program counter calculator PCC 133
read-write logic RWL H59
register access logic RAL 160
register address converter RAC 157
register file 29,76,109,116,154
RESET logic H41
serial-mode controller SMC 137
SHIFT 152
SREG logic H50
statistics TRACE H73,H169
status forwarding logic H47
status pipeline H48
system controller H70
TAKEN multiplexer H57
WORK_UNIT H52

Expert Volume

The RISC Processor TOOBSIE

Supplement to this book

by Ulrich Golze

The present textbook is self-contained. Experts, however, may want to understand the RISC processor design at selected points "down to the last bit", possibly as a base for the development of their own CAD tools, design methods, and experiments. For such experts, there is an expert volume.

It contains a detailed specification of all RISC instructions and a complete printout of the Interpreter Model and the Coarse Structure Model as well as additional comments and simulation results on these models.

Most of all, it contains the complete commented Gate Model with about 150 graphical schematics based on the library of the silicon producer LSI Logic.

The complete disclosure of all details should distinguish the work from other books, but also from large commercial designs. The contents of the book, which has about 400 pages, are given on the next page.

Please use the following order form.

Contents of the Expert Volume

1 Introduction ... 1

2 TOOBSIE Instructions in Detail ... 3

3 The Interpreter Model as VERILOG Code ... 21

4 The Coarse Structure Model ... 39

4.1 The Pipeline Control Unit PCU ... 39
- 4.1.1 RESET Logic ... 41
- 4.1.2 Interrupt Logic ... 43
- 4.1.3 PC_BUS Logic ... 45
- 4.1.4 BCU Logic ... 46
- 4.1.5 Status Forwarding Logic ... 47
- 4.1.6 Status Pipeline ... 48
- 4.1.7 SREG Logic ... 50
- 4.1.8 Module WORK_UNIT ... 52

4.2 The Bus Control Unit BCU ... 53

4.3 The Branch-Target Cache BTC ... 55

4.4 Interrupts ... 63

4.5 The System Environment ... 69
- 4.5.1 Module SYSTEM ... 70
- 4.5.2 Processor Module CHIP ... 71
- 4.5.3 Memory Modules RAM and ROM ... 71
- 4.5.4 Test Support ... 71

4.6 Experiments with the Coarse Structure Model ... 74

4.7 The Coarse Structure Model as VERILOG Code ... 86

5 The Gate Model ... 203

5.1 Hierarchic Structure ... 204

5.2 Processor CHIP (Level 1) ... 209

5.3 Pipeline Stages (Level 2) ... 212

5.4 Caches and Other Submodules (Level 3) ... 222

5.5 Schematics ... 232

Bibliography and Index ... 397

Order Form

Mail to Prof. Ulrich Golze, Dept. of Integrated Circuit Design, Technical University, PO Box 3329, D-38023 Braunschweig, Germany
or fax to: +49 531 / 391-5840

Shipping address:

____

____

____

____

____

NOTE: Please supply a street address, no PO Box.

Billing address (if different):

____

____

____

____

____

____
Daytime phone number

____
Email address

____
Fax number

____
Purchase order # (not required)

METHOD OF PAYMENT

❑ MasterCard ❑ Eurocard
(no others, please)

____
Name

____
Credit card number Exp. date

____
Signature

❑ Send proforma invoice

We require prepayment. A proforma invoice is a bill which is issued to assist in this advance payment process.

❑ Bank transfer

Postbank Hannover, Germany
Route bank # BLZ 250 100 30
Account # 5602 28-302

Important: Please ask your bank to include your name with the wire transfer. Please add DM 30.00 bank charges. Transfer German Marks only.

AMOUNT TO BE PAID

BOOK The RISC Processor TOOBSIE (about $43 *)	DM	65.00
SHIPPING & HANDLING (about $13 *)	DM	20.00
AIR MAIL POSTAGE (DM 20.00) optional (about $13 *)	DM	______
BANK CHARGES (DM 30.00) if no credit card is used (about $20 *)	DM	______
TOTAL (in German Marks)	DM	______

Printing: Mercedesdruck, Berlin
Binding: Buchbinderei Lüderitz & Bauer, Berlin